# THE WORLD CHANGERS

*BOOKS BY BRUCE BLIVEN*

The Men Who Make the Future
Preview for Tomorrow
The World Changers

AS EDITOR

What the Informed Citizen Needs to Know
Twentieth Century Unlimited

# THE WORLD CHANGERS

Bruce Bliven

*ILLUSTRATED WITH PHOTOGRAPHS*

The John Day Company

NEW YORK

*For my grandson*
## FREDERIC BRUCE BLIVEN

*With the hope and the belief that he may grow*
*up into a better world than the one*
*depicted in these pages*

Second Impression

### PHOTOGRAPH CREDITS

*Hitler, Mussolini: Culver Pictures; Churchill: London Daily Express; Chiang*
*Kai-shek, Gandhi, Hirohito, Roosevelt, Stalin: World Wide Photos.*

Copyright © 1965 by Bruce Bliven

Library of Congress Catalogue Card Number: 65-20728

MANUFACTURED IN THE UNITED STATES OF AMERICA

27760

# Contents

# Foreword

THIS BOOK deals with the two decades of the 1930's and 1940's, which were, I believe, the most significant in the history of mankind.

They saw the greatest war of all time, in which Fascism made its bid for world domination and came perilously close to succeeding. They also saw the deepest of all economic depressions, the rise of the welfare state in America—the most powerful nation on earth—and the collapse of colonialism, setting free millions of people in Africa and Asia.

It is of vital importance that we should recall the forces that ruled the world in those fateful decades. While Fascism no longer dominates the three countries that were its centers, it still survives, and impulses toward it remain in every country—including our own. Totalitarianism continues in the form of Communism, which, like Fascism, sacrifices the individual for the supposed welfare of the state, and is a grave challenge to democracy, throughout the world. To understand our present dangers it is necessary to recall the past from which they have sprung.

Since every institution is the lengthened shadow of a man, I have recalled this past by reporting the lives of the eight most important political figures of the Second World War and the decade that preceded it. These eight men played the major role in shaping the modern world. Roosevelt, Churchill, and Gandhi, each within the limitations of his own character, were heroic fighters on the side of democracy. Hitler, Stalin, and Mussolini sought to end freedom for the individual by exalting the state— as personified in their own persons. Chiang Kai-shek, a mixture of good and bad impulses, never succeeded in shaking himself free from the cultural pattern of an Oriental despot, and thereby lost China to the Communists. Emperor Hirohito is the saddest, in some ways the most tragic, of this group; a hereditary ruler whose native instincts were on the side of democracy, whose position would have enabled him to exert a powerful influence on the course of events, but a man who, because of the weakness of his character, plus the inhibitions on his Imperial powers that had been carefully created, could do little to stop the suicidal plunge of Japanese Fascism toward war.

I have written in terms of biography rather than history because by following the career of a single individual it is possible to separate out the various strands of the enormously complicated pattern of events. Since these were the most important men of their time, their collective stories tell the whole history of that era.

This writer was for more than forty years a newspaper or magazine editor in New York, writing daily or weekly comment on every important event everywhere in the world. For thirty years, as editor of *The New Republic*, I had an exceptional opportunity to get behind the scenes of national and international affairs, reporting meetings of the League of Nations in Geneva and Paris, the United Nations in London, San Francisco, and New York, the Naval Disarmament Conference in Washington, and the Organization of American States (long before Castro) in Havana. At various times I interviewed Roosevelt, Churchill, and Gandhi; and I worked as a journalist in Hitler's Germany, Stalin's Russia, and Mussolini's Italy. My firsthand contacts with these dictatorships (and that of Machado in Cuba) drove home to me the lesson that nobody is wise enough to have absolute authority over the life of anyone else, and that with all its notorious weaknesses, democracy is still the best system of government ever devised on this planet.

I wish to acknowledge my debt of gratitude to the Hoover Institution on War, Revolution, and Peace, at Stanford University, and to the libraries of Stanford and Palo Alto. I am also indebted to Dr. Witold Sworakowski of the Hoover Institution, Professors Robert North and Richard Lyman of Stanford, and Dr. Joan Bondurant of the Center for South Asia Studies at the University of California, each of whom read and criticized one or more of the chapters of my manuscript. None of them, of course, is responsible for any of the opinions expressed.

And finally, I must express my heartfelt thanks to my wife, who patiently typed every page several times, and some parts, many.

B.B.

# 1. Roosevelt:
# Father Image from Hyde Park

FRANKLIN DELANO ROOSEVELT played a role of overwhelming importance in the turbulent fourth and fifth decades of the twentieth century. He became President when the deepest economic depression of all history was at its very worst and millions of people were suffering in the richest country in the world, while surrounded by ample quantities, which they were unable to buy, of everything they needed. When the Fascist powers, Germany, Italy, and Japan, made their bid to conquer the world, it was American intervention alone that finally prevented their success, and it was Roosevelt who, almost single-handed, had far in advance prepared the way. It is not incorrect, indeed, to say that he joined the War on the side of the Allies years before his country did, and that his acts during the period when most Americans still wanted to keep out may have been decisive in preventing an early Fascist conquest.

During his lifetime, few Americans were neutral about Roosevelt. He was idolized by many millions of his fellow countrymen, who gave him the most triumphant series of victories at the polls in the nation's history. Correspondingly, he was the object of hatred unparalleled in this generation; though his opponents were far fewer in numbers, they included many men of great wealth and influence, owners of newspapers, magazines and radio stations, who in theory should have been able to influence enormously the attitude of the American people.

Roosevelt's character during the last quarter century of his life can probably be understood only in terms of his struggle with infantile paralysis, which began in August, 1921. Although before that he had achieved some measure of success, as a member of the New York State Senate, Assistant Secretary of the Navy, and Democratic Vice-Presidential candidate with James M. Cox in 1920, hardly anyone saw in him any portent of the towering world figure he was to become. By conquering his terrible physical handicap (a struggle strikingly described by Dore Schary in his play, *Sunrise at Campobello*) he also mastered elements of weakness within himself and thus prepared for his great role on the international stage.

Roosevelt was almost always in his later years supremely self-confident; if he had moments of doubt and pessimism they were few and successfully concealed. Most of the time he was exuberant and optimistic to the point of cockiness; vividly aware of his personal charm, he believed he could manage practically anybody, and he was usually right. With a retentive memory, he loved to store up odd facts and dazzle a visitor with them. He also loved to talk; over and over, people were summoned to the White House to give him information, and found instead that the President spent the whole time telling the visitor about the same subject—or some other. John Gunther, in *Roosevelt in Retrospect,* tells of a typical experience on April 7, 1942, when America had been in the Second World War only four months. The White House staff had told him firmly he could stay only six or seven minutes; the President talked three quarters of an hour, with the conscientious Gunther struggling to get away.

During his twelve years in the White House, Roosevelt was a bad administrator. Partly because of the poor organization of the Executive Branch (since then somewhat improved) but chiefly because of his own temperament, he could delegate little authority; repeatedly he would turn from some great national or

**FRANKLIN DELANO ROOSEVELT**
"Exuberant and optimistic to the point of cockiness, vividly aware of his personal charm, he believed he could manage practically anybody, and he was usually right."

international crisis to settling petty details in one Department or another. Often he appointed several men to vaguely defined responsibilities which overlapped or duplicated one another. Sometimes he did this on purpose, making two men compete for authority and letting the better—or more aggressive—win, but usually it was because he could not bear to make firm decisions if they would hurt someone's feelings. He could never dismiss anybody, from a domestic servant to a Cabinet member, and on occasion he delegated such jobs to others who had no business to do them. On the other hand, he would sometimes turn against an old friend suddenly and permanently; there are people to whom this happened who still do not know why.

In his dealings with those around him he was often tricky and uncandid, with a childish love of secrecy for its own sake. Leon Henderson, one of his aides, did not know he was to be Price Administrator until he heard it on the radio. Conversely, Roosevelt made firm promises to give jobs to certain people and then went back on them.

With his great sensitivity to the moods of those about him he often seemed more in agreement than was the case. There is a famous, probably apocryphal, story that illustrates this. Mrs. Roosevelt is supposed to have been in the room during two visits by important officials. Mr. A outlined a proposal and the President approved, saying, "You're absolutely right." Mr. B came in with exactly the opposite plan, and the President again concurred in the same words.

After Mr. B had left, Mrs. Roosevelt, so the story goes, protested. "Franklin, how can you sit there and agree to two things that are in complete contradiction? You really ought not to do that!"

The President: "Eleanor, you're absolutely right."

In spite of his sensitivity to others, he sometimes showed curious blank spots. In 1940, Dorothy Thompson, the famous columnist, switched from Wendell Willkie to Roosevelt in the middle of the Presidential campaign and lost her job on the New York *Herald Tribune* in consequence. She went to see the President after his victory, to be greeted with: "Dorothy, you lost your job, but I kept mine—ha! ha!" Gunther reports that he would tell a story over and over, even though he must have known that some in his audience had often heard it; Harry Hopkins, who spent much time with him, had listened to some of these stories on thirty or forty occasions.

Roosevelt's famous sense of humor, of which so much has been made, was not very subtle. He loved to tease his intimates roughly and even to play some pretty crude practical jokes on them.

Though he was a great collector of books dealing with things of special interest to him, such as naval history, in adult life he was not a wide-ranging reader—perhaps partly because of the endless burden of documents with which he had to wrestle daily. He read more widely as a boy; Gunther says he used to buy complete sets of authors like Dickens and Scott on the instalment plan from traveling salesmen who visited Hyde Park. He kept these hidden under his bed, but his mother poked there with a stick, found them, and usually forced Franklin to stop the payments and return the volumes. When he became President, he is supposed to have owed money to every second-hand bookstore on Fifty-ninth Street, in New York City; a member of his family went down the street clearing up all these debts before the Inauguration.

If he was careless about paying his bills, it was not for lack of money. The Roosevelts had been well-to-do for generations before Franklin was born. When his mother died he inherited about a million dollars from her, and by the time of his own death this had grown to some $2 million.

When he was in the White House, he followed a consistent daily routine. He woke about seven, had breakfast in bed, and read several newspapers with great care, including the *New York Times*, the *Herald Tribune* and the *Washington Post*. Then followed the daily visit from his doctor, and usually from several of the White House staff or his special confidants among the members of the Cabinet, who came in as a group. He dressed with the assistance of his valet, and was ready for a long day of appointments in his office. He had a small lunch on a tray at his desk.

In the late afternoon he usually swam in the pool that had been constructed for him in the White House basement and was the subject of bitter remarks by wealthy men, most of whom had pools of their own on their country estates and needed them far less than the President, a polio victim with no other means of exercise. There were often guests for dinner, after which, movies were sometimes shown. The President retired about eleven, and read himself to sleep with a book of history or biography or sometimes a murder mystery. It perhaps reveals something of his character that he was a superb sleeper; Mrs. Roosevelt said, "My husband never had a sleepless night."

I saw Franklin Roosevelt in action at the Democratic National Convention of 1920, and also attended some of his weekly press conferences in the White House while he was President, and saw how greatly he had changed over the years. In 1920 he was thin and frail-looking, and appeared even more so because of his height; Hugh Baillie of the United Press describes him at about this time as "a slim, elegant young man with a condescending air." In his autobiography, *High Tension*, Baillie recalls that "He seemed to consider himself not merely superior, but positively infallible—and I never could figure out whether these were his true feelings or whether it was all an act."

When I used to see him in the White House he was still self-confident, but he had changed greatly in other ways. Lacking the use of his legs, he had developed enormous upper arms and shoulders and a barrel chest. His manner was now warm, with the politician's cordiality.

Twenty-five or thirty reporters would crowd into the rather small, white-painted Presidential office and cluster around the big desk with its clutter of toy Democratic donkeys and other trinkets and souvenirs. Most of our group were the regular White House correspondents, nearly all of whom the President called by their first names and with whom, while we were getting assembled, he kept up a crossfire of rather feeble jokes.

When the questioning began, he put on a virtuoso performance: pretending never to have heard of something well-known to all; reproaching a reporter for failing to understand a comment of his that was deliberately phrased in double-talk; answering some questions candidly and fully; refusing to answer others, with elaborate reproaches to the inquirer for failing to remember that he had replied to the same question weeks ago (which may or may not have been true). It was the sort of scene to leave a European breathless with astonishment, yet one thoroughly in the old American tradition—one that Jefferson, Jackson or Lincoln would have understood.

Franklin Roosevelt was born at Hyde Park, New York, January 30, 1882. His father had bought the house in 1867; it had been built in 1826 but extensively remodeled. Both of Franklin's parents came from prosperous old families; contrary to the general impression, only a small proportion of the ancestry was Dutch, being mainly English, with Flemish, German, Italian, French and Swedish elements. The father, James Roosevelt, was a distant cousin of President Theodore Roosevelt, and there were remote and intricate relationships to ten other Presidents: Washington, both the Adamses, Madison, Van Buren, both the Harrisons, Taylor, Grant, and Taft.

James, who was fifty-four when Franklin was born, occupied himself little with business except looking after the family fortune, which came mostly from land ownership and shipping. He was, however, a director of a number of companies, and widely known; he had once been offered the post of American ambassador to the Hague. Sara Roosevelt, Franklin's mother, was just half her husband's age when they were married; she was his second wife, and he already had a thirteen-year-old son. Like other wealthy Americans of that time, the Roosevelts went abroad annually and knew many important people in London, Paris, and Rome; they took Franklin with them annually, from his seventh to his fifteenth year, and on one occasion enrolled him for some time in a school in Germany.

When he was fourteen, Franklin was sent away from home for the first time, to the Groton School in Massachusetts, a famous old institution modeled on the private schools of England. The 150 students lived a life of great austerity, with daily chapel, compulsory athletics and rigid discipline. Young Roosevelt entered in the Third Form (corresponding to the freshman class in high school), at some disadvantage because most of his classmates had already spent two years together. Having been spoiled by his doting mother, he was thoroughly unhappy at school, and an indifferent student; his only recorded prize was an annual medal for punctuality.

On the good side was his contact with the famous headmaster, the Rev. Dr. Endicott Peabody, who influenced generations of Groton students, including such men as Dean Acheson, Francis Biddle, Averell Harriman, Newbold Morris, and Sumner Welles. Dr. Peabody performed Franklin's wedding ceremony, was for many years a guest at Hyde Park every New Year's Eve, and conducted a special service in Washington before each Inauguration. Most Groton alumni are the sons of wealthy men, and while Roosevelt was President, no one abused him more vigorously than they; for many years Dr. Peabody spent much of his time at all alumni gatherings defending the school's most famous graduate.

From Groton, Franklin went to Harvard; here again he was an indifferent student, but he managed to become personally much more popular. He rowed on several minor crews, became president of the *Crimson*, the college newspaper, joined a good club, though not the top-rated one, and became permanent chairman of his class committee.

Graduated in 1904, the next year he married a fifth cousin once removed, whom he had known since childhood, Anna Eleanor Roosevelt; he was twenty-three and she was twenty-one. The bride was given away by President Theodore Roosevelt, who, as might have been expected, dominated the whole affair.

Eleanor Roosevelt, who fifteen years after her husband's death was the best-known woman in the world and a political figure of great importance in her own right, was a shy young person; as she has told us in her autobiographical writings, she was completely lacking in self-confidence. Franklin's mother, Sara, had always dominated her son and took a dim view of his marrying anyone, least of all the diffident and gawky fifth cousin. Sara tried hard to prevent the marriage, and when she failed, sought to rule the young pair. She bought and decorated a house for them in New York, and then moved in next door. It took a long time for her daughter-in-law to muster up the courage to assert her independence, but she finally managed to do so.

In 1907, after studying at Columbia Law School, Franklin passed the state bar examination and went to work for a Wall Street law firm which represented J. P. Morgan and the Astors, among other wealthy clients. Three years later, in 1910, he was asked to run as a Democrat for the New York State Senate for the district embracing Hyde Park. He was chosen because of the Roosevelt name, and because he had money; his other qualifications did not matter, since it was taken for granted he would be defeated. To the surprise of the professional politicians, he worked hard and won; always an innovator, he was the first man in the state to campaign by automobile. Once he got into the Senate he quickly showed that he was no mere rubber stamp for Tammany; he fought the Hall victoriously on more than one occasion. Foreshadowing some of his attitudes of many years later, he displayed an interest in conservation of natural resources and help for the farmers, and opposed the powerful Albany lobby of the big public utilities. He also favored woman suffrage, an unpopular stand at that time in New York.

Roosevelt was reëlected in 1912 with a bigger majority than before, but gave up his seat almost at once to go to Washington as Assistant Secretary of the Navy, a post that had been held by "Uncle Ted" before him. The next year, the First World War began, and while the United States did not join the conflict for nearly three years, it was a tense time for the Navy. Young Franklin worked hard to get our fleet ready in case we should be drawn into the conflict, and was successful. He did take out enough time to seek the Democratic nomination for United States Senator in 1914, but he did little campaigning, and was defeated by James W. Gerard, American Ambassador to Germany, who then went on to lose the election.

Franklin's chief was Josephus Daniels, a newspaper publisher from Raleigh, North Carolina, who is best remembered for removing liquor from American ships and for his mild pacifism. Young Roosevelt, who was developing his lifelong love affair with the sea, and the U.S. Navy in particular, thought Daniels was an old fuddy-duddy and took no special pains to conceal that fact. He conspired behind his chief's back with the admirals to get more and bigger ships, and modern equipment. When the United States joined the War, in April, 1917, Franklin wanted to give up his desk job and get into the fighting, but was overruled by President Wilson.

In 1920, Franklin was sufficiently well-known throughout the country to be nominated as the Democratic running-mate with James M. Cox, a newspaper publisher from Ohio. The compliment may seem more important than it was; a Republican victory was in the cards, and was achieved easily by Warren Harding, another Ohio publisher, chosen by machine politicians in a "smoke-filled room" in Chicago—a phrase that was to become notorious.

Less than a year after the end of the campaign came the great personal tragedy of Roosevelt's life, the attack of polio at the family summer home, Campobello Island, New Brunswick. His legs were almost completely paralyzed; as he afterwards said, "I spent two years lying in bed trying to move my big toe." Never again was he to stand erect without the use of cruel steel braces, a cane, and an arm to lean on.

At first, his life seemed hopelessly ruined; his mother wanted him to give up, become an invalid, and let her care for him as she had done when he was a child. But he developed a streak of stubborn, indomitable courage that seemed inconsistent with his character up to that time. Eleanor Roosevelt was a tower of strength and so was his devoted aide, the wizened little Louis Howe, who had by now been with him for ten years. Before long, Franklin discovered Warm Springs, Georgia, where natural pools of warm water make it easy for polio victims to exercise while immersed, because the tug of gravitation is greatly diminished. By 1924 he was well enough to appear at the National Democratic Convention and nominate his friend, Governor Al Smith of New York, calling him the "Happy Warrior." After a protracted convention struggle between Smith and President Wilson's son-in-law, William G. McAdoo, John W. Davis was nominated and lost the election to President Calvin Coolidge, fifteen million votes to eight.

In 1928, Smith finally got the nomination, but was defeated by Herbert Hoover, twenty-one million votes to fifteen. Roosevelt had been dragooned into running for Governor of New York, the Smith managers believing his popularity would help the national ticket. When the decision was made, Roosevelt was at Warm Springs, where most of the therapeutic facilities were now his personal property. He did not want to run, believing that he could not stand the rigors of the campaign; he refused in repeated long-distance telephone conversations, and only consented when his wife added her voice to all the others. He made a sensation by being elected Governor against the strong Republican tide.

No sooner was he in office than he began having trouble with Al Smith. Smarting from his defeat in the Presidential race, Smith consoled himself with the expectation that he would continue to rule New York, with Roosevelt as his errand boy. The new Governor promptly repudiated any such notion, and the break between the two men was soon complete.

The Governor was also in trouble with Tammany Hall. Jimmy Walker, an irresponsible, happy-go-lucky playboy, was Mayor of New York, and while he was probably not involved personally in the graft, the corruption of his administration had become notorious. The Republican-dominated State Legislature wanted a public exposure and dismissal of Walker, but Roosevelt needed Tammany's support for his state program of legislation and procrastinated; finally, however, he agreed to an investigation by Judge Samuel Seabury, which turned up so much ugly evidence that Walker resigned and fled to Paris.

Roosevelt's opponents often say that the New Deal that he

inaugurated when he became President was a complete improvisation, but this is belied by his record as Governor. His New York program included many of the items later put through on a national scale, including development of water power, aid to the farmers, minimum wages, a workmen's compensation law, ending the abuse of injunctions in labor disputes, the eight-hour day and the forty-hour week.

In 1930, Roosevelt ran again for Governor and won, increasing his majority from 25,000 to 725,000. His Republican opponent was Charles R. Tuttle and Roosevelt infuriated him by blandly ignoring his existence.

By now the Governor had begun to gather around him some of the close advisers who were to stay with him through much or all of his subsequent career. Wanting information about some economic and sociological problems, he made contact with three Columbia University professors, Raymond Moley, Rexford Tugwell, and Adolf Berle, and these men were nicknamed by the Albany correspondent of the *New York Times*, "the Brains Trust" (soon changed to "the Brain Trust"). Other advisers were Judge Samuel Rosenman, Basil O'Connor, Roosevelt's former law partner, Joseph McGoldrick and Lindsay Rogers. James Farley entered the circle as political mentor and quickly taught Roosevelt to keep a card catalogue of political figures all over the country and to correspond with them voluminously. Harry Hopkins, a welfare expert from New York City, was summoned to give advice on unemployment and the administration of relief.

Several of these men broke publicly with Roosevelt at later stages of his career. The first was Raymond Moley, who was sent as an American delegate to the London Economic Conference in 1933, and resigned in anger when he felt, quite correctly, that Roosevelt was failing to support his hard-money, anti-inflationary ideas. James A. Farley broke with Roosevelt in 1940, partly because he was opposed to a third Presidential term, partly because he believed that he himself was a potential candidate for the Democratic nomination. The most important other members of the group continued to serve in one capacity or another until after Roosevelt died, and then drifted away from government.

When Roosevelt was reëlected Governor in 1930, the Great Depression was already a year old. Since it was to bulk so largely in his life, and in that of the American people, it is worthwhile to report the facts about it in some detail. There is endless debate about its causes, which were doubtless complicated, but some of them seem clear. The First World War had been accompanied by a shortage of consumer goods, and when it was over, productive capacity was expanded beyond what was necessary, so that when the legitimate needs had been filled there was a glut. The War was also accompanied by inflation, which always brings a temporary, unhealthy increase in business activity; people try to turn their money into goods before its value has diminished still further. High wartime prices for food fell; millions of acres had been bought at prices so stiff that they could not be tilled at a profit.

During the 1920's, industrial production per man-hour increased greatly, but most of this increase was channeled off into profits, rents, and interest, rather than wages and salaries, so that the great bulk of the people did not have enough additional money to buy back all the things they had produced; while factory productivity rose fifty-five percent, hourly wages were increasing only about two percent. At the same time, private long-term debt, much of it used to increase productive capacity, went up three times as fast as the national income. In the decade of the twenties the share of the national income going to the top one percent of the population increased by fifty percent.

The foreign policy of the United States during this time was similarly incompatible with permanent prosperity. Our allies in the First World War owed us billions of dollars in war debts, and most of them showed little interest in paying. They felt that the War had been as much our affair as theirs, and that we had no real right to ask for the return of the money. The British pointed out that they had made heavy loans to their continental allies, and that it was difficult for them to pay us as long as nobody was paying them.

Large sums can be transferred between countries only in the form of goods (in bilateral or multilateral exchanges), but the United States went in for high tariffs that cut imports to the bone. At the same time, she tried to encourage exports by lending money to foreign governments and to foreign private business with which to buy things manufactured in the United States. Governments, notably in South America, were pressured to accept these loans, and many foreign bonds were sold to individual investors in the United States; when the bubble burst, billions of dollars of these loans went into default.

In the last three years before the Depression, Wall Street gambling went beyond the bounds of reason. This was partly because the Federal Reserve Board insisted on low, inflationary interest rates, partly because of a national insanity like the great tulip-bulb speculation in the Netherlands in the seventeenth century. Stocks could be bought by putting up only ten percent of their value; you could buy a share worth $100 with only $10, and if it went to $200, as many of them did, you had a paper profit of $100, achieved with astonishing ease. Millions of people who had never before invested became stock-exchange gamblers, risking all their savings. If a stock went down, your broker could of course demand extra collateral and if you did not have it, he would sell you out and you lost everything; but very few believed that stocks would ever go down. Many bankers, industrialists, and economists, who should have known better, talked about a "new and permanent plateau of prosperity."

Yet there were warning signs that a few wise men heeded. Agriculture was in trouble; the mortgaged farms of the Middle West had never recovered from the deflation of values in the early 1920's, and neither had the cotton plantations of the South. The New England textile trade was under a cloud during the whole decade. The building of new houses slackened off greatly as early as 1925, and the production of iron, steel and automobiles turned downward in 1927. The railroads were in poor shape, and so was coal. In about 1925, wholesale prices, which are more sensitive than retail ones, began to decline in England and Canada, and there followed a marked lessening of business activity in Australia, Germany, Italy, France, Japan, and other countries. But the danger signals went unnoticed by most people in the United States until 1929.

Even before Mr. Hoover was inaugurated, on March 4, 1929, there were fresh signs of serious trouble. On February 7, the Federal Reserve Board warned that credit was overexpanded, and the stock market broke, though it rallied again. Wholesale prices in some lines turned downward in July. Then in October came the deluge; the market broke seriously on October 4, 21, 23, and 24. On October 29, "Black Tuesday," 16,410,000 shares were thrown on the market amid collapsing prices; some authorities believe unrecorded sales may have added three or four million to this number.

On that day American Telephone and Telegraph and General Electric both lost twenty-eight points, Allied Chemical thirty-five, North American Company twenty-seven, Westinghouse nineteen. In the next two months, in spite of all sorts of efforts to restore confidence, $30 billion had been squeezed out, the equivalent of twice that amount in terms of today's dollars, and in some parts of the country one-quarter of the industrial workers were unemployed.

Yet it took a long time for people to realize what the country was facing. On New Year's Day, 1930, when many prominent men were asked to name the biggest problems of the coming year, unemployment was eighteenth on the list. The first six were, in this order, the administration of justice, prohibition, lawlessness, crime and law enforcement, and world peace; as prohibition had been accompanied by a great increase in crime, the first five of these items were really the same thing.

Since Mr. Hoover was in office when the slump began, he was blamed for it, and was hated by the victims to a degree that seems unbelievable thirty years later. In his *Memoirs* he makes a vigorous, and largely convincing, argument that the Depression resulted from forces beyond his control, and that as Secretary of Commerce during the preceding eight years he had fought hard though unsuccessfully against the inflationary policies of the rest of the government, and notably the Federal Reserve Board. In any case, nothing he did or left undone during the eight months between his inauguration and the crash could have helped very much to ameliorate it.

Another charge that has more justice is that he did little, and did it tardily, to help the victims of the economic storm to keep alive. Always a firm believer in rugged individualism and a minimum of action by the Federal Government, he thought of relief strictly in terms of charity, to be undertaken by the states and cities, though before long, many states and cities were themselves in the red and unable to give the needed help.

A dramatic incident came when a severe drought in 1930 brought a million farm families into deep trouble; Hoover got railroad rates cut on feed for cattle, but ignored the problem of food for the people. When Congress voted $25 million for relief in the drought area, the President encouraged the Red Cross to refuse the money. It may not have been needed, but the story swept over the country and increased the bitterness against the President.

An incident that did much to defeat Hoover in 1932 came in July of that year. In 1931 Congress had voted a veterans' bonus of $1.3 billion, over a Presidential veto, most of it to be paid by instalments during a period of years. The ex-soldiers wanted payment at once, and in June, 1932, thousands of them marched to Washington to try to bring pressure to bear on Congress. They camped in tents just across the Potomac on the Anacostia Flats, and paraded through the city, congesting traffic.

On July 28, they fought a running battle with the Washington city police, in which two veterans were killed and others were wounded. The District of Columbia Commissioners asked the President to call out the Army, which he did; the General in command was Douglas MacArthur and his chief aide was bright young Colonel Dwight D. Eisenhower.

The troops drove the bonus seekers back across the Potomac, their huts and tents were burned, and they were forced to leave the area. Hoover insisted that the whole bonus army was a Communist stunt, that many of its members were not veterans, that the Washington police had fired to save their own lives, that he had not ordered the camp to be burned, and that the veterans had destroyed their own property, but people remembered only that these men had marched on Washington to make a plea to Congress, an action for which there is ample precedent; that some of them were killed, and all of them were dispersed at the point of the bayonet.

How can one describe for those who do not remember it the atmosphere of the Great Depression? A few statistics may help to set the scene. Frederick Allen, in *Only Yesterday*, reminds us of some of the losses in blue-ribbon stocks. From the 1929 highs to the 1932 lows, American Telephone and Telegraph went from 304 down to 70, General Motors from 72 to 8, New York Central from 256 to 8.75, Radio Corporation of America from 101 to 2.5, U.S. Steel from 261 to 21.25.

Industrial production sank from an index number of 125 to 58 and the national income went down even more, by nearly two-thirds. Banks, which had formerly failed at the rate of about 700 a year, stepped up their tempo to 1,300 in 1930, 2,200 in 1931, and more than 4,000 in 1932. Statistics on unemployment were very poor in those days; the accepted figure is 13 million in a population of 122 million, but some people believe as many as 18 million or more may have been out of work.

Great numbers of the unemployed took to the roads, still clinging to the hope that perhaps the hard times were just local, and that jobs might be available somewhere else. Homeless men, and some women, swarmed over freight trains in such numbers that in many places the police in desperation gave up and let them ride. Families abandoned their possessions, except what could be piled into the back of a jalopy, and wandered up and down the nation's highways looking for nonexistent work; often they became mendicants, begging not only for food but for money to buy gasoline "to get out of town." In the big cities apple sellers were on every corner, trying to sell an impossible quantity of fruit—not because of the number of unemployed but because of the vast oversupply of apples.

This writer, preparing a series of magazine articles on the Depression, traveled about the country when things were at their worst and saw something of what was going on. On the Bowery in New York City, I saw long lines of the homeless standing in the street in all kinds of weather, waiting hours for a handout that might be only stale bread and a cup of coffee. Hundreds of men with nowhere else to sleep sought refuge in the municipal lodging-house, where after a compulsory shower, they were given supper, a bed, and breakfast—for three consecutive nights. On the fourth night they begged a nickel, rode back and forth all night on the subway, and were then eligible to apply to the lodging-house again, although nightly hundreds were turned away.

On the railroads, the Pullman cars were almost deserted; the Twentieth Century Limited between New York and Chicago made the daily run with only a handful of passengers, who could look out the windows and see on the outskirts of every town the "Hoovervilles," shanty towns built from old packing-boxes and other scraps of lumber, in which the homeless tried to shelter themselves. In Chicago, in cold October, I saw men sleeping on the ground beneath the partial shelter of the elevated section of Wacker Drive. In Iowa, hundreds of farms were auctioned off by the sheriff on behalf of the mortgage holders; sometimes the neighbors temporarily halted these sales by threatening to lynch the auctioneer.

It was against this background that preparations for the Presidential election of 1932 began. Hoover's general unpopularity made a Democratic victory seem probable and there were a correspondingly large number of candidates for the nomination —Governor Albert C. Ritchie of Maryland, Harry Byrd of Virginia, Alben Barkley of Kentucky, Senator James A. Reed of Missouri, Representative John Garner of Texas, industrialist Owen D. Young, former Secretary of War Newton D. Baker.

Roosevelt was opposed not only by the supporters of all these candidates, but by Al Smith and his friend John J. Raskob, chairman of the Democratic National Committee, by newspaper publisher William Randolph Hearst and by former Secretary of the Treasury William G. McAdoo.

His greatest political strength came from his alliance with James A. Farley, who, as noted, was the first to practice the simple but effective plan of selling a political personality by direct mail. Farley had a card index of 38,000 Democratic officials all over the country and corresponded with them constantly, writing many of them his famous green-ink letters. Roosevelt, who also pursued this policy diligently, entered the Presidential contests in various states, winning in New Hampshire, North Dakota, and Georgia, losing in California, Connecticut, and Massachusetts. He came into the convention stronger than any other candidate and received 666 votes on the first ballot. The Democrats at that time still retained the rule requiring a two-thirds majority, and Roosevelt needed 770.

A key figure was W. R. Hearst, who was supporting Garner, then Speaker of the House of Representatives. Friends of Roosevelt called up Hearst in California and warned him that the nomination might go to Al Smith or even worse, from his point of view, to Newton Baker whom Hearst hated as an "internationalist." With the understanding that Garner would become the Vice-Presidential nominee, Hearst threw his support to Roosevelt. With great difficulty, the Texas delegation was persuaded to come over, and Roosevelt got the nomination on the fourth ballot. The Smith supporters were the only diehards, holding out to the end and refusing to follow old custom and make the nomination unanimous. Roosevelt shattered all precedent by flying out to Chicago from Albany to address the delegates in person, promising that if he were elected America would have a "new deal."

The nominee campaigned vigorously, partly to show the country that while he was a cripple, he was not an invalid. He had to be lifted into and out of automobiles and railroad cars, and as far as possible these actions were kept from the public view. Despite his handicaps, he seemed tireless, wearing out men far younger than himself with day after day of eighteen-hour activity. Television was not yet in use, but he used the radio with enormous skill, beginning every speech with his famous trademark, "My friends." He kept his language simple, spoke slowly and with great emphasis on almost every word; experts agree that few radio orators anywhere have ever succeeded in establishing such a degree of intimacy.

The policies he outlined in his campaign were a curious mixture. Many people agreed with Walter Lippmann, who said:

> Franklin D. Roosevelt is no crusader. He is no tribune of the people. He is no enemy of entrenched privilege. He is a pleasant man, without any important qualifications for the office, who would like very much to be President.

John M. Burns remarks in *Roosevelt: The Lion and the Fox* that he began the campaign with tones of liberalism but then got frightened when Hoover attacked him on this score, and turned more conservative. It is true that one of his chief proposals was a Hoover-like pledge of drastic governmental economy. He promised to cut the government budget by twenty-five percent, and to maintain a sound currency. On the other hand, some of his proposals foreshadowed the New Deal: reduced tariffs, federal aid to the unemployed, regulation of the stock market, and control of the private electric-power industry by means of the threat of federal or state operation.

Perhaps his most famous single address was his speech at the San Francisco Commonwealth Club on September 23, in which he pledged government intervention to guarantee that men should have a chance to work, at improved wages, and promised "economic democracy" and no more "industrial cannon fodder."

Probably what he said was not of much importance. The country was badly frightened, millions were suffering and were fed up with Hoover's appearance of inaction and pessimism.

Although in 1928 the Republicans had won by 6.3 million majority, in 1932 the situation was reversed: Roosevelt was elected by 7.1 million.

There ensued a dangerous period of four months before Inauguration Day, then March 4th, during which things got steadily worse. Business continued to decline, unemployment to rise, the condition of the banks to grow more precarious. The country was shocked by an attempt to kill the President-elect in Miami, Florida; the insane assassin, Joseph Zangara, instead fatally wounded Mayor Anton Cermak of Chicago.

In February the Governor of Michigan closed all the banks in that state, and before the Inauguration the same had been done in Illinois and New York. President Hoover, who still believed his policies were right and indeed essential, tried desperately to get Roosevelt to join him in giving "prompt assurance that there will be no tampering with or inflation of the currency; that the budget will be unquestionably balanced, even if further taxation is necessary; that the government credit will be maintained." Roosevelt, not unnaturally, refused to concur in such a blanket endorsement of the policies of the man he had just overwhelmingly defeated at the polls.

In the midst of the nationwide hysteria, Roosevelt's inaugural address came with an overwhelming sense of reassurance.

> This great nation will endure as it has endured, will revive and will prosper. So, first of all, let me assert my firm belief that the only thing we have to fear is fear itself—nameless, unreasoning, unjustified terror which paralyzes needed efforts to convert retreat into advance.

The Inaugural was a Saturday; the next day, the new President proclaimed a national banking "holiday," forbade all exports of gold and dealing in foreign exchange, and called an emergency meeting of Congress for the following Thursday. A few days later, perhaps to get the nation to think of something else than its monetary woes, he suggested that Congress should legalize the manufacture of beer of such a low alcoholic content as to be legal in spite of the Prohibition Amendment to the Constitution.

Now began the famous period of "The Hundred Days." A new law was rushed through Congress, authorizing the President to reopen those national banks that were sound, keep the unsound ones closed, and appoint receivers to work out the problems of the doubtful ones. The Reconstruction Finance Corporation, created in the closing days of the Hoover Administration, was authorized to buy preferred stocks in banks, to give them badly needed funds. State governments were permitted to take appropriate measures to reopen those with state charters; within a few days, about 5,000 were back in business.

In the following weeks, an agricultural bill was passed to increase farmers' purchasing power and relieve the pressure of farm mortgages. The Civilian Conservation Corps was created to put a quarter of a million men at work in the national forests and on other outdoor public projects, such as flood and erosion control. To aid those threatened by starvation, a Federal Emergency Relief Administration—something Hoover had resolutely opposed—was set up, financed with $500 million from the R.F.C.

To fight the shameful record of dishonesty in Wall Street, a law was passed requiring public disclosure of full information about securities offered for sale across state boundaries. A Tennessee Valley Authority was established for a huge project on the Tennessee River, to provide hydroelectric power, control of floods and erosion, and allied projects. Another law authorized loans to owners of small homes about to be lost through mortgage foreclosure, giving them a longer time to pay, at lower rates of interest, and postponing all payments of principal and interest in hardship cases. A statute was adopted to coördinate railroad activities, to avoid needless duplication of service, cut down other wasteful practices, and reorganize finances.

By the end of The Hundred Days, the mood of the country had changed enormously. Business was beginning to pick up, although another brief setback came in July. On June 16, Congress passed the National Industrial Recovery Act, and peppery

General Hugh Johnson, head of the Moline Plow Company, a West Point man and a lawyer, was chosen to head it. It was an attempt to use voluntary trade associations to stabilize production and prices and put an end to the cutting of wages that had reached fantastic proportions; in effect, it negated the Sherman Act which forbade conspiracy to set prices. More than five hundred codes were written, covering 22 million workers.

Although the codes benefited employers as well as employees, many firms did not like them and procrastinated in putting them into effect, meanwhile rushing through as much work as possible under the old conditions. Since compliance was voluntary, and there were no penalties for refusal, observance soon became spotty and rapidly grew worse. Henry Ford defied the NRA and got away with it; others appealed from its rulings to the Department of Justice or the Federal Trade Commission.

By September, 1934, the whole enterprise was breaking down and Johnson, exhausted by his labors, resigned. In May, 1935, the United States Supreme Court ruled that the Act was unconstitutional, and its famous emblem, the Blue Eagle, became only a memory. Nobody mourned its passing very much; by now its most important provisions, covering minimum wages, maximum working hours, and limitations on child labor, were incorporated into other statutes.

The President's first Cabinet was a curious hodgepodge of liberals and conservatives, personal friends, and appointments in payment of political obligations. James A. Farley came in as Postmaster General, the traditional job for the man who is to keep the political fences mended. Henry A. Wallace, publisher of a successful farm paper in Des Moines, Iowa, and an authority on hybrid corn, became Secretary of Agriculture, a post once held by his father under a Republican administration. Harold Ickes, a progressive Chicago attorney and financier, was appointed Secretary of the Interior. The elderly Senator Cordell Hull from Tennessee became Secretary of State, a rather superfluous job since Roosevelt himself made all important decisions. Miss Frances Perkins, an expert on worker-employer relations from New York State, became Secretary of Labor and the first woman ever to hold a Cabinet post. Lewis Douglas of Arizona, a former Representative and a wealthy copper miner, was made Director of the Budget, largely because he was a close friend of Roosevelt. Fundamentally conservative, he was deeply shocked at the monetary policies of the New Deal, and resigned after about a year.

The turnover in the Cabinet during Roosevelt's three terms and three months in office was large. He had two Secretaries of State, two of the Treasury, three of War, three of the Navy, four of Commerce, two of Agriculture, two Postmasters General and four Attorneys General. The only two members of the original Cabinet to stay to the end were Ickes and Miss Perkins.

Probably more important to the President than any of these was Harry Hopkins, the social-welfare expert from New York City who became the first Administrator of Federal Emergency Relief. Always frail in health (he was a recovered cancer victim) he came from New York with his motherless young daughter, and moved into the White House. By the time Congress had passed the first relief bill and had appropriated $500 million, the need throughout the country was desperate. Even before he had an office, Hopkins sat down at a desk in a public corridor and began sending telegrams setting up state organizations for distributing relief, and authorizing expenditures; in the first two hours he distributed more than $5 million in this way. During his first year in office he spent the then staggering sum of $1.5 billion and cared for seventeen million people, with the aid of a staff of only 121 persons, an unbelievably low figure for Washington, where every bureau chief tries to maximate his own importance by padding his payroll with as many workers as possible.

From the beginning, the effort was made to save the morale of the unemployed, and keep their technical skills from deteriorating through lack of use, by putting as many of them as possible to work in jobs for which they had some sort of training. At first, however, this was not feasible. Thousands of men were therefore assigned to cleaning up parks and the grounds of public buildings, and "leaf-raking" soon became a contemptuous epithet used by the enemies of the New Deal.

These rapidly grew in numbers; before long, the hysterical fear that prevailed in the months before March, 1933, was forgotten, and the country's conservatives began to rail against the "creeping Socialism" of "that man in the White House." Though Roosevelt was in fact trying to save the capitalist system, and succeeded in doing so, the chief beneficiaries of that system were anything but grateful; Roosevelt was hated the more bitterly because he was considered "a traitor to his class." Fantastic stories, many of them scandalous or obscene, were circulated about the President; many Tories really believed that he was insane.

Since in fact Roosevelt probably prevented the sort of revolution by the Left that has been seen in many countries in Europe and Asia, it has always been something of a puzzle why he was the subject of so much obloquy. It is true that he favored regulation of Wall Street, control of corporations, recognition of unions, and stiff income and inheritance taxes, especially after the beginning of the Second World War, but people began to hate him long before these policies became clearly evident. The answer seems to be that he made fun of the "economic royalists," holding them up to ridicule, especially in his famous radio Fireside Chats, and in his campaign speeches. They were not accustomed to being laughed at, and especially by a man of wealth who could not be dismissed as a jealous outsider.

An extraordinary chapter in Roosevelt's life was his financial theories and what he did about them. The United States went off the gold standard through a series of executive orders in March and April, 1933; given the situation, there was probably no alternative to this course. All contracts, public or private, requiring payment in gold were canceled; this included the promises made to the holders of the national debt, then deemed to be dangerously large at $22 billion. (Three decades later it was nearly fourteen times larger.) Congress authorized the President to reduce the theoretical gold content of the dollar as much as fifty percent, and to fix the ratio of value between gold and silver.

But Roosevelt went much beyond the suspension of the gold standard, which by now was almost universal in Europe. In July, 1933, an Economic Conference of the leading Western Powers, including the United States, was held in London; it met under the broad assumption, which had never been publicly contradicted, that this country would coöperate in holding the value of money steady, thus avoiding fluctuations in international exchange, which hamper the flow of goods across boundaries. On the contrary, while the Conference was in session, the President made a declaration, which stunned the delegates, that the United States would go its economic and financial way alone. Under the impact of this suddenly-announced new policy, the Conference broke up in failure.

The President had come under the extraordinary financial ideas of Prof. George Warren of Cornell University. Professor Warren, like a good many other people, believed that the level of prices could be altered by changing the value of gold in the open market. Increasing the value of gold, he thought, would make paper dollars go down, and would therefore cause prices to rise. In October, over the violent opposition of some of his aides, Roosevelt decided to try the Warren experiment. With gold at about $20 an ounce, the Reconstruction Finance Corporation began buying the metal at prices above the world market. Everybody flocked to sell to the United States, and within three months it had gone up about seventy-five percent, to $35 an ounce, which was then made the permanent legal rate.

Unluckily, as far as domestic prices were concerned, the Warren Plan had little or no effect; depressed prices remained depressed, for the obvious reason that there were still far more goods available than there were customers who could afford to buy them.

Inflation of any currency always gives a temporary boost to exports, since it cuts prices to foreign buyers. It discourages imports in the same way, by cheapening the dollars with which foreign goods can be bought. But such influences are never more than temporary, since other countries take defensive measures, either by inflating their own currencies or by setting up embargoes and quotas. In any case, the United States already had a so-called "favorable" balance of trade—an excess of exports over imports—a situation that is in fact less advantageous than one where exports and imports (including "invisible" items) are in balance. It was soon seen that the Warren Plan had not worked.

The decade of the 1930's was marked by one other extraordinary monetary adventure. In 1939, the U.S. Government began buying silver at far above the world price, in some cases at twice that price. This was an internal political movement only; it was done to help the American owners of silver mines. They were certainly aided, but no one else benefited at all. China, which was on a silver basis, was forced off that metal and into a disastrous inflation, in the middle of her war with Japan.

When Roosevelt took office, no segment of the American economy was in worse shape than agriculture. Europeans, who had a depression of their own, had greatly reduced their purchases of American farm products. Changes in food habits in the United States hurt some products, as people cut down on meat, corn and wheat, and switched to vegetables, fruit and milk. The cotton growers in the Old South were particularly hard hit. There was new competition not only from India and Egypt but from the Western states of Arizona and California. Rayon and other synthetics reduced the market, while a practicable mechanical cotton picker threatened unemployment to millions of workers.

All over the country, farms were auctioned off for the benefit of mortgage holders; in other cases, desperate farmers simply abandoned their land, went to the nearest town and got what work they could, often at twenty-five cents an hour or less.

In the mid-thirties, in 1934 and 1936, the plains states were victims of two bad droughts. Arid land, which probably should never have been plowed at all, turned dry and the thin topsoil blew away in vast clouds—"black blizzards" which sometimes reached as far as the Atlantic seaboard. One result was that many farmers, especially sharecroppers, abandoned their farms —notably in Oklahoma and Arkansas—packed their belongings into an old truck or a secondhand Ford, and with their families set out for the promised land of California—a migration strikingly described by John Steinbeck in *The Grapes of Wrath*.

In 1933, an Agricultural Adjustment Administration was set up for emergency measures. The processors of foodstuffs were taxed, and the proceeds were given to the farmers in exchange for agreements to control the production of a long list of items. The plan was optional, but few indeed were the farmers who wanted to stay out. Faced by a huge surplus of hogs, the Administration bought millions of young pigs and sows, slaughtered them and turned them into fertilizer. At the time it seemed the only possible course, but a nation brought up on puritanical notions of avoiding waste was deeply shocked, and the charge that he "killed the little pigs" was thrown at Roosevelt in every political campaign thereafter.

Trying to get cotton under control, the Government rented ten million acres of land from a million farmers, plowed them under, and thus reduced the huge cotton surplus by 4.4 million bales.

Paradoxically, while with one hand Washington sought to reduce farm production, with the other it helped bring about an increase. Hundreds of official experts taught the farmers to get more bushels per acre, more pounds of milk per cow, heavier hogs in a specified length of time. Enormous trouble was taken to teach farmers to do contour plowing, across the face of the hill, instead of vertically which caused topsoil to be lost with every heavy rain.

A Farm Security Administration was eventually set up which made loans at three percent, payable over a long term of years, to tenant farmers and sharecroppers, for machinery, seed, livestock, fertilizer, and repairs to farm buildings. A Federal Crop Insurance Corporation protected farmers against natural disasters such as floods, drought and grasshoppers. The Rural Electrification Administration created coöperatives to bring electricity to the farms; when it began, few farms anywhere had electric light or power, while today few are without these conveniences.

Farm coöperatives were also set up which bought high-quality farm animals for breeding, made possible the use of tractors, combines and other expensive farm machinery, and set up joint irrigation systems. In the arid high plains, "shelterbelts" were started—many millions of young trees, in north-and-south rows hundreds of miles long, to act as windbreaks, help prevent erosion, give winter protection to animals, and conserve water. No aspect of the New Deal was more derided at the time by city people, though the shelterbelts proved a great success and have been widely copied over the world, notably in Communist China.

In 1936, the U.S. Supreme Court, which was methodically throwing out all important aspects of the New Deal, ruled that the AAA was unconstitutional. A new law was hastily passed under which farmers were paid for letting their land lie fallow in the guise of soil conservation. Many thousands of storage warehouses, large and small, were built all over the country; nonperishable farm products, especially wheat and corn, were stored in these, and the Government made loans to the farmers with the stored crops as collateral; a farmer could harvest his corn, put it into cribs of approved design on his own land, and get a check from the Government. Since the loans were often made at prices higher than the market, the farmer usually never bothered to reclaim his produce, and the Government was left with ever-growing surpluses on its hands.

A Food Stamp Plan was presently set up, partly to feed the hungry, partly to whittle down the mountain of surplus food in the Government's hands. Under this scheme, food was distributed to the unemployed, and was also furnished in the form of free lunches for school children, which gave them in many cases their only substantial meal of the day.

Throughout the 1930's the need to deal with unemployment continued. A first and obvious way to do this was through public works—post offices, schools, and courthouses, bridges and dams.

Early in the New Deal a Public Works Administration was started with $3.5 billion and with Secretary of the Interior Harold Ickes in charge. Ickes unfortunately had a merit that proved to be a fault; he was rigidly honest, determined that the Government should get full value for its money. Suspecting, no doubt correctly, that most men taking government contracts would consider it only normal to cheat a little, he moved so slowly that the main purpose—giving as many jobs as possible as soon as possible—was defeated.

In desperation Roosevelt set up the Civil Works Administration (succeeded by the Work Projects Administration) under his pinch hitter, Harry Hopkins, notoriously able to spend money in a hurry. In spite of Ickes' savage opposition, Hopkins promptly gave jobs to four million men, at a cost of $1 billion, building roads, bridges, public buildings, sewers, sidewalks, parks, playgrounds, dams, and erosion-control projects. When it was realized that many white-collar workers, including writers, artists, and others, were unemployed, they were added on. The painters were set to doing frescoes and murals in post offices and court houses—some of them pretty terrible, others of artistic merit. State and city guide books were written for all parts of the country, many of them still in use today and the only comprehensive sources of information for certain areas.

The WPA Theater Project put on plays of its own, employing writers, directors, actors, scenic designers, and stagehands; some of its touring companies played the Civilian Conservation Camps. It is estimated that the WPA gave jobs to a total of about five million of the unemployed; at any given time the number at work was between two and three million. In its first three years, among other tasks, it built 11,000 public buildings and repaired 30,000 more, built 45,000 miles of new roads and repaired 140,000 miles; planted nine million trees, and renovated thirty million library books.

A separate National Youth Administration was also created, which gave part-time jobs to high school and college students to let them go on with their education.

The feud between Hopkins and Ickes, typical of many under

Roosevelt, continued from first to last; for a long time the two men would not speak. Ickes managed to get a law passed saying his rival should undertake no project of more than $25,000; Hopkins cheerfully went ahead with enterprises costing hundreds of thousands, simply breaking them up into a series of undertakings each of which cost $24,999.

The charge is made that Roosevelt's relief program was used for political purposes, and to some extent, this is true. Hopkins, who cared nothing about politics, infuriated Democratic politicians all over the country by hiring the best men he could find to execute his program, without asking about their political affiliations, and Ickes followed in general the same policy. Yet there were compromises with expediency. The work-relief rolls tended to increase before each Presidential or congressional election; the cynical remark was heard that this swelled the Democratic vote since "Nobody is going to shoot Santa Claus." The WPA also yielded to local custom and paid higher wages in the North than in the South.

Harry Hopkins was widely quoted as having said, "We shall tax and tax, spend and spend, elect and elect." I can find no evidence that he, or anyone else in the Roosevelt Administration, made this remark. It is true, however, that Roosevelt did spend—he had to. He also taxed, which he had to. The election results were perhaps inevitable, given the circumstances.

The New Deal was in theory based upon the philosophy of the famous British economist, John Maynard Keynes. Always in the past, depressions had been left to cure themselves. Those who were unemployed had to tighten their belts—to starve, in some cases—and try to sit out the economic storm. When the glut of unsalable, or rather, unpurchasable, goods had gradually subsided, business would slowly revive.

Keynes, who had distinguished himself among economists by applying his theories to the stock market as a young man and speedily making himself a fortune, argued that this period of misery was unnecessary. He held that in times of depression the Government should spend large sums on public works. Not only would this give employment to numbers of the jobless, but the expenditures themselves would help to revive the faltering economy much sooner than would otherwise be the case; he calculated that a dollar spent in this way for wages or raw materials would, because it was itself spent again and chiefly for food, clothing, and shelter, ultimately produce expenditures of about four dollars.

The Keynes theories were brought to Roosevelt by members of his Brain Trust, and it is a matter of dispute how much he understood them. Keynes himself did not meet the President until the New Deal had been in operation for a long time; he complained afterwards that F.D.R. did not seem to know very well what they were talking about, and remarked that his span of attention seemed shockingly short!

To many American critics, including the *New Republic* magazine, of which the writer was then Editor, it seemed that the Keynes theories were never given a full trial because not enough money was spent at any given moment for a real test. When times seemed substantially improved, in 1937, Roosevelt assumed that his troubles were over, listened to the anti-Keynesians, and curtailed government spending sharply; business promptly went into a decline, one of the steepest in history.

Whatever may have been the causal relationship, the national income went up between 1932 and 1936 from $46 billion to $66 billion, recovering about half of the loss since 1929. Gross farm income was nearly doubled, from $4.5 billion to $8.5 billion— and the flight from the land was stopped. Wages and salaries increased from $31 billion to $42 billion, and corporations went from an annual loss of $4 billion to a profit of $6.5 billion.

Ever since the Cold War began, in about 1946, opponents of the New Deal, including in particular most of the leaders of the Republican Party, have charged that the Roosevelt Administration had been infected with Communists, with a strong implication that the President and his top aides knew they were there, did not object, and in fact tacitly approved of their fundamentally revolutionary aims.

Factually, this charge is partly true and partly false; in its implications, it is wholly false.

It is indeed true that some people in the Government at the intermediate level or lower were dedicated Communists who undoubtedly went to Washington to aid the Party. It is also true that the top-level group were warned about the radical affiliations of certain of these individuals and did little or nothing to investigate the charges or to remove these people from their positions. In assessing culpability, several things must be borne in mind.

The first of these is that, beginning early in Roosevelt's Presidency and continuing until the Stalin-Hitler Pact of August, 1939, the Russian Government had ordered Communists all over the world to follow the "United Front" policy. They were to coöperate in every way with liberal and progressive movements; nobody worked harder to further the legitimate purposes of the New Deal than did the Communists in Washington at this time; while some of them stole information and forwarded it to Moscow, apparently only a small percentage engaged in any such illegitimate activity.

We must remember also that in the 1930's many Americans, and especially the liberals, had not yet awakened to the brutal tyranny of the blood-stained Russian regime. They still thought of the Communist Party not as a ruthless conspiracy to destroy all individual freedom but as more or less the inheritor of the mild public-ownership program of the old Socialist Party. Conservative mass-circulation magazines tolerated known Communists among their editors; Hollywood producers hired such men to write motion-picture scripts. It is true that the Communists in these positions rarely succeeded in getting their radical views into the material they prepared for public consumption, but they did what they could to "bore from within."

We must remember also that from the end of the United Front days, in August, 1939, until Russia became a war ally was only about twenty-eight months. Thereafter, during the war years, anybody who had talked about the Russian Government as harshly as everybody was doing in the 1950's would probably have been arrested.

These facts explain, if they do not excuse, the extraordinary slackness of Roosevelt in regard to the American Communists. The conservatives must also bear some of the blame; by calling Roosevelt an ultra-Leftist when he was not, they made it harder for him to take seriously accusations against those who really were ultra-Leftist. In fact, of course, Roosevelt was a conservative in the true sense of that word; he wanted to rescue the capitalist system, not to destroy it, and he succeeded.

Toward the end of the decade, as times got better, the American Tories became more powerful and managed to clip Hopkins' wings. He was forced to agree to dismiss WPA workers who had been on the relief rolls eighteen months; in 1939, 800,-000 were fired under this rule. A check made three months later showed that only twelve percent of these had found jobs, half of them at wages smaller than the pitiful amount the WPA was paying. The remainder of those dismissed were on public charity or using what small savings they had, or were dependent on the neighbors. The median income of the unemployed was $7 a week, but twenty-five percent of them had no income at all.

Most of the states had by now passed laws refusing public assistance to anyone who had not lived there for a specified length of time, often three years. This was a bad blow to transient workers; people feared to move from one state to another, even when jobs opened up, lest they should not prove permanent and relief should be unavailable.

In assessing the results of the New Deal, it is important to remember the tremendous physical improvements that were made and are still in service—Bonneville Dam, the Triborough Bridge over the East River in New York, the many thousands of miles of highways, flood-control ditches and dams, the public buildings and airports all over the country. Millions of people kept up their technical skills who would otherwise have become permanently unemployable except at the lowest level—skills that proved of great value when war came.

The Tennessee Valley Authority greatly reduced for all time the threat of flood damage on the Tennessee, Ohio, and Mississippi Rivers. It saved three million acres that would soon have been destroyed through erosion and brought a new way of life to the inhabitants of a backward mountain area. It also made possible the atomic bomb that ended Japanese resistance in the Second World War, by furnishing at Oak Ridge the large amount of electricity necessary for the extraction of fissionable materials, an amount not available at that time anywhere else in the country.

In June, 1935, began another fruitful period of about three months, often referred to as "The Second Hundred Days." The National Labor Relations Act was passed, and the first Social Security law. Improvements were made in banking, the Tennessee Valley Authority, and the Agricultural Adjustment Administration. New legislation was passed for higher taxes on incomes, inheritances, and corporation profits. The Government undertook to guarantee the safety of bank deposits up to $10,-000. Legislation was passed to strike down holding companies, which controlled the stock of a number of corporations and made possible numerous types of devious manipulations.

It is difficult, a third of a century later, to realize the situation of the worker before Roosevelt took office. Unions had virtually no legal status in most industries, and their membership was confined to a limited number of skilled technicians. Violence in strikes was commonplace, strikers fighting "scabs," police, and company guards who in some cases were practically private armies. The National Labor Relations Act affirmed the right of the majority of the workers in any plant to organize a union and to bargain collectively. A National Labor Relations Board was set up to act as a tribunal to hear complaints from either workers or management, though in many cases its rulings could be appealed to the courts.

Feeling the moral support of the Government for the first time in history, labor now took the bit in its teeth. Some liberal labor leaders who objected to the conservatism of the American Federation of Labor formed the Committee on Industrial Organization, with the avowed purpose of unionizing the comparatively unskilled workers in the mass industries—steel, automobiles, textiles, and others. In 1936, the group broke away from the AFL, and changed its name to the Congress of Industrial Organizations; soon it had nearly four million members. A million of these were taken over from the AFL, which, however, soon expanded enough to replace them, with a total of more than three million. Total union membership had doubled in two years.

While some employers accepted the change with good grace, others fought the unions bitterly. They were outraged when the New Deal pressure forced relief agencies to grant aid to strikers as they did to those unemployed for other reasons. By the end of 1936 there was a huge wave of strikes all over the country, primarily for union recognition; they were a symbol of how far the country had come since the hard times of the Hoover Administration.

About now, the technique was invented of the "sit-down" strike, in which workers stayed in the plant they had struck, eating and sleeping there, and refusing admission to company representatives under the implied threat of damage to valuable machinery. Gathering material for a magazine article, I visited an automobile plant in Flint, Michigan, while such a strike was in progress. It was an eerie experience—the long line of partly assembled automobiles, ranging from the completed car at the front to the mere frame at the back; the strikers in their work clothes, some of them standing guard, others sleeping or preparing meals on camp stoves, in the gloom of the vast shadowy hall, the electricity having been shut off. I entered and left through a ground floor window, having been passed through a picket line on the street after showing my credentials as a journalist. This particular strike was won by the workers, after Governor Frank Murphy of Michigan had outraged the company by refusing to send in state troops to oust the squatters.

Other strikes ended less happily from the viewpoint of the workers. Violence was frequent, and usually aroused little public comment. When the United Automobile Workers sought to organize the Ford plant in Detroit, a union representative, Richard Frankensteen, was beaten almost fatally by strike-breakers.

A climax came when, on Memorial Day, 1937, ten CIO strikers were shot and killed by police in the course of a riot at the Republic Steel plant in South Chicago.

When Roosevelt took office, the United States was lagging far behind the countries of Western Europe and most parts of the British Commonwealth in public assistance for the aged, the unemployed, widows, orphans, and the physically handicapped. Not unnaturally, the Depression spawned a group of radical social and financial reformers in various parts of the country, whose panaceas, whether sound or not, had a strong appeal to millions of Americans who were innocent victims of the economic storm.

Perhaps the best known of the plans put forward was that of Dr. Francis R. Townsend of California, who proposed a nationwide two-percent sales tax to give everybody over sixty $200 a month, on condition that he should stop all productive work, and should spend the whole amount within thirty days. In vain did the experts argue that to do this would eventually require giving half the national income to only eight percent of the people, probably cutting the purchasing power of money by one-third in the process. All over the country millions of elderly people flocked happily into Townsend Clubs. So did large numbers of their grown-up children who looked forward to being relieved of the burden of caring for their parents (about three-quarters of those over sixty-five were without financial resources of any kind). Dr. Townsend speedily became an important political figure.

Another thorn in the side of the New Deal was Father Francis Coughlin of the Shrine of the Little Flower, at Royal Oak, Michigan. Father Coughlin had a persuasive, highly emotional radio personality, and a set of vague financial and economic ideas, never very clear, but believed by many people to have Fascist overtones. A strong opponent of Roosevelt, he rapidly gained enormous power throughout the country. Nobody knows what might have happened had not his superiors in the Catholic Church effectively muzzled him.

Still a third Left demagogue was Governor Huey Long of

Louisiana, a backwoods boy who had come to power on slogans of "Every Man a King," and "Share the Wealth." His administration dripped bribery and corruption, but his promises were rosy, and he really did carry them out to the extent of providing good roads, free textbooks, and some good hospitals. Long quite possibly might have become an Americanized version of Hitler, had he not been assassinated.

A brief but dramatic episode came in California, where in 1934, Upton Sinclair, a Socialist and prolific author of propagandist novels, ran for Governor on a quasi-Socialist promise to "End Poverty in California." His leftwing "EPIC" program frightened the state's conservatives so much that they invested a huge sum in a publicity campaign to defeat him. A freshly created "newsreel" appeared, distributed free to movie theatres throughout the state, containing anti-Sinclair propaganda; among other items, it showed tramps emerging from boxcars in the Los Angeles freight terminals, announcing happily that they had come to live under Governor Sinclair and share the California wealth. The charge was made that these "vagrants" were actors recruited by the Hollywood studios. Although he rolled up an impressive vote, Sinclair was defeated.

Against this background, the Roosevelt Administration introduced the first Social Security legislation, amid powerful opposition from every part of the country. Believers in states' rights objected to federal interference in what they considered local issues. Although the old-age pensions, which were to begin after reserves had been built up, were pitifully small, ranging from a maximum of $85 a month down to $10, employers, especially in the South, wanted to keep old workers on the job at less money, and complained at being required to meet this financial competition.

The bill as finally passed was a hodgepodge of political concessions. Benefits for old-age pensioners and their spouses were kept in a Federal system, but unemployment insurance and all other benefits except care for the disabled were turned over to the states; the Federal Government collected the taxes for these but returned ninety percent of the money to the state agencies. These set their own, widely varying conditions as to the number of weeks in the year unemployment benefits could be drawn and their amount; in many cases these were inadequate. The law also provided for widows, orphans, and the blind. Over the course of years, the statute has been repeatedly modified to provide larger benefits, more liberal terms, and larger taxes on payrolls to provide the needed funds assessed against both employers and workers.

In 1936 Roosevelt was reëlected over Governor Alfred M. Landon of Kansas, in the most sweeping victory in American history. Landon carried only two of the forty-eight states, Maine and Vermont; the electoral vote was 523 to 8. The Republicans said bitterly that the Democrats had bought the election with Federal funds; by now, the WPA had spent $6 billion, the PWA $4 billion, and the AAA was furnishing a large part of the farmers' income. The Social Security system was in effect. The Home Owners' Loan Corporation had made more than one million loans on houses to prevent mortgage foreclosures.

Roosevelt in accepting the nomination added "economic royalists" to the American vocabulary, and thrilled his listeners by saying that we had "a rendezvous with history." Another famous phrase came in his Inaugural address when he said, "I see one-third of a nation ill-housed, ill-clad, ill-nourished." There were certainly many Americans suffering from deep poverty, but nobody knew whether they were one-third of the population; Roosevelt had blithely drawn the figure out of the air.

Only three months after the election, the President's popularity with a large section of the population sank sharply with the announcement of his famous proposal for packing the Supreme Court. This body of nine included four conservatives, Willis Van Devanter, James C. McReynolds, George Sutherland, and Pierce Butler; three liberals, Louis Brandeis, Harlan Stone, and Benjamin Cardozo, and two middle-of-the-road Justices, Owen Roberts and Charles Evans Hughes. Unluckily for Roosevelt, when the constitutionality of New Deal measures came before the Court, the middle-of-the-road men usually sided with the conservatives. By 1937, nine of the eleven most important laws had been thrown out by the Court; the only two that remained were matters as to which it was virtually impossible to "unscramble the eggs"—the devaluation of gold, and the Tennessee Valley Authority. Roosevelt was especially irked because the four conservatives were among the oldest men on the Court, with an average age of seventy-four; they refused to retire precisely because they considered the President a wild radical and felt it was their duty to remain and destroy his program.

Roosevelt, therefore, on February 4, 1937, proposed a plan to raise the number of Justices from nine to a possible fifteen. He wanted the law to authorize him to appoint one new Justice for every man who refused to retire (at full salary) at age seventy. He consulted almost no one before announcing this scheme; many of his loyal supporters both within and without the government were dismayed at this tricky, evasive way of getting a Court that agreed with him, and the proposal was killed by the Judiciary Committee of the Senate. Yet amid the uproar the Court seemed to have taken a fresh look at itself; presently it upheld a minimum wage law in Oregon after having struck down the same law in New York. Deaths and resignations followed, and before long, Roosevelt was able to appoint five new members—Felix Frankfurter, Stanley Reed, William O. Douglas, Frank Murphy, and Robert H. Jackson. The Court now proceeded to approve nearly all the chief provisions of the New Deal program.

The decade of the 1930's, so momentous in domestic affairs for the United States, also saw Fascism make continuing gains throughout the world. Mussolini, seeking to take the minds of the Italian people off their troubles at home, launched his unprovoked war on Ethiopia on the cynical plea that he needed more room for Italian colonization. Japan overran Manchuria and then proceeded to make war on China as the first step in a scheme to dominate all of East Asia and the islands of the Western Pacific, under the plan for the "Greater East Asia Co-

Prosperity Sphere." In Spain, the Fascists rose against the Republican Government and destroyed it after a bitter war in which they were aided by Italy and Germany, and the Republicans were aided (and finally dominated) by Soviet Russia.

Thirty-three days before Roosevelt took office, Adolf Hitler became Nazi Chancellor of Germany; seventeen months later, with the death of the aged German President, General von Hindenburg, he combined the offices of President and Chancellor and became Führer, a word that means "leader" but in this case was used to mean Chancellor. He now began the steady process of extending the boundaries of Germany, occupying first the Rhineland, taken from Germany at the end of the First World War, then Austria, then in two successive bites, Czechoslovakia. In August, 1939, he stunned the world with an agreement with Stalin which freed his hands to begin the Second World War.

The mood of the United States in the mid-thirties was overwhelmingly neutralist if not indeed isolationist or pacifist. For this there were several reasons.

While it is true that America was forced into the First World War for various reasons, one of which was that German submarines sank our ships, this country had entered the War, spurred by President Wilson's idealistic phraseology, in a mood of spiritual fervor; it was to be "the War to end war." The peace-treaty negotiations in Paris in 1919 had brought about a violent revulsion—so violent that the United States subsequently refused by a narrow margin in the Senate to enter the League of Nations, which was Wilson's creation more than any other man's.

At Paris the innocent Americans had seen their European Allies carve up the map of Europe, and scramble for German colonies throughout the world, ignoring the promise to Wilson that subject peoples were to rule their own destiny. The Americans learned, moreover, that the worst revisions of national boundaries had been incorporated into a series of secret treaties signed long before the United States entered the war. It was a hard blow, and one not yet forgotten when Fascism began its aggressions.

Another item that set the mood of the United States in the

1930's was a Senate investigation of the policies of munitions makers, who came to be known popularly as "Merchants of Death." While there was never any evidence that these gentry dictated the policies of the Great Powers, it was revealed that some of them sold ever larger armaments to small nations by building up war scares. As a result of this investigation the United States passed an embargo law forbidding the sale of arms to either side in any future conflict. This law was strictly enforced in the case of the Spanish Civil War.

By the middle of the decade, Roosevelt was far in advance of the great majority of his fellow countrymen in sensing the dangers of Fascist aggression all over the world. He chafed under the restrictions of the Neutrality Act, but as a shrewd politician he refused to get too far in advance of public opinion, or of France and Great Britain, which were keeping hands off the Spanish Civil War.

In October, 1937, the President put out a trial balloon to see whether American opinion had changed. Dedicating a new bridge built in Chicago by the PWA, he borrowed a phrase from Harold Ickes and spoke of the necessity to "quarantine the aggressors." The foundations of civilization, he said, were threatened by international lawlessness, and the United States would eventually be in danger:

> The peace-loving nations must make a concerted effort in opposition to those violations of treaties and those ignorings of human instincts which today are creating a state of international anarchy and instability from which there is no escape through mere isolation or neutrality. . . . The peace, the freedom and security of ninety percent of the population of the world is being jeopardized by the remaining ten percent who are threatening a breakdown of all international law and order. . . . When an epidemic of physical disease starts to spread, the community approves and joins in a quarantine of the patients in order to protect the health of the community against the spread of the disease. . . . We are adopting such measures as will minimize our risk of involvement, but we cannot have

complete protection in a world of disorder in which confidence and security have broken down.

American opinion had not changed; the speech brought strong protest from every part of the country. Pacifists called him a war monger; the AFL passed a resolution against getting involved in foreign wars; not one important Democratic leader spoke out in his support; a poll of Congress showed a heavy majority against any concerted action of any kind with the League of Nations to stop Japanese aggression on the Asiatic mainland. Roosevelt promptly retreated, saying that he had no thought of repudiating neutrality but was only "expanding it."

Although the President was denounced at the time for doing too much and going too fast, today it is more common to complain that he did too little, not lifting a finger to help Ethiopia, Republican Spain, or China. We refused to apply the Neutrality Act in the Far East on the specious plea that, technically, no war existed there. American citizens sold huge amounts of oil and scrap iron to Japan, without which she could not have carried on her war with China; New York City streetcar tracks were torn up, the metal was sold to Japan, and returned a few years later in the form of bullets fired at American boys. Our government snubbed the League of Nations in most of its efforts to maintain peace. Though Roosevelt tried to get British Prime Minister Neville Chamberlain to call a conference of the Powers to head off the impending European war, he refused, against strong urging from some quarters in Britain, to speak out against Chamberlain's fatal appeasement of Hitler at Munich.

While this was true, as the decade wore on Roosevelt did more and more to help Great Britain and France without arousing too much opposition at home. They were permitted to buy munitions in the United States, but at first only on a strict "cash and carry" basis, which meant that they must be paid for before they left our shores and carried only in Allied ships. Later, he devised a plan to exchange fifty American destroyers for long-term leases on several British naval bases in the Western Hemisphere, most of them in the Caribbean. The destroyers were loudly advertised to be "over-age," but they were not so old that the British were not delighted to have them. Finally came the plan for "Lend-Lease"—a phrase achieved after a long struggle for the right words, which simply meant permitting the Allies to buy huge quantities of supplies in the United States with money advanced by our government on no security. When Russia was forced into the War by the German attack in June, 1941, Lend-Lease was extended to her as well, over the strenuous objection of conservative Republicans.

After Dunkirk, the United States rushed supplies to the British: 500,000 rifles, 80,000 machine guns, 130 million rounds of ammunition, 900 seventy-five mm. guns and a million shells. Some historians believe that these supplies, plus the fifty American destroyers, may have prevented a successful invasion of England by Hitler, though of course there were other factors— including the Royal Air Force.

As the storm clouds darkened, the American attitude toward the War began to change. About six months before Pearl Harbor, seventy-five percent of those queried by the Gallup Poll were in favor of America's going to war if Hitler could be defeated in no other way, and eighty percent believed we would get into the War "eventually." Yet isolationism was still strong throughout the country, and especially in the Democratic Party. There were also active pro-Axis elements. The Friends of the New Germany were an openly Nazi group; the German Bund drilled and paraded in Nazi uniforms and used familiar Hitler tactics of administering savage beatings to hecklers at its public meetings. An outcropping appeared of crackpot American Fascist groups, who were against Communists, Catholics, Negroes, and Jews, and probably several million people sympathized with their ideas, openly or covertly.

The isolationists were now bolder than ever; they organized an American First Committee which by demanding neutrality hurt the cause of the Allies. Colonel Charles A. Lindbergh, who had been the subject of adulation thirteen years earlier, was sure that Germany would win, and wanted the United States to keep out. Early in 1941, he said ". . . this War is lost. It is not within our power today to win the War for England, even though we throw the entire resources of our nation into the conflict." Later he added that only "the British, the Jews, and the Roosevelt Administration" wanted the United States to participate in the War—in contradiction of the Gallup Poll.

When, in September, 1940, the first peacetime conscription in American history was established, Roosevelt had to hammer hard on the idea that this was for defensive purposes only. "Your boys," he said, "are not going to be sent into any foreign wars." Judge Rosenman fought hard for a precautionary phrase, "except in case of attack," but Roosevelt refused, saying sensibly that if we were attacked it would be no longer a foreign war.

By 1941 the President felt that he could act more boldly to aid Great Britain, even though the continuance of the draft had passed Congress by only a single vote. An unlimited national emergency was now declared, and a bitter correspondence began with the Germans, warning them that we would shoot back if their submarines continued to attack American ships. United States military bases were set up in Greenland, an Office of Civilian Defense was established, and the sale of oil and steel to Japan was finally stopped after she had acquired vast quantities.

In August, Roosevelt and Churchill held a secret meeting off Newfoundland and signed the Atlantic Charter, which sounded singularly like the document of two nations both at war against a common enemy. The two heads of state agreed that after the victory that was confidently assumed, they would seek no territorial aggrandizement, that there would be no territorial changes unless the inhabitants of an area wanted them, and that all nations that had been conquered would be restored to freedom. Equal access to trade and raw materials was pledged to everyone; the oceans were to be free highways; there must be no more use of force in the world and any future aggressor would be disarmed. When the Allies drew up the United Nations Declaration, on New Year's Day, 1942, the Atlantic Charter was embodied in it.

In October, the convoy system was put into operation in the North Atlantic, and in November, American merchantmen were armed for defense against submarines.

With Russia now in the War, and Lend-Lease extended to her, the President planned to send an American aircraft carrier full of fighter planes to the Persian Gulf, whence these planes could fly to Russian soil. The Navy fought the idea bitterly, however, and he was obliged to send the planes by slow merchant ships to a Russian port on the Arctic Ocean, a route subject to great risk from German attack.

By 1938, Roosevelt's popularity had diminished from the level of 1936 and his stunning victory over Landon. He was hurt somewhat by the Court-packing plan, and probably more by the short but very severe depression in 1937.

He was increasingly harassed by conservative Democrats in Congress, and in 1938 he made the bad mistake of attempting to purge these men in the primary elections, pleading that with the world situation so critical he needed a Congress loyal to his policies. The purge was a dismal failure; as usual, local issues were overriding and the entrenched conservatives in most cases were able to win. In the election that autumn, the Republicans made substantial gains for the first time in ten years; they carried Ohio, almost carried New York, and gained eight seats in the Senate and eighty-two in the House.

As the Presidential election of 1940 came near, the great unanswered question was whether Roosevelt would run for a third term, something never done since Washington set a precedent by refusing a third nomination. Apparently the President himself at first intended to respect the tradition; he told at least three members of his Cabinet that he would not run, and signed a contract with *Collier's Weekly* to contribute a regular column. At the same time, he refused to make his intentions public; at his press conferences, newspapermen laid innumerable traps for him which he laughingly evaded. By now, the Second World War was a year old, the terrible aerial Battle of Britain was in progress, and the President did not dare reduce his political powers by an announcement that he was about to retire. Half a dozen Democrats wanted the nomination, including Vice-President Garner, Postmaster General Farley, and several other members of the Cabinet. The President kept silent until the Democratic National Convention was actually under way; then he sent a message saying:

> The President wishes in all earnestness and sincerity to make it clear that all the delegates to this Convention are free to vote for any candidate.

In the double-talk of politics, this meant that he would run, and he was nominated on the first ballot. Late at night he made an acceptance speech over the long-distance telephone from Washington, broadcast by loudspeakers throughout the hall in Chicago. He said that he did not want a third term but would accept it as a duty and a sacrifice comparable to those he had asked of other citizens. In view of the tense international situation, he announced that he would not have the time or inclination to engage in purely political debate.

The Vice-Presidential candidate was Secretary of Agriculture Henry A. Wallace, an aloof, idealistic man, who spoke a language incomprehensible to most practical politicians, and who was correspondingly disliked by them. Harry Hopkins, Roosevelt's all-purpose messenger boy, had to tell them the President insisted on Wallace before they gloomily accepted him.

Roosevelt's resolution to conduct a passive campaign speedily went out the window because of the aggressive tactics of the Republican candidate. This was a wealthy public-utility official, Wendell Willkie, whose nasal mid-western accent revealed his Indiana origin. Willkie was an amateur in politics, who suddenly appeared out of nowhere when the country had already begun to tire of the other chief contenders, Governors John Bricker of Ohio and Thomas Dewey of New York, and Senators Robert Taft of Ohio and Arthur Vandenberg of Michigan. The new candidate was a man of great charm, ebullience, and energy, though so unskilled in public speaking that he soon wore his voice down to a whisper; he managed to frighten the Democrats so much that soon Roosevelt was "running scared."

Although the Republican nominee did not take an isolationist position, Roosevelt had been so outspokenedly pro-Ally that the America Firsters and pro-Germans flocked to the Willkie banner. So did the American Communists; they had flopped over from being neutralists in the 1930's to being pro-Axis within twenty-four hours after the Stalin-Hitler pact in August, 1939 (they were to flop again in the same length of time in June, 1941, when Hitler treacherously attacked his Russian partner). The Communists and fellow-travelers were insignificant in numbers, but they included many people in the communications industry and had an importance beyond their numbers. Willkie got seven million more votes than Landon had done, but Roosevelt got five million more still; although the Republican carried ten states, he lost in the Electoral College by 449 to 82.

Early in the morning of December 7, 1941, came the worst military disaster in American history. One hundred Japanese planes, accompanied by several midget submarines, made a surprise attack on the American naval base at Pearl Harbor, Oahu, Hawaiian Islands. More than 3,300 Americans were killed, and the naval losses were severe. One battleship was sunk, and seven others were damaged, four of them so badly that repairs seemed hopeless. Corresponding damage was done to six destroyers and a number of military craft. More than 170 of our airplanes were destroyed on the ground. Japan could easily have captured the Hawaiian Islands if she had pushed her advantage.

The American Government of course had long recognized the danger of war, and had sought to mitigate it without conniving at Japan's lawless acts. In the autumn of 1941, President

Roosevelt made a personal appeal to Emperor Hirohito, which came to nothing; Hirohito, in spite of being venerated by the mass of the people, was in fact a palace prisoner of the Fascists; the Government was now under complete military control, with General Hideki Tojo as Premier. In Washington it was common knowledge that the danger of war was great and was increasing. American military and naval forces throughout the world, and in Hawaii especially, were alerted to be on their guard.

Why Pearl Harbor was not properly defended has never been explained, in spite of half a dozen elaborate investigations, including one by Congress. One answer is that all the strategists expected Japan to attack first the Dutch and British possessions in the Western Pacific, perhaps including the Philippines. (In fact, however, many hours after Pearl Harbor, the American forces in the Philippines were also caught napping, and nearly all United States planes there were destroyed on the ground.)

Another explanation, though certainly no excuse, is the traditional rivalry between the United States Army and Navy that has so often hampered our military operations in one war after another. Relations were strained between Admiral Husband Kimmel and General Walter Short, preventing the constant consultation and coöperation that should have taken place.

The United States some time earlier had broken Japan's ultra-secret communication code, and had thus learned of her great military and naval activity in the Western Pacific. She had sent two special envoys to Washington, and on the eve of Pearl Harbor, our intelligence intercepted a long and ominous cable message to one of them. President Roosevelt, reading it in the presence of Harry Hopkins, said, "This means war." Hopkins remarked, "We ought to strike the first blow," to which the President replied, "No, we can't do that. We are a democracy and a peaceful people." Hopkins recorded in his diary that the vulnerability of Pearl Harbor was not discussed, nor any possible date on which the war might begin.

Roosevelt picked up the telephone to call Admiral Harold Stark, Chief of Naval Operations, in Washington. He learned however that the Admiral had gone to the theatre, and decided against having him paged, lest the theatre audience be unduly alarmed!

On the actual morning of Pearl Harbor, Gen. George Marshall, Chief of Staff, did attempt to warn General Short again. He had on his desk a "scrambler" telephone by which he could have reached General Short within a minute or two, but inexplicably, he chose instead to send an ambiguous message by commercial service. It took hours to transmit; long after the attack on Pearl Harbor was over, a Western Union messenger was bicycling with it to General Short's headquarters. Marshall afterward offered the lame excuse that he did not use his telephone because "the Japanese could construe the fact that the Army was alerting its garrisons in Hawaii as a hostile act . . . [They] would have grasped at almost any straw to bring such portions of our public [as] doubted our integrity of action [to feel] that we were committing an act that forced action on their part."

President Roosevelt learned of the attack from Secretary of the Navy Frank Knox at 1:40 P.M. Washington time, about forty-five minutes after the bombing started. Knox phoned that a radio message from Honolulu had been picked up in Washington saying that an air raid was on and that it was "not drill." Hopkins was with Roosevelt, and reported afterward that the President remained calm and talked about the efforts he had made to prevent war. He waited twenty-five minutes before telephoning to Secretary Hull about the attack. Hull had an appointment to see the Japanese envoys later that day, and Roosevelt told him not to mention the attack, but to talk briefly and coldly with the two men; Hull, a hot-tempered mountaineer from Tennessee, on the contrary, gave them a tongue lashing and sent them away. (The two envoys always claimed that they had no advance knowledge of the attack.)

About an hour after Knox's telephone call, and long after every American radio station was broadcasting the news of Pearl Harbor, the President dictated an announcement for the press.

Thirty minutes later he held a short conference with the Secretaries of State, War, and Navy (as the Cabinet was then organized), plus Admiral Stark and General Marshall. That evening he met with the full Cabinet and the leaders of both Houses of Congress, opening the meeting with the remark, "This is the most serious Cabinet session since Lincoln met with the Cabinet at the outbreak of the Civil War." After four hours of planning for emergency action, he broke up the meeting. Next morning he appeared before a joint session of Congress to announce that a state of war existed.

The cult of Roosevelt-hating reached some sort of climax in later years with the charge that the President had deliberately plotted to invite a Japanese attack and thus bring the United States into the World War; whole books have been written arguing this thesis. So far as I am aware there is no evidence of any truth in these charges, which are rejected by the majority of American historians. Quite apart from the fact that only a madman could have undertaken such a diabolical action, to suggest that Roosevelt could have done so under any circumstances is to ignore the fundamental facts of human nature. All his life he was a lover of ships, and above all, of the vessels of the American Navy; it is unthinkable that he should have planned to harm them, even assuming that he did not expect such an overwhelming Japanese success as occurred.

The notion that American policy forced the Japanese into attack conflicts with the historical facts. Everything we know of Fascist psychology, which is very much the same the world over, suggests that they would have struck at us eventually, regardless of anything we did, unless the United States and the chief European Powers were prepared to stand aside and let them have their way.

There was so much controversy over Pearl Harbor that the President appointed a special investigating committee headed by Supreme Court Justice Owen Roberts. The Committee reported early in 1942 and made charges of dereliction of duty against Kimmel and Short. There was talk of a court martial, but it came to nothing; in December, 1944, the Army and Navy made a report of their own, whitewashing these two officers. Next a joint congressional committee was appointed in September, 1945, after Roosevelt's death and the end of the War, to investigate all the charges, including those against the late President. It reported after nearly a year, saying that the charges against Kimmel, Short, and the President were groundless. It did, however, criticise the War and Navy Departments for failing to emphasize sufficiently the danger of armed attack.

Immediately after Pearl Harbor, most of the anger was of course directed against Japan, for its surprise attack without any declaration of war; a fifth of a century later, it is almost impossible for us to realize or remember how deep was the contempt and hatred for the whole Japanese nation. Our military authorities had not yet learned, as they came to do before the War was over, to consult cultural anthropologists about the behavior to be expected of an enemy nation; if they had done so, they would have learned that attack without warning seemed entirely honorable and sensible, in the light of Japanese mores.

The coming of the War greatly increased the already heavy burden on the White House, though it did not improve the President's inefficient work habits. He continued to make many important decisions in a casual, offhand manner, often without consulting the people who had expert knowledge of the problem that was involved.

Within a day or two after Pearl Harbor, all the Allied Powers were legally at war with all those of the Axis, and a setback to any of the partners became a setback for all. A heavy blow was the loss in mid-February, 1942, of the great British naval base at Singapore to Japanese forces which came down (wearing tennis sneakers!) through the supposedly impassable swamps and jungle of the Malay Peninsula and captured the city from the rear; the British, having never contemplated such a thing, had set all their guns immovably looking out to sea in the other direction.

On the following day Roosevelt and Harry Hopkins sat down alone together and sketched out a grand strategy for the War. They decided to reinforce Australia, New Zealand and the Dutch East Indies; to share with Great Britain the defense of Rangoon and the rest of Burma; to give munitions but not troops to Chiang Kai-shek; to step up the antisubmarine warfare in the Atlantic; to send military supplies to Great Britain in larger quantities, and to aid the friendly nations of the Middle East, and some South American countries; to strengthen the defenses of Hawaii and to give first priority to American plants manufacturing high-octane gasoline, airplanes, and ships.

The immediate problems the United States faced upon entering the War were tremendous. The country did not have the resources for simultaneous full-scale attack both in the Pacific and in Europe, and had to decide which theatre should come first. This was also in part a decision between the American Army and Navy, since the European War required many soldiers and fewer naval vessels (though still a huge quantity), while the Pacific War was, in its early stages, almost entirely one of ships and naval aircraft. Roosevelt and Churchill agreed that Hitler must be crushed first, and this course was followed, over such bitter opposition on the part of some elements in the American Navy as to amount almost to insubordination.

Another struggle that continued throughout the War had to do with priorities for military or civilian goods. A generation of Americans who had never known what it was to be unable to buy whatever they wanted, if they had the money, were suddenly forced into wartime austerity, when gasoline, meat, and other things were rationed. Many civilians wanted to have both "guns and butter," and brought pressure to bear on Congress; sometimes this pressure was resisted, sometimes not.

One redeeming aspect of the situation was that the public excoriation of the President stopped, though it is doubtful whether those who hated him actually changed their minds.

For the British, of course, the entrance of the United States into the War meant the difference between the better-than-even chance of ultimate defeat and a good hope of eventual victory. Churchill began his series of extended visits to Washington, during which he was a guest in the White House. His nocturnal habits were a severe trial; when he did not keep the President up until three or four o'clock in the morning, he turned his attention to the even frailer Hopkins; sometimes Roosevelt, not wanting to miss anything, would come back from his bedroom and join the pair.

A story that made the rounds of Washington about this time told how one morning Roosevelt rolled his wheel-chair into Churchill's bedroom just as the Prime Minister, unclothed, came from his bath. The President apologized and started to leave, but Churchill stopped him, saying: "The Prime Minister of Great Britain has nothing to conceal from the President of the United States." Churchill denied this, tongue in cheek, to Robert Sherwood, insisting that he had never met the President while wearing less than a bath towel.

While the War was in progress, propaganda both in Britain and the United States reported that Roosevelt and Churchill had become very close friends, but Sherwood, who had access to Hopkins' private papers, denies this (in *Roosevelt and Hopkins: An Intimate History*). Both of them were too egotistical, too aware of their own importance, for any really close relationship. During most of the War the United States was so powerful, and Britain needed her so desperately, that Roosevelt necessarily had the last word in disputed matters, though Churchill got a partial revenge by repeatedly reopening questions that everyone else thought had been settled.

The two men met several times and of course under conditions of great secrecy—in Washington, Quebec, Casablanca, Cairo, Teheran, and Yalta. It was at Casablanca that Roosevelt made his famous, much-criticized demand that the Axis Powers must surrender unconditionally (later, Italy was excluded). No one is now quite sure whether the idea came to Roosevelt the instant he was speaking, as he afterward remembered, or had been discussed in advance, as Churchill claimed. In any case, there were several arguments in its favor. Stalin feared, or said he feared, that Britain and the United States might make a separate peace; the Western Allies certainly thought that *he* might do so. The grim stipulation also helped warn the Americans they were probably in for a long war. It gave the nations Hitler had conquered some hope that their sufferings would be avenged. Finally, it prevented the Germans from saying, as they had done after the First World War, that they had been tricked into a negotiated peace by promises that were afterward betrayed.

Some historians argue that the demand for unconditional surrender made Germany and Japan fight more desperately and thus prolonged the War. But the leaders of both these countries were fanatics; it is hard to believe that they would have surrended in any case until the last extremity.

Though no one realized it at the time, probably the most important event of the war years was one of which the American public knew nothing until August, 1945: the invention of the atom bomb. Beginning in 1933, a series of experiments by Italian, German, and German-Jewish refugee physicists showed that when the nucleus of a certain type of unstable atom of uranium was bombarded by slowed-down neutrons, it split into two parts, barium and krypton, with the release of an enormous amount of energy. The physicists theorized that if a chain reaction could be set up among the atoms, the bombarded nucleus releasing other neutrons to strike more atoms, an explosive of great power might be developed.

In 1939, this idea was passed along to American physicists. The European experiments were repeated and confirmed in the cyclotron that had been built at the University of California by Dr. Ernest O. Lawrence. It was known that the Germans were continuing experiments with atom smashing, and the scientists in America were alarmed lest they should come up with the answer. It was decided that President Roosevelt should be informed of this danger and should be urged to put up the money for the enormously expensive task of trying to bring about the release of atomic energy.

A letter was therefore prepared setting forth the theory in layman's language, and Dr. Albert Einstein agreed to sign it. He had had little to do with the experimental work, but he was the most famous theoretical physicist in the world, and the author, many years earlier, of the fundamental theory that energy and mass are in a sense interchangeable.

Alexander Sachs, a New York economist and amateur of the physical sciences, undertook to get the letter to Roosevelt's attention. He made an appointment with the President, who as usual started talking to the visitor about other matters. Sachs tried several times to interrupt and finally in despair said: "Mr. President, I paid my own way to come down here, the expense is not tax deductible, and I think the least you can do is to listen." This was enough to catch Roosevelt's attention, and he read the letter.

Impressed, he consulted his own scientific advisers, who confirmed what Einstein had said. A committee was set up, and enormous sums of money (eventually $2 billion) were poured out to separate the unstable type of uranium, U 235, from the stable type that is one hundred and forty times more common, and then to bring about a chain reaction.

This was accomplished on December 2, 1942, in an improvised laboratory under the football stand at the University of Chicago. The uranium had to be dispersed among many tons of ultrapure graphite in order to slow down the neutrons and make a chain reaction possible. When the control rods were slowly withdrawn, the neutron activity increased to a point that spelled success, though it was kept below the critical moment of an explosion. (The scientists could not be sure of this, and some of them feared they might accidentally obliterate Chicago.)

As all the world knows, the first atomic bomb was exploded July 16, 1945, more than three months after Roosevelt's death, at Alamagordo Air Force Base, New Mexico. The President had pushed the project ahead against strong opposition among some of his top advisers, using vast quantities of materials needed for other wartime purposes.

It is interesting to speculate how greatly momentous events sometimes depend upon the character of one man. If the President had been of a different temperament, less inclined to heroic risks, it is quite likely that he would have balked at the tremendous expenditure involved. The scientists tell us that the release of atomic energy was certain to come about sooner or later, but no other country, with the possible exception of Russia, could have risked the diversion of men and money in wartime, and Stalin's temperament makes it seem unlikely that he would have done so. This stupendous scientific discovery, surely one of the two or three most important in all history, might have been delayed for decades, with fateful results for good or ill.

Although the United States sought the utmost secrecy, and the censorship was for the most part loyally obeyed, a tiny break in the dam lost everything. Klaus Fuchs, a German-born British physicist who was a Communist, conspired with others from Canada and the United States to deliver to Stalin many of the technical details of the uranium bomb, information which later also helped to facilitate the development of the hydrogen one—with dreadful consequences with which the world is today all too painfully familiar.

Roosevelt's superb self-confidence, his imperturbability, his power to relax at a moment's notice, stood him in good stead during the terrible strain of the war years. As few other men could, he resisted Stalin's constant demand, that had begun as soon as Russia had been forced into the War, for a "Second Front" in Western Europe; he was equally firm in resisting Churchill's plea that the agreed strategy be changed for a drive up into the "soft underbelly" of Europe from the north shore of the Mediterranean.

Feuds between Roosevelt's subordinates in Washington were a desperate nuisance. Henry Wallace and Jesse Jones were at each other's throats. General William Donovan, head of the Office of Strategic Services, fought furiously both with Elmer Davis, who directed the Office of War Information, and with Nelson Rockefeller, Coördinator of Inter-American Affairs.

Sometimes the President ignored these problems; sometimes he spoke sternly to one or both of the individuals; when things got really desperate he would occasionally kick somebody upstairs to a new job with a resounding title but little responsibility.

In the first days of the War in the Pacific, while America was still stunned by the losses at Pearl Harbor, Japan captured practically all the islands of the western Pacific. It was necessary for the Americans to start the long slow process of island-hopping, beginning with Guadalcanal, in August, 1942. The final defeat of the Japanese Navy came with the greatest naval engagement in all history, the Battle of Leyte Gulf, in the Philippines, in October, 1944. The following February, the island of Iwo Jima was captured, and in April, Japan's last bastion, Okinawa.

By 1944, with the end of Roosevelt's third term coming near, the tide had turned in favor of the Allies, though few believed that the following year would see the winning of the War. In the midst of the conflict, the President hesitated less about running for a fourth term than he had for a third. The dissatisfaction of the practical politicians with Vice-President Wallace was by now too vehement to be ignored, and Roosevelt told the Democrats he must be replaced by Senator Harry Truman of Missouri. Truman, although he had begun his career as the protegé of the Pendergast machine of Kansas City, had made a notable record as chairman of a Senate committee investigating war operations.

When Truman's name was first suggested to Roosevelt, he asked that the attitude of union labor be determined, by consulting Sidney Hillman, head of the Amalgamated Clothing Workers in New York City and a leading figure in the CIO, who had come to Washington and played an important part in the war effort. The Republicans picked up the phrase, "Clear it with Sidney," and attacked Roosevelt as the tool of the unions.

Wendell Willkie, the Republican nominee of four years earlier, tried again for the nomination. He ran in the Wisconsin primary but was defeated and withdrew from the race. Governor Thomas E. Dewey of New York, who had come to fame as a gang-busting district attorney in New York City, was nominated, with Governor John Bricker of Ohio as his running mate. Dewey managed to accumulate twenty-two million votes, but Roosevelt had three and a half million more; he got 452 electoral votes and carried thirty-six states, to Dewey's 99 votes and twelve states. The Democrats had a substantial victory in Congress.

By the autumn of 1944, many people were commenting that Roosevelt looked thin and ill; these stories were discounted, partly because ever since 1932 his enemies had been spreading allegations about his health, including the accusation of insanity. In February, 1945, he journeyed all the way to the Crimea for a conference with Stalin and Churchill at Yalta, the dictator having refused to leave Russian soil.

At this meeting the decision to demand unconditional surrender was confirmed. It was agreed that Germany, when conquered, should be ruled in four zones by the Americans, British, French, and Russians. Reparations in kind were to be collected from Germany for two years; this clause was almost disregarded after the War by the United States and Great Britain, but the Russians stripped their sector of nearly every movable industrial installation.

Russia now agreed to enter the War against Japan three months after Germany's surrender; she did so to the letter, with a token attack against Japan only six days before that country sued for peace.

In exchange, the Western Powers made a series of promises to Stalin. He was given the Kurile Islands and the northern half of Sakhalin Island. The port of Dairen was to be internationalized, Port Arthur was to become a Russian naval base, and it was agreed that the Manchurian railroads should be under joint Chinese-Russian administration. Chiang Kai-shek later said he was not notified of the vital decisions affecting China, to which he was bitterly opposed.

The agreements at Yalta, when they finally became known

in the United States, caused an uproar, and have been used politically against the Democratic Party ever since. It is true, however, that in the conference Stalin lost the argument as to several things. He wanted huge German reparations, and seats in the United Nations for all sixteen of the constituent republics in the USSR. He wanted the French excluded from the postwar control of Germany. He did not want to go to war with Japan. As for the arrangements in the Far East agreed upon at Yalta, while some of these represented naked imperialism, others righted old wrongs perpetrated by Japan after her victory over Russia in 1905. It is also true that most of what Stalin gained in the West he could have taken anyhow, since his army by that time had overrun much of Europe.

Roosevelt agreed to two extra seats for the Soviet Union in the UN, for the Ukraine and Byelorussia, instead of the sixteen Stalin wanted; the American President was reportedly embarrassed in saying No to Stalin by the fact that the British Commonwealth was to have several seats. For some unknown reason, Roosevelt made the bad tactical mistake of trying to keep secret the fact of Russia's extra seats; when it leaked out, it was, naturally, a scandal.

The worst mistake made at Yalta went almost unnoticed at the time—the decision to let the Russians occupy Berlin, which heavily influenced the later decision to extend the Russian zone of influence far to the west of that city. The answer is that nearly everyone in the West then thought the armistice arrangement would last only a few months at most, and that Germany would then be reunited and returned to a new republican government of its own.

Those close to him at the time say that the President was aware that Russia got too much at Yalta, but that he was relying on his personal magnetism to charm Stalin, after the War was over, into relinquishing some of his demands. Roosevelt had done this with other men, notably subordinates in his own administration; but to imagine he could thus influence the Communist dictator was about as sensible as thinking he could persuade one of the carved images on Mt. Rushmore to break into a smile. We can now see in retrospect that Roosevelt misjudged the character and implacable purpose of "Good Old Joe," as he called him—a phrase that was to give endless ammunition to Republican orators at home in subsequent years. There is evidence that Roosevelt himself came to have serious misgivings during the few weeks he had still to live.

Back in America, the President appeared on March first before Congress to report personally on Yalta. For the first time, he spoke from a chair. "I hope you will pardon me for this unusual posture of sitting down. I know that you will realize it makes it a lot easier for me not to have to carry about ten pounds of steel around on the bottom of my legs." Those present in the chambers were shocked to see how thin, frail, and tired he looked. He seemed to have trouble pronouncing some words, and his hands shook. Within a few days, millions of people saw the scene in motion-picture newsreels, and many of them apparently had the same reaction.

A little later, he went to his favorite place, Warm Springs, for a brief rest. On April 12, he was sitting for a portrait by a woman artist, Mme. Elizabeth Shoumatoff. Suddenly he put his hand to his temple, and fell back in his chair. A Filipino houseboy and his valet leaped to help him; murmuring, "I have a terrific headache," he lapsed into unconsciousness. The nearest doctor, two miles away, came as quickly as possible, but could do nothing for him; he had had a massive cerebral hemorrhage, and soon he slipped away.

With the media for mass communication heavily dominated by Roosevelt-haters, many people had failed to realize the true attitude of the country toward him; now it was tardily discovered that many millions of Americans, and people in other lands, had admired and loved him, and were plunged into grief by his passing. Thousands expressed their sense of bereavement in letters to Mrs. Roosevelt; tributes poured in from heads of state all over the world. The train bearing his body moved slowly from Warm Springs to Washington, taking almost twenty-four hours to do so; many thousands of silent mourners stood along the route to see it pass, as had happened eighty years earlier when Lincoln's body went back from Washington to Illinois.

In the White House, the dead President's coffin lay in the East Room, where there was a brief funeral service. The next day it was taken to Hyde Park for burial beneath a simple headstone of his own design. His grave, and the family home which has become the site of the Franklin D. Roosevelt Library, official depository for all his papers, soon were recognized as something of a national shrine, visited annually by many thousands.

It is still too early for a final assessment of Roosevelt's character, or his place in history. As these pages have indicated, he had conspicuous faults and weaknesses. Yet they were combined with elements of greatness—his passion for democracy, his amazing ability to carry his ideas to millions of people, his unfaltering courage and optimism in the face of seemingly overwhelming odds. For great numbers of Americans he presented a comforting father-image in a period of deep anxiety. Though he left in his wake many bruised egos, he was also a matchless politician in dealing with the bulk of the people; as a rule he knew exactly how fast to go in order not to get too far out in front, or to lag behind. He made more changes in the social and economic scene than had appeared for many decades, persuading most of his fellow-citizens that government has a responsibility to police the business community in the interest of the consumer, that workers have a right to organize and, if necessary, to strike, and that the victims of the economic storm are entitled to be helped. These were profound modifications of the social structure, rarely accomplished peacefully in any other country.

And finally, whatever the final verdict on him may be, history will never forget that, with Winston Churchill, he shares the chief credit for preventing worldwide victory by the totalitarian despots.

# 2. Churchill: The Last Bulldog

FEW WILL DENY that Winston Churchill belongs among the top two or three men of the first half of the twentieth century. Nowadays, when we are obsessed with the danger of atomic war, and the chief enemy of the free nations is the Communist bloc, we tend to forget that less than three decades ago there was great danger that the Fascist Powers would conquer the world and that democratic institutions would be extinguished by them for decades if not for centuries. Yet it is true; and Hitler and his jackals in Italy and Japan came close to getting their way.

From September 1, 1939, when the Second World War began, to December 7, 1941, when Japan's attack at Pearl Harbor forced the United States into the War as an active belligerent, only one power stood effectively in their path: Great Britain, and she almost lost the fight. No one can say that the British would have surrendered if Winston Churchill had not existed; but certainly he was a tower of strength to his sorely pressed countrymen. By rallying them to fight on when the odds seemed hopelessly against them, he did more than any other individual of this generation, and perhaps of any generation, to make sure that democratic institutions should not perish. His ordeal began when he was already in his sixty-fifth year, an age when most men begin to think of retirement.

This truly great man has been accused of many faults, but excessive modesty and lack of self-confidence are not among them. All his life he has enjoyed a profound conviction that his ideas on all subjects were excellent and deserved the careful attention of those about him. This was conspicuously true during the days before and in the early stages of the First World War, when he held various posts in the British Cabinet, and his colleagues regularly complained that he bombarded them all with advice as to what they should do or should refrain from doing.

The same self-confidence governed his relations with publishers during his long working career, in which he spent more time as an author than in any other occupation. From the very beginning, he demanded high fees; his editors, perhaps stunned into a state of shock by his audacity, usually gave them, so that for many years he was among the highest-paid authors in the world.

The ample income from his pen has been necessary to support his luxurious way of life. Although during his childhood his family was only moderately well-to-do, as soon as he launched out on his own he began living like a millionaire, whether his resources warranted it or not. Criticized once for his expensive ways, he answered: "Whatever the good earth has to offer, I am willing to take. I am a very simple person and the best is none too good for me."

Among the good things of life that he enjoyed for many years were the products of the distiller's and the vintner's skill. His daily consumption of alcohol has certainly been exaggerated by gossip, but there is also no doubt that it was substantial. He first tasted strong spirits when he went out to India at twenty-one as a subaltern (roughly the equivalent of an American second lieutenant). Many years later, he recorded the facts:

### SIR WINSTON CHURCHILL

"He had a large, round face, his expression impassive but alert . . . [During their terrible ordeal, he would appear before the people of London], his huge cigar freshly lighted, his hand raised with two fingers spread in the famous 'V for Victory' sign . . . He showed the people their Prime Minister just as, before the World Wars, the great maritime powers used to send a battleship to any trouble spot to 'show the flag.'"

Wishing to fit myself for active service conditions, I overcame the ordinary weakness of the flesh. By the end of five days I had completely overcome my repugnance to the taste of whiskey. Nor was this a momentary acquirement. . . . Although I have always practiced true temperance, I have never shrunk when occasion warranted it from the main basic standing refreshment of the white officer in the East.

This may be called a conservative statement. His prowess with liquid refreshment was equaled by his ability to assimilate quantities of food, provided only that it was of superb quality.

Early in his career, he developed a daily routine that he followed thenceforth; it was a good deal of a trial to those around him, including, as noted, President Roosevelt, whenever the Englishman was a guest at the White House during the Second World War. Churchill woke rather late, had his breakfast, and read the morning papers. Then he dictated in bed for several hours before arising. After a late and hearty lunch, washed down with liquid refreshment, he went back to bed again for an invigorating two-hour nap.

By about four in the afternoon he was up once more, recuperated and ready for a bout of work which lasted far into the night and sometimes until three or four o'clock in the morning.

Churchill's self-confidence had all his life permitted him to be careless, not to say eccentric, about his clothes; for many years London was agitated by the question where on earth he could have found his series of extraordinary hats, some of them square-crowned bowlers (derbies) long out of fashion. In the Second World War, he dumbfounded the Russians by turning up in Moscow wearing a "siren suit" of his own invention, a one-piece overall or jumper suit that fitted snugly around his now tremendous girth. Since then, he won added fame by his painting costume, a voluminous floor-length Mother-Hubbard-type smock topped off by a floppy soft hat slightly smaller in circumference than a parasol.

His wedding was one of the high points of the London social season in 1908, and his costume seems to have run true to form. The charge that he wore brown shoes with a morning coat may be a libel, but the coat itself caused a sharp attack by the British trade magazine of the tailoring industry, *Tailor and Cutter*—one of a series of bad notices he was to get from this periodical over many years. Said its critic of the coat: "It was not a success. It did not fit him, neither did it suit him. It was too long and heavy for a morning coat and too short and skimpy for a frock." The critic also spoke frankly of the way the sleeves were set.

As all the world knows, Churchill was a man of the greatest personal courage. Over and over he justified the belief that he simply did not know what fear was. In his early days as a young Army officer (who was also permitted, in those easygoing times, to be a war correspondent), he often ran great risks. In the Second World War, trying to keep him from getting killed was a nightmare to those assigned to his safety. During the air raids of the Battle of Britain he usually declined to take cover, preferring instead to go up on the roof where he could enjoy the view. He had to be almost forcibly restrained, on the battlefield in France, from advancing to the forward lines.

Just after the Second World War, I had the unforgettable experience of interviewing Churchill, as a member of a group of half a dozen journalists. We talked to him early one morning when he had just landed from a ship, but it was not too early for him to be holding a huge, freshly lighted cigar.

He sat slumped comfortably in a canvas chair while we stood in a half-circle before him; his large round face was rather pale in the morning light, his expression impassive but alert. When asked a question, he remained silent and motionless for a long time, until the questioner began to fear he had not been heard. Then with a little preliminary rumbling, as of a volcano about to erupt, out came the answer, very deliberately spoken but in every case in admirable English, discreet when necessary, witty if wit was possible. It was a virtuoso performance, climaxed by a slight wave of the cigar, like Toscanini's baton at the end of one movement of a symphony.

Winston Leonard Spencer Churchill was born November 30, 1874, at Blenheim Castle in Oxfordshire, a splendid pile of more than three hundred rooms. It was built by a grateful Queen Anne for the first Duke of Marlborough, who had capped a brilliant career as a British General by defeating the Army of Louis XIV in the Battle of Blenheim, for which the castle was named. The conflict was important, but it is remembered today chiefly because of the poem by Southey on the folly of fighting, with its famous refrain:

> "But everybody said," quoth he,
> "That 'twas a famous victory."

Winston Churchill was the grandson of the Seventh Duke, and all his life an idolator of the first of the line; in the 1930's he wrote a biography of Marlborough in four big volumes, taking his side in all the many controversies in which he had been engaged. Winston's father was Lord Randolph Churchill, himself an important political figure in Victorian days. He rose to such important posts as Secretary of State for India and Chancellor of the Exchequer. Unfortunately, he developed a habit of resigning one job after another for reasons which the public held to be trivial, and because of this fact, his career went into permanent eclipse. He died in 1895, when Winston was not yet twenty-one.

Churchill's mother was a beautiful American girl, Miss Jeannette Jerome, daughter of a wealthy New York businessman who, among other extensive interests, for a time owned and edited the *New York Times*. Miss Jerome was no naïve Daisy Miller type; she had lived abroad during most of her childhood and moved with familiar ease in high social circles in London, Paris, and Rome. Winston often referred to his half-American ancestry, and capitalized on it when it seemed desirable. On December 16, 1941, just after America entered the Second World War, he made an address to a Joint Session of the United

States Congress, in the course of which he said: "I cannot help reflecting that if my father had been an American and my mother British, instead of the other way round, I might have got here on my own."

Winston was a red-headed baby, rambunctious and aggressive, qualities that remained with him throughout his life. From the beginning, he wanted his own way, and fought hard to get it. One of his early nurses recalled him as the naughtiest small boy she had ever seen. He was a rather lonely little figure; his chief pleasure—and one that seems prophetic in view of his later life—was playing with toy soldiers; of these he had about 1,500, and he conducted elaborate war games that went on for weeks. He attended a series of boarding schools, beginning at the age of seven, and got on badly at all of them. He was especially backward at the three languages considered compulsory for an educated man in those days: Greek, Latin, and French. He finally picked up a smattering of French, largely because of spending much time in France, and spoke it freely, with a barbarous accent, making any word mean whatever he chose, like Humpty Dumpty in *Alice in Wonderland*. On the other hand, he soon began to show the mastery of English prose that was to last him the rest of his life, and before long he was able to make shrewd bargains, offering to write English compositions for his classmates in exchange for Latin translations.

When he was a little older he went to Harrow, one of England's famous old private schools (called there "public schools"). In Harrow, again, he did badly as a student, and was thoroughly miserable; his only recorded achievement was winning the inter-public-school fencing championship. Long afterward he said darkly, "I'm all for the public schools, but I do not want to go there again." Later, when he was preparing for Sandhurst, roughly the equivalent of West Point, he was put into the hands of a private tutor who is supposed to have said, "That lad couldn't have gone through Harrow, he must have gone under it."

Yet there were compensations to his bad scholastic record. In the Third Form (approximately the same as a high school

Freshman class in the United States) the English teacher, Mr. Somervell, was a brilliant man; many years later, Churchill recalled, "I remained in the Third Form three times as long as anyone else," thus getting triple exposure to this brilliant man. "I learnt [English] thoroughly. Thus I got into my bones the essential structure of the ordinary British sentence—which is a noble thing. And when in after years my school fellows who had won prizes and distinction for writing such beautiful Latin poetry and pithy Greek epigrams had to come down again to common English to earn their living or make their way, I did not feel at any disadvantage. . . . I would make [all students] learn English: and then I would let the clever ones learn Latin as an honor and Greek as a treat."

Half a century later, when he was Prime Minister in the terrible early days of the Second World War, he made his peace with Harrow, returning there to give them the advice which at that time he was giving to all Britain, in words and by example. "Never give in," he told the boys, thumping his walking-stick on the floor for emphasis. "Never give in, never, never, never, never. Never yield in any way, great or small, large or petty, except to convictions of honor and good sense. Never yield to force and the apparently overwhelming might of the enemy."

At Sandhurst, Churchill really went to work for the first time in his life; he was fascinated by the studies of the science of war. His first year was clouded by the result of an accident; skylarking during the holidays he tried to jump from a bridge to a tree, missed it, and fell thirty feet to the ground. He was unconscious for three days and an invalid for the better part of the year. In spite of this handicap he managed to graduate eighth in a class of 150.

About this time, he developed an ingenious plan of his own which thenceforth stood him in good stead as a public speaker. In those days, every orator was supposed to interlard his observations with quoted maxims and aphorisms of the great writers of the past, and especially in Latin. Churchill, with the extraordinary memory that almost always goes with high intelligence, got by heart a whole handbook of common Latin quotations, and then went on to do the same with a large part of Bartlett's *Familiar Quotations*, in English. From then on, throughout his life, he was never at a loss for the appropriate text.

Well aware of his weakness in foreign languages, he turned it to good oratorical use. On one occasion, making a long speech in the House of Commons, full of dull statistics, he paused and advised his drowsy audience: "I must now warn the House that I am going to make an unusual departure. I am going to make a Latin quotation." The alarmed Members were relieved to find that the quotation was "Arma virumque cano"—"Arms and the man I sing," the first three words of Virgil's Aeneid, probably the most familiar Latin quotation in the world. After the end of the Second World War, he went to Paris to speak to the liberated French and cautioned them: "Be on your guard! I'm going to speak in French—a formidable undertaking and one which will put great demands upon your friendship for Great Britain."

Early in his life he took his father's advice, and buried himself in Gibbon's famous, massive *Decline and Fall of the Roman Empire*. He also steeped himself in Macaulay's prose and verse, and traces of the orotund phraseology of these two masters remained in his style the rest of his life. Another favorite of his, dating from these early days, was Robert Louis Stevenson's *Treasure Island*, which for a half a century he reread once a year.

In 1894, at the age of twenty, he was graduated from Sandhurst as a cavalry officer, commissioned a subaltern, and assigned to the Fourth Hussars. As was proper for a cavalry officer, he developed a passion for polo, and played it at every opportunity.

Now began a short but remarkable period of active military service. In the next five years he witnessed or participated in fighting in Cuba, in two campaigns on the Northwest Frontier in India, in the Egyptian Sudan, and in the Boer War in South Africa. At the end of that time he was famous in England and abroad, sufficiently well recognized to lecture on his experiences for large fees, not only in Great Britain but in the United States as well.

The Cuban experience was a brief interlude in which he was an observer. Three years before Cuba was to be liberated from Spanish rule by American aid, Cuban rebels were already offering resistance, basing themselves on mountain hideaways as Fidel Castro was to do more than sixty years later. Churchill pulled some wires in Madrid and got himself sent to Cuba with the Spanish forces for a few weeks. Setting up a pattern that was to last for some years, he also got an assignment as war correspondent for the *Daily Graphic* (London). He was greatly aided then, as he was to be many times in the future, by his mother. Lady Churchill knew all the top men in diplomacy and journalism, and happily brought pressure to bear to get for her son whatever he wanted.

The Cuban flames of rebellion having died down temporarily, young Churchill went to India to report for active Army duty. His first encounter with that country was unpropitious: trying to scramble onto a concrete dock from a small boat, he seized an iron ring, the boat fell away from under him, and he managed to dislocate a shoulder. The injury was permanent; it interfered somewhat with his beloved polo, and with all other athletic sports. In fact, the shoulder popped out of place from time to time during the rest of his life—once, while he was making an impassioned speech in the House of Commons.

Things were quiet in India, and the young soldier seized the opportunity to read Plato's *Republic*, Aristotle's *Politics*, and Darwin's *Origin of Species*.

No sooner had he gone back to London on leave than the perennial fighting with wild Pathan (really Afghan) tribes on India's Northwest Frontier broke out again. Churchill's regiment was not one of those assigned to the front, but he wanted to see action. He was told that this was not possible unless he could get a job as war correspondent, as he had done in Cuba. He managed to get an assignment from the Allahabad *Pioneer*, one of whose reporters not very much earlier had been a shy, bespectacled youth named Rudyard Kipling. Lady Churchill again pulled wires and also got him an assignment from the *Daily Telegraph* of London. War correspondents in those days went armed and did not hesitate to join in the fighting. Churchill acquitted himself well enough to be mentioned in dispatches as having "made himself useful at a critical moment." He subsequently made a book out of his experiences, which sold well. Probably thanks to Lady Churchill, the newspaper had paid him at a very high rate, as newspapers were to do for the rest of his life.

The fighting died down in India, and with idle time on his hands, young Churchill proceeded to write a novel, in six weeks. *Savrola, A Tale of the Revolution in Laurania,* was serialized in *Macmillan's Magazine* and published by Longman's in London. It was republished a few years ago, after Churchill had become world famous; critics agreed that worse novels had been written, and also better ones. With this tepid judgment the author agreed, once remarking that he had advised his friends not to read it. It is a story of love, politics, and revolution; Churchill summed it up at the time by calling it "the fortunes of a liberal leader who overthrew an arbitrary government only to be swallowed up by a Socialist revolution." Some people saw in this a remarkable prediction of Churchill's own future nearly fifty years later, since he defeated Hitler's regime in the Second World War and was immediately deposed from power by the (Socialist) Labor Party victory in Great Britain in 1945.

Having polished off his novel, Churchill looked around for a fresh trouble spot, and promptly found one. More than ten years earlier, the famous British General, Charles George ("Chinese") Gordon, had been killed at Khartoum, in the Sudan, by fanatical tribesmen. Herbert Kitchener (afterward Earl Kitchener) had tried to raise the siege but arrived too late; now he was setting out to reconquer the Sudan. Churchill and his mother again importuned everybody of importance in London, trying to get his usual combination of military service and war correspondence. The *Morning Post* gave in to Lady Churchill, but Kitchener was made of sterner stuff. Several times he refused to have young Winston under any circumstances, and only at the last minute did the youth manage to get himself into the expedition.

Here again, he saw dangerous active service, and enjoyed it characteristically. "Talk of fun!" he wrote many years later. "Where would you beat this! On horseback, at daybreak, within shot of an advancing army, seeing everything! . . ." As a matter of fact, Churchill was lucky to come out alive. The fighting was heavy, filled with large numbers of casualties on both sides. His dispatches in the *Morning Post* helped intensify Britain's delight that Chinese Gordon was finally avenged.

His next war experience was in South Africa and was equally serious. With the beginning of the Boer War in 1899, he was on the scene, this time not on active military service but only as a correspondent of the *Morning Post*. He was riding on an armored train when the locomotive broke down, and leaving the scene on foot, he was captured by the Boers. He made a daring escape from prison, was hidden for some days by the English manager of a colliery, and escaped into the neutral territory of Portuguese East Africa. His exploit, duly recorded by himself in the pages of his newspaper, made him even more of a hero than the campaign in the Sudan had done. The Boers had neglected to make Churchill give his word not to fight again, so he returned to the front, this time with a military job as well as his correspondence for the *Morning Post*: he was a lieutenant in the South African Light Horse.

The War dragged on for two years longer, but Churchill cannily cut short his service to return to London and cash in on his popularity. He ran for Parliament as a Conservative (or "stood," as the stubborn British say) and was successful. He wrote another book, about the South African War, which sold well, and made successful lecture trips in Great Britain and the United States. His American lecture manager, who might have been trained as a circus press agent, gave him advance billing as "the hero of five wars, the author of six books, and the future Prime Minister of Great Britain." In one of his few recorded bursts of modesty, Churchill made him withdraw this imaginative citation.

The Boer War having finally ended in a British victory, Churchill to his surprise found himself for some years on the unpopular side of a debate over the question of appropriate punishment for the South Africans, whose only crime, after all, had been a reluctance to be swallowed up and dominated by the horde of British immigrants attracted by newly discovered gold and diamonds. It has always been a rule of all wars that the farther you are from the front the more you hate the enemy; Churchill, who had met a lot of Boers face to face, could not join in the clamor for harsh reprisals against them. His popularity was dimmed for a time, though never eclipsed.

Long before this, many people had begun to notice the potentialities of the young journalist-officer. As early as 1898, an anonymous writer in the *Daily Mail* (London) wrote of him: "In years he is a boy; in temperament he is also a boy; but in intention, in deliberate plan, purpose, adaptation of means to ends, he is already a man. In any other generation but this he would be a child . . . but Mr. Churchill is a man with ambitions fixed, with the steps toward their attainment clearly defined, with a precocious, almost uncanny, judgment as to the efficacy of the means to the end. . . . What he will become, who shall say? At the rate he goes there will hardly be room for him in Parliament at thirty or in England at forty." The author was afterward revealed to be G. W. Steevens, the most popular newspaper columnist of the day; when he wrote, Churchill was twenty-four.

The young man's maiden speech in the House nearly ended in disaster. On the day of his first effort he was preceded by the brilliant young Welshman, David Lloyd George, who had intended to make a motion critical of the Government for its actions in South Africa; instead, he contented himself with a bitter attack and no motion at all. Young Churchill, who had written out and memorized a speech on the opposite assumption, was in a panic and for possibly the only time in his life, practically tongue-tied. Observing his predicament, the man sitting next to him, Thomas Bowles, suggested *sotto voce* that he might begin by saying: "Instead of making his violent speech without moving his moderate amendment, he had better have moved his moderate amendment without making his violent speech." Churchill adopted the suggestion verbatim and the day was saved.

Few would question today that Churchill was the greatest orator of the twentieth century. It could never be said of him as he once did of someone else that "He can best be described as one of those orators who, before they get up, do not know what they are going to say; when they are speaking, do not know what they are saying; and when they have sat down, do not know what they have said." All his public life, he took the greatest pains with his speeches, invariably writing them out and when possible memorizing them. It is a tribute to his skill that although he was afflicted with a slight lisp, no one ever remembered that fact beyond the first few minutes that he was on his feet.

While he was never able to make a whole extemporaneous speech, Churchill soon developed the gift of brilliant spontaneous repartee in the cut and thrust of debate, and all London began quoting him. On one occasion, a fellow member who was making a speech saw Churchill shaking his head in dissent and said angrily: "I see my Right Honorable friend shaking his head. I wish to remind him that I am only expressing my own opinion." To which Churchill replied: "I wish to remind the speaker that I am only shaking my own head."

A heckler in the House was once so excited that he could only gurgle incoherently; Churchill remarked: "My Right Honorable friend should not develop more indignation than he can contain." Criticized in the House for something he had done, he said, "Let us leave the past to history—particularly since I intend to write the history myself."

Much sought after by hostesses, he was already famous as a public monologist. Someone observed: "At dinner he talks and talks, and you can hardly tell when he leaves off quoting his one idol, Macaulay, and begins on his other, Winston Churchill."

George Bernard Shaw once sent him a telegram when a new play of his was opening: "Am reserving two tickets for you for my premiere. Come and bring a friend—if you have a friend." Churchill wired back: "Impossible to be present for the first performance. Will attend the second night—if there is a second night."

In his early manhood, Churchill wore a mustache. At a dinner party an outspoken lady remarked: "I have never cared for your politics, Winston, but my distaste for them is nothing compared to my feelings about your dreadful mustache." Churchill: "I see no earthly reason, Madam, why you should come in contact with either!" In a second acrimonious encounter with a lady said to have been the sharp-tongued Lady Astor, she finally said: "If I were your wife, I'd put poison in your coffee," to which Churchill imperturbably replied, "And if I were your husband, I should drink it."

Within four years, Churchill committed an almost unprecedented political step and one requiring great courage: he changed political parties. The Conservatives, to whom he belonged by inheritance, showed signs of abandoning Free Trade, which had for many years been the foundation stone of British foreign policy. He made the transition successfully without losing his seat in Parliament. In Great Britain, you do not need to live in the district that you represent; if your party considers you valuable, it will shop around and find a "safe" constituency for you; during most of the first twenty years of his career in the House, Churchill represented Dundee, Scotland.

On this as on many other occasions, Churchill was taunted with changing his mind, an accusation he invariably bore with equanimity. On one occasion he remarked, "My views are subject to a harmonious process that keeps them in relation to the current movement of events," and on another he replied calmly, "To improve is to change. To be perfect is to change often."

In 1908, Winston married Miss Clementine Hozier, a granddaughter of the Scottish Countess of Airlie. The marriage was a thoroughly happy one; Mrs. Churchill, brilliant and beautiful, knew how to keep the spotlight directed on her husband. They had five children, of whom one daughter died in infancy. There were three more daughters, Diana, Sarah and Mary, and one son, Randolph.

As the first decade of the twentieth century drew toward its close, Churchill moved farther and farther to the left in his views—something hard for people to believe who remember him only from the firm conservatism of his later years. Lloyd George was coming up rapidly in politics with his demand for higher wages, better housing, and many other improvements in the condition of the working classes—demands that foreshadowed the Welfare State of the Labor Party thirty-five years later, and the American New Deal. Churchill was Lloyd George's loyal lieutenant. In 1906 he was given the post of Undersecretary for the Colonies, and from 1908 to 1910 he was President of the Board of Trade under the famous Liberal Prime Minister, Herbert Asquith. It is hard now to recall that he was damned, along with Lloyd George, as a wild radical and, of course, as "a traitor to his class." Asquith liked him, however, and in quick succession, he became Home Secretary and, in 1911, First Lord of the Admiralty, a position corresponding roughly with Secretary of the Navy in the United States.

Military life and affairs had always been his first love, and now he embraced the sea with equal fervor; it is significant that during the Second World War, his favorite identification in code messages to President Roosevelt was "Former Naval Person." As the shadow of the First World War began to spread across Europe, he worked hard to get the Fleet ready.

He gambled on battleships with guns of increased, untried caliber, and on changing from coal to oil, and he made himself a nuisance to all concerned by harping on the potential value of the airplane. He not only believed in flying machines; he went up in them, and while in the air, frequently took the controls himself. Repeatedly, planes in which he was flying crashed, but he always managed to escape with no more than minor injuries.

In June, 1914, came the event that was to change the world forever. On the 28th of that month Archduke Francis Ferdinand, heir to the throne of Austria-Hungary, was assassinated at Sarajevo, in Bosnia, by a Serbian patriot (Serbia has now been swallowed up in Jugoslavia).

Though it is common to say that the assassination brought on the First World War, in fact the nations of Europe had been moving steadily toward open conflict for many years. For half a century there had been a series of bilateral or multilateral alliances among the Powers, shifting back and forth, until by 1913, in the Triple Entente, France, Great Britain, and Russia were more or less pledged to come to each other's aid, while they were opposed by the Triple Alliance of Germany, Austria-Hungary, and Italy.

Emperor Wilhelm II of Germany was an ardent militarist who believed, as Hitler was to do a quarter of a century later, that German arms were irresistible. Germany was in an expansionist mood, seeking colonies and foreign trade all around the world, and coming into conflict with the British and French empires at many points, notably in North Africa and the Middle East.

The Russians, a Slavic nation, were encouraging political unrest among the Slavs in other countries, and especially those who were suppressed minorities in the great, lumbering Austro-Hungarian Empire, the Czechs, Slovaks, Slovenes, and Croats. The Pan-Slav movement was in fact by now more than sixty years old. It had been pushed by reactionary elements in Russia, and by the Greek Orthodox Church, though in the countries where the Slavs were oppressed, it also appealed to freedom-loving liberals. It played an important part in the revolts of 1848, the Crimean War of 1854–55, and the Russo-Turkish War of 1877–78.

By 1914, Serbia was the chief center of the Pan-Slav movement in the Balkans, constantly stirring up the Austro-Hungarian Slavic minorities, and Austria-Hungary was looking for an excuse to crush the gadfly nation. The assassination of the Archduke offered such an excuse.

On July 24, Austria-Hungary sent an ultimatum to Serbia making a series of demands including the requirement that she be allowed to send her own officials into Serbia to stamp out the secret terrorist organization to which the assassin of the Archduke had belonged. Serbia agreed to all the conditions except this one, which she refused, and the next day Austria declared war.

Russia, with many old quarrels to settle with Austria-Hungary, felt she must come to the aid of her Slavic ally, Serbia, and began mobilizing on the frontier which then existed between herself and Austria-Hungary. Kaiser Wilhelm needed little prodding to throw Germany into the conflict; he sent an ultimatum to the Russians demanding demobilization, and when he had no answer within twenty-four hours, he declared war. Two days later, on the theory that France was about to join the conflict on the side of her Russian ally, he invaded Luxembourg and Belgium on the way to the French border. He seemed to hope that Great Britain, in spite of her obligations to France and Russia, would stay out, but the reckless German actions, and especially the violation of Belgian neutrality, were too much, and the next day England came in. The First World War had begun. Only Italy repudiated the obligations she had undertaken with Austria-Hungary and Germany. She remained neutral for a time and in 1915 joined the War on the side of the Allies.

As the War started, the German battle cruiser *Goeben* eluded the best efforts of the British Fleet to find it, and escaped eastward through the Mediterranean to Turkey where it anchored off Constantinople (now Istanbul). One of Churchill's biographers, Philip Guedalla, attaches great significance to this fact. The *Goeben*, he says, by her threatening presence forced Turkey into the War on the side of Germany. When the Axis Powers lost the War, one result was the destruction of the Turkish Empire, and the rise of the various Arab states —as well as the eventual creation of Israel. Russia was one of the Allies, badly needing munitions from Great Britain and France. The Baltic was sealed off by the Germans, and it would have been a great help if the Tsar's government could have been supplied through the Dardanelles, the Bosporus, and the Black Sea; with Turkey allied to Germany this was impossible. As a result, Guedalla says, the Tsar's government disintegrated and the Bolshevik Revolution ensued. Probably most of these things, and perhaps all of them, would have happened even if the *Goeben* had not eluded the British Navy, but certainly her escape was an important defeat for the Allies.

Churchill by now was riding high. He had become a brilliant orator, and made speeches constantly on every conceivable subject dealing with the conduct of the War. He had persuaded Sir John Fisher, an aged Admiral, to become First Sea Lord, second in command of the Navy after Churchill himself. Sir John was a fanatical early riser, liking to get to his desk at what he considered the reasonable hour of 4 A.M.; by the time Churchill arrived at the office, he had done a twelve-hour stint, and gone home. However, at the end of each day, he wrote the younger man a longish letter telling him what was going on. Sir John commented that he and Winston were very nearly "a perpetual clock." Both of them liked to annotate official documents as they read, Churchill in red ink, Fisher in green; Sir John referred to the pair of them as "the port and starboard lights."

Winston's fertile mind ran off in many directions. He continued to push for the use of the airplane, against embattled opposition. While no one man can claim the invention of the tank, he came as near to having the title as anyone, and without his persistent advocacy it would not have appeared on the battlefield until years later. At about this time he conceived the idea of artificial harbors, which he revived in the Second World War, and which played a significant role in the invasion of Normandy. He is also credited with the invention of smoke screens, and the first ideas about chemical warfare.

Churchill took great pains with his own writing, and bitterly resented the attempts of editors employed by publishers to change it. About this time, he had ended a sentence with a dangling preposition, and someone had awkwardly rephrased the passage to avoid this. Winston wrote in the margin of his proof: "This is arrant nonsense, up with which I will not put."

And now disaster struck; within a few months, after being the most popular young man in Great Britain, he was in disgrace, reduced from his high office as First Lord of the Admiralty to just about the lowest in the Cabinet, an obsolete post with hardly any duties, as Chancellor of the Duchy of Lancaster.

It was a double-barreled misfortune that brought him down, of which the first part was Antwerp. The Germans were thrusting through Belgium, whose resistance was collapsing before them; Antwerp was considered of high importance, and 8,000 British Marines had been rushed there to reënforce the sagging Belgian defenses. Churchill was sent by Lord Kitchener, who was now in charge of the British share of the War, with instructions to do what he could to prevent a Belgian surrender. He worked heroically, but in vain, and the city fell; some of the British forces were unable to get away and were interned in Holland until the War ended three years later.

Military experts today believe that Churchill's services were valuable; the German timetable was seriously upset by the delay he caused. But at the time, the British, alarmed by the triumphant Teutonic march across Belgium and northern France, felt that he was somehow responsible for disaster, and turned against him with a fickleness supposed to be out of character with the phlegmatic members of the Island Race.

The other British setback was a dreadful debacle. With Turkey now in the War on the side of the Axis, Churchill was the chief architect of a plan for a frontal attack on Gallipoli, the peninsula controlling the narrow strait of the Dardanelles, leading from the Aegean Sea into the Sea of Marmara and thence by way of the Bosporus into the Black Sea. Here again, military opinion has now swung around to support Churchill's plan; if the campaign had been rushed through, it had a good chance of success. Unfortunately, Churchill himself was partly to blame for the catastrophe. He rashly made a speech pointing out the great strategic value of the Dardanelles; this was read by the Turks who, respecting him more than did his own countrymen at the time, promptly began fortifying the region.

The rest of the blame must be shared by various British Navy and Army commanders, who never believed in the enterprise and bitterly resented the diversion of men and ships. The first naval sortie into those waters resulted in serious losses from mines, and was not repeated. When troops were finally put ashore, they met with a hail of gunfire, and they never took the peninsula. Total Allied casualties were more than a quarter of a million, about four-fifths of them being British, Australian, and New Zealanders, and the remainder French; the British dead amounted to more than 40,000. One of them was the young poet, Rupert Brooke, who just before his death wrote a poem that ran around the world, the one beginning:

> If I should die, think only this of me:
> That there's some corner of a foreign field
> That is forever England. . .

How many other brilliant young men who might have helped reshape the world were among those 40,000, we do not know. One other name is worth recording: that of Philip Mosley, a young scientist touched with genius, discoverer of X-ray spectroscopy.

The storm that now broke over Churchill was the worst of his whole life. It was hopeless to try to explain to the British public that his plan had been a sound one, involving no more risk than is a normal part of the hazard of war, and that the bungling and vacillation of others had turned it into catastrophe.

Having little to do, he now began what was to prove his greatest lifelong recreation: painting. (He had always been skillful at sketching; a brilliant prizefight drawing is still in existence done at the age of seventeen, when he was at Harrow, and presented to the proprietor of the local candy store in lieu of payment of his bill.) With hardly any instruction, in the characteristic Churchillian way he plunged in and soon became a highly competent amateur; several professional painters, including Picasso, later testified that he could have earned a good living with his brush if he had tried. Some of his pictures signed with a pseudonym were sold about this time for modest prices; now they would command a large sum if put on the market.

His advice given many years later to beginning landscape painters was characteristic. "Splash into the turpentine," he told them. "Wallop into the blue and white, frantic flourish on the palette—clean no longer—and then several large, fierce strokes and slashes of blue on the absolutely cowering canvas."

His second major recreation began about twelve years later, when he happened to lay a few bricks, became fascinated with the operation, and from then on, seized every opportunity to pursue it. He became an "adult apprentice" in the Amalgamated Union of Building Trade Workers, to the horror of many of its members who remembered his strongly anti-labor attitude in the 1926 General Strike.

After Gallipoli, believing his political career to be over, he resigned from the Cabinet, though not from the House, in November, 1915, to join the fighting forces in France. Not unnaturally, officers of the combat troops to whom he was assigned rather resented having an ex-Cabinet member forced upon them, and one, moreover whose bungling was supposed to have cost so many casualties at the Dardanelles. Churchill won them over in a few weeks by his personal fearlessness, his consideration for the welfare of his men, his almost invariable high spirits, and his amazing ability to materialize whiskey, brandy, and champagne seemingly from thin air. Visited by a General who complained that his headquarters seemed to be "a very dangerous place" Lieutenant Colonel Churchill replied, "Yes, sir, but after all, this is a very dangerous war."

His service in the field had not lasted long when in 1916 he was called back to London because his services were felt to be urgently needed in the House of Commons. In June, Lloyd George became War Minister, and in December, head of the government, and he saw to it that his protegé, Churchill, was kept busy. In 1916 Winston was made Secretary of State for Air, a job he held for five years; in August, 1917, he, added the job of Minister of Munitions. In 1918, he switched from Munitions to Secretary of State for War and held this post, plus the Air Ministry, for the next three years.

Following the Russian Revolution of November, 1917, civil war broke out in that country between the Communists and a heterogeneous group of their opponents, ranging all the way from moderate Socialists to Tsarists and other extreme conservatives; and after Germany surrendered in November, 1918, the Allies played an important part in this war. Their troops were not actually engaged, although they had forces on Russian soil, British, French, and American soldiers in Murmansk and Archangel in the Far North, and Japanese (and later, American) soldiers around the port of Vladivostock in Eastern Siberia. What the Allies did was to supply "surplus" uniforms, ammunition and other supplies to the White Russians, and Churchill had a leading role in this action. The Communists won the War, and the Allied part in it has embittered Russia's relations with the West from that time to the present day.

In 1921, Winston became head of the Colonial Office, his

first big job being to clean up a lot of unfinished business in the Near East. His offhand decisions may not have been perfect, but they pleased the strongest critic of British policy, also the strongest European friend of the Arabs—Lawrence of Arabia. Churchill likewise had to deal with the long-continued struggle of Ireland to get free, which resulted in the creation of the Irish Free State in 1921. One of the chief leaders of that struggle was Michael Collins, who later complained crossly to Churchill that when he was hiding from the British in Ireland they had offered a reward of $25,000 for him; Churchill promptly got out the printed notice the Boers had issued when he escaped from their hands, offering $125 for him, and pointed out the implied compliment in holding one Collins to be worth two hundred Churchills. The Irishman seemed appeased.

The next year, 1922, saw the short but savage war between Greece and Turkey, ending in a Turkish triumph. The whole area around Istanbul had been under military occupation by the Allies, and it was Churchill's task, successfully accomplished, to get the British soldiers out. In the same year, the Lloyd George Government, which had seen the World War to a victorious conclusion, at last fell. Even before it did so, a rift had developed between the Prime Minister and Churchill, who was beginning to swing back toward the Conservative Party; one important point of difference was that Churchill regarded Lloyd George as "soft on Russia."

Winston had to stand again for election to the House from Dundee, and just at this time he underwent a complicated appendectomy. He traveled up to Dundee on a stretcher, and for one of his few public speeches, he had to be carried on stage seated in a chair. Characteristically, he did not mention his appendectomy, or explain the novelty of making an election appeal while seated and speaking hardly above a whisper. Perhaps it would not have mattered; the Scots have always loved music, and throughout his attempt to speak much of the audience sang at the top of its lungs. All the accumulated tribulations of the War and the postwar period had build up resentment among the voters and Churchill was turned out of the House, for the first time in twenty-two years. Since it was clear that he was now out of sympathy with the Liberals, there was substance to his remark: "In the twinkling of an eye, I found myself without an office, without a seat, without a party, and even without an appendix."

With nothing else to do, he went back to writing, beginning his great four-volume history of the First World War, *The World Crisis.* This book earned him a sum equivalent to more than $200,000 today. A few years earlier he had inherited, under the will of his great-grandmother, the Marchioness of Londonderry, an income which in today's terms would be about $75,000 a year, so that he no longer needed to worry about what he considered the bare necessities: a very expensive manner of life, including the best of liquor and his huge and costly cigars. With the profits from his book, he bought the country house, Chartwell Manor, in Kent, which was to be his favorite dwelling place from then on.

In 1924 came the first Labor Government in British history, with Ramsay MacDonald at its head. It lasted only nine months, being swept out of office by the furor caused by "the Zinoviev letter." The Government released as an official document the text of a letter supposedly written by Gregory Zinoviev, Russian head of the Communist International, calling for an armed rebellion by British Communists. No one knows to this day whether the letter was a forgery, as the Labor Party insisted; forgery or not, it helped to put them out of power for the next five years.

Churchill, who had been defeated in two more election attempts, in West Leicester and Westminster, was reëlected from Epping in the Conservative sweep that threw out the Laborites. He was now calling himself a Constitutionalist, a tactful way of gently breaking the news that he was returning to the Conservative Party which he had abandoned twenty years earlier. The new Prime Minister was Stanley Baldwin (afterward Earl Baldwin of Bewdley). He promptly made Churchill Chancellor of the Exchequer, a slightly odd post for a man who all his life had assumed that the thing to do with money is to spend it as soon as you can get your hands on it. One theory is that Baldwin regarded Churchill as a possible formidable political enemy and wanted to have him where he could watch his movements closely.

The only remembered action of the new Chancellor of the Exchequer was the serious fiscal blunder of returning to the gold standard. This raised the price of British exports, and caused a reduction in foreign trade—a terribly serious matter to an island nation which for many decades has failed to produce at home enough food for its population, and has to pay for the needed supplement by exports of coal and manufactured goods. With the sale of coal cut down, some mines were closed and masses of miners became unemployed—a fact that helped produce the General Strike of the following year.

Churchill did not seem disconcerted by the bad effects of his policy. About this time Baldwin remarked that "a Cabinet meeting where Winston was present did not have the opportunity of considering its proper agenda, for the reason that invariably it had first to deal with some extremely clever memorandum submitted by him on the work of some department other than his own."

The General Strike of 1926 was a serious matter. Practically all public services were stopped when the workers downed tools, and were restored only in part by volunteers from the middle and upper classes. The country was almost without newspapers, being limited to the *Times* of London, and a paper put out by the strikers, the *British Worker*. Churchill became editor of a temporary four-page sheet, the *British Gazette*; the estimate of professional journalists is that his performance was no more than adequate. Reproached afterward because the paper, which appeared for only a few days, was strongly against the strikers, he replied: "I cannot expect to be impartial between the fire brigade and the fire." Obviously seeking to frighten the instigators of the strike, he told them: "I warn you—I warn you that if ever there is another General Strike we will let loose another *British Gazette.*"

Churchill continued as Chancellor of the Exchequer until the Baldwin Government was forced out in 1929 by the second Labor Government, again under Ramsay MacDonald. During this time he completed the four volumes of *The World Crisis*, was tremendously active in the House, and in general had a finger in every British pie, including some where his participation was bitterly opposed.

When MacDonald came again to office, Churchill resented the fact and took a violent dislike to the man, whom he called the Boneless Wonder, "the greatest living master of falling without hurting himself." He remarked that Ramsay had, "more than any other man, the gift of compressing the largest amount of words into the smallest amount of thought."

Now began the most frustrating ten years of Churchill's life. The Labor Government soon fell, to be succeeded by a so-called National Government dominated by Conservatives but with MacDonald at its head. Churchill might have made his peace with MacDonald and become a member of the Cabinet, even though both Conservatives and Laborites mistrusted him; but he himself made this impossible. The country was deeply agitated over the question of some degree of self-government for India, and Churchill put himself beyond the pale by announcing that he would have nothing to do with any such step.

He was still, of course, in the House of Commons, and still an important figure in the Conservative Party, which came back openly into power in 1935, but he lacked the strategic leverage of a Cabinet post. Between 1930 and 1939 he published nine books, including the great four-volume life of his famous ancestor, the first Duke of Marlborough. He wrote a volume of condensed biographies called *Great Contemporaries*; confirming a general impression that it contained more of Winston than of anyone else, a critic wrote: "Mr. Churchill gleams back at us from twenty-five looking-glasses, formidable, affectionate, and lovable." Other books of the decade were reminiscences and random thoughts on diverse subjects, as well as a volume or two of speeches.

If Churchill had died in the mid-thirties—perhaps from one of the bouts with pneumonia which he experienced from time to time all his life—he would have been recorded in history as a brilliant, erratic, unstable man whose great talents had never come to fruition. The record against him was heavy. He had twice changed his political affiliation. He was believed responsible for one of Britain's worst defeats, Gallipoli. In the first years after the Russian Revolution, it was an open secret that he would have been not unwilling to see his country engaged in full-scale war with the Communists, and he took the lead, as noted above, in giving great aid to the White Russians in the Civil War. His term as Chancellor of the Exchequer was remembered solely by his disastrous return to the gold standard. His stubborn opposition to any concessions to India's desire for freedom at the beginning of the 1930's helped to keep a most troublesome issue alive over many years. Almost everyone in England, including Churchill himself, then thought that his career had come to a decidedly inglorious end.

His popularity in Tory circles was brought even lower toward the end of 1936. Early in that year King George V had died and been succeeded by Edward VIII. But the young bachelor King—he was forty-two—was increasingly unhappy in the sort of life he was forced to live. He had fallen in love with Mrs. Ernest Simpson, a divorced woman, and many straitlaced Englishmen shuddered at the idea of having such a person as the wife of the King. Prime Minister Stanley Baldwin presented Edward with a virtual ultimatium: give up Mrs. Simpson or abdicate. On December 10, 1936, the King chose the second course, and the following day broadcast his affecting farewell speech to his people. "At long last," he began, "I am able to say a few words of my own," and went on, "I have found it impossible to carry the heavy burden of responsibility and to discharge my duties as King, as I wish to do, without the help and support of the woman I love." While millions all over the world listened in tears, he closed: "And now we all have a new King. I wish him and you, his people, happiness and prosperity with all my heart. God bless you all. God save the King!" The new monarch was his younger brother, who took the title of George VI.

Almost alone among British statesmen, Churchill was from beginning to end on Edward's side. He worked for a compromise that would keep Edward on the throne, and for a time it seemed he might succeed. When the end came, he performed a last service by helping the King prepare the abdication broadcast. He has never admitted writing it in toto, saying merely that he touched it up a little, but the legend persists that he was the chief author and that it represents one of his greatest oratorical efforts.

In the early years of the 1930's Churchill had concerned himself with the need for modifying the harsh terms of the Treaty of Versailles imposed on Germany at the end of the First World War, which had left her people angry, impoverished, with a sense of injustice, and in a growing mood to demand revenge. Soon, however, the rise of Hitler, who took power early in 1933, alarmed him. For the next six years he hammered away unceasingly on the doctrine that Hitler was highly dangerous, that his ambition was limitless, and that Britain and France must rearm as quickly and completely as possible. Churchill, who managed to pronounce "Nazis" as though it were "Nazzies," never referred to the German dictator except as Corporal Hitler (his rank in the First World War), or as Schicklgruber, perhaps under the erroneous impression that this was his name. (It was his grandmother's maiden name; his grandfather and grandmother were apparently not married until some time after the birth of his father, but the grandfather's name was Hiedler, or Hitler.)

Churchill was, alas, able to communicate his sense of urgency to almost no one. Most of England was complacent or pacifist or both; it was the time when many college students swore the "Oxford Oath" that they would under no circumstances fight for King and country. Many people, especially in high social circles and the upper echelons of government, shared the view of the Cliveden Set, that was rather pro-Hitler and hoped that if there was to be a war, it would be between Germany and Russia, who would destroy each other.

In the terrible decade of the 1930's Fascism steadily advanced on both sides of the globe. Japan made an unprovoked assault on China, and seized that part of Manchuria she had not already gobbled up, as the first step toward conquering the entire Orient. In Spain, the Fascists revolted against the Republican government, with secret aid from Hitler and Mussolini. Germany reoccupied the Rhineland in violation of both the Versailles Treaty, which had been forced upon her, and the Locarno Pact, which she had signed more or less voluntarily; long afterward it was revealed that the slightest showing of strength by Great Britain and France at this time would have caused Hitler to draw back, and would perhaps have changed the history of the world. Instead, Hitler seized Austria and prepared to carve up Czechoslovakia, sharing a little of the loot with Poland and Hungary. Mussolini planned to make war on the almost defenseless little African country, Ethiopia. The League of Nations, as it was pledged to do, instituted "sanctions" (an economic boycott) against Italy, but the British Government refused to accept the one really effective measure, which would have been to cut off oil, and the boycott fell apart. (Churchill, it must be noted, was at first "soft" on Mussolini; he thought that Italy might be an ally in the war against Germany that he saw coming.)

Neville Chamberlain, now Prime Minister, took his famous umbrella three times on visits to Hitler at Berchtesgaden, Godesberg, and worst of all, at Munich; in exchange for what amounted to giving Hitler carte blanche he came home waving a piece of paper that he said promised "peace in our time."

Churchill, more accurately, said, "We have sustained a defeat without a war," and continued to plead for rearmament with all possible speed. "I have watched," he said at about this time, "this famous island descending incontinently, fecklessly, the stairway which leads to a dark gulf. It is a fine broad stairway at the beginning, but after a bit the carpet ends. A little farther on there are only flagstones and a little farther on these break beneath your feet." Arguing for more military airplanes than he could prove were needed, he recalled "the man whose mother-in-law had died in Brazil, who replied when asked about how the remains could be disposed of: 'Embalm, cremate, and bury. Take no risks!' "

Summarizing the sins of the Tories in a speech after Munich, he said: "They neither prevented Germany from rearming, nor did they rearm ourselves in time. They quarreled with Italy without saving Ethiopia. They exploited and discredited the vast institution of the League of Nations. They neglected to make alliances and combinations which might have repaired previous errors; and thus they left us in the hour of trial without adequate national defense or effective international security." On a more personal level he said of Prime Minister Chamberlain: "See that old town clerk looking at European affairs through the wrong end of a municipal drainpipe!"

Throughout Europe, the tension steadily mounted. In a move that historians now tend to forget, Russia offered a Triple Alliance to Britain and France under which the independence of the states in Central and Eastern Europe would have been guaranteed. Poland, with centuries of ingrained distrust, feared Russia about as much as she did Germany, and Chamberlain as usual vacillated; the alliance never came to pass.

Instead, Stalin made his nonaggression pact with Hitler, news of which stunned the world on August 25, 1939. The

Führer, having thus guaranteed himself against having to fight on two fronts at once, proceeded eight days later to attack Poland, and the Second World War, the bloodiest and most far-reaching ever fought—thus far—was under way. England and France immediately joined the conflict, and just as promptly, Churchill was recalled to the Government in his old post as First Lord of the Admiralty, from which he had been forced in 1915, after the disaster of Gallipoli. At once he called for the same war map that he had been using twenty-four years earlier; it was found, and he calmly sat down in the old chair, at the old table, and went to work.

For the first few months, Hitler contented himself with mopping up on the Eastern Front, so that so far as the West was concerned this period was called the Phony War. But in 1940 he was ready and proceeded to act. On April 8 and 9, Denmark and Norway were invaded; Denmark made no resistance, and Norway was forced to capitulate in two months. On May 10, the Netherlands and Belgium were overrun. One day later, a full-scale attack on France began.

The French had built a tremendous and elaborate line of fortifications known as the Maginot Line, from Switzerland to the Belgian border, and they believed it to be impregnable; ever since then, reliance on some supposedly secure static defense has been known as "Maginot Line psychology." The Germans had more than a touch of the same attitude, having built a corresponding set of fortifications of their own near the Rhine, called the Siegfried Line, but this did not prevent them, when the test came, from bypassing the French fortifications with ridiculous ease. On May 11, they broke through at Sedan (which had been the scene of the final French defeat in the Franco-Prussian War of 1870). The French Government fled from Paris in chaos, and only a month and eleven days later it surrendered.

During this interval, the fast-moving German army raced to the shore of the English Channel, cutting off a large body of French and British troops in Flanders, and around Dunkirk, at the northernmost tip of France. The capture of all these soldiers seemed certain, but most of them were moved to Dunkirk and rescued by sea in a herioc operation during a few days beginning May 26. About 900 British ships, large and small, were employed. While a gallant rearguard sacrificed itself holding off the German troops, and while Hitler's bombers poured death from the sky, the men stood massed on the beaches waiting their turn. In addition to naval vessels, hundreds of civilian craft, some not much bigger than a rowboat, were used, returning again and again across the Channel on missions from which many never returned. About 338,000 soldiers were rescued—123,000 French and the remainder British. The men and their rifles were saved, but all other army equipment, including vehicles and guns—almost everything of this character that Britain possessed—was lost.

Even before this event, the British nation had turned against Prime Minister Chamberlain, whose confident prediction of "peace in our time" was turning out to be such a dreadful mockery. The climax came when, just before the blitzkrieg began in May, 1940, Chamberlain solemnly announced that Hitler had "missed the bus"—meaning, on heaven knows what evidence, that he had lost the advantage in the War. On the day that the Netherlands and Belgium were invaded, May 10, the House repudiated Chamberlain. The King then sent for Churchill and asked him to head the Government. He was to remain in that post more than five years, until after Germany was defeated and the other main antagonist, Japan, was on the point of surrender.

Now began his series of magnificent—and successful—attemps to rally the fighting spirit of his countrymen. Only three days after the attack on Belgium and the Netherlands he gave one of the most famous of his speeches, in the course of which he said:

I have nothing to offer but blood, toil, tears and sweat. . . . You ask, what is our policy? I will say: It is to wage war, by sea, land and air, with all our might and with all the strength that God can give us. . . . You ask, what is our aim? I can answer in one word: Victory—victory at all costs, victory in spite of all terror, victory however long and hard the road may be; for without victory, there is no survival.

These courageous words, uttered under the darkest circumstances, sent a thrill through the sore-pressed British people. As the Germans roared across France, and her government meekly prepared for surrender, Churchill tried to keep her in the War, making an unheard-of offer to consolidate the two nations permanently into one. After Dunkirk, and with the fall of France imminent, his voice continued resolute:

We shall not flag. We shall go on to the end. We shall fight in France, we shall fight on the seas and oceans, we shall fight with growing confidence and growing strength in the air. We shall defend our island whatever the cost may be. We shall fight on the beaches, we shall fight on the landing grounds, we shall fight in the fields and in the streets, we shall fight in the hills. We shall never surrender; and even if, which I do not for a moment believe, this island or a large part of it were subjugated and starving, then our Empire beyond the seas, armed and guarded by the British Fleet, would carry on the struggle until, in God's good time, the New World with all its power and might steps forth to the rescue and liberation of the Old.

This speech was broadcast by radio and the folklore of the time says that after uttering his defiant words, "We shall fight on the beaches," etc., he covered the microphone with his hand to cut himself off the air and added, "but God knows what we'll fight with." Another version has him saying, "And we will hit them over the head with beer bottles, which is about all we have got to work with."

The heroic Battle of Britain, which in cold fact came within a hair's breadth of forcing the island's defenders to their knees, soon began. Day after day and night after night Hitler poured his bombers over London and the other cities. The Royal Air Force was pitifully small but it gallantly rose, twenty-four hours a day, to do battle. British losses were appalling; the life expectancy of a fighter pilot was reduced to only a few months, but these resolute young men never faltered, and Churchill paid tribute to them with a famous phrase: "Never in the field of human conflict was so much owed by so many to so few."

Even before the Battle of Britain, he had foreseen what was coming:

> The whole fury and might of the enemy must very soon be turned on us. Hitler knows that he will have to break us in this island or lose the War. If we can stand up to him, all Europe may be free and the life of the world may move forward into broad, sunlit upland. . . . Let us therefore brace ourselves to our duties and so bear ourselves that, if the British Empire and its Commonwealth last for a thousand years, men will say, "This was their finest hour."

The courage of the Royal Air Force, plus technological advance, finally paid off. In the nick of time, Sir Robert Watson-Watt and his team of brilliant young scientists had developed radar, which not only gave a few minutes' precious warning when the German bombers were leaving the European coast, but also enabled the fighter planes to shoot down enemy aircraft at night or in the heaviest fog almost as readily as in sunshine. To keep the secret, word was allowed to "leak out" that the British pilots were eating massive doses of carrots, which miraculously improved their nighttime vision. Gradually the tide turned, and soon the Germans were suffering such heavy daily losses that they had to end the blitz. The threat from the air was over, for the time being, although throughout the War there were sporadic raids, climaxed by the robot "buzz bombs" of 1944–45.

Those responsible for Churchill's personal safety had a trying time; he would never take sensible precautions. He was irked by the secrecy with which his movements were supposed to be cloaked. On one occasion he was about to go from Washington to Ottawa; forbidden to tell the Canadian Prime Minister, Mackenzie King, his means of travel, he telephoned him and said, "I'm coming by puff-puff, if you know what I mean."

When the bombing of London was at its worst, he would often go out of doors to scowl up at the German planes overhead. On one occasion he went to the roof of a building, and sat down on a small projection to see what was going on; after a while an Air Raid Patrol officer plucked up courage to tell him he was sitting on the smoke vent and the people in the air-raid shelter below—where Churchill should have been —were suffocating. He considered himself a cautious man, contrary to the universal opinion; as he once remarked, "Although always prepared for martyrdom, I prefer that it should be postponed."

While the echoes of the raid were still dying away, he would be out driving through the debris in the streets, sitting up on the back of a convertible car, his bulldog countenance illumined by the flames of the hundreds of fires set by the bomb, his huge cigar freshly lighted, his hand raised with two fingers spread in the famous "V for Victory" sign. (As a matter of fact, while for fifty years he lighted a large number of cigars daily, he rarely smoked more than an inch or two of any of them.) He showed the people their Prime Minister just as, before the World Wars, the great maritime powers used to send a battleship to any trouble spot to "show the flag."

Desperately hard-pressed as he was, Churchill did not allow his spirits to droop, and he continued to toss off phrases that promptly ran around the world. In one of his direct appeals for more aid from the United States he assured the Americans: "We shall not fail or falter; we shall not weaken or tire. Neither the shock of battle nor the long-drawn trials of vigilance and exertion will wear us down. Give us the tools and we will finish the job." He reported to the Canadian Parliament, "When I warned them [the French Government] that Britain would fight on alone whatever they did, their Generals told their Prime Minister and his divided Cabinet:

'In three weeks England will have her neck wrung like a chicken!' Some chicken! Some neck!"

At the time the peril that Britain would be invaded seemed greatest, someone proposed that the church bells should remain silent unless the German forces landed. Churchill observed, "For myself, I cannot help feeling that anything like a serious invasion would be bound to leak out."

In a speech to the United States Congress, he mentioned the theory of the Japanese that their entry into the War would frighten the British into prompt surrender. His comment was, "What kind of people do they think we are."

Churchill of course rejoiced in the help that President Roosevelt was able to give him in the period when the United States was still in theory neutral. In a speech on August 20, 1940, after the beginning of Lend-Lease, he commented:

> Undoubtedly this process means that these two great organizations of the English-speaking democracies—the British Empire and the United States—will have to be somewhat mixed up together in some of their affairs for mutual and general advantage. . . . I do not view the process with any misgivings. I could not stop it if I wished. No one can stop it. Like the Mississippi, it just keeps rolling along. Let it roll. Let it roll on in full flood, inexorable, irresistible, benignant, to broader lands and better days.

In the autumn of 1940 he made a desperate gamble. England had only one armored division left with which to help withstand a cross-Channel invasion by the Germans which it was thought might come at almost any moment. Nevertheless he sent this division to Egypt, in fear that the Axis might seize the Suez Canal, traditionally the lifeline of the British Empire. By this time, Germany's allies included Italy, Hungary, Rumania and Bulgaria. In Southeast Europe only Greece and Jugoslavia resisted, and were finally overrun for their pains.

On June 22, 1941, help came to the Allies when Germany invaded Russia. Allied intelligence knew some time in advance that the attack was coming, and tried to tell Stalin, but he suspected that the warning was a capitalist trick, and was completely unprepared. In the beginning, Hitler's army sliced into the USSR with hardly any opposition, and almost every western military expert assumed that Stalin would have to surrender within a few weeks at most. Churchill, who thought little more of the Communists than he did of the Nazis, immediately welcomed Russia into the War and promised her all possible aid. His private comment was that he would shake hands with the devil himself if at this point the devil seemed to be on his side.

In January of that year, about eleven months before Pearl Harbor, Churchill has recorded, Harry Hopkins, Roosevelt's great friend and confidant, had appeared in London with an amazing message. He told Churchill that "the President is determined that we shall win the War together. Make no mistake about it. He has sent me here to tell you that at all costs and by all means he will carry you through, no matter what happens to him—there is nothing he will not do so far as he has human power."

In August, Roosevelt and Churchill met face to face for the first time on a warship in Placentia Bay, Newfoundland. While the warmth of their subsequent friendship was exaggerated for propaganda purposes during the War, they at once liked and understood each other.

Throughout the War, the fine language of the Atlantic Charter came back to haunt Churchill. The document was intended chiefly as a piece of propaganda to encourage the inhabitants of the countries enslaved by Hitler; it talked about "the right of all peoples to choose the form of government under which they will live." India and other British colonies promptly demanded to know why it did not apply to them, and Churchill was hard put to it to explain. He finally said, in the House of Commons:

At the Atlantic meeting we had in mind, primarily, the restoration of sovereignty, self-government and national life of the states and nations of Europe now under the Nazi yoke, and the principles governing any alterations in their territorial boundaries which may have to be made. So that is quite a separate problem from the progressive evolution of self-governing institutions in the regions and peoples which owe allegiance to the British Crown.

This may have satisfied the Commons, but it certainly did not appease the restive colonial peoples, who remembered with resentment Churchill's "I did not become the King's First Minister to preside over the liquidation of the British Empire."

On December 7th, 1941, came the real turning point in the War, when the Japanese struck without warning almost simultaneously at Pearl Harbor, the Philippines, and Malaysia. The next day war was declared on Japan by the United States, Great Britain, the Netherlands, Australia, Canada, New Zealand, and several Latin American countries. Only three days later, Japanese fliers scored a tremendous success by sinking two important British warships, the battleship *Prince of Wales* and the battle cruiser *Repulse*. Both of them were steaming not far from Singapore, without any air protection; sixteen years later an official British history of the War declared that the decision to send out these two vessels unguarded was a political and not a military one, though in Churchill's own history he denies this.

Winston, with his usual sublime self-confidence, always considered himself a master of military strategy, and worked hard throughout the conflict to get his way. He was never more than partially successful; while Britain was still fighting alone, his own military and naval leaders often resisted him, and after 1941 he had to get the consent of Roosevelt, and sometimes of Stalin as well, for any major change in policy. He conferred with Roosevelt often during the war, once in Newfoundland, four times in Washington, twice in Quebec, and in Casablanca, Cairo, Teheran, and Yalta. He conferred alone in Moscow with Stalin, who was also present at Teheran and, of course, at Yalta.

Long after the War, the chief of the Imperial General Staff,

Viscount Alanbrooke, gave his opinion of Churchill as a strategist, in the book, *The Turn of the Tide,* written by Sir Arthur Bryant but based on Alanbrooke's diaries. The soldier makes it plain that he regarded Churchill's military suggestions as usually unsound, and that on many occasions he resisted what he considered crack-brained suggestions.

He gives us one remarkable portrait of Churchill in action during the War. Winston as usual was driving everyone frantic by insisting on working nearly all night, although his colleagues had to be at their desks early each morning. On one such occasion, Alanbrooke says:

> Finally, at 2:15 A.M. he suggested we should proceed to the hall to have some sandwiches and I hoped this might at last mean bed. But no! He went on till ten of three before he made a move for bed. He had the gramophone turned on and in his many-colored dressing-gown, with a sandwich in one hand and watercress in the other, he trotted round and round the hall, giving occasional little skips to the tune of the gramophone. On each lap near the fireplace he stopped to release some priceless quotation or thought. For instance, he quoted a saying that a man's life is similar to a walk down a long passage with closed windows on either side. As you reach each window, an unknown hand opens it, and the light it lets in only increases by contrast the darkness of the end of the passage.

Field Marshal Montgomery in his *Memoirs* gives much the same poor impression of Churchill as a strategist, though he was deeply impressed by him as a personality. Montgomery always carried an autograph book, and on several great occasions during the War Churchill wrote a few lines in it, which Montgomery proudly quotes. Thus after the great victory in Tunisia in June, 1943, Churchill wrote:

> The total destruction or capture of all enemy forces in Tunisia, culminating in the surrender of 248,000 men, marks the triumphant end of the great enterprises set on foot at Alamein and by the invasion of Northwest Africa. May the future reap in the utmost fullness the rewards of past achievements and new exertions.

Just before the invasion of Normandy he put down:

> On the verge of the greatest Adventure with which these pages have dealt, I record my confidence that:
> *All will be well—*
> And that the organization and equipment of the Army will be worthy of the valor of the soldiers and the genius of their chief.

When the War was ended, after reciting what the British forces had done in its final days, he wrote for the Field Marshal:

> . . . the fame of the Army Group, like that of the Eighth Army, will long shine in history. Other generations besides our own will honor their deeds and above all the character, profound strategy and untiring zeal of their Commander, who marched from Egypt through Tripoli, Tunis, Sicily and southern Italy, and through France, Belgium, Holland and Germany to the Baltic and the Elbe without losing a battle or even a serious action.

It is no wonder that Montgomery cherished his autograph book! He may or may not have known of Churchill's characterization of him: "Indomitable in retreat; invincible in advance; insufferable in victory." Told in 1959 that Montgomery's memoirs in the first few months after publication had already brought in more than $500,000, Winston commented that "the Field Marshal acted in the best tradition of the British Army—he sold his life dearly."

There were three great points in Churchill's strategy for which he was heavily criticized at the time and still is. The first of these was creating a North African front. The second was his opposition to any early attempt to invade France and thus take some of the pressure off Russia. The third was his desire, late in the War, to strike at "the soft underbelly of the Axis." He wanted to use a tenth of the Allied strength in an operation in the Eastern Mediterranean. He pointed out that the air force massed for the defense of Egypt was standing idle, as were several divisions in that part of the world that could not be moved elsewhere because of the shortage of shipping. He suggested an assault on the Island of Rhodes; if it were successful, the whole Aegean would be dominated by the Allies, and there would be direct contact by sea with Turkey, which might force her into the War on the side of the Allies, and open up the Black Sea. It might also have put much of the Balkans under the control of the Western Allies, instead of Russia. Strangely enough, in his book, *Closing the Ring,* he argues that Stalin might have been persuaded to accept this. Roosevelt, however, suspected "a political motive" and would have none of the scheme.

As a part of his strategy, Churchill wanted the Anglo-American troops, when they had conquered Italy, to strike north at once in a bold sweep and capture Vienna, ahead of the oncoming Russians. He preferred this to the second landing in France, at Marseilles, which he thought was unnecessary after the successful invasion of Normandy. Roosevelt was opposed to this plan also, and Churchill dropped it.

Astonishingly, the Prime Minister proposed to Stalin that Russia and Great Britain divide the Balkans into two spheres of influence, offering the Russians Bulgaria and Rumania if Great Britain could have Greece and a share in Jugoslavia. As might be expected, the Americans were furious at this reversion to old-fashioned power politics. Stalin was cold to the idea, probably because he thought he could get most of this area alone, by force of arms, as indeed proved to be the case.

Several other actions of Churchill at about this time severely strained his relations with Washington. For some reason, he was bitterly opposed to any important post in the new post-Fascist government of Italy for Washington's protegé Count Carlo Sforza. Again, when the Germans were forced out of Greece, civil war broke out between the Royalists and the Partisans, who had been underground fighters like the French *Maquis.* Great Britain landed troops "to maintain order," who sided with the Royalists. The Americans, perhaps bemused by their own propaganda, did not seem to realize that the Partisans were mainly Communists, and in their bitterness over the struggle threatened to stop sending badly needed food and other supplies into Greece. The dispute was eventually straightened out. It is worth noting in Churchill's favor that Greece is today the only free country in Southeastern Europe.

In the light of our present knowledge, the criticisms of Churchill's strategy seem less valid than they did at the time. The campaign in North Africa gave invaluable training to green troops, especially the Americans. It prevented a pincers movement by the Axis, striking down through the Balkans and eastward through North Africa, which would have given them control of the entire eastern end of the Mediterranean and, indeed, the whole Middle East. As for the early invasion of Europe, neither the men nor the equipment existed to undertake it for years after Stalin first began to demand it, which was about a week after Russia was invaded in June, 1941. (He tactfully avoided mentioning at the time that it was his alliance with Hitler in August, 1939, that had brought on the War.) When the invasion of Normandy finally did take place on June 6, 1944, it just barely succeeded in establishing a beachhead, helped greatly by accidents of luck, plus a skillful Allied propaganda campaign to trick the Germans into thinking the landing would take place somewhere else.

As for Churchill's idea of getting into the Balkans and Vienna ahead of the Russians, the trouble that has come to the world because Russia got there first and still holds Bulgaria, Hungary, and Rumania makes his plan look much more attractive than it did at the time.

At the Casablanca conference, Churchill supported Roosevelt's demand for unconditional surrender, afterward so much criticised. The demand thoroughly suited Churchill's temperament, and in any case, he had to pay the utmost attention to the President's wishes, since American strength would be the deciding factor.

The lowest moment of the War for the Allies was probably the late summer of 1942. The German armies were sweeping into Egypt; in Russia they had penetrated as far as the Caucasus, and had begun the siege of Stalingrad, while U-boat sinkings in the Atlantic—some of them actually within sight of the American coast—had reached a terrifying level. In the Pacific, the Japanese had made their farthest advances, capturing bases in the Aleutians and New Guinea.

A year later, the picture had enormously brightened. Stalingrad had been relieved and 330,000 Axis troops taken prisoner. The last German and Italian forces were out of Africa. Sicily and Italy had been invaded and on September 3, the Italian government surrendered, although the Germans in that country were to go on fighting almost to the end of the War. In 1943, moreover, the submarine threat in the North Atlantic was virtually ended, while in the Pacific the Americans won the strategically important Solomon Islands.

In 1944 came the long-demanded invasion of Normandy, preceded only two days earlier by the fall of Rome. The Germans began the use of "buzz bombs" against England, a pure terror weapon, since these could not be directed at military targets, but fell indiscriminately on city and countryside alike (just as large atom or hydrogen bombs do). The Russian armies reconquered Byelorussia and the Ukraine, and swept on through the Baltic States and East Poland. On July 22 of that year occurred the abortive attempt by German army officers to kill Hitler with a bomb. Churchill, who thought as poorly of Hitler's military knowledge as his own officers thought of his, congratulated America and Britain on the Führer's escape: "It would be most unfortunate if the Allies were to be deprived in the closing phases of the struggle of that form of warlike genius by which Corporal Schicklgruber has so notably contributed to our victory." Churchill felt about him as military experts, whom he once quoted, did about the Margrave of Baden: "His absence from a battlefield was well worth 15,000 men."

It was usually difficult to give Churchill advice; but when

he decided that someone was worth listening to, he would heed the ideas of that person in spite of all opposition. During the Second World War his adviser on science was F. A. Lindemann, a German-educated physicist, who later became Lord Cherwell. The contrast between the statesman and the scientist was extreme: Lindemann was a vegetarian and an ascetic, solitary and introverted.

Though some people have denied it, there is evidence that throughout the War he carried on a damaging feud with another top British scientist, the chemist, Sir Henry Tizard. Lindemann made some useful suggestions, and helped Churchill to evaluate the flood of technical ideas that poured into the government offices. He also made some bad mistakes. He resisted the development of radar for a long time, and advocated the strategic bombing of Germany; after the War, it was proved that not only had this bombing accomplished far less than Lindemann had predicted, but far less than the bomber crews themselves reported at the time.

By early 1945, the end of the War in Europe was in sight, though Allied intelligence had no idea how close Japan was to surrender. For a week beginning on February 4, Churchill, Roosevelt, and Stalin conferred at Yalta in the Crimea; after Teheran, Stalin had obdurately refused to meet again anywhere except on Russian soil.

Although Churchill and Roosevelt were friends, there were strains from time to time, as was only natural with two high-spirited individuals, the heads of enormously powerful governments in a time of desperate anxiety and tension. Quite early in the War, Roosevelt began to suggest that Churchill's Government should make some strong gesture in the direction of world democracy. He repeatedly hinted that Hong Kong be turned back to the Chinese Government of Chiang Kai-shek. He also proposed from time to time that India should be granted her freedom. Whether Roosevelt really thought Churchill might accede to these suggestions, it is impossible to say.

At Teheran, and also at Yalta, Roosevelt took to teasing

Churchill openly, in front of Stalin, about his cigar smoking, his staying up all night, and his consumption of alcohol. Churchill also heard rumors that secret meetings were taking place between Roosevelt and Stalin; it was almost as if these two men had decided that the world in future belonged to their powers, and that Great Britain no longer counted in quite the same way. It was a difficult time for Churchill but he bore it stolidly.

As the Russian armies began to race westward through Europe, he and many other people became deeply concerned about where they were to meet the Anglo-American forces. Churchill wanted these to go as far as possible toward the east before meeting the Russians, but he encountered stubborn resistance to this policy from both Eisenhower and Roosevelt. The American Army deliberately halted on the border of Czechoslovakia and let the Russians occupy Prague. Montgomery's plea for a quick slash on a narrow front to take Berlin was turned down in what may have been the worst American mistake of the entire War. The Russians moved far west in Germany, accompanied by a wave of rape and looting. Long afterward, Churchill revealed that he had ordered the rifles that were laid down by the surrendering German soldiers to be stacked in such a way that they could quickly be put into use again, if the Russians should forget to stop marching.

Despite their differences on strategy, Churchill had become attached to President Roosevelt; the news of the American President's death was a bad blow.

Less than four weeks later came the end of the European phase of the greatest war in history, a war that cost thirty million lives, including civilians, and altered the face of the world for generations. As the Allies were about to capture Berlin, Hitler and his mistress committed suicide in an air-raid shelter there.

Only two and a half months after the victory, Churchill's government was turned out of office in a stunning defeat;

Winston, who was at Potsdam, Germany, conferring with Stalin and the new American President Harry Truman, was abruptly replaced by the head of the new Labor Government, Clement Attlee (afterward Earl Attlee). There were probably several reasons for the defeat: the British people were tired of the war hardships and, as always happens, tended to blame the party in power. Churchill, who for many years had been interested almost exclusively in foreign affairs, did not have much of a domestic program, whereas the Labor Party made exciting promises to the weary people about many badly needed improvements in their life.

As might be expected, Churchill took the defeat very hard. About this time, being offered the cherished decoration, the Order of the Garter, he is supposed to have said, "Why should I accept the Garter from His Majesty when his people have just given me the boot?" A flash of his familiar humor shone through when he was talking to a lady visitor from a Balkan country, where any newly installed regime liquidates the leading figures of the preceding one. Erroneously applying the political habits of her own country to Great Britain she said, "It is terrible—now they will shoot you." To this he replied bravely: "I have hopes, Madam, that the sentence will be mitigated to a life term at various forms of hard labor."

For the next six years, as leader of the Opposition, he sat in the House and glowered at the Labor Government as it took over coal mines and communication by cable and radio, nationalized the railroads, and instituted free medical care. No trace was now left in him of the brilliant young radical who, three and a half decades earlier, had helped Lloyd George bring about many reforms that pointed in the same direction, and was then called bitterly a traitor to his class. Of Attlee he now remarked, "Indeed he is a modest man— he has a great deal to be modest about." A particular bête noire of his was Sir Stafford Cripps, whose name he always managed to mispronounce with an effect of denigration. Said Churchill: "None of his colleagues can compare with him in that acuteness and energy of mind with which he devotes himself to so many topics injurious to the strength and welfare of the state." About Aneurin Bevan he was briefer, saying merely that he threatened to be as great a burden in peace as he had been "a squalid nuisance in time of war."

When the Labor Government was forced by its own Left Wing to cut the proposed compulsory military service from eighteen months to twelve, Churchill was ironic at the expense of the Minister of Defense, A. V. Alexander, who had to defend the change in the House:

> I have been looking around for something upon which to congratulate the Right Honorable gentleman. After some difficulty I have found at least one point on which I can offer my compliments, and that is the control of his facial expression, which enabled him to deliver the ridiculous and deplorable harangue to which we have listened and yet keep an unsmiling face.

By now, Churchill was probably the highest paid author in the world. Beginning soon after the end of the War, he produced his six-volume history of the struggle, and picked up again an earlier project, a history of the English-speaking peoples. These two books brought him a comfortable fortune, in spite of Britain's very high income taxes; *Life* magazine is reported to have paid him nearly $2 million for the reprint rights to the history of the Second World War, selections from which also appeared in the *New York Times* and in many other newspapers and magazines all over the world. His general feelings at this time are suggested by the subtitle he wrote for the sixth volume: "How the Great Democracies Triumphed and So Were Able to Resume the Follies Which Had So Nearly Cost Them Their Life." But the subtitle for the whole six volumes was more equable: "In War, Resolution; in Defeat, Defiance; in Victory, Magnanimity; in Peace, Good Will."

Only about eight months after the end of the War, when most people's thinking about Russia was still bemused by wartime propaganda, Churchill issued a warning that echoed, clear and ominous, around the globe. Mr. Truman had asked him to come and speak at Westminster College, Fulton, Missouri, and on March 5, 1946, he did so, bluntly warning the West that the Communists intended to conquer the world. "From Stettin in the Baltic to Trieste in the Adriatic an iron curtain has descended across the Continent. Behind that line lie all the capitals of the ancient states of Central and Eastern Europe. . . . The Communist Parties, which were very small in all these Eastern States of Europe, have been raised to preëminence and power far beyond their numbers and are seeking everywhere to obtain totalitarian control. Police government is prevailing in nearly every case, and so far, except in Czechoslovakia, there is no true democracy." (Czechoslovakia was to fall to the Communists in 1948.) Churchill pleaded for the closest possible association between the United States and Great Britain, even going so far as to propose common training for the armed forces, and interchangeable weapons. (The second of these has to a large degree been put into effect.)

Perhaps fearing that America would relapse into isolationism again as she had done after the First World War, Churchill now turned toward the idea of a United States of Europe, to embrace all the noncommunist countries. The Europeans responded warmly to this proposal, which in fact had been agitated for many years by Count Michael Karolyi of Hungary, and others. A Council of Europe was set up, but then Churchill reversed himself and began to pour cold water on the whole idea. With his sensitive political antennae, he felt that there was no enthusiasm for the idea among the British people, except a few liberal intellectuals.

In the general election of 1950, Labor won again, but with its huge majority cut down to only six. This was obviously too narrow a margin to be workable, and the next year the Conservatives came back to power, though their advantage was also narrow, twenty-two votes. Churchill was of course once more Prime Minister.

The next five years were fairly undramatic, compared to the stormy era of the Second World War. Churchill's Government continued to participate in the Korean War that had begun in 1950, as Great Britain was of course bound to do as a member of the United Nations. In spite of the violent attacks during election campaigns on the revolutionary changes by the Labor Government, almost all of them were continued by the Tories; the country had accepted them, and anyhow, unscrambling the eggs would have been an almost impossible task.

In 1952 Great Britain, the United States, and France made peace with West Germany, and withdrew the Allied control groups. Later that year, the first British atom bomb was successfully exploded. On February 6, King George VI died and was succeeded by his daughter, with the title of Elizabeth II. On June 2 of the following year, her coronation took place with the usual elaborate ceremonial pageant; only four days earlier, Mount Everest, the highest mountain in the world, had been conquered by an expedition commanded by the British Colonel Henry Hunt, the actual final climbers being Sir Edmund Hilary of New Zealand and Tenzing, a Sherpa guide. The next year saw the inconclusive Geneva Conference on Far Eastern affairs by the Foreign Ministers of nineteen nations, and the end of the seven-year-long revolt against the French in Indo-China, with a negotiated settlement which turned over to the Communists 77,000 square miles of land and twelve million people. Later in the year, the Southeast Asia Collective Defense Treaty was signed by the United States, Great Britain, Australia, New Zealand, the Philippines, Pakistan, and Thailand.

In Churchill's personal life, 1953 was marked by important events. He received the Nobel Prize in Literature, and for once there were very few dissenting voices. In that year he accepted from the new Queen Elizabeth a Knighthood and the Order of the Garter; it was obvious that he did so chiefly as a token of affection and respect for her. Sir Winston could not rank higher in the esteem of the British people than

"Winnie" already did. In the same year, on June 27, he suffered a stroke, on the eve of going to Bermuda to confer with President Eisenhower. Though rumors of what had happened were widespread, the press loyally kept the secret for another two years, and in time, he seemed almost completely recovered.

His eightieth birthday, in 1954, was celebrated throughout the British Commonwealth; a Birthday Fund of about $14 million was raised, to be devoted to public purposes, and his chair in the House of Commons was replaced by a special one. In his speech on this magnificent occasion, he indulged in a touch of unwonted modesty. He was being over-praised for his role in the dark early days of the War, said Churchill. "It was the nation and the race, dwelling all around the globe, that had the lion's part. I had the luck to be called on to give the roar."

He was still Prime Minister, but paying less and less attention to the onerous details of the job. On April 5, 1955, he was succeeded as Prime Minister by Sir Anthony Eden.

At eighty-one, he now felt entitled to begin to give much of his time to his hobbies; he took winter vacations on the Riviera or in North Africa, where he could paint landscapes with the strong sunlight and the bright colors that he loved. At home at Chartwell he oversaw his farm, augmented recently by the purchase of five hundred additional acres. He made friends of the farm animals—so much so that on one occasion, about to carve a home-grown goose, he handed over the knife to his wife, saying on the verge of tears, "You carve him, Clemmy. He was a friend of mine."

Late in life, his early love of polo was metamorphosed into an interest in racing. He bought some horses, which were remarkably successful. Robert Lewis Taylor in his *Winston Churchill: An Informal Study of Greatness,* suggests that the implacable owner, who has never condoned failure in others, gave his horse a good talking-to just before the race. Taylor quotes one of Churchill's friends as saying, "It might be an exaggeration to describe the horse's face as apprehensive, but

I have noticed the same look from sluggish ministers after a wartime Cabinet meeting. In any case, the horse gets into motion pretty fast and keeps glancing back over its shoulder."

In 1959, Sir Winston had the unusual honor of having a new college named for him. Churchill College at Cambridge is devoted to science; its first head was the noted British physicist, Sir John Cockcroft. The founding cost of the college was $11 million, and Winston himself contributed $70,000 of this amount.

In the same year a general election was called and Sir Winston surprised everyone by announcing, on the eve of his eighty-fifth birthday, that he would stand again, for his old constituency. He did not do much campaigning; he did not need to. His reëlection was a foregone conclusion.

In April, 1962, he was given the extraordinary tribute of being made an honorary citizen of the United States; President Kennedy called him "the most honored man of our time."

In May, 1963, Sir Winston announced his impending retirement from Parliament. He had fallen in his hotel in Monte Carlo a few months earlier and broken his leg, which made it difficult for him to get about. He was eighty-eight, and had been in the House more than sixty years, serving two queens, Victoria and her great-great-granddaughter, Elizabeth II, as well as four kings, Edward VII, George V, Edward VIII and George VI.

During his last few months in the House, Sir Winston attended the sessions only occasionally. His wheelchair was brought to a spot just outside the door of the chamber, but whenever he felt able, he walked the remaining distance to his old place, amid wild cheers of the members. He stayed only briefly, and was soon ensconced in his wheelchair again; somehow, a wheelchair with Churchill in it seemed as powerful, and as almost invincible as a tank on a battlefield.

On July 30, 1964, the House said a formal farewell to him as a parliamentarian. For about forty minutes, friend and foe alike united in eulogizing him. His health did not permit him to be present, but afterward a small delegation of the members called on him at his home in London to report what had happened. They said afterward that he was touched and pleased, and seemed in very good spirits.

In January, 1965, Churchill suffered another stroke. While the whole world waited and watched, he clung to life for almost two weeks and then slipped away. He was given a state funeral—a tribute rarely offered anyone not a monarch. The solemn procession through the streets of London was seen on television by people in many countries, to an estimated total of 250 million—the largest viewing audience in all history, up to that time.

In calling Churchill "The Last Bulldog" I do not mean to belittle the many thousands of other men in the world, in Great Britain and elsewhere, who show great tenacity and resolution. It seems clear, however, that some of the special qualities of this extraordinary man are not likely to be repeated. His unquestioning, wholehearted imperialism is a thing of the past; all the great Empires are finished, or nearly so. From now on, people who attempt to be world conquerors— if there are any more—will seek domination chiefly through the spread of their ideas, as the Nazis did and as the Communists are now doing.

In his way of life, Churchill also belonged to an almost extinct breed. Although he did not become a millionaire until middle age, he always lived luxuriously, in a manner that British very high income and inheritance taxes are making less and less common. His oratorical eloquence and his literary style today seem faintly archaic. Few even of his own class in his own country any longer give one the sense of linkage with the heroes of earlier times that he did. His flamboyance in costume, gesture and personal habit, with a touch of the Renaissance about it, appeared incongruous. It is true that he had great faults, by the standards of the new generation. But he had even greater virtues, for which the free world owes him a boundless debt of gratitude.

# 3. Hitler:
# The Madman as Leader

Of Hitler, as of Stalin, it must be said that no normal human being could have committed his terrible crimes. While he showed none of the usual signs of insanity until the last few months of his life, he was beyond doubt a psychopathic personality.

No tyrant in all history ever set out in colder blood to exterminate whole populations. Not only did he plan to kill all the Jews in Europe, men, women and children; but he intended the same fate for many millions of others, notably the Poles and the Russians. He was relentless in exterminating the gypsies, those nomads, probably of Indian origin, who used to wander all over Europe, and especially Hungary and Rumania.

Many years before he came to power, Hitler was already scheming to destroy the greater part of the population of Poland and Russia. The limited number who would survive would not be permitted to engage in industry; they would be slaves producing food from the soil for the benefit of their German masters. All the chief cities of both countries were to be destroyed, and it was only because Germany lost the Second

**ADOLF HITLER**

"He was always hypnotized by the sound of his own voice. . . . He seemed to convince himself as he went along, and his cynicism . . . appeared to drop away."

World War that these plans were not carried out. When Hitler attacked Russia in June, 1941, he issued orders that Moscow and Leningrad were not to be allowed to surrender but should be destroyed, stone by stone.

Throughout his life, Hitler was subject to fits of hysterical, uncontrollable rage, so violent as almost to resemble an epileptic seizure. There is reliable testimony that during these rages he would sometimes throw himself on the floor and bite the edge of a loose rug. On the other hand, he was also capable of pretending to one of these storms of fury, in order to get his way. He once screamed at the Austrian Premier, Kurt von Schuschnigg for several hours, but as soon as the terrified von Schuschnigg had left the room, he began laughing and slapping his thigh.

How Hitler got started on his pathological hatred of the Jews is still something of a mystery. He himself told a story of a sudden conversion at the age of sixteen in the streets of Vienna, where he came suddenly face to face with one—probably a visitor from Poland or the Ukraine—wearing the traditional long black kaftan and the dangling sidelocks of hair. "The more I gazed at this strange countenance," Hitler wrote many years later, "and examined it section by section, the more the question shaped itself in my brain: Is this a German? I turned to books for help in removing my doubts. For the first time in my life I bought myself some anti-Semitic pamphlets for a few pennies."

This seems too simple and easy a rationalization for the deepest lifelong conviction of a man's whole career. It is true, however, that the newsstands of Vienna in the early years of the century, like those of every other European city, were flooded with anti-Semitic pamphlets that were filled with the wildest possible fabrications against the members of this group. Many people bought these pamphlets, read them, and in some cases doubtless believed them. The fatal difference was that Hitler proceeded to get control of a great modern country in the heart of Europe and to put his beliefs into effect.

There were strong sexual overtones to Hitler's anti-Semitism. He talked constantly about "the sex desires" of the Jews, who "wanted to seduce Aryan girls and adulterate their blood"— as thorough-going nonsense as can be imagined. He said that Negroes had been brought into the Rhineland to bastardize the white race and lower its cultural and political level so that the Jews could dominate; perhaps he referred to African units of the French Army, since no other Negroes came to the Rhineland, and if any had, his friends, the German industrialists, would have been responsible.

He apparently really believed the dreary old nonsense about a Jewish conspiracy to rule the world. Although in any country, the members of the Jewish faith have belonged to various political groups, ranging from conservative to radical, Hitler identified them with internationalism, "humanitarianism," pacifism, and materialism, and thought—or at least, said—that they were seeking to obliterate the heroic qualities of the Nordics.

Nazism was also an anti-Christian movement. Both the Protestant and Catholic churches were persecuted, and any leaders who dared to speak out against Hitler were ruthlessly struck down. Some of his followers actually went back to the ancient Teutonic mythology, but Hitler seems not to have shared this nonsense.

Like many other monomaniacs, Hitler was moderate, almost ascetic, in many aspects of his personal life. He did not smoke, drank almost nothing, ate little meat, and lived simply, in contrast to many of the top Nazis around him who were sybarites indulging in every sort of luxury and vice. Although the Führer had several successive mistresses, he neglected them for months on end. He was fond of art, having been a painter in his youth; his tastes were strictly conservative. Perhaps his greatest esthetic passion was for music, his favorite composer being Wagner. He would turn from ordering the torture death of hundreds of men to listen with tears in his eyes to the tragic story of Tristan and Isolde.

His sadism was illustrated when a group of high Army officers made an unsuccessful attempt to kill him on July 20, 1944. Eight men charged with being among the conspirators were hanged in a manner that involved slow strangulation; a motion picture was made of their last moments and Hitler had it run for him, privately, over and over. He once ordered it shown at a Cadet School; the effect on the students was so bad that it was not exhibited again.

His conceit, from his earliest days, was monumental. His knowledge of the military art was limited; he served as a private and then a corporal in the First World War, and later he read some of the standard textbooks on military strategy. Nevertheless, during the Second World War he insisted his judgment was better than that of all his generals combined—one of the best trained and most skillful groups of professional soldiers in the world. Sometimes, it is true, his reckless gambles paid off, because he had correctly estimated the timidity and vacillation of the enemy.

Because Germany had armed at such a furious pace during the preceding six years, when Hitler started the Second World War in September, 1939, her land and air forces were the strongest anywhere on earth. She came very close indeed to winning the war and might have done so were it not for a series of dreadful military blunders made by the Führer himself against the almost unanimous advice of all his generals. One of these mistakes was the unnecessary attack on Russia which forced Germany into fighting on two fronts. Another was his insistence on killing civilians in London with indiscriminate aerial bombing, instead of directing his attack against military installations on the British coast, an attack that could have greatly delayed or perhaps even prevented the Allied invasion of France. A third was his failure to invade Great Britain promptly after gaining possession of the whole European coastline from Denmark to the Spanish border. He also sent his soldiers to face a Russian winter clad in summer uniforms; and he insisted that the entire French coast be guarded, instead of keeping his troops at a few strong points where they could be moved quickly to any threatened area.

Perhaps his worst single fault as a military man was his monomaniacal insistence that his troops should never retreat, no matter how desperate their situation or how certain they were to lose. Over and over this cost him hundreds of thousands of his best men, killed or captured—in North Africa, at Stalingrad in Russia, and in France after the Allied invasion. This senseless procedure was the outgrowth of nothing but egoism; these men were *his* soldiers and they must maintain at any cost the fiction of his invincibility.

Hitler was one of the most colossal egoists whom history records. When "Heil Hitler" was the standard salutation in Germany, he used it himself. Nobody with a sense of humor could possibly have done so; but then, it is unlikely that anyone with a sense of humor could have raised himself from obscurity to control of a great nation in only ten years and gone on, in another ten, to come dangerously near to control of the whole world. Arguing with his General Staff in 1939 as to why Poland must be attacked at once, he told them, "Essentially it depends on me, on my existence, on my political ability. Probably no one will ever again have the confidence of the German people as I have."

His egoism and lack of humor led him to extremes of fatuousness. An example was the order he issued on the day Normandy was invaded by the Allies, June 6, 1944. He commanded that the enemy must be "annihilated by evening, since there exists the danger of additional sea and airborne landings for support." There did indeed.

His egoism also displayed itself in the fact that he could not endure to be questioned or contradicted by anyone. In the early days of the Nazi Party there were other people in it, like the brothers, Gregor and Otto Strasser, who disagreed with him on questions of policy and said so; Hitler's strategy was to answer at once that if he could not have his way he would resign from the Party. Since he had already demonstrated his magnetic attraction for certain elements in the German population, this tactic silenced the opposition.

In those days anyone who questioned him or disputed any factual statement he made threw him into painful confusion and anger. Later on, when his power was complete, he dismissed from office or even executed many who showed independence. General Franz Halder, Chief of the General Staff, tried to warn Hitler in the middle of the Russian phase of the War that Germany's military position was untenable. According to Alan Bullock, in *Hitler: A Study in Tyranny*, Halder recorded one scene where an officer was reading aloud to the Führer a report that Russia still had large reserves, including many tanks:

> Hitler flew at the man who was reading, with clenched fists and foam in the corners of his mouth and forbade him to read any more of such idiotic twaddle.

Shortly thereafter, Halder himself joined the procession of generals who were dismissed for failing to support Hitler completely in all of his fantastic refusals to face the truth.

He was one of the most skillful propagandists who ever lived, and his rules are probably just as effective today as they were when he first used them. You should, he said, expound only a few ideas, of the utmost simplicity, and these must be repeated over and over and not changed even though they are out of date. Never hesitate or qualify or concede anything. Make everything black and white. Above all, use the technique of the big lie. Bullock quotes him:

> In the big lie there is always a certain force of credibility, because the broad masses of a nation are always more easily corrupted in the deeper strata of their emotional nature than consciously or voluntarily and thus in the primitive simplicity of their minds they more readily fall victims to the big lie than the small lie, since they themselves often tell small lies in little matters, but would be ashamed to resort to large-scale falsehoods. . . . The grossly impudent lie always leaves traces behind it, even after it has been nailed down.

Hitler was one of the first to use effectively the saturation technique in propaganda. Newspapers, magazines, motion pictures, radio were all forbidden to breathe the slightest opposition to his policies. School teachers and college professors were dismissed for any infraction of this rule, or even if their past history suggested they might have independent ideas of their own. (Television had not yet come to Germany; one trembles to think what use Hitler might have made of it, though it is hard to see how he could have been more successful than he was in mobilizing public opinion.)

His public speeches and those of his followers were deliberately filled with violent language, with words like "beat," "kill," "smash," and "destroy." The Nazi bullies who roamed the streets had orders—which they hardly needed—to beat people up; Hitler believed that violence has a certain attraction of its own even to those whose first reaction is repulsion. Before he was strong enough to banish all opposition political parties, the Nazis regularly attended all public meetings of such parties and disrupted them.

The Führer carried this philosophy of force into his private life. Bullock describes how, in his Munich days in the early 1920's, he carried a heavy riding whip of hippopotamus hide, and planned his every move like an actor, to suggest force, decision, and will. A record remains of a social gathering in Munich in about 1923 to which he was invited. He came very late, looking pale and not very well, with an expressionless face. He sat silent for a long time, then suddenly got up and began to harangue the group as though at a street-corner meeting. After a lengthy speech, he abruptly left.

The truth is that Hitler, who in his youth was what would now be called a beatnik and went straight from the slums of Vienna into the German Army, was keenly conscious of his ignorance of polite manners. One of the reasons for the long tension between himself and the High Command of the German Army is that the wellborn officers of the latter secretly despised him as a guttersnipe, and he knew and resented this.

He was always hypnotized by the sound of his own voice, and this fact probably helped to create his extraordinary ability to hypnotize others, especially in large public meetings. When he had to make a speech, he usually wrote it out in advance, but he would put off this task of preparation until the last possible moment. Then he would begin to dictate, shouting at the stenographer as though addressing ten thousand people. (He shouted so hard that twice in his life surgeons had to remove a polyp from his vocal cords, once in 1935, and again shortly before his death in 1945.) He seemed to convince himself as he went along, and the cynicism which we know was usually his predominant state of mind appeared to drop away.

It is a striking fact that he sometimes appeared to be sucked in by his own propaganda even when he knew that this propaganda was false. His successive invasions of Austria, Czechoslovakia and Poland were preceded in every case by the planting of stories that Germans in these countries had been mistreated—though in fact there is no evidence of any such incidents or any reason to believe that Hitler would have cared. Thriftily, he used the same propaganda stories in each case—pregnant German women beaten on the street, German students knocked down and trampled, and so forth. Yet when the press, in obedience to his orders, printed these lies he seemed to forget that he had ordered them, and to become genuinely indignant.

Though as a soldier in the First World War, Hitler was awarded the Iron Cross twice, both First and Second Class, and saw some dangerous duty carrying messages, in later life he showed evidence of physical cowardice. In the Munich Beer Hall Putsch in 1923, when the Nazis tried to seize control of Bavaria, he fled from the field when the police started shooting. When he had become master of all Germany, attempts were made to excuse him by saying he was pulled to the ground by a man standing next to him, and that he had a dislocated shoulder, but the fact remained that he deserted his comrades in a crisis. Late in the Second World War he was once in a bunker on the Western Front, and a V-2 rocket on its way to London accidentally turned around and came down on top of the shelter. No one was injured, but he left the front in a panic and retired to his mountain retreat at Berchtesgaden.

Toward the end of the War, when he mistrusted nearly everyone, an armed guard stood behind the chair of every German general at military conferences with Hitler, ready to shoot at a second's notice. It is hardly surprising that he should by now have been somewhat nervous; in the course of time there had been seven major attempts on his life, one of which missed killing him only by a narrow accident that would occur only once in a thousand times.

All his life, Hitler was a hypochondriac. For years he clung to a quack doctor, Theodor Morell, who fed him a great variety of nostrums; a phalanx of pill bottles accompanied him everywhere. While most of these were harmless, in 1942 he began taking strychnine and belladonna, and this continued until the end of his life; during this time he was being slowly poisoned, and so were most of the other top Nazis, who dutifully took the same pills. In 1944, a competent doctor who examined him tried to warn him, and was exiled from the Hitler circle for his pains.

Hitler was like his arch enemy, Churchill, in that he liked to sleep late in the morning and then work far into the night. He would breakfast at ten or eleven, and lunch any time between two and five. Dinner was also a movable feast, beginning as early as eight or as late as midnight. After dinner, he went on working, sometimes until four A.M. Before the War began, his routine was less strenuous and in the evenings he sometimes looked at movies, including many foreign ones which the German people were forbidden to see, or he listened to phonograph records of Wagner and Beethoven. He never took exercise beyond an occasional walk late at night with his dog.

Hitler seems to have been deeply in love with only one woman, Geli Raubal, the daughter of his half-sister. She had a room in his apartment in Munich, and there in 1931 she was found dead, presumably a suicide. For weeks afterward he appeared to be in a state of shock, and all his life, tears came into his eyes whenever her name was mentioned.

For the last twelve years of his life his mistress was Eva Braun, twenty years younger than he, whom he first met when she was an assistant to the official Nazi photographer, Heinrich Hoffmann. For most of this time, Hitler kept her out of public sight, but about a year before the end, her sister married Hermann Fegelein, a prominent Nazi, and Eva was then permitted to be more conspicuous on the excuse that she was Fegelein's sister-in-law. She seems to have been genuinely fond of Hitler; at any rate she showed signs of jealousy when he developed a passing interest in other women. Twice she attempted suicide, or pretended to. She herself was not averse to flirting, and had to conceal these episodes from Hitler— as well as the fact that she liked to drink and smoke, two things he strictly forbade. She is described as a stupid blonde, fond of athletics such as skiing and swimming, and commonplace in her tastes, fond of new dresses and the movies.

Hitler was born April 20, 1889, in a town called Braunau am Inn in Austria, on the Bavarian border, the third son of his father's third marriage. His father, Alois Hitler, had been an illegitimate child, and for many years went by his mother's maiden name, Schicklgruber. The grandfather acknowledged Alois as his son only when eighty-four years old, and then only to help him obtain an inheritance from an uncle. Adolf Hitler all his life congratulated himself that he was entitled to his surname, doubting that any man named Schicklgruber could become the leader of a great nation.

Alois Hitler was a restless man, who moved often from town to town; Adolf went to five schools in nine years. He did badly in the Austrian equivalent of high school, and dropped out. When he was fourteen, his father died, and for several years the widowed mother supported the son; she had a small pension, and also did some work. In later years, Nazi propagandists exaggerated the poverty of this period. At sixteen, threatened with tuberculosis, Hitler had to spend a year in idleness; after his health was restored he went back to school, but only briefly. For the next couple of years he did nothing but read omnivorously, go for long solitary walks, and idle about the streets of the town where his mother was living. He stubbornly refused to look for a steady job.

With a very modest talent as a painter, he tried at eighteen to enter the Vienna Academy of Fine Arts, and with his strong conceit, he was greatly taken aback when the Academy twice rejected him. Soon his mother died, and he moved to Vienna.

From his twentieth to his twenty-fourth year he lived here in the greatest poverty, dressed in threadbare hand-me-downs, living in municipal lodging-houses or the most miserable of rented rooms, often going hungry. Though he still refused to try to get a steady job, he worked intermittently at all sorts of humble tasks—shoveling snow, beating carpets, carrying bags at the railroad station, helping on construction jobs. Once in a while he managed to sell a hand-lettered advertising poster to a shopkeeper; at other times, he painted postcards of Vienna scenes and peddled them himself on the streets. He copied famous paintings and sold them for a pittance to art dealers, who used them for the humiliating purpose of displaying frames which were then sold to surround better paintings, while Hitler's were discarded.

Though in later life no one was more lyrical about the glories of war, Hitler at this early stage did not practice what he was to preach. In Vienna, he dodged compulsory military service for years, helped by his semi-mendicant life with no fixed address. At twenty-four, when the authorities seemed hot on his trail, he managed to get across the border to Munich, Germany, where as an Austrian citizen he was not subject to the draft. Yet at some time in the next few months he must have had a change of heart, for as soon as the First World War started in 1914, he asked and obtained permission to volunteer in the German Army.

His army record, if undistinguished, was also unblemished; he was shot in the leg in 1916 and was gassed in 1918. He was in hospital, temporarily blinded from gas, when news came that Kaiser Wilhelm had abdicated, one day before Germany surrendered. He himself said later that he was deeply moved by the news and resolved then that he would try to go into politics.

Nevertheless, when he did so it was more or less by accident. In 1919, while still in the Army, he was assigned to investigate several little radical political groups in Munich. One of these, the German Workers Party, had a program that appealed to him and he abandoned investigating it to become its seventh member. A year later, by sheer power of personality, he had become the dominant influence. After long thought, he changed the name to the National Socialist German Workers Party, nicknamed the Nazis. He adopted the famous swastika, the hooked cross, again after long deliberation; it is a symbol that goes far back in time to ancient India, China, and Egypt.

The program of the Party at this time was radical indeed. All incomes from property ownership were to be abolished. Trusts would be nationalized, and land rent and land speculation ended. Big industries of every sort were to be taken over by the state, some of them being rented back to private operators for modest sums. Anti-Semitism was an important element. Jews would be forbidden to be citizens or to hold public office, and all of them who had come to Germany later than the beginning of the First World War would be expelled. The party platform, like that of all other political groups in Germany at this time, denounced the terms imposed by the victorious Allies in 1919.

At the end of a year, the Nazi Party had attracted only about sixty members, but the soil was well prepared for the sort of agitation Hitler conducted. Long before, he had come to realize that his best chance lay with the lower middle class. The wealthy, of course, did not desire to change anything, and most of the workers were loyal to Socialism or Communism. The lower middle class, on the other hand, suffered severely from the aftermath of the First World War. They were humiliated by the defeat, hurt by the inflation of currency in the early 1920's, and they resented the fact that Germany was now regarded as a pariah nation.

Hitler's propaganda was ideally suited to restore the self-esteem of this group. The Germans had not lost the War, he told them; they had been betrayed at home by the radicals and the Jews. He preached against the Versailles Treaty, aided by the fact that that Treaty was indeed unjust, with many unfair and unworkable clauses. To the Army officers, frustrated by the Treaty provision that Germany could have only a small "police force," he preached secret rearmament.

In 1923 he was helped greatly by the action of the French in occupying the Ruhr, Germany's invaluable coal and steel district. The French marched in on January 11, on the charge that the defeated foe was defaulting on her deliveries of timber for reparations. Their action cut off most of Germany's supplies of coal, steel, and iron, and brought her attempted industrial recovery to a grinding stop. It helped to bring on the dreadful inflation of that year, which her government did nothing to halt. The inflation resulted in money's sometimes losing half its value in a single day and wiped out hundreds of thousands of owners of securities.

Internally, Germany was racked by dissension, with various groups fighting for control. The Catholic church and the wealthy owners of heavy industry were nearly as powerful as the central government, and the Socialists and Communists were also strong. It was this situation that made the Nazi attempt to take over Bavaria, in November, 1923, less hare-brained than it might seem.

Hitler himself had no enthusiasm for the attempted *Putsch*. He was forced into it by a very strange ally indeed, General Erich Ludendorff, a military hero of the First World War.

The egotistical Ludendorff overestimated his own popularity; he thought that the Munich police would not dare to fire on an advancing force of Nazis with himself at its head. He was wrong. The police did fire, a number of Nazis were killed, and the *Putsch* was defeated. As a result, Hitler was sentenced to five years in jail, but he was so popular that the authorities released him in less than nine months.

His imprisonment was more like being under house arrest; he was permitted unlimited visitors and correspondence, and he busily conducted the affairs of the party. He also wrote the greater part of his book, *Mein Kampf,* in which he revealed practically every idea and intention of his later life. One of the world's great mysteries is why nobody either in Germany or among the Allies, paid any real attention to this book. Probably the answer is that the intentions he described seemed so fantastic it was impossible to take them seriously. By the time people discovered that he was in deadly earnest it was too late to stop him.

*Mein Kampf* sold badly for the first few years. Not until 1930 did the sale go as high as 10,000 copies a year. It had been declining for several years until he really emerged on the national scene in that year, when it jumped to 54,000. While he was in power the sales soared into the millions, and his royalties into hundreds of thousands of dollars; great numbers of people bought his book because they were afraid they might be asked whether they owned a copy.

When Hitler emerged from prison, the Nazi Party seemed to be in a decline, and this remained true for the next few years. In an election in 1928, the Party got only 810,000 votes out of 31 million; at that time there were about 100,000 members. This was a hectic time in Germany, nearly as hectic as the days of the inflation in 1922. Trying to put the country on its feet, the Allies, and especially the United States, made huge government loans, and private money was also available, though at high interest rates. The German Federal Government, the various states, the large cities, and heavy industry all borrowed vast sums and spent them recklessly. Many German factories had been destroyed in the War and some others were taken away by the French as reparations; they had been rebuilt or replaced with the latest machines, giving Germany a strong competitive advantage in the world market.

The Great Depression, which began in 1929, hit the country hard and gave Hitler his first real opportunity. There were tremendous numbers of unemployed, and many of these accepted the Nazi doctrines. The able-bodied young men among them became members of the Brown Shirts, lived in Party barracks, and were fed and clothed and given a little pocket money from Party funds. They spent much of their time in the streets, rioting at public meetings of other parties, preventing any reprisals at Nazi gatherings, and beating up Jews—or people who looked as though they might be Jews.

With the Depression continuing, the power of the Party rapidly increased. Hitler had two important principles. The first of these was always to keep friendly with the German Army, which meant, in practice, with the officer class, and in this he was on the whole successful. The second was to try to complete the Nazi revolution before taking power. This would not have been possible if he had really believed, as the Strasser brothers did, in the expropriation of wealth and the setting up of a quasi-Socialist regime.

Though he was tactfully silent, Hitler cared not a whit for these ideas. His revolution was in the emotions; he wanted to engender belief that the Germans were a master race, that Jews, Slavs, Negroes, and Asiatics were subhuman, that all people of Teutonic origin should form one country, and that this country should have virtually unlimited *lebensraum*—living space. Circumstances forced him to take office before this revolution was completed, and he managed, indeed, to get control of the country with the support of far less than a majority. Once in power, he was able to use his propaganda machinery to spread his ideas much more widely.

A man is known by the company he keeps, and it is significant that so far as is known, not one decent human being ever voluntarily became a member of the Hitler inner circle. It is worth while to look briefly at a few of the men who helped him degrade Germany into the least civilized nation on earth.

The person closest to him for many years, and perhaps the only one who could really be called a friend was Captain Ernst Roehm, a professional soldier, a homosexual, and a thoroughgoing blackguard and bully. It was Roehm who was chiefly responsible for building up the Brown Shirt Army that contributed so greatly to Hitler's success; nevertheless the Führer had him killed without any compunction in the great blood purge of June 30, 1934.

The person who was perhaps of greatest usefulness in bringing Germany completely under Hitler's rule was Dr. Paul Joseph Goebbels, a little man only five feet five inches tall, who limped from an operation on one foot as a child and was commonly, though erroneously, believed to be clubfooted. Goebbels wandered into a Nazi meeting in 1922, was instantly converted, and soon became one of Hitler's most important aides. He had a real genius for propaganda; it was he who invented the idea of tremendous Nazi mass meetings, usually at night and in the open air. These were spectacular pageants, with hundreds of massed flags carried down the aisles or thousands of lighted torches borne by men in close-order drill. Hitler would arrive very late, and march down the aisle surrounded by a bodyguard, under a spotlight, to mount the platform and be greeted by thousands chanting in unison "Sieg Heil!"

Goebbels also invented the public burning of books written by Jews or anti-Nazis. Another of his triumphs was the creation of the Horst Wessel legend. Wessel was an unsavory young man living in a poor quarter of Berlin, off the earnings of a prostitute. He was an officer in the Brown Shirts, so zealous that he was cordially hated by his neighbors, many of them Communists. One night three men entered his room and shot him; since the only doctor available was a Jew, Wessel refused his services and died (which might of course have taken place even with medical aid). He had written a song with a catchy air, and Goebbels made it immediately popular with the Nazis, at the same time glorifying Wessel into a sacred martyr of the cause. Rightly or wrongly, his death was blamed on the German Communists, and this accusation helped feed the fires of Nazi hatred.

After Hitler came to power, it was Goebbels who made sure that every instrumentality of education and of communication was devoted one hundred percent to the Nazi line. Anyone who deviated was instantly dismissed, and was lucky to stay alive.

Probably next in usefulness was Hermann Goering, Hitler's chief military adviser. Goering, immensely fat, brutal, sadistic, an egoist whose fondness for self-devised uniforms was the subject of universal surreptitious joking, had been Germany's third ranking aviator in the First World War. At one time he was a morphine addict, but he managed to break the habit. His vanity was proverbial; when Mussolini gave the Nazi Foreign Minister, Joachim von Ribbentrop, a fancy decoration, the Collar of the Annunziata, Goering burst into tears and said he had to have one, too.

During the Second World War, he was ruthless in looting the art treasures of the countries overrun by Germany; his stolen collection was worth millions of dollars. Toward the end of the War, his faculties seemed impaired, perhaps by his gross and long-continued debauchery, and he had little part in the activities of its closing days.

The man chiefly responsible for the mass murder of the Jews, Poles, and Russians, after Hitler himself, was Heinrich Himmler, who looked like a village schoolmaster, with his prim nose glasses. He was in fact an ex-poultry farmer, and his humble exterior hid a monumental sadistic cruelty and indifference to human life. Himmler, captured by the British just after the end of the War, committed suicide by taking cyanide of potassium, a capsule of which he had managed to conceal in his mouth during a supposedly thorough search of his person. Goering, also, managed to kill himself while under sentence of death, swallowing poison that had been smuggled into his cell.

Rudolf Hess, at one time Hitler's private secretary, drew worldwide attention to himself when, during the War, he flew an airplane to Scotland in a fantastic private attempt to persuade Great Britain to make a separate peace. He would probably have been executed after the War by the Allies, if they had not decided that he was insane and sent him to prison under a life sentence.

Most vocal of all the anti-Semites in the group close to Hitler was Julius Streicher, editor of a gutter weekly, *Der Stürmer*. Streicher, who had begun life as a teacher, was infamous for his sadism and lechery, even among the Nazi leaders—no mean achievement. His paper was so pornographic that it turned the stomachs of some who sympathized with his anti-Semitism.

Most of the chief Nazis came from the gutter, but Franz von Papen was different. A career Army man, he achieved notoriety in the United States during the First World War when he permitted American espionage agents to steal a briefcase bulging with damning documents about German espionage and sabotage in that country; the United States promptly demanded his recall. An aristocrat and a Catholic, he entered politics in the 1920's in the Catholic Center Party, and in June, 1932, he became German Chancellor; he was tremendously valuable to the Nazis when he lifted the legal ban on the Brown Shirts.

His government lasted only a few months, but after it was ended he played an important role in persuading the aged and senile President and former war hero, Paul von Hindenburg, to make Hitler Chancellor; he was rewarded by the post of Vice-Chancellor. Appointed ambassador to Austria in

1934, he helped to bring about the conquest of that country in 1938. He stayed clear of the deep internal divisions inside Germany during the Second World War by spending nearly the whole period as Ambassador to Turkey. He was acquitted as a war criminal by the Allies in 1946, but was then sentenced to eight years of hard labor by a German "denazification" court. As with so many others, his sentence was soon canceled. As late as 1960 he was still acting like a genuinely convinced Nazi and talking the Hitler jargon of thirty years earlier.

Another important figure who did not fit the typical Nazi pattern was Dr. Hjalmar Horace Greeley Schacht. He has often been called a financial wizard, and it is true that he accomplished remarkable feats. In 1923 when German paper currency had become valueless, he introduced a new and stable German mark, based on a mortgage on all the nation's land and industry. He stopped the inflation and soon managed to balance the budget; two years later, aided by a foreign loan under the Dawes Plan, Germany was back on the gold standard. Schacht was by now President of the Reichsbank, a post he held until 1930, when he resigned because of his opposition to the Young Plan with its demand for at least token continuance of reparations payments.

He met Hitler the next year and appeared to be captivated by him, though Schacht was an opportunist whose sincerity has often been questioned. At any rate, he played a tremendously important role in bringing Hitler into contact with the big industrialists and bankers who gave him huge sums under the erroneous idea that they could thenceforth control him.

When Hitler became Chancellor, Schacht again took charge of the Reichsbank, and soon added the job of Minister of Economics. He invented the fantastic scheme of barter agreements all over the world by which Germany exchanged her manufactures for the raw materials needed for the rearmament program. He resigned as Minister of Economics in 1937 when Goering was given a post as his superior, but continued as head of the Reichsbank two years longer. He had long been protesting Hitler's utter disregard of financial responsibility, and in 1939 he was forced out, chiefly because Hitler by now would have no one around him who raised the slightest question about his actions. Schacht's face was saved by a six months' journey to the Far East "to study economic conditions."

There is no doubt that he was for some years a member of the group, composed mostly of high Army officers, who plotted to get rid of Hitler. Schacht swore that he had no part in the bomb plot of July 20, 1944, but this did not save him from arrest. Under sentence of death, he was one of a group of Hitler's prisoners who were moved from place to place repeatedly to keep ahead of the advancing American Army, which finally, on May 4, 1945, rescued him in the nick of time. He promptly went from a German prison into an Allied one, was tried as a war criminal at Nuremburg, but was acquitted.

When the Great Depression began in 1929, Germany was in a sorry condition politically. There were ten political parties, each with more than one million votes, but none of them big enough to dominate. Von Hindenburg, the popular idol, was before long almost completely senile; his mind was fairly clear for only an hour or two early each morning, and the men really running the Government sought to get all necessary decisions at that time. With the Reichstag stalemated by the multiplicity of parties, the Government had to rule chiefly by the use of von Hindenburg's special powers; successive Chancellors had to have the coöperation of the Nazis to exercise these powers, and this fact played into Hitler's hands.

The Social Democrats (the Socialists), who had played a great role in Germany in past decades, had leaders who were old and tired. The Communists were more vigorous, and were important because they received constant moral and financial support from Soviet Russia. Many people feared another Communist uprising like the Spartacide rebellion of 1919; the

Nazis themselves thought this was possible and were prepared to rise at once in a counter-revolution. Election after election was held, with no real change in the situation and with no party anywhere near a majority.

Stalin was more responsible than any other individual except Hitler himself for the latter's coming to power. The German Communists and Social Democrats on the whole had more things in common than in disagreement; if they had stood together they could have blocked the Nazi ambition. On the contrary, Stalin ordered a ruthless Communist attack on the Social Democrats, in the Reichstag and out of it, and thereby opened the door to Hitler. Stalin expected that the Nazis would get control, but he assumed that they would soon fade away and that the Communists could take power. It was one of the worst mistakes of his whole career.

In this juncture there occurred the famous Reichstag fire of February 27, 1933. Who actually set this fire is still something of a mystery. A feeble-minded Netherlander, Marinus Van der Lubbe, a known pyromaniac, was in the building that night, and confessed that he had done so. However, William L. Shirer points out in *The Rise and Fall of the Third Reich* that several witnesses at the postwar Nuremberg trials said that the Nazis had burned the building. Hans Gisevius, who was at the time an official in the Prussian Ministry of the Interior, claims that Goebbels had plotted it. The chief of the Gestapo, Rudolf Diels, said that Goering knew of it in advance, and told him to prepare a list of the people to be arrested after it took place.

General Halder reported that Goering boasted at a party on Hitler's birthday in 1942 that he himself had done it:

> I heard with my own ears when Goering interrupted the conversation and shouted, "The only one who really knows about the Reichstag is I, because I set it on fire." With that, he slapped his thigh with the flat of his hand.

On all other occasions, however, Goering denied any complicity.

Shirer points out that although Van der Lubbe had only his shirt for tinder, the main hall of the building was burning fiercely within three minutes after the pyromaniac went to work. Experts said later that large quantities of chemicals and gasoline had been used to set the fire. Goering wanted Van der Lubbe to be hanged at once, which suggests that he wished to dispose of a man who might make indiscreet revelations; but the Netherlander was tried before being decapitated.

A German trade-unionist who had been a victim of the Nazis, Fritz Tobias, set to work in 1955 to make a painstaking investigation of the fire and in 1959 published his conclusion that Van der Lubbe was solely responsible. (His book was published in the United States in 1964 under the title, *The Reichstag Fire*.) If Tobias is correct, this was very nearly the most convenient coincidence in history. The Netherlander had once had a tenuous connection with a Communist youth organization in his native country, and this helped the Nazis to say that the Communists had burned the building, though it is hard to see how doing so would have benefited them. At any rate, every leading Communist in Germany was at once thrown into jail. Tobias thinks that the Nazis actually feared a Communist uprising, and that later on, evidence was skillfully planted by Stalin to make it appear that the Nazis were guilty. If they were not, they worked with amazing speed to capitalize on their lucky break.

In this atmosphere of hysteria occurred the election of March 5. The Nazis still did not have a majority, but they were close enough to it to enable Hitler to be made Chancellor. He had been a German citizen only for a short time, having gone through the legal farce of appointment to a minor provincial post that carried with it automatic citizenship. At last, he was in the driver's seat.

From 1933 to 1939, Hitler's life followed a repetitive pattern. In his official contacts with the victorious Allies in the First World War he was for a few years humble and subservient. He wanted only peace, he said; no one talked more eloquently of the folly and horror of war than this man whose whole ambition was to engage in that folly and horror. He was furiously engaged in secretly building up a new Army and Air Force and as far as he dared, a new Navy; firms supposed to be manufacturing baby buggies or children's toys were in reality making machine-gun parts and other war implements. "Amateur glider clubs" were training fighter pilots. Much of Hitler's new Army was completely motorized, the first such force in the history of the world.

Although his military leaders considered him foolhardy and constantly protested that their forces were not strong enough for what he wanted to do, he was in fact reasonably careful most of the time. When Austrian Nazis attempted to seize that country, in July, 1934, and were defeated, Hitler sat by and saw them punished. When he sent his troops into the demilitarized Rhineland, in violation of treaties Germany had signed, the commanders had orders to pull back if the French showed any signs of mobilizing to resist the action. Actually, the French wanted to stop the movement by force; the French Foreign Minister flew to London and begged the British to join in turning the Germans back, but the British refused. As one high government official said, "The Germans, after all, are only going into their own back garden."

When the Spanish Civil War broke out a few months later, Hitler promptly agreed to help his fellow-dictator, Francisco Franco. Germany spent 500 million marks—a huge sum for her in those days—and sent thousands of men, especially from the Air Force, but the operation was kept as secret as possible; the soldiers traveled in civilian dress and were officially designated as tourists.

The seizure of Austria in 1938 was preceded by a heavy barrage of propaganda in a pattern that became typical. Hitler summoned Austrian Chancellor Kurt von Schuschnigg to Berchtesgaden and attacked him, as mentioned above, in an outburst of simulated furious rage that lasted for hours. He said that Austria was plotting against him, that Austrian Nazis were being persecuted, and that other German citizens in Austria were being abused—all statements that were false.

He laid down an ultimatum: The Nazi Party must be made legal, and all the Nazis still in prison because of the abortive revolution three years earlier were to be released. An Austrian Nazi was to be made Minister of the Interior, with control of police and security, and another, Minister of War. As was to happen again in the future, Hitler did not want his ultimatum to be accepted; he wanted to invade the country by force. He dictated a telegram that was to be sent to him by the Austrian Nazis, telling how they were persecuted and asking for help. Then he marched in. All the leading Austrians who might resist were thrown into German concentration camps; the Nazis took particular pleasure in abusing von Schuschnigg, who was imprisoned and compelled to do degrading forms of labor.

The pattern was again displayed in regard to Czechoslovakia. The northeastern part of the country, the Sudetenland, contained German-speaking inhabitants; Hitler now proceeded to charge that these "former German citizens" (which they were not) were being cruelly abused by the Czechs, who are of Slavic origin. The standard atrocity stories were trotted out again.

By now the Allies, though very slow to react, were beginning to get alarmed at Hitler's seizures of territory, each of which was followed by the assurance that it was the last, that henceforth he wanted nothing but peace. Great Britain and France finally warned that his course might lead to war. He was so furious that he flounced off to Berchtesgaden and sulked there for a week; then he pulled himself together and went on with his plans.

There was in fact not much reason to be afraid of the old Alliance. Both Britain and France distrusted Russia, a distrust that Stalin heartily reciprocated. Czechoslovakia's independence was guaranteed by France and Russia, but Russia could not come to the aid of the Czechs unless she got the consent of Poland and Rumania to send troops across their territory, which it was practically certain they would not give. Russia did not have to act unless France did, and France was imbued with "Maginot Line psychology." Having built the most elaborate frontier fortifications in history, she had by now a strong impulse to hide behind them and await events. Great Britain had let her army dwindle to a low point, and her will to fight was rotted by almost universal pacifism, exemplified in the famous Oxford Oath "under no circumstances to fight for King and country."

The British Prime Minister, Neville Chamberlain, became the spokesman for the Allies in dealing with Hitler, whose fantastic determination to conquer Europe and ultimately the world he was incapable of grasping. In a few weeks, as noted, he flew to Germany three times, to Berchtesgaden, Godesberg, and finally to Munich. His long conversations with Hitler were hardly more than hysterical monologues by the Führer, insisting that Czechoslovakia was treating the Germans outrageously, was a menace to world peace, and so on. These accusations were of course false; Czechoslovakia, under two successive very able Presidents, Thomas Masaryk and Eduard Beneš, was much the most civilized state in Central Europe, and behaved with scrupulous correctness toward all her neighbors.

Hitler wanted the Czech state destroyed for a reason that he did not mention to Chamberlain. Many months earlier he had called together his top military leaders and had told them that Germany must go to war with the Allies. He did not bother to justify this war in any attempted rational terms; instead, he merely argued that Germany was now powerful in a military sense, while the Allies were weak. But, he said, Germany's new equipment would begin to be obsolete in the early 1940's, while the Allies would be rearming themselves with newer weapons. He estimated that 1945 was the latest date on which he could safely begin hostilities.

This he did not dare to do until Czechoslovakia was out

of the way, and this was especially true in the case of a campaign against Poland and Soviet Russia. The Czechs had an excellent though small army. They had a huge, efficient arms plant, the Skoda works, and their border defenses, modeled on the Maginot line, were good. Germany would not dare to move until this threat to her flank was wiped out.

The final scene of the Czech tragedy, at Munich, was a grim one. Beneš had done everything possible to conciliate the Germans. The Nazis in the Sudentenland were heavily subsidized by Hitler with orders to make impossible demands on the Czech government. At one time Beneš told their leader, Konrad Heinlein, to write down his demands, promising that they would be met; when Heinlein did so, he was embarrassed to find that these demands had been met in full by the Czechs some time earlier—also in writing.

Chamberlain got France and Russia to agree that their treaty of mutual assistance with Czechoslovakia would be canceled, but when the British Prime Minister told Hitler this, he refused to accept the offered agreement and instead ordered Beneš to sign a blank-check agreement with Germany within six days or take the consequences. He hoped for a refusal, because he wanted to fight and to make a triumphal entry into Prague as he had done at Vienna. But he was temporarily thwarted; the Sudetenland was handed over to him.

The result was ruinous to Czechoslovakia; her border fortifications were lost, her industry crippled, her railway network thrown into confusion, and 11,000 square miles of territory taken away. Because the new frontier was drawn to be military and not ethnographic, Hitler got control of 800,000 Czechs who did not speak German, while he left out 250,000 who did.

Chamberlain returned from the disaster at Munich jubilantly believing that he had done well. He came down the steps of his airplane, pulled from his pocket a piece of paper bearing Hitler's signature, waved it and told the waiting crowd that at Munich he had achieved "peace in our time"—one of the worst prophecies of the century.

Why had Hitler taken only the Sudetenland? One reason

was that he was not sure whether the German people were really behind him; military parades in Berlin had recently been greeted with stony silence. He was also doubtful about the support of Mussolini, with whom he now had a supposedly firm alliance. In his heart, he despised Mussolini, and—with good reason—he thought poorly of the Italian Army but if his Ally turned against him the result could be serious.

Although at Munich he had told the Western Allies he was now satisfied and would make no further demands, he instantly resumed his pressure on the reduced state of Czechoslovakia. With Mussolini's attitude cleared up, his demands grew stronger and stronger, and a few months later, in March, 1939, the country surrendered. Hitler made the triumphal entry into Prague of which Chamberlain had cheated him in September. Hungary seized some Czech territory; and other parts, Bohemia and Moravia became German protectorates. The strongest bastion of the West in Middle Europe was gone.

From the time Hitler took power in 1933, the plight of the German Jews grew steadily worse. In a series of statutes they were excluded from German citizenship; from holding public office; from employment in the civil service; from farming, teaching, journalism, the theatre, the radio, and the movies. They were forbidden to trade on the stock exchanges, and German Aryans were told to boycott them in law, medicine, and business; in 1938 they were formally excluded from these occupations as well. Intermarriage was forbidden, and Aryans could not be employed as servants by Jews. Jews found it difficult to buy needed medicine, or milk for their babies, or even food. Hotels excluded them as guests. Typical of the times were the highway signs which said "Drive carefully! Sharp curve! Jews seventy-five miles an hour!" (When the 1936 Olympics were held in Germany, many of these signs were taken down to avoid offending the sensibilities of the foreigners.)

The first pogrom actually organized by the German Government was "the week of the broken glass," which began on

November 9, 1938. The ostensible reason was that a minor employee of the German Embassy in Paris was shot by a seventeen-year-old German Jewish refugee whose father had been shoved into a boxcar in Germany and deported to Poland, one of a group of 10,000. Actually, the murder seems to have been another coincidence utilized by the Nazis, who had already planned a wholesale attack on the Jews to coincide with the fifteenth anniversary of the Munich *Putsch*.

All over Germany the windows of Jewish homes and places of business were broken. Synagogues, homes, and stores were burned, and people were shot trying to escape from the flames. It is believed that one hundred or more were murdered, and at least a thousand buildings destroyed. Twenty thousand Jews, leaders or potential leaders, were arrested.

Most of the broken glass was insured, and its total worth ran into millions of dollars. The insurance companies, not yet indoctrinated with Hitler's scorn of the law, were worried, but the Nazis solved the problem. The Jews were paid for their glass, the money was then confiscated by the state, and about a fifth of it was given back to the insurance companies. Because of what Goering called "their abominable crimes," the nature of which was not specified, the German Jewish community was also fined several hundred million marks.

In practice, the campaign against the Jews tended to overlap with hostile actions against the Communists, the Socialists, and the Christian churches, especially the Catholic. The public book burnings included volumes banned for various reasons; among the authors were Thomas Mann, Stefan Zweig, Erich Maria Remarque, Albert Einstein, Jack London, Upton Sinclair, H. G. Wells, Havelock Ellis, Arthur Schnitzler, Sigmund Freud, André Gide, Emile Zola, and Marcel Proust. Because Hitler did not like modern art, the paintings of Cezanne, Van Gogh, Gauguin, Matisse, and Picasso were forbidden.

The Nazis boasted of their repudiation of the great works of the past. "When someone mentions the word 'culture,' I want to reach for my revolver," said Hans Johst, an unsuccessful playwright whom Hitler had placed in charge of all theatrical productions throughout Germany. (The remark is often attributed to Goering, and he might have agreed with its spirit, though he avidly looted the museums and private collections of all conquered countries for his personal benefit.) During all this time most of the German people seemed to approve of what was being done, though after the War many thousands of them insisted that they had never been Nazis at heart, but had not dared to protest.

Life was hard for most people in Germany during the 1930's. Wages were low; for most workers the average was only $6 or $7 a week, and taxes and "voluntary" contributions sometimes took as much as one-third of this amount.

Hitler was shrewd enough to follow the custom of Roman dictators of two thousand years earlier, and give the people "bread and circuses." His frantic campaign for rearmament meant high employment; if a job was not available, a good Nazi could always join the Brown Shirts and be sure of food, clothing and shelter. The Government arranged vacations for the workers at astonishingly low prices and probably at a loss. Ships were specially fitted for ocean cruises; you could take a week's cruise to Madeira for only $25, or a special vacation in the mountains for $11 a week. Those properly certified as loyal Nazis got especially cheap tickets to theatres and the opera.

The Germans, very few of whom had any form of private transportation beyond a bicycle, were overjoyed to learn that an inexpensive automobile, costing less than $400, was to be put on the market. This "people's car" (Volkswagen), excellently designed by an Austrian engineer, Ferdinand Porsche, was to be marketed by the million as soon as more pressing obligations of rearmament were out of the way. Hundreds of thousands of people began buying it on the instalment plan; after about half the price had been paid, the individual got a serial number, and was to have his car when this number was reached. Actually, nobody ever got one during the Hitler era, and all the huge sum invested was used by the German Government for other purposes.

Hitler and Goebbels realized that it was important to get hold of children as early as possible, and all boys and girls were enrolled in Nazi organizations from the age of six. They wore uniforms, learned military tactics, and were heavily indoctrinated with the Nazi ideology. So effective was this training that occasionally some denounced their own parents as enemies of the state.

The Hitler Youth organizations embraced ages six to eighteen, at which time everybody had to serve a period in the army or a labor force. Hundreds of thousands of girls had to do one year of service on a farm or in domestic service for persons of Aryan stock in the cities. On the farms, some of them lived with the farm family and others were gathered into work camps. As might be expected, many thousands of them got pregnant. The Hitler regime, planning ahead for huge armies twenty years hence, welcomed this development; no stigma was attached to bearing an illegitimate child who would grow up to be a good Nazi. Indeed, at one time, young women were openly encouraged to bear as many children as possible with selected Nazis as the fathers.

Hitler's philosophy held that the Germans were the destined rulers of the world, but within their Nordic ranks there were some who were even better, the elite of the elite. Boys who qualified for this category were sent to very special schools for rigorous training to be the leaders of the future German Reich (which, Hitler said, would last a thousand years). Life in these schools was a severe ordeal; to harden them, the students were forced to live like medieval monks and were worked mercilessly from dawn to dark. In the closing days of the War, thousands of the boys, some still in their early teens, were thrown into the front lines of Hitler's dwindling army, where their losses were especially heavy.

Two practices of the Nazis are worth noting. They habitually sterilized the feeble-minded, and soon extended the practice to some others who, they felt, ought not to have descendants. They also began putting to death certain helpless old people who were a burden on the state. Before long, of course, this policy became an insignificant detail of the wholesale slaughter of Jews, Poles, Russians, and others who, Hitler felt, were unworthy to continue living.

Among those strongly affected by the Nazi regime were the farmers. They were bound to the land, not permitted to seek any other occupation except under very special circumstances. No one was allowed to own a farm unless he could prove his family was pure Aryan for a period of at least a century. A farm could be inherited, but small holdings could not be mortgaged, divided among several heirs, or sold. This policy of course required that the farmer be guaranteed at least a subsistence wage for himself and his family.

Just when Hitler decided to start a general European War is not certain—unless you assume that *Mein Kampf*, begun in 1923, was an announcement of such an intention. On November 5, 1937, he called together the top military leaders of the country in a secret meeting and announced that Germany must have more "living space" and that this must be obtained, by a war, right at home in middle Europe, not in remote colonies around the world. In order to make his flanks secure for this war, he had to seize Austria and Czechoslovakia. It was also necessary to persuade Russia to stand aloof, and this was done with the notorious Hitler-Stalin Pact of August 23, 1939, secret clauses of which divided Poland and the Baltic states, Estonia, Latvia, and Lithuania, between the two dictators.

The ground was also prepared, as usual, with a series of lying propaganda accusations against the Poles, who were accused of mistreating German civilians, of threatening to make war on Germany, and so on. There was a German radio station near the Polish border; Hitler arranged to dress a number of condemned German prisoners in Polish army uniforms, kill them with injections, fire bullets into their bodies and leave them lying around the grounds of the station and even inside the building. The radio program was to be interrupted by a man with an unfamiliar voice, shouting incendiary demands in Polish and pretending to be a Polish soldier. This scheme was carried out, and Hitler then announced a Polish-army invasion of German territory in a frustrated attempt to seize the radio station; this was reported all over the world, in good faith, by foreign correspondents in Berlin.

The Führer made various demands on Poland at various times; they included the return of Danzig—a port on the Baltic lost by Germany after the First World War—and a super-highway and a railroad across the Danzig Corridor, a strip of Polish territory that separated Germany from East Prussia. Finally, he used his customary pressure, demanding that Poland send to Berlin within one day an emissary authorized to agree to any and all German demands. Following the death of the dictator, Marshal Joseph Pilsudski, Poland was ruled by a clique of army officers, even more inept at politics than they proved to be in twentieth-century warfare, and it was inevitable that they should refuse.

The approach of the war was accompanied by frantic struggles in the chancellories of the world to maintain the peace. President Roosevelt appealed to Hitler not to commit any aggressive act against a long list of nations, specified by name; the Führer reduced a meeting of the Reichstag to howls of laughter by reading the letter aloud. He assured his assembled stooges that he wanted only peace.

Mussolini was bound by a secret treaty to go to war if Hitler did. He now sent an urgent message asking that the war be postponed several years, or if this was not possible, to release him from his promise; the Italian dictator pleaded that his country was not ready either militarily or in economic strength to join the fighting. Hitler was forced to agree that Italy should stay out.

Great Britain and France were bound by treaty to come to Poland's aid, but as noted above, neither was ready to do so effectively. Great Britain's army was small, and her navy could do little to aid Poland. France did not want to venture beyond the Maginot Line if she could help it.

Hitler, of course, had no intention of letting anybody or anything divert him from his plans. He did postpone the date of the war by a couple of days because of Mussolini's action, but on the night of August 31, 1939, his troops moved across the border to begin the greatest war in history and one that was to affect the fate of the world.

In the course of their secret rearmament, the Germans had changed the entire technique of war. The dive bomber had been much improved, and squadrons of these deadly airplanes now attacked Polish cities with terrible effect. For the first time, noncombatant civilians were regarded as legitimate targets on a massive scale; Poland's cities soon lay almost in ruins. Reduced to a secondary role was the foot-slogging infantry that went back in time to the dawn of history and beyond; the brunt of battle was now carried by motorized divisions in which soldiers, guns, and all equipment were carried by vehicles capable of rapid movement by road or even across country, in not-too-rough terrain. Poland was pitifully ill-equipped to meet such a challenge; in some cases, she sent against Hitler's tanks and self-propelled guns cavalry armed with sabres. The war lasted only six weeks.

Great Britain and France had entered the conflict forty-eight hours after it began, but they could do almost nothing to help the Poles. France sent her troops into the Maginot Line; Great Britain set up a sea patrol in the North Sea to blockade Germany—a blockade rendered ineffective by the fact that Hitler could use all of Russia's seaports for imported materials. So valuable were these ports that Hitler ordered goods being sold to Russia as part of the bargain of the Hitler-Stalin Pact to have priority over supplies going to his own front lines.

With the surrender of Poland began the period of the "phony war" on the Western Front. Until the following April, there was a stalemate with hardly any activity. At the time, the reason for Hitler's inactivity was a mystery, but after the War it was discovered that he had used up his armored vehicles in Poland so completely that a long pause was needed for repairs and the manufacture of new equipment.

But the Eastern Front was far from quiet. On November 30, 1939, Russia invaded Finland on the pretext that her own safety was menaced. Hitler was furious at this; Germany and Finland had always been good friends. However, he could do nothing—at the moment; he still needed Russia, though he was already planning to start a war against her.

In Poland, meanwhile, he began the mass murder that was to become so familiar, a dreadful exhibition of brutality on a par with Stalin's extermination of the Russian peasants at the beginning of the 1930's. About 1.2 million Poles and 300,000 Jews were dumped by the Germans into Russia in the course of a few months; they were rounded up without warning, herded into boxcars without food, water, or sanitary facilities, and started off; Hitler neither knew nor cared what provision would be made for them by the Russians. Many of these deportations took place in winter, sometimes at forty degrees below zero, and uncounted thousands froze or starved on the way.

Of those who were left behind many suffered an equally harsh fate. Since Hitler intended that Poland should be reduced to an agricultural community producing food for the Germans, he set out to exterminate all potential leaders, including intellectuals, the clergy, and the nobility, as well as all the Jews. This plan had the code name of "The Housecleaning." Killing the intellectuals, as a special subdivision of the enterprise, was called "The Extraordinary Pacification Action."

Only one exception was presently made to this general rule. Hitler decided to leave some of the Polish Roman Catholic clergy alive, on the ground that religion, in Lenin's phrase, was "the opiate of the people," and that the Poles would be meeker and more obedient if the churches were kept open.

By April, 1940, Hitler's armies were again ready to strike,

and the war in the West came to life. On April 9, he invaded Norway and Denmark. Denmark offered no real resistance, and Norway, despite some fierce fighting, was speedily overcome. About a month later, on May 10, he struck at the Low Countries—the Netherlands, Belgium, and Luxembourg, and bypassed the left end of the Maginot Line to invade France. The three little countries offered only brief resistance, and the armies were soon free to concentrate on France, which capitulated on June 22.

The speed of the German advance, unparalleled in modern experience, caught the Allies napping. As noted, more than 300,000 men, mostly English but with some other troops included, was surrounded at the little town of Dunkirk, on the French coast near the Belgian border, and it looked as though they would be captured with all their equipment. Their amazing rescue by hundreds of British ships and boats of every size and character is one of the heroic feats of the War.

The failure to capture the Allied forces at Dunkirk was one of Hitler's series of errors that eventually cost him the War; at the time, the whole world was puzzled by his delay in pushing forward after Allied resistance had all but collapsed. Three reasons have been advanced, and all of them may be true in varying degrees.

Whereas during most of the War, Hitler was reckless and his Generals timid, in this case the opposite was momentarily true. The movement of his armies into France was so rapid that Hitler simply could not believe it. Several times he ordered a brief halt, over the strong protest of his military men, and this was true of one of the German forces advancing in a pincers movement on Dunkirk. The delay was only forty-eight hours, but that was enough for the evacuation to get under way.

Hitler waited also because Goering boasted that he could knock out the Allied forces by the use of air power alone, a promise he was unable to keep.

Third, it is at least possible that the German hesitated for political reasons to wipe out the last remnant of Great Britain's Army. Throughout the War, he kept trying from time to time to make a separate peace with the British, a people whom he admired for their indomitable character and whom he wanted to have as an Ally. After France was conquered he again made definite proposals for peace to the British, who now stood alone. He offered to guarantee the future of their Empire if Germany had her colonies restored and was recognized as the dominant power on the Continent; he was amazed and angered each time that his proposals for peace were rejected.

The year 1940 was a busy one for the Führer in many ways. After the French surrender, a dummy government was set up with headquarters at Vichy and the aged, half-senile French Marshal Pétain was put at its head; for some time, only the northern part of France was formally under German rule.

Hitler tried hard to get General Francisco Franco, the Spanish dictator, to enter the War. After Dunkirk, when Great Britain seemed to be finished, Franco agreed to do this, but when the British went on fighting he got frightened and stayed out. Franco wanted French Morocco as the price of his entrance, but the Führer refused to agree. He was dreaming of a huge German colony in Central Africa and he felt that French Morocco was a suitable gateway to this colony.

Hitler was also worried about his Russian Ally. Stalin had invaded all three of the Baltic states and Eastern Poland, and now occupied a big area of Rumania, consisting of Bessarabia and Northern Bukovina; Bessarabia had been Russian territory until the end of the First World War, but Bukovina had been Austrian.

Since Rumania no longer had the protection of France, her Ally for many years, she was vulnerable to her greedy neighbors; both Bulgaria and Hungary proceeded to take large sections. Italy, too, wanted to join the game of seizing territory; Hitler had to put severe pressure on Mussolini not to move into Jugoslavia. Italy was active in North Africa during this year; in September Mussolini invaded Egypt from the west, and in October he attacked Greece. Hitler was furious, foreseeing quite correctly that the Italian Army would get into trouble and he would have to come to its aid. He feared that Bulgaria, Jugoslavia, and Russia might also now seize the chance to fish in troubled waters, and that Great Britain would use the excuse to land troops—who would be hard to dislodge—in Greece. He had to remain friends with Mussolini, however; he still needed Italian help.

At the end of his life, Hitler blamed his Italian ally for causing him to lose the War. F. W. Deakin, in his book on the relation between the two dictators, *The Brutal Friendship,* quotes his complaint that Italy's attack on Greece upset Hitler's timetable and delayed the attack on Russia by "exactly five weeks . . . and I lost them because of the confidence which I had placed in my dearest and most admired friend, Mussolini." In another passage, which gave Mr. Deakin the title for his book, the Führer observed, "My attachment to the person of the Duce has not changed . . . but I regret not having listened to reason which imposed on me a brutal friendship in regard to Italy." In other words, he should have been tougher on the Italians than he was.

Following the French surrender, the whole world was waiting for Germany to invade England by sea. Although 338,000 British and Allied troops got away from Dunkirk, they came with hardly more than the clothes they stood in, plus in some cases small arms and a few rounds of ammunition. Britain was stripped of her big mobile guns and nearly all other military equipment, though most of her Navy was intact.

The long delay in attempting the invasion, and the final cancellation of the plans for it, were not Hitler's fault but that of his military and naval leaders. First of all, there was a serious shortage of landing craft. It was proposed that German canal boats be used for this purpose, but the men in charge of the domestic economy pleaded that they must have these boats to keep up production of munitions and other essentials.

Second, the Army and Navy quarreled furiously over the technique of the landing. The Army wanted to land on a very wide front, and the Navy said this was impossible. Nazi intelligence seems to have been faulty; no German realized how utterly defenseless Britain was on land during the last half of 1940.

Third, Goering again made boasts about his airpower that proved fallacious; he said he could knock England out of the War by bombing, alone.

Fourth, when large quantities of landing craft were assembled in a French port, great damage was done by fire bombs dropped from British planes.

Even so, Hitler continued to keep ordering the invasion of Britain, and his military commanders kept postponing the operation, usually on the pretext of unfavorable weather. Not until he became engrossed in the coming invasion of Russia, in June, 1941, did he give up the plan.

Another of his great military blunders was his shift from daylight bombing of military targets in Great Britain to mass terror raids on London at night. For all his admiration for the British people, Hitler failed to understand that they could not be frightened into surrender.

The turning point in the Battle of Britain came on September 15, 1940, when the Germans made a daylight raid on London. The Royal Air Force shot down thirty-four German bombers and twenty-two fighter planes, at a loss to themselves of only twenty-six fighters; this was a ratio of destruction the Germans could not afford to continue. It also meant that invasion would be enormously more difficult, since it would necessarily have to take place during daylight hours, and air cover would be essential.

Hitler's plans for the eventuality of the invasion being successful are an indication of his character. The able-bodied male population of Great Britain between the ages of seventeen and forty-five was to be transported across the Channel to prisons on the Continent. All property of every sort except limited household necessities was to be confiscated, and the slightest resistance was to be met with death.

Hitler had compiled a list of more than two thousand persons who were to be arrested immediately. They included not only every important political figure, but writers whom he did not like, such as Noel Coward, Aldous Huxley, J. B. Priestley, Bertrand Russell, C. P. Snow, H. G. Wells, and Rebecca West. His list also had on it the names of a number of foreigners who were or had recently been in England: Ignace Paderewski, the famous Polish pianist and one-time Premier; Sigmund Freud, the Jewish psychiatrist from Vienna; Eduard Beneš, the former Czechoslovak Premier; and a curious collection of Americans, including John Gunther and Louis Fischer, writers on current history, Paul Robeson, Negro singer with Leftist political views, and Bernard Baruch, the financier.

Hitler was so far from reality that he actually thought the Duke of Windsor, the former Edward VIII, who had been appointed Governor of the Bahama Islands, could be induced to come back to Great Britain and become Germany's puppet ruler. The Duke had got out of France and was in Lisbon waiting for a ship to take him to the Bahamas, and in a weird seriocomic episode, Hitler agents were sent there to try to get him to come back. With true Nazi logic, they tried first to soften him up with threats of death. The threats did not work, and the Duke and Duchess sailed for the Bahamas on an American ship on August 1, 1940. Afterward, the Duke said no actual offer to return to Great Britain as a Nazi stooge was ever made; he was simply threatened regarding his leaving Lisbon to cross the Atlantic.

Hitler was painfully inept in his attempt at diplomacy with the other Fascist states. He tried hard but unsuccessfully to get the Japanese to attack Singapore, believing that this would knock Great Britain out of the conflict. He also proposed a division of a great part of the world among the Powers with whom he was then allied. Germany herself was to have Western Europe and Central Africa. Italy would get North Africa, part of which she controlled already. Russia was to have Afghanistan, India, and control of the Indian Ocean. Japan was to get Southeast Asia.

Russia replied by making much heavier demands for herself. She wanted Finland; the southern part of Sakhalin Island, north of Japan; and the oil fields of the Middle East, which would mean a special position for herself in Eastern Turkey, Iraq, and Iran. Hitler, who had already decided to destroy Russia, amiably agreed to all this.

A fantastic scheme by the Führer was to capture the Azores and use them as a base from which to bomb the United States. Germany did not then possess a single airplane capable of carrying bombs across the Atlantic—to say nothing of a round trip.

The same man who cooked up this plan insisted that his Navy must not sink without warning the merchant vessels of the United States, still technically neutral. When the Navy suggested it might destroy American ships "by mistake" he still said No.

Despite the weird character of some of his own ideas, he was intolerant of similar lapses by others. When his trusted lieutenant, at one time Number Three in the Nazi hierarchy, Rudolf Hess, flew a plane to Scotland with the idea of negotiating a separate peace with Great Britain, Hitler would undoubtedly have shot him out of hand had Hess not remained a prisoner in England for the rest of the war.

One of the dictator's classic blunders came when Jugoslavia, after agreeing to join forces with him, repudiated that agreement twenty-four hours later, following a palace revolution. Hysterical with rage, Hitler vowed to get his revenge. He attacked Jugoslavia and for three days his airplanes bombed the almost undefended capital, Belgrade, practically at rooftop level. The city was destroyed, and 17,000 civilians were killed; but the enterprise took more than a month of time, and the attack on Russia was set back accordingly. If he had started the Russian War on schedule he might have taken Moscow and Leningrad before the winter closed in.

Hitler now overran Greece without too much trouble. Military history was made when the island of Crete was captured by the use of air power alone.

In North Africa, the forces on either side seesawed back and forth. The Italians, after managing to invade Egypt, were thrown back by British forces under Archibald Wavell in a brilliant campaign that has been almost forgotten because of Bernard Montgomery's later achievements in the same area. Wavell took 130,000 prisoners in two months, at almost no cost, and pushed Mussolini's men back 500 miles. The Germans once again had to rescue the Italians; Field Marshal Erwin Rommel, "the Desert Fox," came in and drove the British back again over most of the territory they had captured. Finally, Montgomery pushed the Germans west once more, breaking the back—with the aid of the Americans who had landed in their rear—of the Axis forces in Africa.

Hitler did not tell Mussolini of the plan to invade Russia until his troops were already on the march, offering the excuse that the decision had been made only at the last minute. He did not tell Japan about the invasion at all, and the result was the fall of the Japanese Cabinet headed by Yosuke Matsuoka, Hitler's good friend. The angry Japanese now began keeping their own secrets. The German diplomats did not have wit enough to understand the meaning of the change when the government of the liberal Prince Fumimaro Konoye fell and was replaced by the belligerent, militaristic government of General Hideki Tojo; and they had no advance warning of the attack on the United States at Pearl Harbor. Hitler quickly rallied from the shock, however, and himself declared war on the United States, gratuitously getting himself into trouble, since his treaty with Japan bound him to come to her aid only if she were attacked.

He made one of his worst blunders when his troops entered Russia on June 22, 1941. There were at that time millions of people in the Soviet Union who were bitterly hostile to the Communist government, and this was especially true in the Ukraine, where only about twelve years earlier Stalin had remorselessly starved millions of peasants to death. The Ukrainians met the Germans with joy, greeting them as liberators, and if Hitler had only treated them decently, an uprising would have occurred that Stalin might not have been able to withstand. The Führer, however, was obsessed with the idea of slaughtering the "subhuman" Slavs; he promptly introduced his terror tactics, and before long, the unhappy Ukrainians were forming guerrilla bands in the hills to help the Communist government which they hated.

The invasion of Russia was accompanied by a frank abandonment of all the supposed civilized restraints on warfare. The German Army was told explicitly to ignore all the rules of war. Any captured Russian, soldier or civilian, could be shot without trial by any German officer, with no fear of punishment. Beyond this, cold-blooded plans were laid to starve millions of Russians to death. A month before the invasion began, an official Nazi memorandum pointed out that large amounts of food would be removed from Russia to Germany, and added that "many millions of people in the industrial areas [will become] redundant and will either have to die or emigrate to Siberia." Emigration on any such scale would of course be out of the question.

After the war was under way, these plans were carried out as far as the Germans could manage. Thousands of Russian prisoners were collected into open fields, with no shelter of any kind, and held there within a ring of guns until they died of hunger and exposure. When the war was five months old, Goering remarked with satisfaction, "In the camps for Russian prisoners they have begun to eat each other. This year between twenty and thirty million persons will die of hunger in Russia. Perhaps it is well that it should be so, for certain nations must be decimated."

It was in Russia that Hitler lost the War, by stubbornly

insisting on his own ideas against the advice of his military leaders. He refused to prepare for a winter campaign, because his intuition told him the fighting would be over before the cold weather began. The Generals wanted to strike hard in a single thrust for Moscow; Hitler insisted on a double drive, toward Leningrad in the north and the oil fields of the Caucasus in the south. When any officer protested, no matter how high he was in the chain of command, Hitler fired him. He would permit no retreat, and was outraged and contemptuous when anybody was reluctant to get the chance to die gloriously for Hitler's honor in a hopeless fight.

The result should have been foreseen. The German Army, hitherto invincible, now began to crack. Its espionage in Russia in advance of hostilities had turned out to be bad: the Germans did not know of the existence of the T-34 tank, so heavily armored that German shells bounced off it; the number of Russian fighter planes was seriously underestimated; and worst of all, Hitler was told the Russians had only 200 divisions, though they had 360.

The turning point of the whole War was the Germans' failure to capture Stalingrad. Field Marshal Friedrich Paulus, in charge of the siege, reported to Hitler in January of 1943:

> Troops without ammunition or food. Effective command no longer possible. . . . Eighteen thousand wounded without any supplies or dressings or drugs. . . . Further defense senseless. Collapse inevitable. Army requests immediate permission to surrender in order to save lives of remaining troops.

Hitler cared nothing for the suffering of the men who had been trapped because of his own stupidity. He answered:

> Surrender is forbidden. Sixth Army will hold their positions to the last man and the last round and by their heroic endurance will make an unforgettable contribution toward the establishment of a defensive front and the salvation of the Western World.

But in fact the entire Army was forced to surrender. Only 91,000 were left, of 285,000 on that front, only a short time earlier; and of the 91,000 only about 5,000 ever saw Germany again, the remainder dying in Russian prisons.

Hitler was also largely responsible for Rommel's defeat in North Africa. The British attacked with such ferocity and skill that Rommel felt he needed a strategic retreat for regrouping, and asked Hitler permission to do this. He refused:

> In the situation in which you now find yourself, there can be no other consideration save that of holding fast, of not retreating one step, of throwing every gun and every man into the battle. . . . You can show your troops no other way than that which leads to victory or to death.

Rommel obeyed for three days and then decided he must retreat, but by then it was too late. In the next few weeks he was thrown back 700 miles with huge losses of men and materials.

Nothing revealed Hitler's essential character better than his treatment of civilians in the countries his armies overran. Only in the East did he order wholesale extermination, but even in the West, his brutality staggers the imagination. As is always true in war, there was some underground resistance in the occupied lands, and Hitler tried to stop this by terror.

In Denmark, the "Night and Fog" technique was employed. If a German were killed, five prominent Danish citizens disappeared overnight and were never heard of again. All inquiries by their families or by anyone else were met by grim silence.

In other areas, such as France, the technique was simpler, though even more drastic: if harm befell a German, one hundred hostages were shot. It is estimated that sixty thousand French died in this way.

For the most part the rules of war were respected in regard to British and American prisoners, but this was not always true; on a number of occasions, uniformed officers and men were shot in cold blood. There was a terrible scene in a stone quarry at a place called Mauthausen, late in the War, where forty-seven American, British, and Dutch officers were tortured by being forced to carry heavy loads of stone up a steep hill, while being beaten with clubs. Some of them died under this treatment and the remainder were then shot.

In another case, seventy-one American prisoners were shot near Malmédy during the Battle of the Bulge in December, 1944. Some of the men guilty of this atrocity were captured, tried, and sentenced by the Allies. For some mysterious reason, the late Joseph McCarthy, after he had become a U.S. Senator in 1947, intervened on behalf of these men; the only cause that has ever been suggested is that Wisconsin has a heavy German-American population. While it is hard to prove any direct connection, it is a fact that following his intervention, nearly all of forty-three Germans who had been found guilty were released after serving short prison sentences.

Two examples of Hitler's terrorism received worldwide attention. In May, 1942, Reinhard Heydrich, Chief of the German Security Police, who was in charge of Czechoslovakia, was the victim of a bomb thrown by members of an underground Czech organization and died a few days later. Hitler seized about 4,500 Czech citizens, of whom 3,000 were Jews, and shot them, and he made a special example of the little Czech town of Lidice, chosen at random. It was surrounded by troops in the early morning and all the inhabitants seized. All males over sixteen and seven women were shot. Nearly 200 other women were sent to concentration camps, where about one quarter of them died or were killed. Four pregnant women gave birth to babies, who were promptly murdered and the mothers sent off to camp. The children who were under sixteen were sent to various places in Germany to be brought up as Nazis; after the end of the War, only about a fifth of them could be discovered and reunited with their mothers, if the latter had survived.

Lidice became world famous, and a new town of the same name was built after the War, but there were other places in half a dozen occupied countries, of which the world never heard, that were treated the same way.

Another town that became well known was the French village of Oradour, near Limoges. On the charge that the French underground, the Maquis, had hidden explosives in the village, the 650 inhabitants were rounded up, the men in a barn and the women and children in a church. Both buildings were set on fire and nearly all within were burned to death. Those who ran out the doors were killed by machine gunners who had been stationed there for this purpose. The only survivors were about ten people who, badly burned, had the fortitude to pretend to be dead, and then escaped after night fell.

Twenty Germans involved in this ghastly deed were captured and tried by the Allies. Two of them were executed, but the other eighteen, who had been given prison sentences, were soon released.

Nearly everything done to anybody else pales before the nightmare treatment of the Jews. With the outbreak of the War, the censorship on what was happening became complete, and Hitler could vent his sadism to the full. How many Jews were methodically murdered it is difficult to say; the World Jewish Congress after a careful study estimates that 5.6 million were done to death. Adolf Eichmann, who fifteen years after the War was found hiding in Argentina, taken to Israel, and tried and executed there, boasted toward the close of the War that he had caused the deaths of five million.

At first, the Nazis were clumsy in their technique of execution. In Russia, five thousand Jews were marched to the outskirts of the town of Dubno, in the Ukraine, where they were forced to dig a large pit. Then all of them—men, women, and children—undressed, piled their clothing in orderly rows, climbed into the pit, and lay down to be shot. This was accomplished by an SS man who sat on the edge of one end of the pit, smoking a cigarette and using a machine gun.

Beside the favored technique of shooting, others were killed by injecting air or gasoline into their veins. Many were packed into trucks, with tubes leading from the exhaust pipe to the interior, and were killed with carbon monoxide. Execution by firing was soon largely abandoned, partly to save ammunition, and partly because of an incident in Minsk, Russia, late in August of 1941. Heinrich Himmler, head of the Gestapo, the dreaded German secret police, visited the prison camp at Minsk and expressed curiosity to see how the Jews were being killed. The local Nazi officials, eager to please, brought out one hundred and shot them on the spot. Himmler, for once in his life, seems to have been dismayed by what he saw; the marksmanship was bad, and some of the prisoners were only wounded. He gave orders that henceforth the women and children, at least, should be killed only with gas.

The final technique that was used was to spray people with the fumes from crystallized prussic acid. They were first stripped, the clothing being methodically sorted and saved. Jewelry, watches, and rings were also saved; the economical government sold them through the municipally-operated pawnshops, but there were so many that the market was soon glutted.

The naked victims were crowded into large extermination chambers, and the gas was turned on. It took from three to fifteen minutes to kill them, according to the weather conditions; Rudolf Hoess, commander of the camp at Auschwitz, explained that "we knew when the people were dead because their screaming stopped." Other prisoners were used to remove the bodies and to extract gold-filled teeth, after which most of the bodies were burned. Testimony at Nuremberg proved that in some cases the corpses were used for fertilizer or in the manufacture of soap. The prisoners who did this grisly work were promised that their lives would be spared, but in fact they were replaced at frequent intervals and were all killed, lest some word of what was happening should leak to the outside world.

After the War, Germans living close to the prison camps and whose daughters regularly went out in the evenings with the young SS guards, uniformly professed that they had no idea that the mass murders were taking place.

Those who were executed in the gas chambers were in a way the lucky ones; thousands of others suffered dreadful tortures before they died. A wave of sadism seems to have swept over many members of the medical profession in Germany at this time; they performed many hundreds of so-called scientific experiments which resulted in horrible suffering on the part of the victims, and as far as can be learned, no scientific results of any value. It is worthy of note that not a single protest from any German doctor is on record against these meaningless barbarities.

All Hitler's reasons for the slaughter of the Jews were of course nonsense. The myths of anti-Semitism have been exposed too often to need further discussion today. In regard to the German Jews in particular, it is not true that they conspired in any way against the rest of the German population. On the contrary, they thought of themselves more as Germans than as Jews. The German habit of obedience to orders may be one of the reasons why they meekly allowed themselves to be marched into the execution chambers.

One of the few places where there was any sort of resistance was in the ghetto of Warsaw, Poland. About 400,000 Jews lived in this area, around which the Nazis built a wall and then proceeded methodically to remove the inhabitants for execution. After about 310,000 had been killed in only a few months, the remnant began to resist; the story of their desperate, futile struggle is told with close adherence to the facts, by John Hersey in his fine novel, *The Wall*. In the end, only a few managed to escape, by tunneling into the sewer system.

An unsolved mystery is where the many thousands of German sadists came from who went out of their way to torture innocent and helpless victims "above and beyond the call of duty." While there are some incidents in which Germans helped Jews, even at serious risk to themselves, there is a sorry catalogue of other cases where the opportunity to cause pain seems to have been irresistible. The strain of hidden sadism in humanity is wider and deeper than is generally recognized.

From the moment Hitler took office in 1933, opposition to

him developed, although the efficient methods of his police required that it be secret. Some of this opposition was personal, some came from those who believed he was leading Germany toward destruction, but the strongest and most important hostility came from a group of high Army and Navy officers, who hated him for various reasons—because of his humble origin, because he obviously despised them, and because he usurped their authority. Through the years the conspirators, loosely linked into several groups, kept plotting, sometimes merely to have him deposed, at other times to kill him. They made repeated efforts to come to an understanding with the Allies as to the terms of a settlement if Hitler were out of the way, and they were disheartened by the Casablanca Declaration demanding unconditional surrender.

A number of successive plots to imprison or assassinate Hitler were badly bungled. A bomb was planted in a hall in Munich, but went off only after he had left. Several good chances to kill him were passed because the plotters, with Teutonic thoroughness, decided they must get rid of all the other high Nazis at the same moment, and almost never were they all together in one room.

The plan that came nearest to succeeding was the famous bomb plot of July 20, 1944. Its moving spirit was a man of extraordinary personality and courage, Count Klaus von Stauffenberg, whose indomitable spirit was indicated by the fact that he had insisted on returning to active Army duty, though war wounds had cost him his left eye, his right hand, and two fingers of his left hand.

Count von Stauffenberg was under orders to make a report to a conference of top officials at Supreme Headquarters. He carried in a briefcase a powerful bomb that could be activated by breaking a small bottle of acid to eat through a wire; it would then explode after ten minutes. Von Stauffenberg entered the room where Hitler and a dozen other men were grouped around a heavy table; just before he did so, he had broken the bottle of acid. He set his briefcase under the table near Hitler, and then, murmuring an excuse, left the room as though he had forgotten something and would be back in a moment. One of Hitler's aides sat down, found the briefcase in his way, and moved it behind a heavy partition beneath the table, an act that undoubtedly saved Hitler's life. When the bomb went off four men were killed or fatally wounded, and Hitler himself slightly wounded and severely shaken up.

The explosion took place before von Stauffenberg had cleared the final series of sentries who guarded the Head-quarters; with superb sangfroid, he talked his way through the guards, and started a flight, in a slow plane with no radio, to Berlin, several hours away. While he was in the air, news of the attempted assassination was broadcast throughout Germany, and Hitler himself went on the air to demonstrate that he was still alive. Von Stauffenberg's fellow conspirators in Berlin sat around in an agony of indecision, making no attempt to disrupt communications or to get control of broadcasting facili-ties. When he arrived, he insisted that Hitler must surely be dead or dying, and a half-hearted attempt was made to go on with the insurrection. Before long, it had been snuffed out and the leaders captured.

Now followed a blood bath as terrible as those of Stalin. Some of the conspirators, or supposed conspirators, were shot without trial. Others were tried, but were not allowed to make any defense, being executed solely on a basis of the Gestapo records about them. Field Marshal Erwin Rommel was a mem-ber of the conspiracy, but he was such a great popular hero that the Nazis did not dare to make a public charge against him. He was forced to commit suicide and the story was given out that he had died of a heart attack. Out of about 7,000 persons arrested, nearly 5,000 were killed and many others given long prison terms. It is a safe assumption that many were executed who were not involved in the conspiracy, but had incurred the hostility of someone in power.

The autumn of 1942 was the high point of the War for Germany; from then on, things got steadily worse. Hitler's Army was thrown back in Russia with terrible losses. Rommel was defeated in North Africa, and the Allies invaded first Sicily and then the Italian mainland. Mussolini was overthrown, and Italy dropped out of the War, though the Germans there continued to resist the Allied advance with great tenacity and technical skill.

In the North Atlantic, the tide also turned. With the use of radar and other new devices, the war against the German submarines became much more effective. In three months, early in 1943, Hitler lost thirty-seven submarines to sink only fifty Allied merchant vessels, a ratio of loss he could not afford to continue. The air bombardment around the clock of Germany itself was also doing bad damage. The British mass raids on the cities at night were less useful than was supposed at the time, but daylight raids on military targets, chiefly by American bombers, were effective, especially those on ball-bearing plants, on other factories, and on refineries for making synthetic gasoline.

By now, Hitler had come to realize the folly of the mass murder of Russians and Poles and began using them instead as slave labor. About 7.5 million foreign civilians were brought to Germany for this purpose, most of them kidnaped and removed by force; sometimes the German soldiers would lie in wait outside a church or movie house and capture everybody as they came out. In Russia, a village would sometimes be surrounded during the night and all the houses burned to the ground, the inhabitants being seized; about three million Russian civilians were removed to Germany. Hitler had some curious reluctance to use women in factories, even Germans who might have been willing to volunteer. A million and a half Russian women, brought to Germany, were used instead as household labor in the homes of good Nazi families. They worked long hours, seven days a week, and were permitted no appeal to anybody, no matter what indignities were heaped upon them. To prevent escape, they were forbidden to travel on railroads or buses unless accompanied by the German "employer."

The record of the Russians taken as prisoners of war is a

grim one. Of about six million, one-fifth joined the German army, or were used as slave labor, one-fifth were rescued from prison by the Allies at the end of the War, and three-fifths died, most of them from starvation or abuse by their jailers.

As the triumph of the Allies grew ever more probable, Hitler's military advisers wanted to bring their scattered armies home to defend Germany itself, but the Führer refused. He gave various specious reasons, but the real one was his old, stubborn feeling that no German must ever retreat. He still kept the complete direction of the war entirely in his own control; he dictated orders covering everything in the most minute detail and wrote on them with his own hand, "Not to be altered."

Hitler suffered the delusion that he could still divide the Allies and triumph. He believed that the British would not tolerate seeing the Russians sweep west across Germany, that they would make a separate peace and then join him in a war against Stalin.

The group of high army officers who were plotting against Hitler had the same delusion. They entered into secret negotiations with the Allies through Allen Dulles, in Switzerland. They wanted something less than unconditional surrender, with Hitler arrested and the Nazi regime destroyed. They hoped, however, to make peace in the West while still continuing to fight Russia. Dulles told them there could be no separate peace and that the demand for unconditional surrender still stood.

The closing days of the war, in early 1945, intensified the melodrama with which Hitler had always surrounded himself. He retired to a deep bunker in Berlin, and issued orders from there for the fighting on all fronts. Goering and Himmler got out of Berlin and were active in the field. Both of them still thought that victory might be achieved, and they intrigued against each other to seize power when Hitler, whose star was obviously setting, should let it slip through his fingers. Himmler opened his own secret negotiations with the

Allies, and Hitler, told of this, ordered him shot—an order that was disobeyed.

Four years earlier, Hitler had decreed that if he were to die, Goering was next in line to succeed him. When the Führer indicated that he would stay in Berlin and go down to disaster with the city, Goering believed it was time for him to assume command. He therefore telegraphed to Hitler in terms of the utmost respect, but saying that unless he received a negative reply by ten o'clock that evening he would "take over at once the total leadership of the Reich."

This threw the egomaniacal Hitler into a fury. He dictated a telegram to Goering, accusing him of high treason, for which the penalty was death, but saying his life would be spared if he resigned all offices at once. Martin Bormann, a third contestant for supreme power, on his own initiative ordered Goering and his staff, who were at Berchtesgaden, arrested on the charge of treason; and this was done.

Hitler's cold-blooded fury was illustrated by his treatment of Hermann Fegelein, married to Eva Braun's sister, who was in the Führer's bunker as liaison officer for Himmler. In spite of the close personal tie, Hitler responded to Himmler's attempt to make a separate peace by ordering Fegelein shot. It is true that Fegelein had left the bunker and gone to his home in Berlin, where he had put on civilian clothes, but there is no evidence at all that he participated in Himmler's secret peace negotiations.

The Russians were now in the outskirts of Berlin, and it was apparent to almost everyone that the final defeat of the German Army was not far away. In Hitler's mind, which was now beyond doubt seriously disordered, there could be but one end for an honorable Nazi: self-destruction. He invited several leading members of his regime to take this course, and was surprised and hurt when only one of them accepted. (Several others committed suicide later, Himmler when he had been captured and identified, Goering in his prison cell on the eve of execution.) The immediate exception was the little propaganda expert, Goebbels. He was in the bunker with Hitler, with his wife and their six young children; when the last hope was gone, he had a doctor poison his six children; the same doctor had obligingly killed Hitler's favorite dog. Then at Goebbels' request, a soldier shot him and his wife in the back of the head.

Hitler had not waited for the last act of his faithful follower. Having married Eva Braun, he wrote his last testament, a whining document without a word of regret for the fearful, useless suffering he had inflicted on so many. He blamed the defeat on the German people, who had "played him false," and repeated all the cheap lies of his entire career. He had wanted only peace; the nations he had attacked had been so aggressive that he had had no alternative to war; nearly all of those closest to him had turned out to be traitors. He argued that Mussolini's invasion of Greece, where the Italian Army had to be rescued, had delayed the invasion of Russia and cost him the War. He and Eva now retired to a private apartment, where she took poison and Hitler shot himself in the mouth.

While the Russian guns thundered far above the deep bunker, the bodies were put in a shell hole in the garden, covered with gasoline, and set on fire. The witnesses watched them burning for a few minutes but then hastily retreated into the shelter for fear of Russian shells.

The policy of falsehood was maintained even beyond Hitler's death. Admiral Karl Doenitz took over the government, and had an announcement read over the radio: "Our Führer, Adolf Hitler, fighting to the last breath against Bolshevism, fell for Germany this afternoon in his operational headquarters in the Reich Chancellory." Doenitz then went on the air and spoke of Hitler's "hero's death."

A week later, on May 7, 1945, Germany signed an unconditional surrender; and at midnight on May 8, hostilities ended.

# 4. Stalin:
# Caligula in a Sack Suit

JOSEPH STALIN was one of the two worst mass murderers of the twentieth century, the other being Adolph Hitler; if you assume that they were sane—and it is a rather dubious assumption—they were among the two most odious criminals who ever functioned as heads of states. Many men before them had been brutal tyrants, casually killing their victims without compunction; but these earlier practitioners of genocide lived at times and places where such conduct was taken for granted and sometimes, indeed, had social approval. By the fourth decade of the twentieth century, when the Russian and the German were in power, Western culture had risen far above the level of a Caligula or a Genghis Khan. The crime of Hitler and Stalin is that they turned their backs on the prevailing standards of behavior professed by the cultures of which they were a part.

Like many other powerful individuals throughout history, Stalin was short of stature, not much over five feet. He had a rather large head for his size, covered with thick hair which he wore brushed straight back, a fashion common among the Russians. He had rather small eyes which darted quickly from side to side as he checked the impression he was making on those around him. He wore a big mustache and smoked a pipe with a curved stem and large bowl, usually giving the appearance of placidity common to pipe smokers, though he was capable of violent fits of rage, which may or may not have been genuine. He could also employ a coldly hostile demeanor, with tirades of vituperation, ironic, sarcastic, or contemptuous, as when, during the Second World War, he told Sir Winston Churchill that the failure of the British to establish a second front earlier than they did was due to simple cowardice.

Like other Russians of his generation, Stalin ate and drank prodigiously, though in his last years his doctors forced him to be more abstemious. It is possible that at public banquets, with foreign diplomats present, where many toasts were drunk, he may have been given a watered-down substitute for the huge quantity of liquor every individual present was supposed to consume; it was a standard technique to try to get the foreign diplomats drunk in the hope that they would then blurt out state secrets. Another Russian characteristic Stalin shared was the habit of rising late in the morning, and then working far into the night; many of his important engagements with callers were around midnight.

Of his personal life in his latter years, surprising little is known. He had what was probably the best secret police organization in history, and he used it to keep obscure many facts about himself; for example, although his second wife died twenty-one years before he did, no one seems really sure whether he married again; the sister of Lazar Kaganovich was often seen in the Kremlin in those years but her exact status is in doubt.

Stalin was born a peasant, was poorly educated as a boy, and retained these characteristics all his life. In the arts, and notably in music, painting, and sculpture, he had no understanding of modern trends, and forced Russian artists to conform to his ideas. He was equally ignorant of science, which made him an easy victim for the mountebank geneticist,

**JOSEF STALIN**
"He had a rather large head for his size . . . with small eyes which darted quickly from side to side as he checked the impression he was making on those around him."

Trofim Lysenko, who insisted, in opposition to the opinion of all competent scientists throughout the world, that acquired characteristics of an organism can be inherited, and that he could manipulate matters to bring this about.

He was a poor and dull writer and speaker; he was read or listened to only because of the power he came to possess as an individual. He had few if any original ideas, and until he had gathered the reins of power firmly into his own hands, he was obsequious and fawning, especially to Lenin. In the early days, both before and after the Russian Revolution, his colleagues were half amused, half contemptuous of this stolid-seeming peasant; not until it was too late did they awake to the fact that he had an endless thirst for power; shrewdness and cunning in getting his way; and the resoluteness of character that brings men to dominance.

Stalin was born December 21, 1879, in the small town of Gori in Georgia, a part of Russia lying in the Caucasus Mountains, between the Black and Caspian Seas. His name was Joseph Vissarionovich Djugashvili; "Stalin," which means "man of steel," was a pseudonym that he did not adopt until he was about thirty. Before that, he had used fifteen or twenty others; the best known of these was the first, adopted when he was about eighteen. It was "Koba," the name of the hero of a popular Georgian novel of that time.

The Caucasus has been one of the great crossroads of history, repeatedly invaded and conquered, and populated by what was eventually a conglomeration of races. Mount Ararat, where the Bible says Noah's Ark came to rest, is in the Turkish part of the area. Here, legend says, Jason sought the Golden Fleece and Medea, who lived as his wife for many years, killed her two children when his roving glance turned elsewhere. The region was conquered many times—by Alexander, Pompey, Genghis Khan, and Tamerlane, among others; it was controlled by Armenia from the sixth to the nineteenth centuries. Late in the eighteenth century, Georgia had to appeal to Russia for help to fight off the triple threat of the

Afghans, Persians, and Turks; the Russians, having been invited in, stayed, and the last Georgian king abdicated in 1801 in favor of the Tsar. Traditionally, the Georgians always seemed like a Mediterranean people, which indeed they probably were, in part—artistic, musical, and fond of consuming their own excellent native wine. This culture has now been partly obliterated by the Communist discipline imposed on it from above.

Eighty years ago, the Caucasus was a wild, rather remote region, with a turbulent and lawless population. Highwaymen often held up and sometimes murdered travelers. Blood feuds between families, similar to the famous American private war between the Hatfields and McCoys, were frequent. Not many of the inhabitants could read and write or saw any necessity for doing so. Although Russian was the compulsory language in school, and students were severely punished when caught speaking any of the forty other tongues that were in use (in an area smaller than Texas), Georgians never spoke it in the home if they could help it.

All of Russia presented an ugly picture to the world at this time. The peasants had been made virtual slaves by Ivan the Terrible, in the sixteenth century; in 1861 they were set free by Tsar Alexander II, but the great landowners were very slow in putting his edict into effect; and even eighteen years later, when Stalin was born, millions of peasants continued to be tied to the land in one way or another. His own grandparents had still been serfs when his father and mother were born; his father, however, had escaped from farm life and had become a cobbler. He was a Georgian, but married beneath him: Stalin's mother was an Ossete, one of a group looked down upon by the fairly crude and primitive Georgians as being even more so.

In the 1870's, Russia was a land of great wealth and great poverty. There was almost no middle class, and very few industrial workers; the overwhelming majority of the people were peasants, most of them living in poverty and ignorance:

the illiteracy rate was eighty or eighty-five per cent. Russia was ruled by three groups. The Court was tyrannical, bureaucratic, and in most matters desperately inefficient. The Russian Orthodox Church was reactionary; it possessed enormous wealth, and its higher officials lived in luxury which, however, did not as a rule extend to the local priests; great sums were extracted annually from the poverty-stricken peasantry. The landowners were also medieval in their outlook, exploiting the land and the farm workers.

The repression which successive Tsars and their police exerted on Russia over the centuries had generated an opposition, as it almost always does in such countries. The opposition was split into various groups which quarreled with one another and disagreed as to what ought to be done. Some of them believed in immediate direct action, the assassination of government officials. Others wanted to wait until they were strong enough and then bring about a forcible revolution. A few hoped for democratic reforms through the ballot box, on the Western model.

For many decades there was a continuous guerrilla warfare between the revolutionists and the Tsar's secret police, who were almost the only fairly efficient arm of the government, particularly adept in planting spies in the revolutionary ranks. Seeking to turn the pent-up emotions of the people away from the repressions of the government, the police tolerated and sometimes instigated pogroms—outbursts against the Jews—in which rioters invaded the ghettos in various cities, beating any Jew they could catch, looting, sometimes burning their homes, and occasionally resorting to outright murder.

Stalin was born in great poverty; the house of his parents, which has been preserved as a museum, is only one small room with an alcove for cooking. His father could not earn a living at his trade as a cobbler and usually worked for miserable wages in a shoe factory in the nearby city of Tiflis; his mother took in laundry and did mending for the neighbors. The father was a drunkard, who beat his son mercilessly on many occasions. The boy had smallpox at the age of six or seven; he recovered, but his face was thenceforth pockmarked. Some historians say that he had a severe ulceration of the left arm, which resulted in permanent damage and may have caused him to be exempt from military service; others believe that the defect was congenital.

At the age of nine, Stalin was sent by his deeply religious mother to an ecclesiastical school of the Orthodox Church at Gori. The students resented being forced to speak, read, and write only Russian; the slightest display of Georgian patriotism was severely punished, and even among these children there were sometimes riots in school.

At fifteen, Stalin transferred to the Orthodox Theological Seminary in Tiflis, where he remained for five years and where matters were even worse. Political radicalism had made inroads among the students and the authorities responded by treating them more as prisoners than as scholars. Their rooms were frequently searched in their absence, and they were severely punished for possessing not merely revolutionary literature but any book outside the highly limited range of reading matter that was permitted. Stalin became a subscriber to the "cheap library" in Tiflis, and was disciplined repeatedly for borrowing and reading such books as *The Life of Jesus,* by Renan, and Victor Hugo's novels, *Toilers of the Sea* and *Ninety-Three.*

Within four years he had been converted by fellow students to Socialism. Many years later he told an interviewer, "I became a Marxist because of my social position (my father was a worker in a shoe factory and my mother was also a working woman) but also . . . because of the harsh intolerance and Jesuitical discipline that crushed me so mercilessly at the Seminary. . . . The atmosphere in which I lived was saturated with hatred against Tsarist oppression." Psychologists have speculated that he was probably also subject to the influences that have often created rebels in other societies: a tyrannical father and great poverty, so that he felt himself to be an outsider from an early age.

At the age of twenty he left the Theological Seminary; there is some dispute as to whether he was expelled for political activities, or quit voluntarily. At any rate, he was now out in the world on his own, and began devoting almost his full time to Socialist activities. For a few months he had a trifling job in a local astronomical observatory; it gave him barely enough money to rent a room and feed and clothe himself, but he was pleased because the room was a place to hold conspiratorial meetings. He soon lost his job, however, and never again sought private employment.

For many years, he lived the typical life of a revolutionary. When he wasn't in prison, the Social Democratic (Socialist) Party kept him fed and clothed, after a fashion. His lodging was usually in the home of some one of the comrades, and since he was always on the run from the police, he changed his abode as frequently as he did his name. Between 1905 and 1917 he was arrested and sentenced to prison or exile six times; five times he escaped, and the sixth time he was liberated by the general amnesty of the Lvov-Kerensky government, which took over after the abdication of the Tsar, in March, 1917. Even so, he was in prison or in exile slightly more than half the time during these twelve years.

When Stalin became a revolutionary, there was only one important Socialist movement throughout the world. In spite of the fact that it included terrorists in Russia and some other countries, it preached, on the whole, a mild, Utopian doctrine. Socialism was supposed to come gradually, by orderly legal means, through reform movements in all countries. The Socialists paid lip service to Marx and Engels, but in Western Europe, Great Britain, and the United States, they showed very little intention of planning violent revolution, or setting up a dictatorship of the proletariat. Their propaganda was conducted in the open; a good example was the gradualist Fabian Society in Great Britain, for which famous writers like H. G. Wells and George Bernard Shaw produced very skillful and appealing propaganda books and pamphlets, and from which came much of the impetus for the Labor Party.

In Russia there were two opposing groups within the Social Democratic Party, one of which wanted violent revolution while the other preferred a Fabian policy. In July, 1903, the Russian Social Democrats held a conference; because of the vigilance of the Tsar's police it had to take place in a foreign country, meeting clandestinely, first in Brussels and then in London.

The radical wing was led by a young Russian, Vladimir Ulyanov, who used the pen name, Lenin. He was the son of a middle-class bureaucrat in the school system; in 1887 his brother had been executed for attempting to kill Tsar Alexander III, and soon Vladimir also became a radical. He studied law at the universities of Kazan and St. Petersburg, but before long he was arrested and sentenced to exile for his revolutionary activities. After being released and exiled again, he fled his homeland in 1900, and spent the next seventeen years in Western Europe, devoting his full time to fomenting revolutionary Socialism in Russia by conference and correspondence with others who had stayed at home.

At the Brussels-London meeting the two wings of the Social Democratic Party argued furiously with each other. The milder group had a large majority in the conference as well as in Russia itself, but on one minor vote, Lenin's group happened to win by a narrow margin. Throughout the rest of the conference, it was called "the Bolsheviki," or majority, and the moderates were addressed as "the Mensheviki," or minority. The two titles stuck and were used from then on.

The agitation of the radicals in Russia was helped by the increasing misery of the mass of the people. In 1904, the Tsar's government—arrogant, stupid, and greatly overrating its own military strength—blundered into a war with Japan, in which it sustained a crushing defeat the following year. On Sunday, January 22, 1905, a huge crowd of demonstrators in St. Petersburg, the capital, marched on the Winter Palace, the residence of Tsar Nicholas II. As far as is known, they intended no harm to anyone; they were merely trying to emphasize to the "Little Father," the Tsar, the fact that they were miserably poor and wretched. They were led by a singular character, Georgi Gapon, a Russian Orthodox priest; later he was proved to be a spy of the Tsar's secret police, and this may even have been true on "Bloody Sunday." In any case, the soldiers suddenly and without warning began firing at the crowd, killing and wounding thousands.

The incident caused the gathering tension to mount even higher, and the Tsar's government, really frightened for the first time, made a few concessions. Elections were permitted for representatives in a national parliament called the Duma; while its powers were severely limited, it was a first feeble step toward liberalism. The Socialists boycotted the elections and the parties actually represented in it were all farther to the right, the strongest one being the Constitutional Democrats. The abstention of the Social Democratic Party was preceded by a bitter debate within its ranks; the Mensheviki wanted to participate. Lenin, controlling the Party from his self-imposed exile by sheer power of personality, was in favor of abstention, which was in fact the general policy of most Socialists in all countries at that time; they believed that if they entered coalition governments the lines of demarcation would be blurred, and their pure doctrine would be weakened in the public mind.

Stalin was still working primarily in his native Caucasus, but he was by now sufficiently well known to have his views recorded. He agreed with Lenin, arguing that the creators of the coming revolution could not afford to waste their time on petty side issues. The Mensheviki, he said, reminded him of "the convict who, when he was about to put his head into the hangman's noose, implored the hangman not to scratch the pimple on his neck."

The victory of the intransigents was temporary, however. At the next election, in 1907, the Menshevik majority had got its way and the Social Democratic party participated.

The partial reformation of the Tsar's government was also

temporary. As soon as the creation of the Duma had soothed the country somewhat, the autocracy was restored, and before long repression was as complete as it had been before the beginning of the Russo-Japanese War.

In the Caucasus, Stalin, still calling himself Koba, was busy with his standard occupation. He held meetings, sometimes public, but more often secret. He helped to write, edit, and publish revolutionary pamphlets and newspapers. Foreign capital was pouring into the region to develop the recently discovered oil fields; the workers were exploited, and they offered a ready field for revolutionary propaganda.

In 1903, the youthful radical married an illiterate young girl, Catherine Svanidze, who died of tuberculosis after about four years, leaving a son, Yasha. Since Stalin was obviously in no position to care for a child, the boy was brought up by his mother's parents. When he was grown, he lived for a time with his father in the Kremlin, but they were never very sympathetic and Yasha finally drifted away.

At this time the radical group of which Stalin was one used a singular method of raising money for their revolutionary activities: bank robbery. This was not Stalin's own idea, nor did he operate alone, as is often charged. The technique had been employed for a long time by various political and other groups. So far as is known, Stalin never participated in person in any of these activities; he directed some of them, but from a distance.

A sensational incident took place in June, 1907, when an armed band fell upon messengers carrying money from the Tiflis post office to a bank; a large sum was captured in a pitched battle in which three were killed and fifty were wounded. A good deal of the money was in bank notes of big denominations, and the conspirators smuggled them out of the country and tried to exchange them in various banks in Western Europe. These banks had been warned, and several of the men engaged in the operation were arrested, including Maxim Litvinov, who was to become Commissar of Foreign Affairs in the Communist government many years later—about the same post as the American Secretary of State.

Many reminiscences have been written about the seven years that Stalin spent in prison or in exile. These are usually of two kinds: adulation by his followers or expressions of contempt from his enemies—if they were outside the country and able to speak frankly. Enough of this material is reliable, however, to give us a solid picture of what he was like. He was extraordinarily self-willed and intolerant of opposition—characteristics that became more marked as he grew older. He would never argue about politics with one or two men alone, insisting on getting a large group together and making speeches. The Tsar's police, the Okhrana, had a habit of planting spies among political prisoners, and fairly often men suspected of this were murdered by their fellow-prisoners. Stalin's enemies now say that several times he denounced and had killed other men against whom he had a grudge, even though their guilt was in doubt.

How he looked at this time has been described by a fellow prisoner, Semion Vereshchak. Apparently there were no prison uniforms, because Vereshchak says, "He wore a blue satin smock, with a wide open collar, without a belt. His head was bare. A *bashlyk*—a sort of detached hood with two tapering scarves—was thrown across his shoulders. He always carried a book. . . . He walked with a slow, catlike tread. He was slender, with a pointed face, pockmarked skin, sharp nose and small eyes looking out from under a narrow forehead, slightly indented." Vereshchak says that he defied the regulations which forbade intermingling between political prisoners and petty criminals, and associated constantly with the latter.

In the period of his greatest adulation, an anecdote was told dating back to this time. In 1908, it was said, he was in prison, and the guards, in the course of a little impromptu celebration of their own, decided to make a number of the prisoners run the gauntlet. The guards lined up in two long rows facing each other, and as the prisoners were forced to run down the line between them, they beat them over the head with their fists. Stalin alone, the story said, refused to quicken his steps but sauntered along, ignoring the blows, a book under his arm. The best guess today is that this is probably a pure fabrication, and that Stalin was, as Nikita Khrushchev called him after his death, always physically a coward.

In the interval between prison sentences, he went on with the routine life of a revolutionist. The claim is made—and denied—that he attended a Social Democratic Conference in Tammerfors, Finland, in 1905, where Lenin was also present. It is true, however, that he did go to similar meetings outside the Russian border once or twice, the only occasions on which he left Russian soil until he went to Teheran during the Second World War to confer with Churchill and Roosevelt.

By now, the third leader of the revolutionary forces to reach worldwide notoriety had also emerged on the scene. Lev Davidovich Bronstein, who called himself Leon Trotsky, had become an important figure in the leadership of the Social Democrats. Like Lenin, he came from the middle class; Stalin was the only important figure in the first decade of the revolutionary movement who was of peasant stock. Trotsky, who was Jewish, had become a revolutionist at the age of seventeen, had been arrested for the first time at nineteen, and two years later was exiled to Siberia. At twenty-three he escaped and fled abroad where, like Lenin, he worked in France, Belgium, Germany, and England. For a time he and Lenin jointly edited in London the revolutionary newspaper *Iskra* (the *Spark*). Unlike Lenin and Stalin, who were in the radical wing of the Social Democratic Party from the beginning, Trotsky was for many years close to the Mensheviks—a fact afterward repeatedly used against him.

Three men more unlike one another in appearance and temperament than this trio would be hard to imagine. Lenin, partially bald even early in life, wearing a short, pointed beard, was slant-eyed and furtive in appearance. Stalin, as noted, was short and bulky, his face expressionless, his darting eyes small and crafty. Trotsky had a small tuft of chin whiskers and startled, protruding eyes behind thick eyeglasses. Lenin was a pragmatist; he sensibly modified the rigid Communist doctrine when necessary to meet an emergency. Stalin had practically no principles at all, except an abiding interest in advancing his own fortunes; he twisted and turned continually in his efforts to get ahead. Trotsky was a true, fanatical doctrinaire; he devoted his life to the belief that communism could not succeed in one country alone, that the Russian Revolution must be part of "the continuing revolution," in all countries. To be sure, this was the orthodox opinion of all radicals at the time. Marx had taught that the revolution must come first in a highly industrialized country, through the efforts of the exploited factory workers, and that a nation of peasants—like Russia—would be the last in which there could be any hope of success.

Trotsky, still chiefly a collaborator with the Mensheviks, remained in this attitude until after the Russian Revolution in 1917, opposed at first to Lenin's efforts to win control of the party and to adopt a policy of immediate revolution. Stalin, as always, had no policy of his own, but followed Lenin. In 1912, the Lenin group held a meeting in Prague and announced its determination either to capture control of the Social Democratic Party or, if this proved impossible, to start a new one of their own. The efficiency of the Tsar's secret police is shown by the fact that of the dozen or so followers of Lenin who met in Prague, at least three were spies.

A little later, in St. Petersburg, several of the leading figures in the Bolshevik faction of the Social Democratic Party were Tsarist spies, including an important member of the Duma, Roman Malinovsky. In fact, this man was so trusted that when Stalin was about to be arrested, Lenin turned to him to arrange an escape. Malinovsky was one of those who wrote the secret code by which the Bolsheviks communicated; he promptly turned over a copy to the police. When the First World War began, in August, 1914, the Tsar's agents were readily able to arrest every leading Bolshevik who was still in the country. With Lenin's writings used to support a charge of conspiracy, they were all found guilty of treason and exiled to Siberia. (When the files of the Tsar's secret police were opened after the Revolution of March, 1917, Malinovsky's actions came to light; in 1918 he was arrested, tried and executed by the Communist Government.)

Was Stalin himself a secret Tsarist spy for a number of years before the First World War? Some people think so; Isaac Don Levine has listed the evidence. Several friends and co-conspirators of his were arrested, at various times, when Stalin was one of a few people, or the only one, to know where they were hiding. On some occasions after he himself had been arrested and exiled, his escapes appear to have been ridiculously easy. In one case he returned home illegally from exile and although he was conspicuous because of his activities, he was not rearrested for more than four years. More than once, he was given an extremely light sentence, and instead of being sent to Siberia, was "exiled" to fairly nearby places in European Russia. On one occasion, the records indicate, he was arrested and released the same day, and turned up only about a week later for a Party meeting in Stockholm. Unless the books were juggled to misstate the date of his arrest, it is extraordinary that the Tsar's police should have let him leave the country immediately after being arrested.

Alexander Orlov, who was Stalin's top confidential agent in Spain during the Civil War, and who defected shortly thereafter and came to the United States, believes that Stalin was a Tsarist spy. In an article in *Life* magazine in April, 1956, Orlov states that the execution of Marshal Tukhachevsky and practically the entire high command of the Red Army in 1937 was because the Marshal had come across documents from the files of the Okhrana, in Stalin's own handwriting, exposing fellow Bolsheviks as conspirators. Orlov's theory is that the Marshal was so angered by the revelations that he plotted to overthrow Stalin who, however, got wind of the plan and acted first. Orlov says the file of old Okhrana documents was discovered in about 1936 by a man named Stein, who showed them to various important people, all of whom were liquidated by Stalin in the next few years.

Tremendous events took place in Russia in the years that began with the outbreak of the First World War in August, 1914. Since Stalin played little or no part in most of these, we may pass over them rapidly.

When the War began, the Russian bureaucracy, probably the most inefficient in the world, was as unprepared for the conflict as it had been ten years earlier. Huge masses of Russian soldiers were slaughtered in battle after battle, and behind the lines the country was rapidly falling to pieces. Early in 1917, a bloodless coup transferred power to the hands of a new government headed by Prince George Lvov, in which a brilliant young Socialist, Alexander Kerensky, was Minister of Justice. It decreeded a general amnesty for political prisoners, and Stalin, who was in exile in Siberia, was one of many Bolsheviks who came hurrying home.

Lenin also came home from Switzerland, with the help of the German Government, which believed that attempts at a Russian revolution would hasten the complete collapse of military resistance. When Lenin arrived at the St. Petersburg station of the railroad from Finland, he was greeted by a delegation of Moderate Socialists, who believed that their aims were also his. But as soon as he stepped off the train, he disillusioned them, and indicated they were to play no part in his ambitious plans. Pointedly ignoring the flower-bearing committee members, he turned his back on them, and addressed the crowd of bystanders, hailing them in significant words:

> Dear Comrades, Soldiers, Sailors and Workers! I am happy to greet in your persons the victorious Russian Revolution and greet you as the vanguard of the worldwide proletarian army. . . . Long live the worldwide Socialist Revolution!

In July, Lenin tried to implement his words with an uprising against the Lvov Provisional Government. The effort failed, a number of Bolsheviks were arrested, and Lenin had to retreat temporarily to Finland. Among those arrested for a time was Trotsky, who had now thrown in his lot with Lenin.

Prince Lvov now stepped down as Prime Minister, and was succeeded by Kerensky, who two months later had to deal with another attempted uprising, this one led by Cossack General Lavr Kornilov and composed of various right-wing elements.

Despite the setback in July, the Bolsheviks were growing in power and managing to arm themselves. Lenin came back from Finland, disguised by a bloody bandage around his head, and on November 7 a new uprising took place. The Bolshevik forces, including soldiers, sailors, and civilians, seized the key points in St. Petersburg, the railroad stations, bridges, power house, and telephone buildings. The seat of Kerensky's government was the Winter Palace; when expected reénforcements of troops loyal to him did not arrive, he went in search of them, and in his absence the Winter Palace was stormed by a force that was more an undisciplined mob than a military formation.

A few days later, there was an indecisive brush between small contingents of military forces of the two sides. Soon the elements loyal to Kerensky in the Kremlin in Moscow surrendered, and the Communists were in control. Kerensky was forced to go into hiding and fled the country.

The Kerensky regime was not the only center of resistance to the Bolsheviks. The Mensheviks joined with other parties to oppose Lenin. The Union of Railway Workers was hostile, and Tsarist elements began an uprising far away from St. Petersburg, on the Don River in the south. (The Bolsheviks at this time probably numbered about 100,000 in a population of 175 million.)

The Kerensky government had arranged for nationwide elections for the Constituent Assembly, or Parliament, on November 25, and the Communists, though they did not like the idea, were afraid to cancel the plan; they got 9.8 million votes out of 41.6 million. When the new Constituent Assembly met, Communist soldiers ringed the building, the gates of which were locked and guarded by the soldiers. The delegates managed to get in, but they worked in an atmosphere of Communist-created terrorism; they brought food and candles, expecting the lights to be cut off and access interrupted. Armed Communist guards were inside the meeting hall as well as outside, but in spite of this, the anti-Communist delegates passed a series of liberal resolutions. At four o'clock in the morning, one of the Communist guards interrupted a speaker, saying that the meeting had gone on long enough; that the guards were tired and everyone must go home. Thus undramatically ended the democratic government of Russia, which had lasted about eight months; the Constituent Assembly never met again.

Stalin now reappeared in the new government headed by Lenin; he was put in charge of minorities, which seemed an appropriate post in view of his Georgian origin. He played a minor role in the dramatic events of the next phase—the harsh peace treaty with Germany, which would have cost Russia dearly had the Central Powers been victorious; the desperate civil war with the White Russians, who got huge supplies from the victorious Allies; and the conflict with Poland that ended in a stalemate. Although Russian history books were later rewritten to conceal the fact, Trotsky was the hero of the military defense of the Revolution.

Conditions were now deteriorating rapidly. Industry was almost in a state of collapse, which meant that very few consumer goods were being manufactured to exchange for food from the farms. Starvation was endemic in the cities, where production was only twenty percent of prewar, on the average; steel was down to only five percent. The inflated paper ruble was almost worthless. Trotsky felt it was necessary to put the Army to work on civilian tasks, and to comandeer citizens for forced labor.

Factories began paying their workers in products which they

could take to the country and barter for food, a dreadfully time-consuming process. The Government confiscated food from the villages, which deeply angered the peasants. They themselves were half-starved in the confusion and inefficiency that followed the breaking up of the big estates.

When the Revolution was less than four years old, sailors at the naval base of Kronstadt, a few miles from St. Petersburg, which had helped the Communists greatly in the first days, revolted. The rebellious sailors were aided by other dissident elements—the Whites, some Anarchists, and even some dissatisfied Bolsheviks. The Communist Government suppressed the uprising and executed many of the participants.

At about the same time, famine threatened the lives of some fifteen million people in Russia; it was caused by drought, governmental inefficiency, and the mounting hostility of the peasants. The Government apparently planned to let these people die rather than reveal its own weakness by asking the outside world for help, but Maxim Gorki reported the crisis and asked for aid. Herbert Hoover, then Secretary of Commerce of the United States, who had fed the Belgians during the War and the people of the Central Powers after it ended, responded. More than ten million Russians, one-third of them children, were fed until the next fairly good harvest, in the autumn of 1922.

The Communist Government did much to hamper this operation. With great difficulty, Hoover got the Soviet Government to release about a hundred Americans whom they were holding on various political charges. The Russians tried hard to prevent the food from carrying any identification of its American origin, trying to pretend to the illiterate peasants that the Communists deserved all the credit. The secret police hounded the Americans, interfering with their operations so seriously that Hoover had to threaten to withdraw the aid; and at one point the shipments actually were stopped. Russia still refuses to admit the role the United States played; her history books say that the main source of assistance was "the working class in foreign countries," which did indeed help—to the extent of about one-fiftieth of the total.

When Lenin perceived in 1921 that things were going from bad to worse, he reversed himself and established the famous NEP—New Economic Policy. The ruble was stabilized; the confiscation of food was stopped; and the peasants instead were assessed for taxes which they could afford to pay, at first in kind and later in money. Small and medium-sized industry and trade were permitted to be privately owned, and foreign capital was invited to come back into Russia, even on a large scale.

Strong ideological differences were developing among the leaders of the Revolution. A powerful movement developed to give the trade unions a real voice in managing the country; Trotsky, on the contrary, wanted the unions stripped of all power and made a part of the Government. Lenin tried to compromise the issue and succeeded temporarily, although Trotsky's plan was the one finally put into effect.

The Central Committee of the Communist Party was now authorized to expel those who disagreed with "the majority" —which meant in practice Lenin and the little group immediately surrounding him. To be expelled from the Party was a terrible punishment; it meant a forced resignation from your job, cancellation of all privileges, quite possibly including your family's ration cards for food, and ostracism by friends and acquaintances who feared being identified in any way with the pariah. Trotsky concurred in this new policy, not seeing that he was signing what would eventually prove to be his own death warrant.

Gradually Stalin, the colorless nonentity sucking his pipe in the background, Lenin's yes-man, began to emerge as a figure of importance. He never stuck his neck out, never took a strong line of his own, but waited to see how Lenin was going and then agreed with him. By now, the Georgian had several important posts. He was Commissar of Nationalities, riding herd on the rough, wild tribesmen of the Urals and beyond.

He was a powerful figure in the huge network of the secret police, an organization so unpopular that it kept changing its name—Cheka, OGPU, NKVD, MVD, KGB. He was influential in the Political Bureau, the "Politburo," which had been set up casually in an absent-minded moment, without anyone's realizing that it would eventually be more influential than the nominal government itself. The writings of Marx were considered infallible, and it was necessary for somebody to reconcile every important action of the Communist Government with them. The Politburo served this purpose and became all-powerful by doing so.

In spite of his holding several key posts, people still did not take Stalin very seriously. He had been quarreling with Trotsky ever since they had collided during the Civil War, and Lenin continued to arbitrate disputes between them. Trotsky was contemptuous of the silent, opportunistic Georgian as only a highly articulate theoretician could be, and took no trouble to hide it.

A great asset for Stalin was his ability to listen quietly and with seemingly no impatience while other people went on talking. As Isaac Deutscher, author of an authoritative biography of the Russian dictator, remarked, by sitting there smoking his pipe and never saying a word, he avoided making embarrassing promises while giving those who poured out their troubles a feeling that they had a friend at court.

The year 1922 saw several fateful events. Early in April, Stalin became General Secretary of the Communist Party, the only official position he was to hold until he became Premier in the great emergency of the Second World War. All the multitudinous strings of Russian political and economic life now ran through his eager fingers. An Organization Bureau had been set up to take full control of party personnel; Stalin was the only link between this and the Politburo. A Central Control Commission was set up to purge the Party of crooks and careerists; again, Stalin was the only link between this and the Central Committee of the Communist Party; ex-officio, he conducted the purges, imprisoning or shooting people with a liberal hand. It always turned out that the crooks and careerists were people who were at least suspected by him of being enemies of his own. He prepared an elaborate card catalogue which gave many details about each of the 20,000 top Communists in the country, an invaluable help to him in later years in deciding who was ambitious and should therefore be shot.

He prepared the agenda for every meeting of the Politburo, and then interpreted its formal actions as he pleased. He engaged, promoted, and dismissed at his pleasure many thousands of local bureaucrats all over the country, whose loyalty while in office was primarily to him. The other high-ranking Communists were glad to have him do the dirty work, especially the imprisonment or execution of old comrades-in-arms who had supposedly gone astray; by the time they realized how much power he had quietly gathered up, it was too late. Trotsky said afterwards that Lenin was worried about him and had remarked, "This cook can only serve peppery dishes"; but even Lenin was not at this time prepared for a showdown.

A few weeks after Stalin became General Secretary, such a showdown became impossible. Toward the end of May, Lenin suffered the first of three strokes which were to cause his death about two years later on January 21, 1924. While there were periods when he could do some work, he was always during this period an invalid who must nurse his health, avoid excitement, be not more than one-tenth of the man he had been.

Trotsky long afterward accused Stalin of having poisoned Lenin, but there is no evidence that this is true. It is quite possible, however, that Stalin did try to hasten Lenin's death by more circuitous means.

On December 25, 1922, Lenin dictated his famous "Testament," in which he passed judgment on several of the people closest to him, and on January 4, 1923, he added a postscript.

He said that Stalin and Trotsky were "the two most able leaders of the present Central Committee" (of the Communist Party). However, Stalin "has concentrated an enormous power in his hands; and I am not sure that he always knows how to use that power with sufficient caution." Trotsky "is personally the most able man in the Central Committee" but has "too far-reaching self-confidence and a disposition to be too much attracted by the purely administrative side of affairs." Lenin feared that these qualities of the two men "might, quite innocently, lead to a split," and urged that measures be taken to avoid this, without saying what those measures should be.

In his postscript, he engaged in a breath-taking attack upon the Georgian: "Stalin is too rude, and this fault, entirely supportable in relations among us Communists, becomes insupportable in the office of General Secretary. Therefore, I propose to the Comrades to find a way to remove Stalin from that position and appoint to it another man who in all respects differs from Stalin only in superiority—namely, more patient, more loyal, more polite and more attentive to comrades, less capricious, etc."

This amazing doctrine has never yet been published in full inside Soviet Russia, though it was mentioned by Khrushchev in his famous speech attacking Stalin at the Twentieth Congress of the Communist Party on February 25, 1956. When Trotsky was kicked out of Russia, he took with him a copy of Lenin's Testament; he turned it over to the American journalist, Max Eastman, who gave it to the *New York Times*, where it appeared October 18, 1926. For the next thirty years nobody in Russia dared admit it existed.

In Khrushchev's 1956 speech, he revealed the full text of another astonishing document, a letter from Krupskaya, Lenin's wife, on December 23, 1922, to Kamenev, one of her husband's closest friends, then nominal head of the Politburo. Lenin had just suffered his second stroke, and was forbidden by the doctors to take more than an absolute minimum of interest in public affairs. All communication with him was channeled through Krupskaya. Lenin knew that Stalin was concealing important information from him, as he was from everyone else, and asked his wife to try to get some of these facts from Stalin. She says in her letter to Kamenev:

> Because of a short letter which I had written in words dictated to me by Vladimir Ilyich [Lenin] by permission of the doctors, Stalin allowed himself yesterday an unusually rude outburst directed at me. . . . During all these thirty years I have never heard from any [other] Comrade one word of rudeness. The business of the Party and of Ilyich are not less dear to me than to Stalin. . . . I beg you to protect me from rude interference with my private life and from vile invectives and threats. . . .

Stalin evidently continued to abuse Krupskaya, for on March 5 of the following year, Lenin himself wrote to the Georgian, sending copies to Kamenev and to another important Communist leader, Grigori Zinoviev:

> Dear Comrade Stalin: You permitted yourself a rude summons of my wife to the telephone and a rude reprimand of her. . . . I consider as directed against me that which is being done against my wife. I ask you, therefore, that you weigh carefully whether you are agreeable to retracting your words and apologizing or whether you prefer the severance of relations between us.

Commenting on this correspondence in the *New Leader* of July 16, 1956, Boris Nicolaevsky, a well-known authority on Russian affairs, formerly of the Marx-Engels Institute of Moscow, says:

> To appraise Stalin's motives, one must remember that he possessed extraordinary self-restraint, knew how to conceal his true feelings when necessary and could skillfully play whatever role he had decided to assume. If, nevertheless, Stalin was rude toward Krupskaya, knowing that this upset Lenin and might bring on another stroke, he did so deliberately.

The death of Lenin marked the end of an epoch. His survivors were now free to struggle openly among themselves to see who would succeed to his shoes, but the battle had little reality. Stalin had laid his plans so well, had entrenched himself so carefully, was so much shrewder and more ruthless than anyone else, that his rise to power was inevitable.

His oration at Lenin's funeral was a piece of emotional adulation of the departed leader whose death he had certainly desired and quite possibly, as noted above, had helped to hasten. He intoned what amounted to a long, quasi-religious litany:

> In leaving us, Comrade Lenin charged us to hold high and keep pure the great title of Member of the Party. We vow to thee, Comrade Lenin, that we shall honorably fulfill this, thy commandment. . .
>
> In leaving us, Comrade Lenin charged us to guard the unity of our Party like the apple of our eye. We vow to thee, Comrade Lenin, that we shall fulfill honorably this, thy commandment.

And so on and on, with repetitions of the same paragraph, with only a few words changed.

One of Stalin's skillful strokes against Trotsky came in connection with the funeral. Trotsky, nearly broken down with overwork, was on his way to the Caucasus for a rest. On the news of Lenin's death he telegraphed back to the Kremlin asking when the funeral would take place, since he wished to return for it. This was a tremendously important matter; not to be seen at the state funeral of the most important man in the whole Communist world would be a very black mark indeed. Stalin telegraphed back: "The funeral takes place on Saturday. You will not be able to return in time. The Politburo thinks that because of the state of your health you must proceed to Sukhum."

The telegram contained two falsehoods. The date of the funeral had been set for Sunday, and Trotsky could easily have returned in time. Also, whenever Stalin quoted the opinion of the Politburo, he was giving merely his own ideas. During the few remaining years before Trotsky was exiled (and eventually assassinated) by Stalin his absence from Lenin's funeral was over and over brought up against him. However, as Louis Fischer sensibly remarks in his biography of Stalin, Trotsky should have turned around and gone back to Moscow without waiting for word from anybody.

Stalin went on with his quiet, implacable campaign to get rid of every possible rival for power, beginning with Trotsky, still the strongest of them all. There were half a dozen others who were members of the intimate ring, and during the next few years, several combinations and recombinations were made. Not yet feeling strong enough to take over the Government alone, Stalin at first worked with two other men, Kamenev, and Zinoviev, the fat, nervous, natural orator. When this triumvirate had served its purpose, Stalin got rid of the other two members, and began to work with Nikolai Bukharin, Alexei Rykov, and Michael Tomsky. Bukharin, erudite but erratic, was an editor of *Pravda*, with a following among the young. Rykov had been close to Lenin and had been the first Commissar for the Interior after the 1917 Revolution; as a reward for siding with Stalin against Trotsky he was made Chairman of the Council of Commissars, roughly equivalent to Premier. Tomsky, once head of the formerly powerful Russian trade-union movement, was the only man of either group who was not executed by Stalin a few years later; he killed himself when he was about to be arrested.

There is little point in discussing the details of the ideological differences between Trotsky and Stalin during the five years that the former was still (with one interlude of Siberian exile) permitted to stay in Russia; Stalin was determined to get rid of his rival and would have done so regardless of their respective political positions. Both men had for many years advocated world revolution, but Stalin now changed his tune and began to talk about "Socialism in one country." As was so often the case with him, he had several reasons for doing this. One of these was to reassure France and Great Britain, who feared Communist propaganda within their borders. As E. H. Carr points out in *Socialism in One Country*, the new line flattered Russia and made Trotsky's attitude seem contemptuous; it appealed to patriotism and thus brought support from some anti-Bolshevik elements. It made possible the resumption of forced-draft industrialization, which had slowed down with the introduction of Lenin's New Economic Policy. It also helped to answer those critics who had said that the NEP was really a step away from Socialism, toward state capitalism. The NEP had favored the "rich" peasants, the Kulaks, but the plan was not working out, and Stalin's revision made it possible to crack down on them. It served to revive the flagging enthusiasm of the Bolsheviks themselves.

In later years, of course, Stalin would advocate or soft-pedal the world revolution from time to time, as temporary expedience dictated.

One immediate disagreement with Trotsky was over the latter's protest that Stalin, Zinoviev and Kamenev, when they were the ruling triumvirate, were too harsh in their restrictive measures. Trotsky said you could have both stern dictatorship and some degree of freedom simultaneously, expanding one or the other according to the situation, and seeking to make the dictatorship milder as time went by. Stalin thought this was nonsense, that the masses must be kept down remorselessly, lest they revolt.

Trotsky, always the impractical, fiery revolutionist, began making speeches trying to appeal to the country over the heads of the triumvirate; he made the bad blunder of calling himself "an old Bolshevik," the highest accolade anyone could have at this time. This gave Stalin the chance to remind everyone that Trotsky had in fact been close to the Mensheviks right up to the 1917 Revolution; by 1924 the Mensheviks were considered a pack of counter-revolutionary scoundrels. A national conference was called to arbitrate the dispute; it consisted of officials of local branches of the Communist Party, most of them Stalin's appointees. When Stalin asked Trotsky whether he proposed to change the rules of the late and sainted Lenin, Trotsky was afraid to answer yes or no. (In fact, Lenin himself had been on both sides of many questions, and while he was still alive plenty of people had disagreed with him.)

Stalin further consolidated his power by sending out of the country as ambassadors men likely to oppose him. But it was Zinoviev, not Stalin, who brought forward the idea that one could be punished for "dangerous thoughts," and demanded that Trotsky should make a public recantation. (Twelve years later, Stalin shot Zinoviev for himself having dangerous thoughts.) The persecution of Trotsky continued; his books and pamphlets were suppressed and on one occasion when he tried to address a throng from a hotel balcony, it is reported that members of the police ruthlessly hauled him back into the room.

At this time Russia's economic difficulties were about as great as ever, and the peasants were withholding grain and meat from the cities, largely because food was desperately scarce in any case, and industrial production was still so low that the city dwellers had little to offer in exchange.

Although he handled his own career with maximum ineptitude, Trotsky was still too powerful to be executed out of hand; he was yet remembered in Russia and throughout the world as the second man of the Revolution. Stalin managed to get him removed as War Commissar, and then gave him several small but harassing simultaneous jobs, loading him with work and then complaining sharply if any detail went wrong, as it was sure to do.

Zinoviev and Kamenev were closer to Trotsky ideologically than they were to Stalin, and finally came out openly on his side. They tried to warn the Communist Party of Stalin's egomania and ambition, but it was too late; they had kept silent too long. Trotsky was soon removed from the Politburo, and presently he and Zinoviev were expelled from the Party; both of them, and some others among Trotsky's sympathizers, were forced to sign confessions that they had held erroneous beliefs, and to promise to drop them. In all, about seventy-five prominent Communists, suspected or known by Stalin to be hostile to him, were expelled from the Party. Before long Trotsky was exiled to Siberia. Stalin, having used Bukharin, Rykov, and Tomsky to get rid of Trotsky, Zinoviev, and Kamenev, now turned against his three new collaborators in the same way. At last he stood alone.

It is difficult for Americans to realize the fawning adulation of the dictator that now began and continued until the day of his death. Seven cities were named for him, with slight variations in the names, as well as thousands of schools, factories, farms, ships, rivers and lakes. On his birthday, every Russian newspaper printed only a few lines of news and many pages of personal praise. An American traveling in a remote part of the country tried to send a telegram to Stalin, and the telegraph office refused to accept it until he added after Stalin's name a few flattering words—"Hero of the Revolution," "Leader of the Russian People," or something of the sort.

The *Daily Worker*, the Communist paper in New York City, solemnly published a poem translated from the Russian by an American Communist, Isidore Schneider:

> Above the valley the mountain peak.
> Above the peak the sky.
> But Stalin, skies have no height to equal you.
> Only your thoughts rise higher.
> The stars, the moon, pale before the sun
> That pales in turn before your shining mind.

The dictator was considered omniscient, which he was not, as well as omnipotent, which he very nearly was—inside Russia. A magazine solemnly announced, "Certain pronouncements of Aristotle have only been fully deciphered and expressed by Stalin."

The propaganda machine both glorified the Georgian and belittled all other members of the original revolutionary group. Although at the beginning he had played only a minor role, it was not hard to swing the balance the other way. A photograph existed showing Lenin standing between two men, one of whom was Stalin; the third man was snipped out and the edited picture was circulated by tens of millions. Stalin also remembered to publicize little humanizing touches; a snapshot was taken showing an attractive small girl handing him a bouquet of flowers, an appealing scene, and this was also circulated by the million. Yet he did not let sentiment interfere with what he considered to be business; a short time later, he became suspicious of the father of the little girl, one Markizov, and had him shot.

With all this power in his hands, Stalin continued some policies of Lenin's time, abandoned others, and instituted some new ones of his own. The steady hostility to all non-Communist countries—which at that time meant every other government in the world—was continued, though its surface manifestations were altered from time to time under the pressure of expediency. All Communist parties everywhere were under strict Moscow control, and every change in Stalin's policy, of which there were a number, was instantly followed, no matter how ridiculous this might make foreign Communist leaders appear. Large amounts were spent for espionage, especially in the United States, and for Communist propaganda, but these sums were smaller than was generally assumed at the time; the Communist leaders and spies were in most cases fanatics who lived happily on small wages. Almost never did Moscow trouble to inform them in advance about important policy decisions, and they learned of shifts in the party line only from dispatches sent to non-Communist newspapers by the correspondents of such papers in the USSR.

The enforced poverty of Communist leaders elsewhere was in marked contrast to the luxurious life enjoyed by top bureaucrats inside Russia itself. Their nominal salaries remained low, but they gave themselves special privileges and a standard of living available in other countries only to the very wealthy. While most of the population lived in crowded quarters, with inadequate food and clothing, Stalin and his favorites dined luxuriously, enjoyed ample quarters, had country homes and fleets of limousines at their disposal—all, of course, at the expense of the State.

From the beginning, political opponents of the regime had been treated harshly, and with Stalin in full power, their punishment was now made more severe than ever. Those suspected rightly or wrongly of hostility to the regime were arrested in the dead of night, given perfunctory trials or none, and sent to prison or to the notorious slave-labor camps, most of them situated far north, near the shore of the Arctic.

The few who have escaped from these camps and managed to make their way out to the non-Communist world have given careful, documented evidence of the living hell that the inmates experience. It was a deliberate policy of the Soviet Government to work these political prisoners, most of them white-collar intellectuals, to death. The hardest sort of labor was enforced from dawn to dusk; food was inadequate to sustain life; clothing was never proper protection against the bitter Arctic cold. Slave labor was used for some huge engineering projects, including a canal from the Baltic to the White Sea and double tracks for the Trans-Siberian Railway. No one knows how many men and women died in these slave camps or under the equally cruel treatment in Stalin's prisons, but the number is undoubtedly huge; some estimates go as high as fifteen million.

From the beginning of the Revolution, religion was strongly opposed by the Communists. Priests were subjected to great hardships; many churches were closed and were turned into anti-religious museums. Not until the middle of the Second World War was the Orthodox Church again given legal status, and then only as another puppet of the Government. The action was taken for several reasons: one was strong pressure from the Western Allies; another was that the Bolshevik Government had been shocked to find, when it called the young men to the colors, that in spite of all the indoctrination with atheism, many of them still remained Christians.

Members of the former middle class led a miserable existence. It was difficult for them to get employment or to obtain ration cards, and for some time their children were not permitted to go to school. Naturally, they tried to assume the protective coloration of the proletariat, and as the years went on, with some success.

By 1929, Stalin had decided Trotsky was too dangerous to be allowed to remain inside Soviet Russia. He still feared to shoot him, but Trotsky was exiled and went to live on Prinkipo Island, near Istanbul, Turkey. Since he still had many friends inside the USSR, much important information was smuggled out to him; he printed it in a magazine which was in turn smuggled back inside the country and which enjoyed a wide, if surreptitious, circulation. Anyone caught with a copy in his possession was in danger of being shot out of hand.

Stalin, who must by now have bitterly regretted allowing Trotsky to escape (a mistake he never made again with any other important person) hounded him from country to country, by bullying the Government of each in turn with threats of economic reprisals. In the next eleven years, Trotsky was forced to move from Turkey to France, to Norway, to Mexico. In the last-named country he was murdered in August, 1940, by a man who called himself variously Frank Jacson, a Canadian, or Jacques Mornard, a Frenchman; he has been identified by fingerprints and photographs as a Spaniard named Ramon Mercader, apparently a loyal Stalinist who had been trained in Moscow for the job of killing Trotsky. Mercader had spent years ingratiating himself with Trotskyists in Paris, so that he came to Mexico City carrying what seemed to be irreproachable recommendations.

With the banishment of Trotsky began one of the most fantastic aspects of life in the Communist State, and one that continues to the present day—the rewriting of history to downgrade fallen heroes and to glorify those who at the moment are on top. All the textbooks and other historical works dealing with the Russian Revolution were modified to belittle Trotsky and to magnify Stalin's insignificant contribution beyond all reason; old copies were required to be turned in and destroyed. The writer was in Russia shortly after Trotsky had been expelled, and saw in the Museum of the Revolution how far the falsifiers would go. At the moment of victory in 1917, a group photograph was taken of the small handful of top leaders, and this picture was prominently displayed in the Museum. The head of Trotsky had, however, been cut out of the picture, another head substituted, and the whole thing rephotographed; it had been done so clumsily that the substitution was readily apparent.

Throughout Stalin's regime this process went on as he turned against one old comrade after another. Perhaps the height of absurdity came when every subscriber to the *Great Soviet Encyclopedia* received new pages with instructions to cut out and destroy the old ones and paste in the substitutes.

With Trotsky out of the way came a terrible episode. The peasants were still withholding grain and resisting collectivization, and Stalin embarked upon a policy of unflinching extermination of them, especially in the Ukraine, always a center of resistance to Moscow (to which the capital had some years earlier been moved from St. Petersburg, now renamed Leningrad). The food produced by the peasants and hidden away by them was remorselessly sought out and confiscated. Thousands of them were shot, but the number executed was negligible compared to those who died of enforced starvation. Stalin's excuse was that efficient methods of agriculture required large-scale operations, that these could only be done on collective or state-owned farms, and that the peasants refused to give up their little individual holdings. Long afterward, during the Second World War, the dictator one night had dinner alone with Winston Churchill, and tried to defend his actions. He said:

> The collective farm policy was a terrible struggle. . . . I had to deal with ten million people. It was fearful. Four years it lasted. It was absolutely necessary for Russia, if we were to

avoid periodic famines, to plow the land with tractors. We must mechanize our agriculture. When we gave tractors to the peasants they were all spoiled in a few months. Only collective farms with workshops could handle tractors. We took the greatest trouble to explain it to the peasants. It was no use arguing with them. After you have said all you can to a peasant he says he must go home and consult his wife and he must consult his herder. . . . After he has talked it over with them he always answers that he does not want the collective farm and he would rather do without the tractors. . . . It was all very bad and difficult—but necessary.

Isaac Deutscher recalls:

In that critical period the author traveled in Russia and the Ukraine. He remembers a striking account of the collectivization that was given to him in a railway carriage on the way from Moscow to Kharkov, by a Colonel of the GPU. The Colonel was completely broken in spirit by his recent experiences in the countryside. "I am an old Bolshevik," he said, almost sobbing. "I worked in the underground against the Tsar and then I fought in the Civil War. Did I do all that in order that I should now surround villages with machine guns and order my men to fire indiscriminately into crowds of peasants? Oh, no, no!"

On the other hand, this writer also traveled, unchaperoned, through the Ukraine about the same time, and talked on trains (in bad high school German) with various people, not one of whom—presumably in fear—said anything against the regime.

How many people were killed by Stalin in the purge of the peasants, nobody knows or will ever know; the estimates range from three to ten million. There were at this time three types of peasants. The richest, the Kulaks, were those who not only worked on their own land but hired labor to help them; there were about one and a half or two million of these. A "middle peasant" worked his land aided by his family only, and these numbered fifteen to eighteen million. A poor peasant, of whom there were five to eight million, was one who could not support himself by work on his own land but had to supplement his income by hiring out for wages part of the time; most of these were so poverty-stricken they could not afford an iron plow, but used a wooden one. In theory, Stalin's purge was directed only against the Kulaks but in fact, in large areas almost everyone was wiped out.

During the struggle, the starving peasants slaughtered many of their livestock for food. More than half of the horses were killed, nearly half the cattle, and two-thirds of the sheep and goats.

When the orgy of mass murder of the peasants was over, Stalin tried to escape the responsibility by announcing that the misdeeds had been the work of his wicked subordinates. Whether anyone believed him, it is now impossible to say.

In 1932 a tragic incident occurred. In 1918, Stalin had married for a second time, Nadezhda Alliluyev, the daughter of a friend in St. Petersburg, Serge Alliluyev, whose home had long been a rallying point for the Bolsheviks hiding from the police. In November, 1932, the dictator and his wife are supposed to have had an ugly public quarrel in the course of a party at the home of Voroshilov. She is reported to have reproached Stalin for letting so many peasants die, and for the prevailing atmosphere of terror. He is said to have scolded her very sharply, with the result that she went home and committed suicide. (There are apocryphal stories that he killed her, or had her killed, but there is no evidence that this is true.)

Stalin and Nadezhda had a daughter, Svetlana, who has been described as "a sweet girl." They also had a son, Vasili, who grew up to be a worthless young roisterer. By nepotism unalloyed by any merit, he became a General in the Soviet Air Force.

The urgent problems at home were paralleled by complications abroad. By now Soviet Russia had formal diplomatic relations with many other countries, with large embassy or consulate staffs. (Special schools were set up in Moscow to train future diplomats in the table manners and other customs of the countries to which they would be assigned.) Every Soviet Embassy and every other Russian official group abroad was, as it is to this day, a nest of spies. At about this time, Great Britain had discovered that the Soviet Trade Delegation in London was engaged in espionage, and had broken off diplomatic relations—a grave blow to Russian prestige.

The British storm finally blew over, but another more serious one developed. In China the dictator Generalissimo Chiang Kai-shek had had a firm alliance with the Chinese Communists for some years; now he repudiated this agreement and began imprisoning or executing all of them he could lay his hands on. Stalin had defended the alliance with the "bourgeois" Christian Generalissimo against the advice of Russian skeptics, and now he had to perform a quick change of policy; since all Communists throughout the world were under Russian tutelage, he was criticized when anything went wrong.

At home, things continued to be bad. The ruble had lost about ninety-seven percent of its value, and production of all kinds of goods was still lagging, in spite of efforts to pull the country up by its bootstraps in a series of Five-Year Plans, each setting higher goals than the one before. The factories reintroduced the hated piecework system, with punishment for those who failed to meet their quotas, and bonuses for those who did. You could not quit your job without permission, or move from one city to another. The borders of the workers' paradise were now guarded with bloodhounds. To divert people's minds from their lack of food, clothes, and housing, Stalin, like many another dictator, raised the spectre of possible attack on Soviet Russia by the capitalist powers. The story was plausible because people remembered how France, Great Britain, and the United States had aided the White Russians in the civil war a decade earlier.

Since Russia needed production so desperately, the dictator began using the carrot as well as the whip. A young coal miner named Aleksey Stakhanov, by heroic endeavor, greatly exceeded the production expected of him, and his name was soon applied to people doing any sort of work, who managed to outproduce everyone else by a wide margin. The Stakhanovites were given decorations and glorified in the newspapers; so many tried to emulate them that production was in fact substantially expanded. Standards of work had been so low in the old Russia, however, that even the Stakhanovites frequently did no more than approach the normal output of an American worker.

Soon there came the first large formal treason trial, a pilot model for those that were to rock Russia a few years later. The production of coal was going badly, and about fifty leading engineers were arrested and accused of sabotaging production, installing defective machinery, and conspiring with foreign capitalists to undermine the Soviet economy. As was to happen regularly in the future, nearly all the accused men made formal confessions; in their desperate plight they not only admitted the crimes with which they were charged but others—some of which they could not possibly have committed.

Early in 1933, Hitler took control of Germany, a development for which Stalin, as noted earlier, was largely responsible. With the Führer in the saddle, Stalin's problem soon became acute. The Russians feared the French and the Germans more than anyone else; they consistently overrated the former, and for a time they underrated the latter. Hitler in his early days was playing a double game; he tried to persuade the Western Powers that he was a barrier against the Red Tide from the East, while at the same time he emphasized to the Russians the "Socialist" aspect of his National Socialist (Nazi) regime and its supposed hostility to private capitalism. Some commentators believe that the Western Powers secretly encouraged Hitler's rearmament in the hope that he would in fact prove a bulwark against the Communists, but far more important in the mild policy of the West toward Hitler was war weariness and the quasi-religious pacifism of many of the rising generation.

Stalin, as might be expected, was completely opportunistic

in his foreign policy. He permitted Hitler to conduct on Russian soil military exercises and experiments which were still forbidden in Germany itself by the Treaty of Versailles of 1919. The Georgian did his best to be friendly with Mussolini, ignoring his merciless persecution of Italian Communists. When the Duce launched his unprovoked war against Ethiopia, Russia sold the Italians airplane gasoline, though most of the Western Powers were refusing to do so. Stalin's efforts at friendship were thwarted when the three chief Fascist Powers formed an anti-Communist alliance: the Berlin-Rome-Tokyo Axis.

The Russian dictator now felt that he must have more friends in the democracies, and accordingly executed a right-about-face with the creation of the "Popular Front." Communists all over the world who had been bitterly fighting the moderate Socialists were suddenly ordered by Moscow to begin fraternizing with them, and tamely proceeded to do so. The idea of world revolution was now ostentatiously dropped. When Roy Howard, head of the United Press, asked Stalin whether this objective had really been abandoned, Stalin replied with a thumping falsehood: "We never had such plans and intentions. . . . This is the product of a misunderstanding. Not a tragic one; a comical one—or perhaps, tragi-comic."

While Stalin was still fearful of Hitler in the West and the Japanese Fascists in the East, the Spanish Civil War broke out, the Fascists rising against the coalition government which was elected in 1936 and was supported by Republicans, Socialists, Communists, and Syndicalists. Germany and Italy immediately came to the aid of the Fascists, who were headed by General Francisco Franco; with as much secrecy as possible under the circumstances they sent soldiers, airplanes, arms, and ammunition to Spain. Stalin was forced by the pressure of Communist opinion throughout the world to give aid to the Spanish Popular Front. He was unhappy about it; fearing a German attack on Russia, he did not want a Communist or quasi-Communist government in Spain, which might help to divide Western Europe, increase the fears of the British and French, and make it less likely that these Powers would help him out. He therefore ordered the Spanish Communists to soft-pedal their revolutionary aims and made this a condition of Russian aid to the hard-pressed Spanish Loyalists.

But unfortunately, he could not control all the left-wing elements among the Loyalists. In Catalonia, a center of resistance to the Fascists, there existed a large semi-Trotskyist organization, the POUM, and the Anarchists and Anarcho-Syndicalists were also powerful. These groups wanted far-reaching radical measures when the War was over. Stalin thereupon ordered their leaders liquidated, and he had enough power among the Spanish Communists to have this done; in a dreadful blood-bath, a war within the War, his bidding was carried out. His errand boy was one Antonov-Ovseenko; when this man returned to Russia, Stalin had him shot so that he could not in the future bear witness to what had been done.

Two years before the Spanish Civil War there had begun the terrible Stalin purge inside Russia itself. One of his loyal supporters, S. M. Kirov, who had been sent to Leningrad to rule that area, was assassinated; there are various theories as to the cause. One explanation is that he was killed by enemies in the Government, and another, that he was shot in a quarrel over a girl. The hypothesis is also advanced that Stalin himself had Kirov assassinated, in order to give an excuse for the wholesale bloodletting that now followed.

Whatever the facts, there is no doubt that the dictator took the excuse to destroy every man who might possibly be a rival for supreme power, and then went on to kill all who he thought were loyal to any of these leaders. "He is," commented Trotsky, "like a man who seeks to slake his thirst with salt water." Before he was through, all the chief leaders from the days of the Revolution had been executed or had committed suicide, except himself and Trotsky, who was at the moment beyond his reach. Kamenev, Zinoviev, Rykov, Bukharin, and Marshal Tukhachevsky were among the old comrades whom he killed. Much of the so-called "evidence" was assembled for him by the head of the secret police, G. G. Yagoda; when the time was ripe, Stalin had Yagoda himself arrested and shot. The evidence against Yagoda was assembled by his successor, N. Yezhov, and he too was presently sent to his grave. Of forty members of Stalin's own personal bodyguard two were shot and the remainder were put into prison, some of them for long terms. The purge was particularly severe in the Army; estimates of the number of officers executed range as high as 20,000

The charge in all these cases was conspiring with various Western Powers and with Trotsky to overthrow the Russian government. The series of trials went on for several years, and some men who were at first found innocent were later retried and executed. Everyone who appeared in public confessed his guilt and recited elaborate details of what he had done; those who gave signs of being "difficult" were secretly executed without trial. One man made the unlikely confession that he had "arranged" hundreds of train wrecks in Siberia. Former Commissar of Finance Grinka confessed that Prime Minister Rykov had told him to underpay large numbers of government employees in order to create discontent.

In almost every case it is quite certain that these men were innocent and their confessions a tissue of lies. They had been Communists all their lives; most of them had suffered in the Tsar's prisons and had worked themselves half to death during the two decades since the Revolution, trying to make it a success.

Why then did they confess, and especially when they knew that they would be shot in any case? Various complicated hypotheses have been brought forward to explain their actions, but it is probable that the real reasons are fairly simple. In 1934 Stalin ordered that whenever a confession was desired the prisoner should be tortured until he gave it; in an unguarded moment the dictator boasted of his technique: "Beat, beat, and beat again." Other methods were also used;

men were half-starved, half-frozen, prevented from sleeping, interrogated ceaselessly day and night, forced to remain standing until they fainted, whereupon they were revived and the torture continued.

The victims knew that if they did not talk in the open court as they had been instructed to do they would go back to the cells and the torture would continue. Some of them hoped that if they were "coöperative" their families might be spared similar treatment—a hope that was frequently vain. And finally, some of the prisoners, clinging as doomed men will to the last faint hope, however spurious, may have believed that if they coöperated fully their lives might after all be spared.

We know from the lips of Nikita Khrushchev in his 1956 denunciation of Stalin how elaborate were the preparations for these public confessions. Men were coached and drilled daily for many months in names, dates, and details. Great pains were taken to see that the falsehoods told by one man fitted in with those told by another. Even so, there were some slips. One man told of conspiring with Trotsky in a Copenhagen hotel which did not exist at the time he specified; and another mentioned meeting a conspirator at an airfield where records proved he could not have done so. From his exile, Trotsky made public record after record showing that he could not have plotted with the supposed traitors on the dates and in the places specified.

In 1936 and 1937 the public confessions told of plotting chiefly with Trotsky and Hitler; in 1938, France, Great Britain, and the United States were included. Eugene Lyons in his biography of Stalin suggests that in the first two years Stalin still hoped to make some sort of deal with the democratic Western Powers, and therefore omitted them from the trumped-up confessions; in 1938, Lyons thinks, he had given up this hope. The testimony that almost all these victims were guiltless comes from the best possible source—Stalin's successor. In his 1956 speech, Khrushchev flatly asserted their innocence. "Actually," he said, "they were never enemies, spies, wreckers, et cetera, but they were always honest Communists; they were only so stigmatized, and often, no longer able to bear barbaric tortures, they charged themselves (at the order of the investigative judges—falsifiers) with all sorts of grave and unlikely crimes." Khrushchev reported that of 139 members of the Central Committee of the Communist Party, 98 were shot. Of 1,966 delegates to the Seventeenth Party Congress, 1,108 were arrested, and presumably most or all of them were shot.

Khrushchev says that confessions were obtained "with the help of cruel and inhuman torture." He quotes a letter written by one of these men, an old Bolshevist named Robert Eikhe, to Stalin:

> Not being able to suffer the tortures to which I was submitted by Ushakov and Nikolayev [NKVD investigators]—and especially by the first one—who utilized the knowledge that my broken ribs had not properly mended, and have caused me great pain, I have been forced to accuse myself and others.

This confession of guilt, he says, was dictated to him and then altered many times to get the "facts" to fit each other.

> I have never betrayed you or the Party. I know that I perish because of vile and mean work of the enemies of the Party and of the people, who fabricated the provocation against me.

In court, however, Eikhe managed somehow to muster up his courage and repudiated his confession.

> The most important thing for me is to tell the Court, the Party and Stalin that I am not guilty. I have never been guilty of any conspiracy. I will die believing in the truth of Party policy as I have believed in it during my whole life.

Stalin was not impressed by this plea. Forty-eight hours later Eikhe was shot.

Sometimes the police were quite frank with their victims.

A man named Rozenblum was brought before Leonid Zakovsky of the secret police, who told him:

> You yourself will not need to invent anything. The NKVD will prepare for you a ready outline for every branch of the center [for treasonable activities]; you will have to study it carefully and be ready [for trial] in four or five months or perhaps half a year. During all this time you will be preparing yourself so that you will not compromise the investigation and yourself. Your future will depend on how the trial goes and on its results.

Zakovsky then explained to the victim the slightly ambiguous phrase, "your future." If Rozenblum did badly in the trial, he would be subjected to additional torture before he was shot. If he did well, he would be shot without extra suffering.

With the purge concluded, Stalin had done away with every man who had the slightest spark of independence; he was now surrounded by those who could be depended upon to do his bidding: Vyacheslav Molotov, Lazar Kaganovich, Klimenti Voroshilov, Nikita Khrushchev, Anastas Mikoyan, Andrei Gromyko, Jacob Malik, Georgi Malenkov, Andrei Zhdanov. There was now no one left who dared tell him he had made a mistake.

From about 1935, Stalin had to divide his attention between the process of trying and executing all of his oldest friends and comrades in arms and seeking to keep Russia safe in view of the general war which he correctly sensed was impending. He feared the Fascist and the democratic powers about equally; he also feared an alliance between both groups, aimed at the Soviet Union. At the same time he wanted the Western countries to be strong in a military sense, in case they should finally come in with him and against the Fascists. The Communists everywhere had been taking a pacifist line; where they were members of national legislatures they voted against budgets for armaments. Stalin now ordered this policy reversed, and to emphasize that he meant business he shot a few pacifist Communists at home who were unable to make the 180-degree turn as quickly as he wished.

In 1935, the Russian dictator signed an inconclusive and more or less meaningless mutual-security pact with France. When Pierre Laval visited Moscow in the course of these negotiations, he urged Stalin to treat the Roman Catholics in Russia a little better, which Laval said would ease France's relations with the Pope. "The Pope!" Stalin is supposed to have said. "How many divisions has *he* got?" (Stalin may have made this rather grim joke on various occasions; both Churchill and de Gaulle claimed to have heard him say the same thing.)

In 1938, Russian Foreign Minister Maxim Litvinov told the Czechs that the USSR would fight to protect them from Germany if France would agree to do the same; but France, in the paralysis of will that afflicted both that country and Great Britain at this time, refused any such obligation. (Perhaps she distrusted the Russians' promise.) Both Poland and Rumania, fearing Hitler, announced that they would not permit Russian troops to cross their territory on the way to help Czechoslovakia. Poland, in fact, refused to join an anti-German pact with Russia on the ground that if there were war, the Poles would be too busy protecting their own country to turn in and help the Soviet Union as well! The low opinion of the Russian Army thus indicated was shared by all the Western Powers and by the United States; it was generally believed that by shooting thousands of Red Army officers in the great purge, Stalin had fatally weakened its efficiency.

A conference of the Powers opposed to Hitler met in Moscow but came to nothing. Prime Minister Neville Chamberlain later asked Russia to guarantee the frontiers of Poland and Rumania, but he offered no *quid pro quo* from the West.

Stalin now began making overtures to Hitler, even though the German dictator as far back as September, 1936, had announced his intention of annexing not only the Ukraine, in Western Russia, but Siberia. To placate the German, Stalin dismissed Foreign Minister Litvinov, a Jew, replacing him by the indubitably Aryan Molotov. The Russian dictator suddenly began to make speeches from which he omitted his customary vituperation of Hitler, and the latter took the hint. After months of negotiation, the German Foreign Minister, Joachim von Ribbentrop, saw Stalin, on August 23, 1939, and the notorious German-Russian pact was announced.

By guaranteeing Hitler against having to fight on two fronts at once, it made the Second World War not only possible, but inevitable; the conflict began a week later. Ostensibly, the pact merely said that each country would remain neutral if the other got into a war; in fact, however, there was a secret protocol which divided up vast territories in Eastern Europe. Russia got Poland as far west as Warsaw; three independent countries, Finland, Estonia and Latvia; and the Rumanian province of Bessarabia. Hitler, whose ambitions temporarily ran in other directions, contented himself with Lithuania.

The Communists in other parts of the world had been given no warning of this shattering shift in policy, but managed as usual to reverse themselves overnight. Until that moment, Hitler had been "a degenerate beast"; now he was presented in a favorable light and it was the Western Powers who were "capitalistic degenerates."

Many people profess bewilderment that the Communists in foreign countries should surrender all independence of judgment and abandon the dictates of common sense, to parrot whatever is the Soviet line at any given moment. This is certainly not, in most cases, because they are "hired by Moscow gold"; as noted, most of them get little or no financial reward, and indeed, they often continue in the Party at heavy financial sacrifice.

One thing to remember is the psychology that turns men and women to the ranks of Communism. In a country like Russia, where it is in control, the people with unusual initiative and aggressiveness, who would be leaders in any society, turn almost automatically to Party membership. This may also be true in a country of great poverty, where there is little opportunity for individual advancement; in India, for example, the Party finds many recruits among university graduates who can get either no job or a poor one.

In the United States the situation is different. Here very

few seek Party membership except those who feel rejected for one reason or another—the misfits, the people who turn their personal psychological difficulties into defiance of prevailing authority, political or economic. Such individuals are often seeking a father image, and they find it in Communism, which does all their thinking for them, answers all questions, and exerts tremendous moral pressure against any independence of spirit. Once they have made this intellectual commitment, the Communists have nowhere else to go. If they were to admit that what Moscow orders is wrong, that its analysis of what is going on in the world is often naïve or bull-headedly ignorant, they would be admitting that they themselves had been acting like a pack of fools. Such avowal of error is always hard.

However, Moscow's frequent reversals of policy have in fact disgusted beyond endurance many thousands of individuals, especially in the United States and the countries of the British Commonwealth. The Party in America lost a large section of its membership overnight when the Hitler-Stalin Pact of 1939 was announced; by 1960, it was estimated that it had not more than a quarter of the strength it enjoyed in the mid-thirties, when the Great Depression was at its worst and capitalism really did seem to many superficial observers to be tottering.

When Poland was conquered by the Germans in about three weeks, Stalin proceeded to occupy all the territory he dared to, including the three Baltic states. On November 30, 1939, when the World War was three months old, Russia attacked Finland, announcing that the Finnish Army had invaded the USSR; as Eugene Lyons remarks, we were asked to believe that a nation of 4 million started a war against one of 180 million.

Stalin's propagandists, who by now did not dare tell him the truth about anything, had assured him that the Finnish Communists were so strong that as soon as a token force of the Red Army had crossed the frontier they would rise and seize the country. On the contrary, the brave Finns put up such a resistance that they rocked the Russians back on their heels. The Western Allies did very little to help the Finns, pleading that Norway and Sweden, who feared Hitler's wrath, would not let Allied troops cross their territory; they ignored the ice-free Finnish port of Petsamo on the Arctic Ocean (now Pechenga, in the USSR). It is possible that the Allies were inactive in the hope that Russia might still come over to their side. In about four months the Finns succumbed under the overwhelming weight of numbers, and sued for peace in March, 1940. Russia was expelled from the League of Nations for her assault on Finland.

Throughout 1940, Stalin continued to consolidate his position in Eastern Europe. He occupied Bessarabia and another Rumanian province, North Bukovina. Hitler was now showing more interest in that part of the world, sending German troops into Rumania and Finland, "to guard," he explained to Stalin, "against the English menace." Seeking to make sure that Russia would remain quiescent until Germany was ready to go to war in the East as well as the West, he offered Stalin India and large chunks of other parts of the British Empire, which he described loosely as "forty million square kilometers."

Stalin, equally hypocritical, offered to join the German-Italian-Japanese Axis, provided Hitler would turn over Bulgaria to Russia and help Stalin get a lengthy lease on bases in the Dardanelles, to make possible Russia's centuries-long dream of access to the seven seas through an ice-free port. Taking a lesson from Hitler, Russia early in 1941 signed a neutrality pact with Japan, which saved her from having to fight on two fronts—and incidentally freed Japan's hands and thereby made Pearl Harbor possible.

The espionage service of the Allies learned, as noted earlier, that Hitler, ignoring his treaty, was planning to attack Russia; Churchill even gave Stalin the date, but the Russian refused to believe it and was caught completely by surprise when the invasion began on June 22, 1941. Just as had happened after the Russian Revolution in 1917, German troops rolled eastward through the Ukraine; most Western military experts were sure that this phase of the War would end within a month or two.

In the first thirty days the Germans advanced 450 miles; in a short time they had taken 500,000 Russian prisoners on the Dnieper River, had cut off and blockaded Leningrad, had occupied almost the entire Ukraine, and were at the gates of Moscow. They had captured forty percent of the Russian population, two-thirds of the facilities for coal and pig iron, nearly two-thirds of those for steel and aluminum, forty percent of the grain, eighty percent of the sugar production, and forty percent of the railroad mileage. Industrial output available to Stalin was down by one-half, steel by two-thirds, ball bearings by ninety-five percent. The Government had to flee from Moscow far east to Kuibyshev, and 1,600 factories were transported complete to new sites beyond the Volga.

While Stalin was still in power, Russian propaganda made much of the idea that when his government left he had stayed behind in Moscow to conduct in person the defense of the beleaguered city; but in 1956 Khrushchev denied that this was true. He said that the dictator always kept far from the front. On the other hand, Averell Harriman, former American Ambassador to Russia, in his book *Peace with Russia?* speaks of conferring with Stalin in Moscow when the German attack was at its height.

Khrushchev also belittled Stalin as a military leader. Khrushchev cited an instance when he was with the army that was under orders to attempt to retake the city of Kharkov. The officers in the field decided that it would be fatal to attempt this and Khrushchev tried to get Stalin on the telephone and tell him so. The dictator refused to answer the phone at this critical moment, merely sending word by a secretary that the original plans must be carried out. As a result, "the Germans surrounded our army concentrations and we lost hundreds of thousands of our soldiers." Khrushchev said that Stalin did his military planning by means of a globe, refusing to use a large-scale map. He intimated strongly that the dictator was such a coward he concentrated masses of weapons at places where they would protect his own person, leaving the soldiers in the field to shift as best they could.

A very different picture of Stalin as a strategist is painted by Winston Churchill, himself, as reported, an amateur of military science. In his history of the Second World War, he tells of discussing with Stalin the proposed landings in North Africa, and of how quickly the Russian grasped half a dozen important implications of the campaign.

A more important witness on Stalin's side is Lord Alanbrooke, chief of the British Imperial General Staff and Chairman of the Allied Chiefs of Staff Committee. In the book, *Triumph in the West,* based on his diaries, Alanbrooke says of Stalin's part in the discussions at Teheran, at which he was present:

> I rapidly grew to appreciate the fact that he had a military brain of the very highest calibre. Never once in any of his statements did he make any strategic error, nor did he ever fail to appreciate all the implications of a situation with a quick and unerring eye.

At another meeting in Moscow, Alanbrooke asked Stalin about the possibility of a campaign against the Japanese in Eastern Siberia.

> He displayed an astounding knowledge of technical railway details, had read the past history of fighting in that theatre, and from this knowledge drew very sound deductions. I was more than ever impressed by his military ability.

As an ally, Stalin was certainly difficult almost beyond belief. When the War began he was in such a panic that he begged Roosevelt to send American troops, led by American generals, to fight on Russian soil; but as soon as he had recovered his balance, he refused to let the Allies use Russian territory under any circumstances or for any purpose. The war effort was severely crippled because Allied bombers were not allowed to shuttle across Germany between Great Britain and Russia. Stalin began to demand a second front within a few days after the Germans invaded his territory, and repeated the demand in a towering rage (simulated or real), whenever he met any important official of an Allied government, ignoring the fact that such an attempt was impossible with the limited men and supplies then available. It was at this time that in the presence of Churchill and his aides the Russian several times accused the British of cowardice and said that if their troops could only muster up enough courage to meet the Germans face to face as the Soviet soldiers had done, they "would not be so frightened of them."

Colonel Louis Reichers, of the United States Air Force, flew a dangerous mission from Scotland to Moscow, carrying Averell Harriman (who was to arrange for Lend-Lease materials for Russia) plus a group of technical experts and Constantine Oumansky, then Russian Ambassador to the United States. In his book, *The Flying Years,* Reichers gives a detailed description of the Russians' seeming efforts to make the flight end in disaster. They refused to send in advance vitally necessary weather information (to avoid the Germans, the route looped above the Scandinavian Peninsula). The Russians told Reichers to land at Archangel, on a field which was under water and out of use, so that he had to continue non-stop—unexpectedly—to Moscow. The Russian military radio never answered any of his signals during the flight across Russian territory, but several Russian fighter planes came up and gave every evidence of intending to shoot down the American plane; they were scared off only when the tail gunner trained his weapon on them and acted as though he were about to fire. Arriving over Moscow, Reichers selected an airport at random and landed.

Nobody ever explained the extraordinary behavior of the Russians. There has been speculation that Stalin had come to distrust Oumansky, did not want to go through the formality of trying him, and hoped that he would die in "an airplane accident"—indifferent to the fate of the members of the Lend-Lease commission and the crew of the plane. (Oumansky did in fact die in an unexplained airplane accident some time later, just after taking off from Mexico City.)

Once Russia was in the War, the Allies sent her enormous masses of material; there can be little doubt that without this help she would have been forced to capitulate. Some of this came up through Iran, but a large part was sent by ship around the Scandinavian Peninsula to Murmansk or Archangel. The losses on this route by enemy action were heavy; of 34 British freighters sent in one convoy from Iceland to Archangel in 1942, 23 were sunk, with a loss of nearly all members of their crews. In a three months' period in the same year, of 84 ships which sailed from the United States for Murmansk, 33 were lost in storms or because of enemy action.

Whatever may have been Stalin's faults as a military leader, some of his Generals must have been very good indeed—aided, certainly, by Hitler's arrogance, which led him into bad blunders. The siege of Moscow was lifted, as I have said, partly because Hitler neglected to issue winter uniforms to his troops, or to realize that his vehicles could not operate in deep snow, or run at all in winter, unless specially equipped for operation at low temperatures.

There were numerous Russian centers of hostility to the Communist government, where people fraternized with the Germans, or tried to. As soon as he was able, Stalin inflicted Carthaginian punishment on whole areas inhabited by national minorities, including, of course, many thousands of completely innocent people. On the Volga there was a centuries-old German settlement; it was destroyed, and those inhabitants not executed were sent to exile in the Siberian wastes. This was also done to the Crimean Republic, and to the Chechen, Ingush, Karachai, Kalmyk, and Balkar tribes.

The turning point of the War in the East was the successful defense of Stalingrad. Partly because the city had been renamed for him (it was formerly Tsaritsyn), partly because he had himself operated there in the early days of the Revolution, Stalin ordered that it be held, regardless of the cost in human life. The city was smashed by bombardment, but the Red Army and many of the civilian inhabitants went on fighting in the rubble. All bridges across the Volga having been destroyed, supports for a new one were put down by men who worked at night, often in bitter cold; to keep the Germans from knowing about the bridge, nothing was allowed to show above the surface until the last minute. The German generals were frantically asking Hitler for winter uniforms, food, and ammunition, but he sent them only token amounts. Finally the Russians struck from behind the city with a pincers movement which encircled the Germans simultaneously from the north and south. On February 1, 1943 came the surrender which involved 285,000 German soldiers, Field Marshal von Paulus, and 23 Nazi generals.

From that day on, Hitler never managed to recover his balance in the East. In January, 1944, the siege of Leningrad was lifted, and every month thereafter saw fresh Russian successes; in the spring the Crimea was recaptured. By August, the Russian troops were in Rumania; in the next two months they overran Estonia and Latvia; and by the end of 1944, they were in Budapest. In January, 1945, Red soldiers entered East Prussia and Czechoslovakia, and on April 25, Russian and American patrols made an historic and emotional contact at Torgau, in Saxony. On May 2, the Russians captured Berlin, Hitler having committed a Wagnerian suicide the day before. In the next forty-eight hours, all the German forces surrendered and the European phase of the War was over.

Berlin was put under joint control of the Allies, but the Russian zone of influence extended many miles to the west, leaving the German capital as an enclave far inside Red territory. Bitter controversy broke out almost at once—and continues to the present day—over the fact that the Allies had held their troops back and permitted the Russians to come far to the west. British Field Marshal Montgomery, as already recorded, believed he could have made a quick slash through to Berlin and has never forgiven the Americans for refusing to permit this. On April 22, 1945, Drew Pearson, the American newspaper columnist, wrote that on April 13, American patrols were in Potsdam, a suburb of Berlin, but were then withdrawn to the River Elbe, fifty miles away, because of an agreement made at Yalta that the Russians were to occupy Berlin. Harry Hopkins commented indignantly:

> This story by Drew Pearson is absolutely untrue. There was no agreement made at Yalta whatever that the Russians should enter Berlin first. Indeed, there was no discussion of that whatever. The Chiefs of Staffs had agreed with the Russian Chiefs of Staff and Stalin on the general strategy which was that both of us were going to push as hard as we could.

Hopkins admits that General Omar Bradley, commanding the American forces, did get a division "well out toward Potsdam" but says it had "far outreached itself," ran short of supplies, and had to fall back.

General Eisenhower, Commander-in-Chief of all Allied Forces, was in a difficult position. His orders were to pursue and destroy the German Army, not to take action for political purposes. When he asked the Joint Chiefs of Staff for instructions as to the course he was to follow, they did not answer him.

Nobody realized how fast the German resistance was disintegrating, and how rapidly the Allies would be able to move forward. It is also true that hardly anybody—Winston Churchill was among the few exceptions—attached much importance to where the line of demarcation between East and West was drawn. Nearly everyone took it for granted that a peace conference would soon be held, following which all foreign troops would withdraw from German soil, and the country would go back to its prewar status, except for some readjustment of the eastern boundary.

Finland, smarting under the defeat by the Russians in

March, 1940, took advantage of Hitler's attack in June, 1941, and came into the war on Germany's side. In September, 1944, the Finns were again defeated by the Russians, who once more imposed harsh terms. The little country had to pay $300 million in reparations, and also lost substantial amounts of territory on or near the Russian border. (In 1948, as a gesture useful in political propaganda elsewhere, Stalin cancelled $75 million of the bill for reparations and returned some territory.)

Throughout the War, Stalin constantly accused the Western Allies of seeking to make a separate peace with Hitler, at Russia's expense. He repeatedly charged that their postwar plans included the permanent alienation of Russian territory. In spite of the huge masses of material he received, the delivery of which cost many thousands of lives, he also said that "they want us to bleed in order to dictate to us their terms later on." Whenever possible, the origin of foreign military goods was concealed and the Russian people were told that the tanks, trucks, guns, and planes had come from their own factories.

Russia's losses in the War were certainly huge. As her armies retreated in the early days of the conflict, Stalin ordered a "scorched earth" policy, destroying as much as possible so that it should not fall into the enemy's hands. Whatever the Russians had left, the Germans wrecked when they in turn retreated. Officially, the Russians said that they had lost 3 million soldiers and 7 million civilians. In 1959, long after the end of the War, an American research organization, the Population Reference Bureau of Washington, D.C., after careful study, announced that the number killed was more like 15 to 20 million, with 45 to 60 million wounded, many of them permanently disabled. The Russians, with their usual psychotic fear of a possible attack by their late Allies, had understated their losses in order to conceal their military weakness.

Both during and after the War, Stalin was jealous of brilliant military leaders like Marshals Georgi Zhukov, Semyon Timoshenko, and Klimenti Voroshilov, and tried to belittle their part in the War. In 1949 he ordered a motion picture made, *The Fall of Berlin,* dealing with the capture of that city —a victory accomplished with great skill by Marshal Zhukov. In the picture, all the credit goes to Stalin; Zhukov appears only for a few seconds, taking orders from the dictator.

Stalin also circulated slanderous attacks on Zhukov's military competence. One was the utterly baseless charge that "before each operation at the Front, Zhukov used to take a handful of earth, smell it, and say, 'We can begin the attack,' or the opposite, 'The planned operation cannot be carried out.' "

Another propaganda motion picture made at Stalin's orders to be shown inside Russia portrayed that country as having won the war against Japan single-handed. It included the American newsreel scene showing the Japanese envoys signing the surrender to General MacArthur on board the U.S. Battleship *Missouri;* the Russian commentary suggested that these were Soviet officers receiving the surrender on board a Russian battleship.

In 1943 it was discovered that about 10,000 Polish Army officers had been massacred in the Katyn Forest near Smolensk. Hitler and Stalin promptly accused each other of having murdered these men; a careful investigation after the end of the War leaves no doubt that the Russians were guilty. Stalin, however, never admitted his guilt, and when the Polish Government-in-Exile, in London, refused to fall in with his explanation, he used this as a pretext to do what he would certainly soon have done in any case: he set up a competing puppet government of his own.

In 1944, Warsaw was in the hands of the Germans, but many of the inhabitants had secret caches of arms, and had been authorized by the London Polish Government to stage an uprising whenever the right moment seemed to have arrived. On July 20 came the news of the attempt by German army officers to kill Hitler, suggesting widespread unrest. At about the same time the Allies, who had landed in Normandy on June 6, broke out of the beachhead and started to fight their way across France. The Poles intercepted radio messages from the German High Command to their troops on the eastern front ordering them to fall back west of the Vistula River, which flows through Warsaw; they did so, and the Russians advanced until they were only a few miles from the city. The Poles in Warsaw, commanded by General Bor-Komorowski, decided that the time had arrived for them to revolt, and bitter house-to-house and hand-to-hand fighting broke out all over the city. But now Stalin ordered his troops to stop, and they stood idle, week after week, while the reinforced German garrison proceeded to slaughter thousands of the people of Warsaw. Stalin's unadmitted reason was that the Polish guerrillas were taking orders from the non-Communist government in London and not from his own puppet regime in Lublin.

The British and Americans proposed to send planes to drop arms, ammunition, and supplies to the Poles; the round trip from the western front was too long for the aircraft of that era, and they planned to have them land in Russia and refuel for the return trip. Stalin, as before, refused to permit this. He denounced the Polish guerrillas, saying: "Sooner or later the truth about the group of criminals who have embarked on the Warsaw adventure in order to seize power will become known to everybody." Repeatedly, Roosevelt and Churchill asked him to change his attitude; repeatedly he refused. Churchill was sorely tempted to suggest to the Americans that all Lend-Lease to Russia be stopped, as a means of bringing pressure to bear upon the dictator, but he knew that this was impossible. As he commented later, "Everyone has to keep in mind the fortunes of millions of men fighting in a worldwide struggle and that terrible and even humbling submissions must at times be made to the general aim."

Six weeks later, when he was sure that most of the Warsaw patriots were dead, Stalin made a pretense of modifying his policy a little. On September 10, the Russians lobbed a few shells onto German positions in the eastern part of the city. Red troops got as far as the suburbs, but then halted again.

Beginning on September 14, Russian planes dropped a few supplies, but whether by accident or design, most of the parachutes failed to open and the packages were smashed. The Germans were finally driven out of Warsaw, but not until many of those Poles whom Stalin considered unfriendly to him had been liquidated.

At the successive meetings with top British and American leaders, Stalin made various sweeping demands on behalf of the USSR. He wanted postwar control of Rumania and Bulgaria, and a large share of eastern Poland—both of which ambitions he later achieved by force of arms. He proposed that after victory 50,000 leading Germans, both civilians and military men, should be shot in order to cripple that country for a long time to come. He wanted a return to the infamous secret treaties of the First World War, through which Great Britain, France, Italy, and Russia agreed to carve up most of Europe—and many other parts of the world—to suit themselves. These proposals were rejected. At Yalta, in February, 1945, as already reported, he made still more demands, some of which were accepted.

The next meeting of the Allied chiefs of state was held July 17 to August 2 at Potsdam, Germany, after the German surrender and less than a month before Japan capitulated. Harry Truman was now the American President; and in the middle of the conference, Churchill's government fell and he was succeeded as Prime Minister by Clement Attlee, of the Labor Party.

Stalin made still more new and extreme demands. Hinting that he intended to do as he pleased in Poland, the Balkans, and Greece, he asked for some territory that would be taken from Turkey, control of the Dardanelles, control of one of the former Italian colonies in North Africa, and partial control of the Ruhr, in Western Germany, with its rich coal and steel resources.

Truman and Attlee were more hard-boiled than Roosevelt and Churchill had been, and they said no to most of these demands. They did agree, however, to a Russian scheme that sowed the seeds of unending trouble. A large section of Eastern Poland was given to Russia, and to compensate the Poles they were given a corresponding part of East Germany; in other words, the whole Polish state was moved toward the west. Among other things this meant that between nine and ten million Germans living in the newly confiscated areas had all their property taken and had to flee in haste and confusion into West Germany.

The first successful atom-bomb explosion took place in the New Mexican desert on July 16, and Truman was notified of it at Potsdam (the coded telegram he received read, "babies satisfactorily born"). At the end of one formal session, he drew Stalin aside and solemnly told him of the existence of the bomb; Stalin sucked at his always-present pipe and asked no questions, which struck Truman as singular. As we know, Stalin had stolen the secrets of the atom bomb some time earlier, through a group of spies headed by Klaus Fuchs, a German-born devoted Communist working at Los Alamos as a member of a British delegation of physicists; the Churchill Government, with an amazing lapse, had failed to check his background.

At the Potsdam Conference, Stalin told Truman that the Japanese Emperor had made a peace offer through his ambassador at Moscow, Naotake Sato; not until fifteen years after the end of the War were the facts about the negotiations (revealed from papers in the American State Department) first published by two newspapermen, Fletcher Knebel and Charles W. Bailey, in the *Des Moines Register and Tribune*. According to this account, Stalin asked the American President what sort of reply should be made, pointing out that the peace offer could be accepted or rejected, or an equivocal reply could be sent. Truman remarked that he did not trust the Japanese. After some further discussion it was decided—about three weeks before the bomb was dropped on Hiroshima—to "stall off" the Emperor. The Allies sent a reply reiterating the demand for unconditional surrender and threatening as an alternative "inevitable and complete destruction," which was a very vague reference indeed to the existence of the bomb. Premier Admiral Kantaro Susuki answered indirectly by announcing that Japan would ignore this offer. Ironically, when the surrender finally came, it was not unconditional; the Allies acceded to the Japanese request that Emperor Hirohito be retained on the throne.

Before Potsdam, recognition had been withdrawn from the Polish Government-in-Exile. It was succeeded by a coalition government consisting partly of Russian puppets and partly of individuals acceptable to the West. Before very long, the non-Communists were forced out and Poland was a full-fledged Russian satellite.

With the end of the War, Stalin was freed from many restraints and enabled to return to his own true character. The Comintern, the organization devoted to fomenting revolution in other countries, had been turned on and off like a light several times during the previous decade, to suit the political policy of the moment; now it was turned on again and the dictator, in effect, declared war—a cold war—on the whole non-Communist world. The three Baltic countries, Estonia, Latvia, and Lithuania, having been forcibly incorporated into the Soviet Union, she tightened her grip on the satellites, Poland, Rumania, Hungary, Bulgaria, Albania—and soon, Czechoslovakia.

Only Yugoslavia was to slip from Stalin's control. The Yugoslavs had a dictator of their own, Tito, who had led the Communist Partisans to victory in the War. The Russian dictator insisted he should rule the Yugoslav Army and the secret police, and Tito refused. Stalin told Khrushchev: "I will shake my little finger—and there will be no more Tito. He will fall." But he was wrong; Tito defied him and got away with it.

As the Russian armies tramped westward in the closing months of the War, they and the West got a good look at each other, and both sights were equally revealing. The soldiers were young men who had grown up as victims of the Russian propaganda which said that no matter how poor and miserable they were, the people of the West were still more so. Now they saw that this was not true. Even Eastern Europe, where the standard of living had always been low and the countryside was devastated by six years of war, looked like paradise. The West, on the contrary, saw a horde of near-savages whose conduct was like that of the Goths. They stole everything they could get their hands on; they indulged in rape and drunkenness, their officers making little attempt to restrain them. (Among the art treasures carted off to Russia and never returned was the priceless mass of ancient golden implements found in the ruins of Troy by the famous explorer, Heinrich Schliemann.)

The impact that the West made on the Russians who saw it for themselves was so serious that Stalin had to bend all his efforts towards counteracting it. He set up brain-washing centers—some of them in Siberia—at which Russians returning home could be reindoctrinated and somehow persuaded that what they had seen was not a reality.

During the War, about ten million Russians had been sent to the West, most of them as German war prisoners or slave laborers, a few as refugees. The Allied governments now agreed to Stalin's demands that those who had survived should be forcibly returned to Russia. American and other Allied soldiers helped the Russians to round up a million and a half people who were jammed into freight cars and sent back to the Soviet tyranny. Very few of them wanted to return; some of them had met and married citizens of West European countries and had children. Families were torn apart, never to see each other again; Russians threw themselves on their knees, pleading to be allowed to remain in the West. Numbers—how large, no one will ever know—committed suicide rather than go back.

Even more than in the past, Stalin now dominated every phase of Russian life. No one was permitted to express disagreement with the weird genetic theories of Lysenko; a number of distinguished scientists who proved recalcitrant disappeared and have never been heard of again, presumably having been exiled or shot. A gifted composer of music, Dmitri Shostakovich, whose style in composing tends toward the modern, wrote an opera, *Lady Macbeth of Mzensk,* which ran for two years to packed houses in dozen of theatres all over the USSR before Stalin got around to seeing it. The Caucasian peasant, whose musical taste ran to folksongs, did not like it, and instantly not only this opera but every other work of Shostakovich was banned throughout the country. Only by abject confession of "error" did the composer save himself and manage, after years, to get back into favor.

Stalin was equally the autocrat of painting, sculpture, and writing, in all of which fields his taste was so bad that it could be called nonexistent. His eager hatchet-men waited vigilantly to denounce any creative worker whose product departed from the Stalinist line of the moment.

Toward the end of his life the Georgian, who had killed millions without compunction, got into a panic about his own impending end. The newspapers that he saw accordingly began to print many articles about people who had lived to tremendous ages; such stories seemed to comfort him.

Always suspicious of those around him, he now became more so than ever. In Khrushchev's 1956 speech he calls Stalin "sickly suspicious." The dictator would say to those about him, "Why are your eyes so shifty today?" Or, "Why are you turning so much today and avoiding to look me directly in the eyes?" He distrusted, Khrushchev said, "even eminent party workers whom he had known for years," and called nearly everybody "enemies, two-facers and spies."

In 1948 there appeared a biography of Stalin written, naturally, in terms of servile flattery; but no flattery could satisfy the megalomania of the man, and on the galley proofs he added supplementary praise in his own handwriting. He wrote of himself, in the third person, that he

> upheld the great banner of Lenin, rallied the Party behind Lenin's behest, and brought the Soviet people into the broad

road of industrializing the country and collectivizing the rural economy [as] the guiding force of the Party and the State. . . . Although he performed his task as leader of the Party and the people with consummate skill and enjoyed the unreserved support of the entire Soviet people, Stalin never allowed his work to be marred by the slightest hint of vanity, conceit or self-adulation. . . . Stalin is the worthy continuer of Lenin's work or, as it is said in our Party, Stalin is the Lenin of today.

One of the more ridiculous aspects of Stalin's internal propaganda was the campaign to tell the people that most of the important inventions of the last hundred years had come from Russians. Thus Popov, not Marconi, invented radio; Schilling, not Morse, was responsible for the telegraph; Yablochkov had done the work on the electric light commonly credited to Edison. Other Russian inventions: steam and gasoline engines, the balloon and the airplane, the submarine and the helicopter. These claims seem absurd to us, but the Russians, living all their lives cut off from the rest of the world, probably believe some or all of them.

Having gone back to the doctrine of world revolution, Stalin now began to make trouble everywhere that he could. He seized some territory in northern Iran, and was dislodged with great difficulty only by pressure from the free world. With his support, the Greek Communists broke into open civil war, and Russia seriously threatened Turkey. America's response was the Truman Doctrine, under which the United States offered to supply arms, military instruction, and other help to any country threatened by Communist aggression. It was followed by the Marshall Plan, which gave urgently needed economic aid to the war-crippled countries of Europe. Stalin forbade any of the satellite countries to accept this help, thus dooming millions of people to needless additional misery over a period of years.

Marxian theory, as now interpreted in Russia, said that the United States, which has always been Russia's chief rival and the object of her bitterest hatred, was sure to have a bad depression after the end of the War—a depression that might well be the beginning of the final collapse of capitalism. The Russians confidently built their plans on this expectation, but at the same time, by their truculence in many parts of the world, they frightened the United States into a fairly rapid rearmament. Whatever possibility there may have been of a major American depression was soon counteracted by the huge government expenditures on preparedness, which before long were running at the annual rate of about $40 billion or more.

The fact that the Western Allies controlled West Berlin was a profound irritant to Stalin. Private initiative had restored that section of the ruined city in record time after the War, and its prosperity contrasted with the hunger and misery of East Berlin under the puppet East German Government. Since the Communists controlled all of Germany itself to a point 200 miles west of the city, all goods entering Berlin by rail or road had to pass through Communist territory; in 1948, the Russian dictator decided to force the West out of Berlin and set up a blockade. The city would soon have been starved out, but for the United States and British Air Forces. They proceeded to supply Berlin with everything it needed by means of an air lift, the Americans carrying the heavier part of the load; planes departed every few minutes from West German points, flying in all kinds of weather, and after some months Stalin had to admit defeat.

Two years later began the most serious conflict thus far between the Communist and non-Communist sections of the world—the Korean War. In theory, Stalin had nothing to do with this struggle, which started as a clash between the rival governments of North and South Korea and ended as a war between the Chinese Communists and North Koreans on one side and the United Nations forces, principally American, on the other. In fact, however, all the world knew that Stalin probably instigated the war, and that certainly it could not have begun without his approval. All the Communist warplanes and much of the other materiel were Russian, and whether this equipment was given, loaned, or sold to North Korea and China by the Russians is not important; the Communists never do anything without a political motive.

The fighting, which began on June 24, 1950, had ended by July 10, 1951. Stalin did not live to see the signing of the armistice, which took place more than two years later on July 26, 1953.

The last important episode in the dictator's life was also one of the ugliest. It was the notorious "doctors' purge" of the winter of 1952–53, which was also the worst overt expression of his anti-Semitism. All his life, Stalin was prejudiced against the Jews, but not until about 1948 did this attitude become an official doctrine of the Soviet Government. The censorship was so strong that many people outside Russia still believe his hostility to the Jewish race was an insane aberration of the last few weeks of his life. On the contrary, it had received violent expression for at least the previous four years. Hundreds of outstanding Jews in all walks of life were arrested, tortured, given long prison sentences, or sent into exile, without any shadow of justification. The Yiddish newspapers and publishing house were shut down, and the Yiddish theatres throughout the Soviet Union were closed.

In the doctors' purge several dozen leading physicians of Jewish birth were arrested, including top specialists of the Kremlin Hospital who regularly treated Stalin and all the other leaders of the Government. They were accused of having murdered Zhdanov and Alexander S. Shcherbakov and of attempting to poison Marshal Konev and a number of other people. Several of these physicians were tortured; one of them committed suicide; and one is supposed to have died of a heart attack.

The man responsible for this persecution did not long survive his victims. For some time, Stalin had had a heart ailment, and on March 5, 1953, he died. Reports were afterward circulated that he had been murdered by his associates; a television drama giving this version was shown in the United

States in 1958, and brought bitter repercussions in Russia. In this version, Stalin is shown in a room with several other leaders of the Government; when he suffers a heart attack, urgently needed medicine is brought to him; Khrushchev dashes it to the ground, and Stalin dies.

There is, however, no reason, as far as I can learn, to assume that this story is true. In the summer of 1959, Khrushchev had a talk with Averell Harriman, former American Ambassador to the USSR, and gave him a circumstantial story of Stalin's death. On March 2, according to Khrushchev, Stalin was at his *dacha* (country house) outside Moscow and his head bodyguard called up the Kremlin to say that he was "not well." Four of the chief leaders went at once to the *dacha*— Khrushchev, Lavrenti Beria, Nikolai Bulganin, and Malenkov. They found that the dictator had had a stroke that had paralyzed his arm, leg, and tongue. He lingered for three days, most of the time in a coma, but toward the end he became conscious. On the wall of his bedroom was a painting of a little girl feeding a lamb with a spoon; Stalin pointed to it and gestured to indicate he was now as helpless as the lamb. Khrushchev told Harriman: "A few minutes later he died." Although in 1956 Khrushchev had excoriated Stalin in a philippic rarely matched in modern history, he now seemed to have changed his mind. He told Harriman: "I wept. . . . Like Peter the Great, he fought barbarism with barbarism. But he was a great man."

Harriman asked whom the dictator had chosen to be his successor.

"He never selected anyone. He thought he would live forever."

Was Stalin insane? This is a difficult question to answer, since there are various definitions of insanity. In the United States, the law says you are insane if you are unable to distinguish right from wrong—a definition with which most psychiatrists are in strong disagreement, believing that it results in severe punishment being given people in many cases who are not actually responsible for their acts. In this technical sense, Stalin presumably was sane to the day of his death; certainly he never lost his shrewd grasp of the total situation by which he was confronted. On the other hand, his conduct in the last four or five years of his life suggests delusions of persecution and a flight from reality; some of the men he accused—many of whom were shot—were not only innocent but were in no position to do him any harm. Khrushchev apparently believed that Stalin suffered a marked mental deterioration about the time that Kirov was assassinated in 1934; but years earlier, the dictator had already ordered the death of several million men, women, and children.

We must remember that few of the men who made the Russian Revolution had any compunction about the wholesale slaughter of their enemies. If they did not wade to power through seas of blood, they maintained themselves in control by repeated killings, probably far more than were necessary even under their own brutal philosophy. Their indifference to human life smacks of the Orient, with which in fact Old Russia always had more ties than she had with the West.

Dramatic events followed rapidly upon Stalin's death. The surviving doctors who were in prison were immediately released. A search now began through the slave-labor camps and prisons of the USSR for survivors of the great purges of 1934–38, and those who were still alive were set free; nearly all of them had died, including all the well-known old Bolsheviks. A total of 7,679 persons were officially "rehabilitated," most of them posthumously. Those who were still alive and were released included the Jews who had been persecuted since 1948; pensions were ordered for the families of those who had been killed.

One more chapter remains to the Stalin story. In February, 1956, came the Twentieth Congress of the (Russian) Communist Party. On the 25th, the 1,355 delegates met in an extraordinary secret session at which Khrushchev made his six-hour speech denouncing Stalin. He did his best to keep it secret, and for a time he succeeded, but the U.S. State Department obtained a copy and made it public on June 4. It caused a sensation all over the world. As usual, the servile Communist Parties in other countries were caught unawares, and had to make their customary 180-degree turn, from abject flattery of Stalin to proclaiming that they had known all along that he was no good.

Why did Khrushchev decide after three years to attack the memory of the man who as far as anyone knows was still considered second only to Lenin? Probably there were several reasons. He may have feared that someone else would tell this terrible story and would point out—as is true—that Khrushchev himself and all the other leaders had stood by and condoned crime after crime of the dictator. Perhaps even more important, he felt it was urgently necessary to modify the tremendous tension that had built up between the USSR and the non-Communist world; Stalin was the author of the Cold War, and by repudiating him it was easier to modify his policy.

In his speech, Khrushchev told of the conditions in the Kremlin in Stalin's last years. If Stalin summoned you, he observed, you said goodbye to your family on the assumption that you might never return.

A voice from the hall: "Why didn't you kill him?"

Khrushchev: "What could we do? There was a reign of terror."

Following the speech, the Government began the familiar process of again trying to rewrite history. As had happened before, the *Great Soviet Encyclopedia* had to be modified, the article on Stalin entirely rewritten, and many hundreds of references to old Bolsheviks had to be changed from "traitors" to "heroes." The Stalin Auto Works became the Moscow Auto Works, and parallel changes were made in other names. Numerous projects that involved the glorification of the dictator were dropped or modified—so many that it is reported throngs of people began to visit the joint Lenin-Stalin tomb in Red Square, Moscow, under the Kremlin wall, to see whether Stalin's body was still there. It was, but not for long. On October 31, 1961, Khrushchev, who had come out victorious in several successive bitter struggles for power, had the body removed to a modest grave in a group of several, in a nearby spot just outside the Kremlin wall. No act could have more strikingly symbolized the end of the Stalin era.

In October, 1964, Khrushchev was himself ruthlessly removed from office, but not because of the process of de-Stalinization that he had pursued for eleven years. He was overthrown for a variety of reasons—worsening relations with China, the tendency of Communist parties in other countries to act independently, the failure of his agricultural policy to provide sufficient food. While isolated individuals continued to look back nostalgically to Stalin, the era of the bloody tyrant from the Caucasus was, and had long been, a closed book.

# 5. Mussolini:
# Jackal in the Lion's Skin

IT IS STARTLING to see how the images of Hitler and Mussolini are diverging with the passage of time. The more Hitler recedes, the more terrifying he seems, as we learn further details about his monomania, his indifference to human suffering —indeed, his sadist gloating over it. Mussolini, on the other hand, who once seemed a formidable figure, is being steadily reduced to the status of a comic-opera clown, with his silly vanity, his essential futility, his yielding to Hitler's dominance as soon as the German had hit his stride.

To be sure, Mussolini did not seem a comical figure to contemporary Italian anti-Fascists who were imprisoned, beaten, forced to drink castor oil, exiled to waterless Mediterranean islands. Their tortures were sometimes as severe as those suffered by the victims of any tyrant, anywhere.

Hitler had never had any real occupation until he learned something of the art of war in the German Army. His ambition to be a painter or architect had failed; as an artist he never rose above the level of colored postcards that he sold for a few pennies. Mussolini, on the other hand, had been a successful left-wing journalist, flowery and bombastic by Anglo-Saxon standards but well suited to the audience he was trying to reach, which is all there is to success in journalism. He never lost his love of printer's ink; throughout the dictatorship he continued to write unsigned articles for his old paper in Milan. While these were sometimes useful in turning popular opinion in a desired direction, he had other and more effective means of doing this, and he wrote chiefly just because he wanted to.

He looked irresistibly like an actor pretending to be a dictator, throwing his head back, squaring his big jaw, looking down his nose, turning smiles and frowns on and off like an electric light. During the years that he was in the limelight he was a puritan in many ways, except as to sex, where he was possessed by satyriasis, having relations with scores of women on the most sordid and casual basis. For many years he thought he had a stomach ulcer, and ate a sparse diet consisting mostly of fruit and milk; an autopsy after his death revealed damage to his stomach so slight that we can only conclude most of his severe and prolonged stomach pains were psychosomatic.

He had a morbid fear of shaking hands, which he generalized into a rule that good Fascists were to abandon the custom on the ground that it was a waste of time. In many other ways he tried to transform the easygoing, relaxed, and pleasure-loving Italians into imitations of the hard-working, rather gloomy Nazis, but the climate was against him and he never succeeded. He himself, though he gave the impression of tremendously hard work, accomplished very little of a routine character; it was hard to get him to read any lengthy document, or to make a decision of any kind.

He was a show-off. He loved to exhibit himself in public, especially to the photographers, in a fancy uniform or—equally impressive—one of marked simplicity. When the wheat harvest began, he would appear in a field long enough to be photographed stripped to the waist—he was vain about his sturdy build and took every excuse to display it. As soon as the photographs had been taken, he would go away and leave the real work to be done by others. He was a good horseman,

**BENITO MUSSOLINI**
"He looked irresistibly like an actor pretending to be a dictator, throwing his head back, squaring his big jaw, looking down his nose, turning smiles and frowns on and off like an electric light."

or managed to give that impression to the press; he learned to fence and to fly an airplane; he once took a frightened Hitler up, an ordeal that the German did not soon forget. The Duce romped for the photographers with a pair of lion cubs, seeking to leave the impression that he would have been equally fearless if they were full grown.

Throughout the decade of association with Hitler he seethed inwardly, because the German was the master and the whole world knew it. Over and over, as the Führer made his successive sudden coups, Mussolini was not notified until the very last minute; Hitler always had some excuse, believable or not, but the real reason was that he thought the Italian and his entourage were incapable of keeping a secret.

The Duce's disastrous attack on Greece was probably one of the things that caused Hitler to lose the War; the men and equipment Germany had to divert to rescue the Italians were desperately needed on other fronts; yet Hitler was mild in his reproaches. Weak and incompetent as Mussolini was, at the time the Führer still needed him badly, and both of them knew it.

The Italian's adventure in Greece, like his conquest of Ethiopia, was chiefly megalomania, the desire to play the conquering Alexander. There was no good reason for either of these ventures even from the most sordid and mercenary point of view. In the case of Ethiopia, Mussolini pleaded that he needed new land to take care of the overflow Italian population, but even in the mid-thirties few any longer took seriously the idea that overpopulation can be solved by emigration. In the case of Greece, her interference in Albania was made the pretext, though it seems likely that the war would have been initiated even if Albania had never existed.

Mussolini shared with Hitler an utter indifference to suffering by others if it could advance him on the path of glory. He hastily brought Italy into the Second World War when France had been beaten to her knees, with the observation that he needed "a few thousand dead in order to be able to sit at the Peace Conference as a belligerent"—ignoring all the misery that would come to many thousands of Italians because of what he did. On the other hand, he tried to postpone the beginning of the War, on the ground that Italy could not be ready until at least 1945. He told Hitler that for Italy to be able to fight she would need huge quantities of supplies, quantities that he thought Germany could not possibly supply—six million tons of coal, two million tons of steel, and so on. Hitler was furious but managed to control himself; he coldly told Mussolini to stay out of the War for the present, that Germany would go it alone.

Mussolini was born in 1885 in Predappio, a village in east central Italy, an area whose inhabitants are notoriously independent and hostile to all authority. His ancestors for many generations had been peasants, a fact he often mentioned in his speeches. His father, however, was a blacksmith. He was also an atheist and a radical, like millions of others throughout Europe in those times. Though his mother was middle class, a school teacher, and a devout Catholic, she stood by her husband loyally when he was in trouble with the police, as was often the case. Benito Amilcare Andrea was their oldest child; he was named for Benito Juarez, the Mexican revolutionary who rose against Emperor Maximilian, and for two early Italan Socialists.

In a poor region, the Mussolinis were among the poorest. There was often no money for winter fuel, and sometimes not even bread; like the poor the world over, they existed in these times chiefly on the charity of neighbors almost as badly off as themselves. Mrs. Mussolini tried to earn money as a teacher, but her husband's notorious radicalism was a handicap. Nevertheless the family always insisted at this time that they were lower middle class and not of the peasantry.

Benito grew up a stubborn, sullen boy, a street fighter, and a petty thief. He scorned books, and was expelled from one school after another, both for poor scholarship and for his belligerence toward the teachers and his fellow students. At the age of nine he was sent to a church boarding school which took children of the well-to-do as well as the poor. The second group sat at a separate table and were fed on scraps, a bitter experience that may have contributed, in addition to his father's beliefs, to making him a radical from an early age.

Benito learned easily but was handicapped by his continued truculence; his first job, at eighteen, was as an elementary school teacher, at $10 a month. At this period of his life he had almost no friends. At the age of nineteen, on impulse, he gave up his position as a teacher and went to Switzerland, with no money, no skills that were of any use to him there, and no friends. Here for some time he led an existence as miserable as that of Hitler a few years later in Vienna. He did odd jobs, including heavy manual labor for which he was unfitted, went hungry, slept under a bridge, sometimes begged, and once snatched food from two elderly ladies lunching in the park. He soon made contact with other radicals, and they helped him get small jobs of editing and writing.

He also began making speeches, and when he exhorted his listeners to join in a general strike, and argued in favor of violence, the Swiss arrested him, kept him in jail a few days, and then returned him forcibly to Italy. He immediately came back to a different Swiss canton, which was not against the law, but when he went on making radical speeches he was arrested again and was discovered to be carrying an altered passport. By now he was old enough for his compulsory military service in Italy, and since he remained in Switzerland, he was sentenced by the Italian authorities to a year in prison, *in absentia.*

The Swiss disliked deporting anybody into the arms of the law, and permitted him to go by a roundabout route to France. He had told the Swiss police that he was a Revolutionary Socialist, and not an Anarchist who would have been subject to automatic expulsion.

When Benito was twenty-one, a first son was born to the

King of Italy, and amid the general rejoicing, Army "deserters" were given amnesty if they would surrender themselves. Mussolini took advantage of the offer, came back and did about twenty months' service. He was now a grown man, he had learned German and French—though his knowledge of these tongues was never as good as he thought—and had definitely settled on a journalistic career.

By the age of twenty-six, he was editor on a Socialist paper in Trent, then a part of Austria. His writing attracted attention, and before long he became editor of *Avanti* in Milan. He had been tremendously influenced during the past few years by a brilliant Russian Socialist woman living in exile in Italy, Angelica Balabanoff, and he insisted that she be named co-editor.

Until the beginning of the First World War, Mussolini lived the typical life of an Italian radical agitator. He made inflammatory speeches, wrote editorials, and was in and out of prison. He opposed the Libyan War of 1912, and went to jail in consequence. (Some people think that his claustrophobia which, for example, caused him to refuse to enter the Blue Grotto at Capri, may have resulted from his being locked up.) For a time, between journalistic jobs he went back to teaching school, but he was so rough and brutal with his students that he was highly unpopular.

Italy at this time had a large and growing Socialist movement, split, as in other parts of Europe, between those who wanted an orderly, legal process of bringing in a collectivized state, and those who wanted direct and violent revolution. Mussolini was in the second camp, and helped to purge the Italian Socialist movement of gradualist intellectuals. The direct-actionists were growing more numerous, more powerful, and more threatening. Frequent ugly demonstrations against the Government took place. There was great poverty in Italy at this time, with large numbers of unemployed and widespread unrest on which radicals like Mussolini capitalized. The movement was also anti-clerical. In June, 1914, there were demonstrations which resulted in some deaths; churches were set on fire, and city halls and trains were attacked in various places. During the demonstrations in Milan, Mussolini, who had spurred them on in every possible way, stayed mostly inside his newspaper office, though he came out once and, as he later boasted, got hit on the head by a policeman.

When the First World War began, it was assumed that the Socialists would oppose it as an adventure of the capitalists with which they should have nothing to do. To everyone's surprise, Mussolini advocated Italy's entrance on the side of Great Britain and France, in spite of the fact that Italy was a member of the Triple Alliance with Germany and Austria and theoretically under an obligation to come to their aid. It was widely believed at the time that he had been bribed by somebody to change his mind. The French might have done this, and there were powerful elements in Italy itself that wanted the country to join the Entente or at least, to remain neutral.

No one knows whether Mussolini was bribed, but on the whole, circumstantial evidence seems against it. His arguments in favor of joining the Entente seemed sincere—or as sincere as he was capable of being. He never in his life showed any avarice: when he was dictator his only real source of income was $1,500 a week from the Hearst newspapers in the United States for writing them a weekly article. (It is true, however, that he greatly enjoyed the "fringe benefits" of his position— the cars, planes, houses, and other things that were put at his disposal.)

Because of his position, he was expelled from the Socialist Party and fired as editor of *Avanti*. He promptly founded a paper of his own, *Il Popolo d'Italia,* in which he carried on a bitter running duel with his recent comrades in the Socialist Party.

By now he had married Rachele Guide, with whom he had been living for some time. A short, fat, bovine woman, she bore him five children, managing to shut her eyes to the dozens of affairs, long and short, he was already having with other women. In these early years his home life was stormy. When he moved to Milan, he left her behind, and tried to prevent her coming there to live with him. The testimony of his children is that he would beat her and the children as well; his daughter Edda has told that when she was only a baby her father threw shoes at her to stop her crying.

Italy stayed out of the First World War for about ten months, and then in May, 1915, entered on the side of Britain and France, as Mussolini had wanted. He was now drafted, a fact that he tried to conceal after he became dictator, pretending he had volunteered. He saw active service against Austria in rugged mountain terrain, and he seems to have acquitted himself well—as Hitler was doing at the same time in the German Army. In February, 1917, an officer ordered him to continue firing a howitzer that had become red hot from overuse. When he obeyed, it exploded. Five men were killed, and Mussolini was severely wounded, getting about forty splinters in his body; he was in the hospital for months.

With the end of the War in November, 1918, Italy's economic predicament, already bad enough, became even worse. There was again widespread unemployment, almost universal poverty, and little industrial activity. Mussolini, the veteran political agitator, was in the forefront of those attacking the Government and the war profiteers.

He had made many friends in the Army among a special unit of commandos called the *Arditi*, or "daring men"; they wore black fezzes and sweaters, carried black flags and were sometimes called "the Black Flames." In March, 1919, Mussolini called together a group of these former soldiers in a palazzo in Milan and proposed a new organization to be called the *Fasci di Combattimento*. "Fascism" came from the bundles of sticks, or *fasces*, carried by the ancient Roman authorities as a sign of office; they had the symbolic significance that while one stick can be broken easily, a bundle of them is strong. Mussolini was not the first to resurrect the word in modern times; it was employed by restless peasants in Sicily in the 1890's. He himself had used it as far back as 1915 for groups he helped organize which were demanding that Italy enter the War on the side of the Allies.

This first organization had no particular program except a vague radicalism; John Gunther has remarked that Hitler came to power with a concrete set of proposals and abandoned them, while Mussolini came to power and then improvised a philosophy. The Fascists of 1919 announced that they opposed all imperialism, and especially that hostile to Italy. They advocated a League of Nations, and demanded that Fiume and Dalmatia should be turned over to Italy. They also expressed their opposition to all "neutralists"—a word that meant Socialists, from whom the Communists had not yet, in Italy, completely parted company. Mussolini thus broke with his prewar past. As early as August, 1918, he had stopped calling his paper a Socialist daily and began describing it as the organ of the "Fighters and Producers." Unlike the Russian Communists, who had by then been in power for about nine months, Mussolini at this time explicitly said that under Fascism there would be room for capitalists.

By the autumn of 1918, he was one of the two most important men in Italy outside the Government. The other was Gabriele D'Annunzio, a mediocre poet but a swashbuckling self-advertiser of the first water, who was best known because of his love affair—loudly advertised by himself—with the famous actress, Eleonora Duse.

In 1919 both D'Annunzio and Mussolini became greatly exercised over the question of Fiume. This city, on the eastern shore of the Adriatic, not far from its northern end, with an excellent harbor, had been an important seaport for Hungary before the First World War. In the secret treaties made during that War, it was promised to Italy, but after the War's end, there was a strong disposition to give it to Yugoslavia—which was not then, of course, a Communist country. D'Annunzio saw a chance to express his jingoistic patriotism to the full, accompanied by plenty of publicity. He secretly raised an armed force and seized the city on behalf of Italy, among roars of approval from most Italians and from practically nobody else in the world. Mussolini was in on the plot from the beginning and had promised to raise money for D'Annunzio and to help him in other ways, but when it came to the test, he did neither. He remained safe in Milan, his only aid consisting of spirited editorials in his paper.

After about a year, Italy and Yugoslavia signed a treaty dividing up various territories that were in dispute; Fiume was to be made an independent state. D'Annunzio refused to surrender, and when the Italian government sent troops and blockaded the city, he and his handful of followers declared war! There was some desultory fighting, a few men were killed, and D'Annunzio himself was slightly wounded, enabling him to retire with honor from the battlefield.

Many people believed at this time that Mussolini's lackadaisical attitude was the result of a secret bargain with Prime Minister Giovanni Giolitti, and this belief was strengthened when the Fascist leader announced that he was satisfied with the outcome in Fiume. The settlement, however, did not prove permanent; after changing hands several times in the next few decades, the city became a part of Yugoslavia, its name changed to Rijeka.

If there was a bargain between Mussolini and the Italian Government, it was that if he would refrain from violent public criticism, his Fascist bands would be let alone, unless they misbehaved too violently. These bands were rapidly growing in numbers and in truculence. They wore black shirts and fezzes, copied from the uniforms of the Arditi. The Fascist salute of the clenched fist over the head seems to have been invented by D'Annunzio, though it was later used by various left-wing groups in other countries.

Whether Mussolini had a compact with the Prime Minister or not, his Fascists grew steadily bolder, beating people up, staging food riots, and in general threatening the Government in vague ways. As early as 1920, Mussolini began talking about a march on Rome that would overthrow the regime. At this time he was a republican, and proposed to do away with the monarchy.

If the Fascists were truculent, the left-wing Socialists, now calling themselves Communists, were equally so. In areas where they were strong enough, they were openly confiscating factories and taking over and dividing up the estates of the great landowners. Not unnaturally, this threw the landowners and the big capitalists in general into an uneasy alliance with the Fascists, paralleling the similar development a decade later in Germany.

The Army, as is true of most armies the world over, was reactionary, and strongly favored the Fascists, so many of whom were their own ex-comrades-in-arms.

By the spring of 1921, the Fascists were so strong that Prime Minister Giolitti made what was certainly a bargain with them; he dissolved Parliament, called for elections, and invited the Fascists to enter the coalition of which he was head. Mussolini agreed, and about thirty-five Fascists, of whom he was one, were elected to Parliament. In the past, Mussolini had always said Fascism would never become a political party but would always remain only "a band of brothers"; but now the policy was abruptly abandoned. The movement at this time had about 320,000 hard-core members, but its sympathizers ran into millions, especially among the war veterans.

The famous March on Rome was triggered by a general strike called by left-wing Socialists in August, 1922. The strike did not amount to much, but it enabled the Fascists to come forward and operate some of the essential services. Mussolini now gave an ultimatum to the Government. While he did not demand that he be made Premier, he did ask that Fascists should head several of the Ministries; his demands were refused. He was angered, and began taking steps to seize control of the Government, though many of the men around him felt the movement was not yet strong enough.

Mussolini was now the leading political figure in Italy. His quarrel with D'Annunzio was intensified when the latter proposed to dethrone King Victor Emmanuel and substitute the King's cousin, the Duke d'Aosta; Mussolini had abandoned his republicanism of a short time before and now wanted to keep the King on the throne. D'Annunzio's public career came to an end when he suffered an accidental fall from a window, injuring his head and making him an invalid the rest of his life.

Although Mussolini was the man best known to the public, he was an inefficient executive, and the Fascist Party was actually run by others. The "big four" were Michele Bianchi, Secretary General of the Party, with a background in journalism; General Emilio de Bono, an older man with a good record in the First World War, who had (illegally) become an important figure in the Fascist Militia while still serving in the regular army; Captain Cesare Maria de Vecchi, an ultra-conservative monarchist and land owner who was also a lawyer, amateur painter, and poet; and finally, the only one of the four whose name is still remembered, Italo Balbo, an aviator with a brilliant record in the First World War, and a general in the Fascist Militia.

The actual march was preceded by Fascist rallies throughout the country. Engineered by the four men mentioned, the action had to get along without any actual participation by Mussolini; as in the case of D'Annunzio's adventure in Fiume, he stayed behind in Milan and wrote burning editorials.

The situation was chaotic. Some elements of the Army were pro-Fascist, others wanted to fight them. Prime Minister Luigi Facta wished the King to declare a state of siege, but the monarch declined, and the Army was finally ordered not to fight. With the Fascists coming nearer, the Cabinet resigned. The King telephoned to Mussolini in Milan and offered him the Premiership; Benito, always the skeptic, refused to believe the offer was genuine until it was confirmed by telegram. Finally, two days late, he joined the March on Rome—by means of a compartment in a sleeping car. He arrived the next morning, dirty and fatigued, called on the King, and accepted the position as Premier. The Fascists were in control.

Yet, like Hitler in Germany, Mussolini did not try to gather all the reins into his hands until he was sure of himself; in his first Cabinet, only four of fourteen Ministers were Fascists, the others being Social Democrats, Catholics, and Liberals. He himself was Minister of Foreign Affairs and of the Interior.

Though other and abler men managed the Fascist Party and for that matter Mussolini himself, he was indispensable to them at this time. He was a skillful orator and writer, with an intuitive feeling for the mood of his audience at all times and for that of the country as a whole. Like all modern dictators, he went in for an orgy of monumental public works: great highways for people most of whom were kept too poor to drive on them, the restoration of ancient monuments, vast new amphitheaters. A pet project of his was draining the noxious marshes around Rome. Hitler assured the Germans they had not lost the First World War but had been defeated by traitors at home; Mussolini told the Italians they were the inheritors of the glories of ancient Rome, that they must restore the old Roman Empire, or as much of it as was practicable in modern times. As far as he could, he reintroduced the old Roman salute and forms of address. Small boys who were to be trained up for the Fascist militia were called "Sons of the She Wolf," to link them to Romulus and Remus, the legendary founders of Rome.

The greatest scandal of Mussolini's whole career was the Matteotti affair, and this fact itself indicates how much milder Italian Fascism was than its German counterpart; Hitler did scores of things equally reprehensible, and they caused hardly a ripple at home or abroad.

Giacomo Matteotti, who was thirty-nine in 1924, was a Socialist deputy, a wealthy man coming from a land-owning family. He had watched with growing dismay the movement of Fascism away from even the pretense of legality, and on May 30, 1924, he made a speech strongly protesting the numerous uses of brute force by the Fascists in the recent election. The Fascists had received only sixty-five percent of the votes in this election, but Matteotti pointed out that Mussolini had already indicated he would not be bound by the results. Il Duce, furious, remarked to some of his associates, "This man, after this speech, should not be allowed to go around."

Whether he meant that Matteotti should be killed is not clear, but the Fascists thought so, kidnaped the Deputy and murdered him. Two months later his body was found in a shallow grave in a wooded area fifteen miles north of Rome.

The guilty men, all Fascists, were identified without much trouble; one of them had in a suitcase Matteotti's bloodstained trousers, and the bloodstained upholstery that had been cut from the kidnap car. In the meantime, Mussolini's opponents withdrew from Parliament until law and order should be restored. Several prominent officials implicated in the murder were forced to resign.

The assassins were tried, and pleaded that Matteotti's death was an accident; they received no punishment. The affair was so sharply criticized in the anti-Fascist newspapers that Mussolini responded by suppressing them all. His opponents were still strong enough so that if they had risen against him, they might have swung the scales the other way; but while they hesitated, Mussolini consolidated his power, and soon it was too late.

The real dictatorship now began in earnest. New laws were passed destroying freedom of speech and of the press; the King became even more of a mere figurehead than in the past. Hundreds of critics of Fascism were imprisoned for long terms, being tortured, starved, and sometimes forced to drink massive doses of castor oil, with results that were nearly fatal. Many of them were sent to a small, waterless, "escape-proof" island in the Mediterranean where their life was extremely hard.

During the next few months there were at least four attempts to kill Mussolini. One was made by a former Socialist deputy who stationed himself for a time in a hotel room, with a high-powered rifle, across the street from the Ministry of Foreign Affairs; but he was discovered. An elderly English-woman, mentally unstable, shot the Duce in the nose, inflicting a superficial flesh wound. A young anarchist threw a bomb at his passing automobile; it bounced back and exploded after the car had passed. A fourth person shot at him in a moving automobile but missed; the infuriated crowd seized and lynched a bystander, a fifteen-year-old boy who was almost certainly innocent. Mussolini himself described the would-be assassin as bearing no resemblance to the boy who was killed.

By now, Italy was a police state, with as much terrorism as the national temperament made possible. The secret police, the "Ovra," were everywhere. Capital punishment was employed freely, and special political courts were set up from whose findings there was no appeal.

Mussolini throughout this period was admired by many Americans and citizens of other Western democracies. For some reason a great many people outside Italy were enormously impressed by the argument: "He made the trains run on time." The claim was only partly true, and in any case, punctuality of the railroads can be bought at too high a price. It is a fact, however, that he had ended the virtual civil war by which Italy had been rent ever since 1918. Strikes were forbidden under his "Corporate State." This was a scheme through which, in theory, the country was to be governed by a series of corporations. The number of these varied from time to time but in general, most of them were economic, representing agriculture, heavy industry, commerce, and so forth. One included the professions; another, all employes of the state, including the teachers in the public schools. Most of the corporations were represented in the national legislature, through separate organizations for employers and workers.

This grandiose scheme never worked very well, and Mussolini soon lost interest in it. The country was ruled, down to its minutest detail, by the Fascists, and the Duce's word was law. A popular Fascist slogan was, "Credere, Ubbidire, Combattere"

—believe, obey, fight. Another slogan was, "Mussolini is always right."

As Hitler did later, Mussolini enhanced his popularity with social measures. The poor got summer camps for their children, some free meals and clothing, and free medical care. He attempted sanitary measures to reduce the high incidence of tuberculosis and other diseases, and sought unsuccessfully to improve agricultural production, notably of wheat. Like all dictators, he wanted to increase the birth rate, and as always happens, he was unsuccessful in this. In 1933, as a publicity gesture, he brought to Rome and feted ninety-three mothers who among them had produced more than 1,300 children.

Mussolini's press agents tried to make a great triumph out of the agreement with the Roman Catholic Church in 1929. For centuries, certain secular powers and the actual control of some territories had been claimed and exercised by successive Popes. The agreement with Mussolini reduced the territory over which the Pope had control to the 108 acres of Vatican City.

It is not at all certain, however, that the outcome was a victory for the Fascists. The Church was in fact glad to end the dispute over secular powers which had meant little in recent years. Under the agreement, religious instruction continued to be compulsory in all the schools, an important matter in the eyes of the Vatican. A point of difference that was not resolved was Fascist infiltration of the parochial schools, and the political activities of the lay organization, Catholic Action. Nine years later, when Mussolini, prodded by Hitler, introduced active anti-Semitism in Italy, the Church objected on principle.

In the beginning, Hitler considered himself Mussolini's pupil and imitated him in many small ways, while the Duce was patronizing and condescending toward him. When they first met, in June, 1934, Mussolini had been in power more than a decade and Hitler not much more than a year. Hitler flew to their meeting, just outside Venice. He had been airsick during the flight, and was pale and tired. Moreover, he was wearing a dirty raincoat and a battered soft hat. Mussolini, on the other hand, was resplendent in a full-dress uniform. Hitler was furious at the contrast and savagely reproached his advisers, who had not warned him what to expect.

It did not take long for the roles of the two men to be reversed. Only two weeks after the first meeting in Venice, Hitler conducted the terrible blood purge of the Nazi Party, and Mussolini was appalled at the callous and bloodthirsty way in which the Führer killed men who had been his old comrades.

As Hitler, over the years, executed one bold coup after another, Mussolini was angered because he was never notified in advance. The Italian people quickly realized that the Duce was being kept in the dark, and his prestige was reduced. On the occasion of one of Hitler's dramatic strokes, Mussolini remarked, "The Italians will laugh at me; every time Hitler occupies a country, he sends me a message." When the Italians invaded Greece, the Duce kept it a secret from Hitler, with the observation, "Hitler always faces me with a *fait accompli.* This time I'm going to pay him back in his own coin. He will find out from the newspapers that I have occupied Greece. In this way the equilibrium will be reëstablished."

In the early days of Hitler's rule, the two dictators were divided because of Austria. Engelburt Dollfuss, the Austrian leader, took lessons in one-man rule from Mussolini, and it was the Duce who urged him to crack down on the Austrian Nazis in 1934. Dollfuss' family was visiting Mussolini in Italy when Hitler ordered him killed, and the Italian had to break the news that he was dead.

In spite of differences, Mussolini and Hitler stuck together to the end, chiefly because they had to. In May, 1938, Hitler made a state visit to Rome; Mussolini had all the houses near the whole length of the railroad track freshly whitewashed and painted with welcoming signs. On a few occasions, Mussolini succeeded in causing Hitler to modify his course slightly, victories that looked much more important at the moment than later. He was unsuccessful in the greatest effort of all, to postpone the beginning of the Second World War.

Mussolini's attack on Ethiopia in 1935 was a piece of naked imperialism. Though there had been a few minor clashes between Ethiopians and Italians on the border of Somaliland, they were of no importance, and Mussolini would certainly have acted without them. He seized Ethiopia because he wanted to make modern Italy into an Empire on the old Roman model.

The African kingdom was betrayed and abandoned by the European Great Powers, and by the League of Nations in which these Powers were paramount. The French Foreign Minister, Pierre Laval, went to Rome and made a secret agreement with Mussolini, giving him a free hand in Ethiopia if he would stay out of Tunisia. A special committee of the League Council, dominated by England and France, tried to appease Mussolini by giving him part of Ethiopia, sparsely populated and with poor soil. The Duce indignantly refused, remarking, "Italy's need for expansion in East Africa is not to be satisfied by a cession of a couple of deserts, one of salt, one of stone. . . . The League Council seems to think I am a collector of deserts." Laval and Sir Samuel Hoare, British Foreign Minister, made a secret agreement that would have given nearly all of Ethiopia to Italy; both their governments approved the plan, but when it leaked out, such a storm of public protest developed that it had to be withdrawn.

The Ethiopian Emperor, Haile Selassie, made his way to Geneva and appeared before the League to make a dramatic personal plea for his country; he was greeted with a storm of boos and jeers, obviously arranged in advance, by representatives of all the Fascist countries.

The League made a halfhearted attempt to apply mild economic sanctions to Italy, sanctions that would have been ineffectual even if the chief powers had applied them conscientiously. She was permitted to continue to import oil, without which her whole economy would have come to a halt. She was allowed to use the Suez Canal, then under British control. England and France, in a hypocritical gesture of impartiality, embargoed arms to both Italy and Ethiopia; the embargo hurt Mussolini not at all, since he could readily obtain weapons from his Fascist allies, but it was almost fatal to Ethiopia.

The outcome of the war was never in doubt. Italy used nearly 300,000 trained, highly equipped troops, plus 60,000 African natives. Ethiopia had only 35,000 troops with rifles, plus a large number of tribesmen armed with swords, spears, and a few muskets. To speed up the war, Mussolini bombed the opposing troops with mustard gas. His airmen also bombed clearly marked Red Cross hospitals. The callous brutality of the Italians was illustrated by Mussolini's son, Vittorio, a pilot in the Italian Air Force, who called bombing the natives "magnificent sport." In a book about his experiences he observed, "One group of horsemen gave me the impression of a budding rose unfolding as the bombs fell in their midst and blew them up. It was exceptionally good fun." The war lasted only seven months, and ended in the surrender of Ethiopia in May, 1936.

The Italian occupation continued until 1941, when the country was set free by British forces in the course of the Second World War. Like most modern colonies, Ethiopia was of doubtful value to the conquerors. Seeking to justify his actions, the Duce spent large sums building roads, factories, and power plants. Schools were started, with separate classrooms for Christians and Moslems. Although Mussolini's official excuse for conquering the country was Italy's expanding population at home, he had the greatest difficulty in persuading any of his fellow countrymen to emigrate to the region. The few who did so had to travel in groups in the daytime and stay indoors at night, for fear of being murdered.

Haile Selassie had escaped when the capital, Addis Ababa, was captured; and when the Italians were driven out, he was restored to the throne.

After the Ethiopian War, Italy's economic plight was worse than ever. Taxes were heavy, productivity was low, profiteering, corruption, monopolistic practices, and burdensome bureaucracy were universal. Mussolini's own popularity, however, continued high; as often happens, the people made a distinction between the head of the state and the unhappy results of the policies for which he was responsible.

Hugh Baillie, former head of the United Press, describes Mussolini at about this time in his autobiography, *High Tension*. He saw the Duce appear on his famous balcony at the Palazzo Venezia to address a huge, cheering crowd below. He stood, Baillie says, on a little platform invisible from the street, to make him seem taller than he was.

> He delivered his speech in short bursts, interrupted by deafening roars, during which he set his arms akimbo, popped his eyes, nodded and wagged his head. Sometimes he leaned over the balustrade, resting his weight on hands spread far apart, stared down at the people just below, and flashed a big, toothy grin. Sometimes he leaned far back and gave a mirthless laugh.

A few days later Baillie had an interview with the Duce in his famous office, a huge room with no furniture except at one end where there was a long antique table and two chairs. Any visitor had to walk the whole length of the room while Mussolini ignored him; the effect was intended to make the caller feel as inferior as possible.

In Baillie's case, Mussolini let him stand and wait for a long time without looking up; Baillie had plenty of time to notice that he was bald, fat, needed a shave, and wore a rumpled suit.

> Abruptly, as if suddenly becoming aware of me, Il Duce rose, folded his arms high on his chest, reared his head back and popped his eyes. "Hah!" he ejaculated.

Baillie thought someone had played a joke on him and that this could not be the ruler of Italy. Presently, however, he began to feel the genuine power of the man. He also felt that the Duce was not one to permit neutrality; if you were not his warm supporter, you were an enemy. Baillie decided that the coldness at the beginning of the interview was just a piece of showmanship to alarm the visitor and reduce him to docility.

> [As they talked] Il Duce went through other parts of his act, grimacing and batting his eyes, grinning and then turning off the grin abruptly and frowning fiercely. He was a showoff.

During this period of his life, Mussolini was a lonely man, as all dictators must be. Most of the men who had been his close associates if not his friends, in the days of the March on Rome, were gone. Some were dead, a few had turned against him. Anyone who showed signs of being a real rival was quietly removed in one way or another. The most popular man in Italy next to Mussolini was probably Italo Balbo, good-looking, with pleasant manners and a host of friends; Mussolini packed him off to Libya. D'Annunzio, now an invalid, made overtures to Mussolini but they were rejected; when he died in 1938, Mussolini showed no grief.

The Duce's daughter, Edda, fell in love with a youth who was a suitable match in every way except that he was Jewish. Although anti-Semitism in Italy had not yet attained the height it later reached, Mussolini broke up the match. In 1930 he married her off to Count Galeazzo Ciano, a young man with little to recommend him. Ciano promptly took advantage of his family relationship to throw his weight around. He helped to create the Rome-Berlin Axis, and encouraged the ill-fated attack on Greece. Late in the Second World War, Mussolini turned against him and shunted him off into the unimportant post of Ambassador to the Vatican.

After the successful invasion of Italy by the Allied forces, a meeting of the Fascist Grand Council was held, which resulted in Mussolini's downfall. Ciano voted against his father-in-law at that meeting, a fact that some time later resulted in his death. He was arrested by the Germans, turned over by them to the Fascists, and was one of a group of former Fascist officials who were executed.

For many years Ciano had kept a diary, and when he was arrested he sought to gain immunity by threatening to have it published; the threat did not work. However, Edda managed to smuggle the manuscript into Switzerland and it was published in the United States in 1945. It paints an extraordinary picture of the inner workings of Fascism for fifteen years.

For many years, Mussolini left his wife and children in Milan while he lived in Rome, and he resented it when Rachele insisted on moving down to the capital. As usual, Mussolini was involved with a series of mistresses and an even longer series of women with whom he had brief and sordid relationships. One of his mistresses, Margharita Sarfatti, is supposed to have ghostwritten some of his articles, including those for American newspapers.

Though he was brought up an atheist and presumably remained one all his life, Mussolini was surprisingly superstitious. He believed in astrology and, like the Italian peasant that he was, he feared the Evil Eye.

Those around him took advantage of his gullibility in many ways. Though he told Hitler Italy was not ready to fight, he did not himself realize in what poor shape she was. When he was shown a field with hundreds of airplanes on it, he was satisfied with the sight and did not bother to learn that almost none of them was in condition to fly. His soldiers who invaded Albania early in 1939 wore shoes with cardboard soles. For the great military parades in Rome, of which he was so fond, the Army borrowed armored cars from the police, painted them over with military insignia, and after the parade was ended, repainted them and gave them back.

Mussolini was reluctant to introduce strict anti-Semitism among his easygoing compatriots, and did so only after Hitler had brought great pressure upon him. Laura Fermi in her biography of Mussolini suggests that Hitler had to promise to keep hands off the South Tyrol, which contained many German-speaking people. Mussolini had tried to distinguish between "the international Jewish problem"—a phrase borrowed from Hitler, since of course no such problem existed—and the situation in Italy. At first he promised that Italian Jews would not be molested if they were not hostile to the Fascists, but soon he yielded to Hitler's pressure. Jews were forbidden to hold government offices, or to practice journalism or other professions. Mussolini said that the Jews were only one tenth of one percent of the population, so they should be restricted to that proportion of the national activity.

The Duce decided that the Italians were Aryans, after all.

> We must get it into our minds that we are not Hamites, we are not Semites, we are not Mongols. If we are none of these races, we are evidently Aryans . . . of Mediterranean type, pure.

By now, those around him were worrying about Mussolini's health; his stomach pains were severe and almost incessant, and he showed signs of mental and physical deterioration. The American Ambassador, William Phillips, found it necessary to read to him in English very slowly, as Mussolini seemed to be losing his sparse knowledge of that language. At a meeting with Hitler, the Duce got into trouble because he pretended to understand German when he did not.

He was now under tremendous strain, partly because he was sending men and weapons in considerable quantities to aid Franco to put down the Spanish Revolution; Italy itself was in serious straits and could not afford this adventure. Perhaps because his judgment was clouded, Mussolini put through additional legislation even more stupid than some of the earlier laws. Bachelors had their careers severely limited; one army officer was promoted to General, and then when Mussolini discovered he was not married, he canceled the promotion, remarking, "A General must be the first to realize that without men one cannot make divisions." Copying Hitler again, he tried to prevent Italian women from having careers outside the home. No Italian was permitted to marry any foreigner. All civil servants were required to wear Fascist uniforms.

At the same time, his dream of Empire became more

grandiose. He wanted to seize from France Tunisia in North Africa; the island of Corsica; Savoy, the French province on the Italian border; and even the Riviera. He took advantage of the approaching Second World War to invade Albania in April, 1939, and then attacked Greece in 1940. The Greek War was deliberately timed to begin on October 28—the anniversary of the march on Rome.

Mussolini, as already noted, after first trying unsuccessfully to postpone the beginning of the Second World War, hastily entered it on June 10, 1940, when France was about to be overrun, in order to earn himself a place at the peace conference which he thought would come very soon.

Beneath the surface, the stresses between Italy and Germany were becoming more serious. Italians sent to Germany as a labor force were abused by the Nazis as though they were prisoners of war. When Mussolini invaded North Africa, Hitler offered him troops which the Duce haughtily refused; he was so confident of victory over the hard-pressed British forces defending Egypt that he made elaborate preparations for his victorious entrance into Alexandria. When his soldiers were thrown back, the Germans had to rescue them, as also happened in Greece.

The Duce insisted on sending 250,000 men to aid the Germans in Russia—men who, if they had been sent to Africa instead, might have conquered Egypt. When the Germans were forced back, both in Russia and in North Africa, they contemptuously left the Italians to escape as best they could; the Nazis commandeered all the vehicles, and Mussolini's men had to walk.

The Duce was deeply angered because Hitler used to call him into conference without warning and always by telephone.

> These conferences called by ringing a bell are not to my liking; a bell is rung when people call their servants. And besides, what kind of conferences are these? For five hours I am forced to listen to a monologue which is quite fruitless and boring.

So bitter was he that when the British and Americans began to wreak havoc by aerial bombing of German cities, he privately expressed his satisfaction that Hitler would be taken down a peg or two—sentiments that he was of course careful not to express in public.

With the Allied invasions of first Sicily and then the Italian mainland, in 1943, Mussolini became more than ever the prisoner of the Germans. It was their soldiers who put up the fierce resistance south of Rome. Italian officials, except Mussolini, saw that defeat was inevitable; at a meeting of the Fascist Grand Council on July 24, votes were taken that meant Mussolini must be deposed. The Duce went to the King, confidently expecting his support, but he did not get it; Victor Emmanuel on the contrary said only that he would see that Mussolini was "protected"; he sent him from the Palace hidden in a Red Cross ambulance; it took the fallen Dictator some time to realize that he was in fact under arrest.

He was moved from place to place under guard; one of his temporary prisons was the same little island to which he had exiled so many of his political opponents. Finally he was sent with his guard to a spot considered safe—a summer hotel on the top of a high peak in the Apennines, reached only by a funicular railway.

However, the place was not as unreachable as it seemed. Hitler gave orders that the Duce should be rescued, and this was done. A small plane, trailing a glider filled with German soldiers, managed to land on the tiny flat area by the hotel. The surprised Italian guards put up little resistance, Mussolini was hustled into the plane, and a dangerous takeoff was just barely accomplished.

He was now moved to Vienna, and shortly thereafter a new puppet government was set up under complete German domination, in the small part of northern Italy not yet conquered by the Allies. Mussolini was now a crushed, defeated man, walking as in a dream; when he spoke on the radio, people thoroughly familiar with his voice refused to believe that it was he.

The new Government had almost no program and its head had little to do. He made a few half-hearted attempts to liberalize his rule; there were not many newspapers in the area he controlled, but he ordered some degree of freedom of the press—canceling the orders very soon when these journals began to utter hostile criticism. In a sop to the radical industrial workers, he had factories nationalized; but the workers remembered that as head of the Fascist Government he had taken away the right to strike, destroyed the unions, and persecuted leading Socialists, and they were not appeased.

As the Allies advanced steadily up the Italian peninsula, and as Hitler's situation grew more and more desperate on all fronts, the Germans in control in Italy opened secret peace talks with the Allies, behind the backs of both Hitler and Mussolini. The Duce at the same time started his own secret negotiations with the Allies, of which the Germans were not informed. In both cases the reply was only: "Unconditional surrender."

Mussolini's Government continued to dwindle as its members went into hiding or fled for their lives into Switzerland. The anti-Fascist Italian underground, the Partisans, among whom Italian Communists played an important role, grew steadily bolder and more active. They had arms, ammunition, and even vehicles that were supplied to them by the American and British forces fighting their way north; before long, Partisan motorized columns took Milan, while the inhabitants of the city cheered wildly—as though they had not a few years earlier cheered with equal enthusiasm for Mussolini. His rump government moved from town to town, trying to keep ahead of the Allied forces; soon there came the news that the Germans in Italy had surrendered.

Though his wife was near by, Mussolini made no attempt to see her. He did write her a letter and then called her on the telephone, saying, "There is no one any more. I am alone, Rachele, and I see that this is the end of everything." By now, even his own personal bodyguard had abandoned him.

Only one person in all the world now seemed to have any

personal attachment to him. This was Clara Petacci, the last of his long series of mistresses. He had met her in 1933, a young girl many years his junior, who was engaged to be married. She seems to have fallen in love with him at first sight; whether he ever really cared for her is not known, but shortly after the Ethiopian War she became his mistress. She was pretty and stupid, and possessed a large family which promptly capitalized on the relationship in every possible way, peddling her supposed influence, accepting bribes, and demanding all sorts of special privileges.

When he set up the new puppet government, she managed to get through the lines and came to live nearby. While Mussolini was moving his government hither and yon they were separated, but finally she managed to join him again. The Duce was traveling north with a few German soldiers, hoping to get out of the country; now, dazed and haggard, he tried to disguise himself in a German overcoat. Just as Clara had succeeded in joining him, he was recognized and captured by a band of Partisans. The two were put under guard, and kept overnight in the house of a peasant; and early next morning Mussolini was informed that he had been tried by a military court and that he and seventeen other captured important Fascist officials had been sentenced to death.

Clara could probably have escaped, but she chose to die with him. They were taken a short distance from the farmhouse to a villa hidden in trees, and the pair were placed in front of a low wall. The terms of the death sentence were read aloud, and they were both shot.

The following day, anti-Fascist feeling was demonstrated in a gruesome form in Milan. The two bodies and those of other executed Fascists were taken to the Piazzale Loreto and hung up by the heels, at a spot not far from that where the Fascist Party had its beginnings; the proprieties were observed with a rope tied around Clara's legs to keep her skirt in place. Thousands of Milanese gathered to jeer the corpses. It would be hard to conceive a more sordid and miserable end to Mussolini's career.

In the case of a modern dictator, it is amazing how quickly the signs of his rule disappear, with nothing left but the great automobile highways and the formidable public buildings in which such men delight. This was true in Italy. When the conquering Allied Armies overran the country it became almost impossible to find anybody who would admit to having been a voluntary Fascist, unless he was so high in the Government that he had put himself irrevocably on record. It turned out that the great crowds who had gathered wherever Mussolini made a public appearance, giving the Fascist salute of the clenched fist overhead and shouting "Duce! Duce! Duce!" had always hated him and his regime and wanted only to live under democratic institutions.

All the suffering for so many years, the suppression of every liberty, the thousands of young Italians killed in needless wars, had gone for naught; the Fascist regime vanished into nothing and soon the very memories of its leader had grown dim.

# 6. Gandhi:
# Politician and Saint

His name was Mohandas Karamchand Gandhi, but he was, and is, known all over the world as Mahatma Gandhi, a title that may be translated roughly as "Great Soul" or "Great Teacher." (He disliked this title, but was unable to prevent people from using it; he wanted to be called *Bhai*, brother, or perhaps *Bapu*, father.) He was one of the very few men in modern times to be venerated as a saint while still alive, and he was the key figure in what may well prove to be the most important world development of the twentieth century—the death of colonialism in Africa and Asia.

He was a small man, only a little more than five feet tall and never weighing much more than one hundred pounds; he was dark in color, and during the part of his life when he was world famous, almost bald and toothless. He wore steel-rimmed spectacles, sometimes pushed down on his nose. At first glance, with his big ears sticking out, his wide mouth, and his round smooth skull, he seemed superlatively ugly, but in the next instant the keen intelligence, the warm friendliness, and the fearless confidence that shone from his brown eyes obliterated any other impression.

I once spent half a day with Gandhi, including several hours of private conversation, and it is one of the great ex-

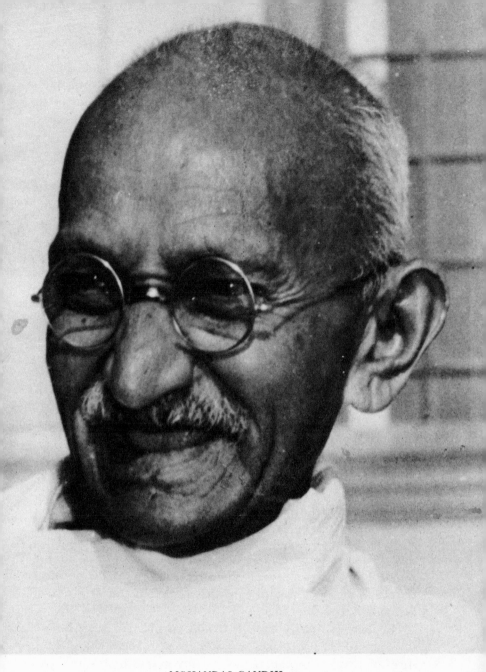

### MOHANDAS GANDHI

"A small man . . . almost bald and toothless. At first glance he seemed superlatively ugly, but in the next instant the keen intelligence, the warm friendliness and the fearless confidence that shone from his brown eyes obliterated any other impression."

periences of my life. During the whole time of our talk, Gandhi sat cross-legged on the floor. He was wearing his usual loin cloth and sandals, with no doubt his old-fashioned, large tinny watch with a dangling fob concealed somewhere in a loin-cloth pocket. The day was chilly, and he was wrapped in a huge, beautiful, white wool blanket, from which his little dark head protruded in striking contrast. Following the standard custom of the journalist, I asked him as many embarrassing questions as I could; but he was not embarrassed. In his high, soft, sometimes almost squeaky voice, he instantly and skillfully evaded all the traps I set for him, sometimes chuckling a little at his own dexterity.

Of all the characteristics of this remarkable man, perhaps the most notable was his personal courage. Repeatedly, he took great risks without seeming to consider for a moment the possible consequences to himself. During the Boer War he raised a voluntary ambulance corps and served with it on the battlefield, often exposing himself under heavy fire to rescue a wounded man. At least twice in his life he was savagely beaten, making no attempt either to defend himself or to escape. In his last days, when it was obvious that fanatical Indian Nationalists were seeking to assassinate him, the police begged to be allowed to check for concealed weapons the people who came to his meetings; his refusal may have cost him his life. For many years he walked barefoot through open fields infested with poisonous snakes and insects; the fact that he was never bitten seemed to his followers proof that he was under God's special protection. He was always thin to the point of emaciation; several times when he fasted for political purposes, the doctors told him that he might die as a result; he ignored their warnings.

His diet was barely enough to sustain life. For years he ate the same meal three times a day—a glass of goat's milk, three slices of toast, two oranges and twenty grapes or raisins. The other foods he took occasionally were sparse servings of bananas, peanuts, lime juice, and olive oil.

His daily routine was equally ascetic. Although he was often kept busy with pressing political problems far into the night, he frequently rose after only a couple of hours' sleep to pray, write letters or read the newspapers. A second short nap in the early morning, and he was ready for another twenty-hour day.

In spite of his courage, he was fascinated by the details of his health, and seemed to Western eyes something of a hypochondriac and medical faddist (perhaps partly because he followed native Indian medicine). He experimented with salt, eating large or small quantities or none at all for long periods of time. He was convinced of the miraculous power of mud packs and of high colonic irrigation. At one time he got interested in some sort of weird electrical device for improving health, writing to one of his disciples about it: "You asked me what the electrical treatment was. It is called high frequency —it consists in rubbing with a flat glass bulb charged with violet rays. Exposure to the early morning sun should serve the same purpose except that these instrumental rays are hot."

Though he apparently thought that his own health was precarious, he performed extraordinary feats of physical endurance, including long overland marches on foot during which much younger men fell by the wayside. For many years, whenever he appeared in public he was soon surrounded by a throng of hysterical admirers; even to survive their attentions was an exhausting ordeal. After such occasions he would return to his lodging place with his feet and ankles cut and bleeding from the violent embraces of hundreds of persons who had thrown themselves into the dust to pay this homage.

While he became the greatest exemplar in modern times of the doctrine of nonresistance, in his youth he had a violent temper, sometimes quarreling bitterly with his wife. On one occasion early in his married life, when he was living in South Africa and was already the leader of the Indian colony there, he actually pushed her out of the house, intending in anger that the parting should be permanent. He reconsidered, abashed, when he saw a group of hero-worshipping Hindus watching near the doorstep.

Perhaps because he was always so urgently preoccupied with political problems, he seems to have been indifferently successful as a father. The only one of his children to make any real success in life was his son, Motilal, who grew up to be an important leader in the South African Indian colony.

That Gandhi was not infallible he was the first to admit; when he made a mistake, he laughingly admitted, it was sometimes "a Himalayan miscalculation." While he stuck to his essential main principles of truth and love, he sometimes made political compromises, yielding to the ideas of those around him even though he believed they were mistaken.

Whenever a great man arises in a time of national crisis, the question is asked: Do the events create the leaders or do natural leaders shape the course of history? In Gandhi's case, we can only say that the man and the events interacted upon each other. In his youth he was shy, timid, ineffectual, filled with such deep feelings of inferiority that for a long time he was incapable of practicing as a lawyer because of his inability to speak in public. Until he went to South Africa, where his fellow countrymen were being subjected to wholesale injustice, he showed hardly any signs of the greatness which grew steadily in him until the day of his death. Yet when the test came, he rose to it.

Gandhi was born in 1869, at Porbandar, India, a town which now has about 60,000 inhabitants, near the shore of the Arabian Sea, roughly 160 miles northwest of Bombay. His was a well-to-do family, which in the Western world would be described as middle class; his father and grandfather had been important civil servants in the employ of various small native states. Gandhi was deeply influenced by his mother, who—an extraordinary fact for that day and place—actually had political ideas of her own; she was an idealistic, Utopian Socialist.

The family, devoutly religious, belonged to a group called Modh Bania, one of the many branches of the Hindu caste, the Vaisyas. Strict as was his own sect, Gandhi was brought up surrounded and strongly influenced by members of an even stricter one, the Jains, which broke away from Hinduism many centuries ago and is scrupulously careful never to take the life of any creature if it can be avoided.

There was little sign in Gandhi's early life of the spiritual development that was to come when he was mature. He was studious, markedly shy, and outwardly obedient, although, as he reported long afterward, sometimes inwardly rebellious. His religion forbade him to eat meat or to smoke tobacco, and naturally forbidden things had a great attraction for him, especially since there was a superstitious idea that the strength and dominance of the British came because they were meat eaters. Gandhi hid himself in the deep woods and tried both of the illicit practices with no serious ill effects. He soon gave them up, however, because he did not wish to continue to lie to his parents.

One incident from his boyhood foreshadows the stubborn, undeviating personal honesty of his mature life. A visiting inspector came to the classroom and checked the boys' spelling by having them write down five words from his dictation. The instructor, eager to make a good impression, hinted strongly that everybody should copy the spelling of the brightest boy in the class, but Gandhi would not. "The teacher," he wrote long afterward, "tried to prompt me with the point of his boot, but I would not be prompted." Everybody spelled everything correctly—except Gandhi.

In his autobiography, *The Story of My Experiments with Truth,* Gandhi says that a life pattern of importance was set for him by a poem he read as a boy. "Its precept—return good for evil—became my guiding principle. It became such a passion with me that I began numerous experiments in it." He read it in his native language, Gujarati; in English translation it says:

> For a bowl of water give a goodly meal;
> For a kindly greeting bow thou down with zeal;
> For a single penny pay thou back with gold.
> If thy life be rescued, life do not withhold.

Thus the words and actions of the wise regard;
Every little service tenfold they reward.
But the truly noble know all men as one,
And return with gladness good for evil done.

When he was in his early teens Gandhi was married to a girl of the same age, the marriage being arranged by the parents of the young couple—a proceeding quite customary at that time and place. Despite their youth this was a real marriage in every sense, including the sexual. Though they had been strangers, they soon became devotedly attached to one another and had a happy life together for sixty-two years; Kasturbai Gandhi died on February 22, 1944, and her husband mourned her passing on the twenty-second day of each month during the four years he had still to live.

In 1887, at the age of eighteen, young Gandhi went to England to study law. The journey overseas was a violation of the strict rules of his caste, and even though a priest swore him to abstain from "wine, women and meat," he was formally exiled from it, a ban that was never fully revoked in later life.

His life in London was a deeply disturbing emotional experience to the religious, earnest young Hindu. He was, of course, a vegetarian, as he was to remain all his life, and he nearly starved before he found a vegetarian restaurant in London which used no animal fats in cooking. Wanting to cling to his Indian ways, at the same time he wished to be assimilated to the British, whom he admired; he tried to wear Western clothes, and to learn to play the violin and to dance. So shy that he was unable to speak extemporaneously in public or even read aloud a prepared speech, he took lessons in elocution, which proved of little value. Within a few months, his common sense reasserted itself and he went back to most of his Hindu ways. He studied hard and in three years he passed his bar examinations.

The experience had been revolutionary in many ways. Brought up in the rigidity of Indian society, even the disciplined and orderly British life toward the end of the nineteenth century seemed to him amazingly free. The ideas of individual liberty that he first glimpsed at this time were to remain with him until his death, more than half a century later.

Gandhi returned immediately to India, and there began the most dismally ineffectual part of his whole career. He tried to practice law in Bombay, but his shyness in public appearances militated against him, and he was a failure. In 1893, at twenty-four, he was offered a small legal post in the Indian community in South Africa, on one year's tenure. As it turned out, he stayed twenty years, and before he returned to India he was the most famous member of his race in the world.

The separate states of South Africa, the Cape, Natal, the Orange Free State, and the Transvaal, then still seventeen years away from federation, were already beginning to practice the severe restrictions against all nonwhites that are so notorious today. Indians had been imported, beginning about a quarter of a century earlier, to do manual labor in mines and on farms. They arrived under contracts requiring them to serve for five years, but the South African whites then wanted them either to sign up for another five years or to go back to India, and passed a law saying that if they refused, they must live henceforth in what amounted to perpetual serfdom.

In one state or another, or in all of them, the Indians were forbidden to vote, or to own property, or to be traders, a restriction planned to force the bulk of them to work for starvation wages for white employers. They could only travel second or third class in public conveyances and were not allowed (even if they could afford it, as most of them could not) to live in hotels or eat in restaurants frequented by whites. An Indian walking on a sidewalk who encountered a European would be well advised to detour into the street around him. A pass was needed to be out of doors after nine P.M. One of the worst features was the law in Natal requiring every Indian to pay a poll tax of £25 ($125), about twice an Indian's annual average earnings. By heroic efforts, Gandhi got the tax reduced to £3 ($15), though even this amount was impossibly high for many members of the community.

The chief grievance of the white South Africans against the Indians as free enterprisers was the familiar complaint against recent immigrants the world over: that they worked too hard, lived too economically, competed too fiercely. Lionel Curtis, the distinguished British publicist, was at one time head of the Asiatic Department of the Transvaal Republic. He reported that Gandhi came to see him and "started by trying to convince me of the good points in the character of his countrymen, their industry, their frugality, their patience." Curtis replied: "Mr. Gandhi, you are preaching to the converted. It is not the vices of Indians that Europeans in this country fear, but their virtues."

Most of the Indians in South Africa accepted the discriminatory practices, however bitter they may have felt; but Gandhi had a stubborn independence and it was hard to break his spirit. When he was still a young man in India he was once bodily expelled by orders of an Englishman from an office where he was trying to intercede for his brother on some minor matter. He afterward wrote that "this changed the course of my entire life." Several times in South Africa, protesting unfair treatment, he was severely beaten by men who may have weighed twice his ninety or one hundred pounds.

On one occasion he had bought a ticket for a horse-drawn stagecoach; the conductor, who was supposed to ride outside with the driver, ordered Gandhi to change places with him, partly because of the color of the Indian's skin and partly because it was a cold night and he himself preferred to ride inside. At first Gandhi yielded in order not to make a scene. After awhile the conductor decided he wanted to smoke; when the stage stopped he got out and ordered Gandhi to sit on the floor between the feet of the driver, so that the would-be smoker could occupy his seat. The Indian refused, and the man began to beat him. Gandhi made no effort to defend himself, but finally, perhaps in fear that he would be killed, some of the male passengers made his assailant stop.

On another occasion, Gandhi bought a first-class train ticket. The conductor ordered him to ride second class, and when he refused, put him off the train in the middle of the night at a small way station. All his baggage, including his overcoat, was thrown after him, and the station master, who naturally sided with the train conductor, seized all his possessions and locked them up. It was bitterly cold and Gandhi, clad in lightweight Hindu clothing, nearly froze as he spent the night in the deserted waiting room.

His native intelligence and the force of character he began to demonstrate as soon as he had conquered his original shyness, soon made him an outstanding leader in the Indian community in South Africa. He was the first Hindu, and in fact the first non-European of any sort, admitted to practice before the Supreme Court of Natal. By an arbitrary ruling, he was ordered to remove his turban in court, although Moslems were permitted to retain theirs—a piece of discrimination that deeply offended his sense of justice. He had, however, no choice but to obey, and as a result he abandoned the turban completely; for the rest of his life he went bareheaded or wore only the little white Gandhi cap, now familiar to us chiefly in pictures of the late Indian Prime Minister Jawaharlal Nehru.

Gandhi announced that he was willing to be the spokesman for all Indians who were in trouble with the law—of whom there were a great many. He took the case of a Hindu indentured servant whose master habitually beat him; the man having been freed, Gandhi naturally was flooded with cases of other indentured servants, none of whom had any money to pay him. He cheerfully helped them, as well as developing a law practice among more prosperous individuals. In spite of all his charity work, within a short time he was a highly successful lawyer, earning an income of $25,000 to $30,000 a year —a sum with a purchasing power several times greater than the same amount today, and with practically no income tax.

It was Gandhi's invariable custom to settle every case out of court if he possibly could, and he usually succeeded.

After he had been in South Africa three years he returned to India to get his family. While he was home, he made some speeches and gave some interviews denouncing the mistreatment of the Indians by the South African Government. Garbled reports of what he had said were cabled back to South Africa and aroused the white community to fury. They recognized that he was their strongest opponent, and decided to crush him.

When he finally returned, he was at first detained on the ship for five days while legal efforts were made to bar him from the country. When these failed, he went ashore and was confronted by an angry mob bent on a lynching. He probably would have been killed had not an Englishwoman, Mrs. Alexander, the wife of a police superintendent, happened by and with remarkable courage faced down the mob and rescued him. Sticks and stones were flying, but Mrs. Alexander, who sounds as though she might have posed for a statue of Britannia, raised an umbrella to shield him, and managed to get him into her house.

Later that day, an even bigger and uglier mob gathered outside with the avowed intention of burning down the building if Gandhi were not turned over to them. With characteristic intrepidity, which all his life long seemed to others to amount to foolhardiness, Gandhi wanted to go out and argue with the mob; he was half persuaded, half compelled not to do so. Finally he put on a constable's uniform; two real constables were then disguised as Indians, to make it seem that one tiny policeman was arresting two stalwart Hindus. The trio escaped safely by means of the back door.

For twenty years the little Indian stayed in South Africa, fighting discrimination by every means at his command. The ambulance corps he helped to establish during the Boer War, which operated with the British Army, was a pathetic attempt to ingratiate the Indians with the white race—an attempt that so far as the evidence shows failed of its purpose.

In South Africa, Gandhi developed many of the personal habits—some of them fairly described as idiosyncrasies—that were to stay with him the rest of his life. He was sometimes difficult indeed in the role of husband and father. While his children were still quite young, he insisted at one time that the whole family should adopt Western ways, to the extent of wearing shoes and stockings and eating at the table with knives and forks. The shoes were badly fitted and the wearers were miserable, especially in the midsummer heat; the knife and fork were hard to get used to. Then abruptly Gandhi reversed himself, and the family was permitted to go back to Hindu ways.

For a long time he insisted, as a matter of principle, that he and his wife should together perform many menial household tasks. His wife, who came from a high caste, was horrified by the prospect, especially since many of these duties were forbidden to her by her religion. They were equally inappropriate to a busy, hard-pressed lawyer, with a large annual income. He bought a book on laundry work and another on baking, and insisted that the family should perform these functions, even the children helping as they could. They learned barbering and cut each other's hair. He abandoned his life insurance and went without it for many years because, so he said, to have it "seemed to show a lack of trust in God."

From Mrs. Gandhi's point of view, the worst of the household tasks he insisted on performing was cleaning the latrines. This work in India has always been the function of the Untouchables; Mrs. Gandhi not only would never have dreamed of doing it, but the slightest physical contact with one of the men who did would have necessitated elaborate and time-consuming purification ceremonies. Yet because this was her husband whom she loved and trusted, she uncomplainingly followed a course that must often have seemed to her close to madness.

All his life, Gandhi struggled to rise above the claims of the flesh. His health was always frail, and for many years the doctors worked to persuade him to eat enough to keep going under the heavy burden of activity that he decreed for himself (or that was forced upon him by events). In India, cows are cruelly treated to get the last ounce of milk from the udder, and because of this, Gandhi would drink no cow's milk; it was a great triumph for his family when he was persuaded to use goat's milk instead.

His asceticism, which of course grew out of his religion, was not confined to himself, or to his own household. He once deeply offended a friendly family with whom he was staying by trying, in dead earnest, to convert their five-year-old son to vegetarianism. Taking a long ocean voyage with an English friend, he observed that the man was much attached to a pair of expensive binoculars; Gandhi did not rest until he had persuaded him that for the sake of his soul he should throw them overboard—which he did!

In 1906, at the age of thirty-seven, Gandhi, a man of strong sexual desires, decided that henceforth he would live in chastity. By then he was devoting his full time to leading the Hindus both in practical matters and spiritually, having given up his private law practice in 1900, and he felt that such a leader must renounce all the claims of the flesh. He had arrived at the great principles which were to guide him until his death: dedication to *Satyagraha*, which can be translated as soul force or truth, and *Ahimsa*, or nonviolence. He now added to these *Brahmacharya*, or absolute chastity of body and mind. Mrs. Gandhi, herself a deeply religious woman, understood and sympathized with his attitude.

In theory, he was an orthodox Hindu, but actually there were other elements in his belief. Deeply impressed by the Hindu sacred book, the *Bhagavad Gita*, he was hardly less influenced by the teachings of Jesus, and especially the Sermon on the Mount. He once said: "I have regarded Jesus of Nazareth as one amongst the mightiest teachers that the world has had. Those who today call themselves Christians do not know the true message of Jesus." Christ's doctrine of pacifism fitted in with and reënforced his own ideas.

Though skeptical in so many things, he firmly believed in the Hindu doctrine of reincarnation. He wrote to one of his disciples: "It is Nature's kindness that we do not remember past births. Where is the good of knowing in detail the numberless births we have gone through? Life would be a burden if we carried such a tremendous load of memories."

Gandhi was also deeply influenced by Ruskin and Tolstoy. Ruskin confirmed him in his determination to perform for himself menial household duties that most Indians of his class left to others; Tolstoy was another factor reënforcing his pacifism.

During most of his life, Gandhi had very little time for reading, or for recreation of any sort. He never saw a movie until 1944, at the age of seventy-five; his first one was *Mission to Moscow*, and his innate puritanism came to the fore, causing him to criticize the ballroom dancing by "flimsily clad" women in the picture.

The doctrine of nonviolent resistance spread rapidly among the Hindus in South Africa with Gandhi at their head. The law said you could not cross the border between two states without a permit; Gandhi deliberately defied this statute, but since he was already a famous personage the police looked the other way. Thereupon Mrs. Gandhi and fifteen other people did the same thing and were sentenced to three months' imprisonment at hard labor. When there was a strike of several thousand miners, hundreds of them crossed the forbidden border in a protest march. The Government herded them into a concentration camp surrounded by barbed wire, where many were cruelly beaten. News of this action was reported in the press all over the world; public opinion, not yet inured to cruelty as it was to become forty years later, responded with a wave of indignation that caused the white South Africans to yield a little. About the time that Gandhi returned to India in 1914, some of the worst restrictions on the Hindus were removed. Among them were the poll tax and a law that said marriages performed according to Hindu customs were illegal;

technically this had made every Hindu wife a concubine and her children illegitimate.

Nonviolent noncoöperation as practiced by Gandhi and his followers required enormous courage. It meant that you accepted the beatings by your enemy without following the normal human instinct of seeking to hit back. To prevent a train from moving, hundreds lay down on the track in its path. Gandhi exhorted his followers: Never start passive resistance unless you are perfectly sure you have enough force of character to go through with it.

There was no visible trace of masochism in his doctrine. "The mice," he once remarked, "which helplessly find themselves between the cat's teeth acquire no merit from their enforced sacrifice. . . . It is the right of the citizen to withdraw his coöperation from the state when that coöperation means his degradation. . . . Nonviolence is the greatest force at the disposal of mankind. It is the summit of bravery. I am a noncompromising opponent of violent methods even to serve the noblest of causes. To win independence you have to learn the art of dying without killing."

The nonviolent noncoöperation of South Africa developed into the full-fledged *Satyagraha* of later years during the Indian resistance to British rule. Since it played such an enormous part in Gandhi's life and that of his followers, it deserves a word of explanation. Most people think of it as merely refusal to coöperate, boycotting goods, striking for political reasons, closing shops, and so on. While these elements were included, to the Indians, *Satyagraha* went far beyond such matters.

As Dr. Joan Bondurant points out in her thoughtful book, *Conquest of Violence,* it is a struggle for positive objectives and for fundamental change. Gandhi called it an "experiment with truth"; you find out what is truth through the suffering you undergo at the hands of your opponents. The principles involved are nonviolence, truth, and the dignity of labor; the objectives are independence and moving toward the ideal society; the means is refusal in every way to coöperate with the oppressor. (Since Gandhi's death, there have been added to the general concept the system of voluntary gifts of land to peasant groups, a movement headed by an extraordinary Indian named Vinoba Bhave, and a scheme for basic education centered around learning a single craft.) Supplementary policies that Gandhi stressed were abolition of Untouchability, and social and political decentralization—more power to the villages—which would move toward the ideal society.

A typical *Satyagraha* campaign in Gandhi's later years in India embraced several stages. First of all he developed a large group of loyal lieutenants, devoted to his ideals and willing to endure any hardship for the cause. Then he began by seeking to persuade the opponent (in most cases the British Government of India) to modify the onerous conditions in question. If this did not work, as it never did, civil disobedience was begun, after full notification of what was coming, including in some cases giving the Government in advance the names and addresses of the leading participants!

Though Gandhi emphasized that "God is Truth," and also, with some difference in meaning, "Truth is God," he himself never claimed to possess any absolute truth. "What appears to be truth to the one," he remarked, "may appear to be error to the other. . . . For me the only certain means of knowing God is nonviolence—*Ahimsa*—love." One involved in *Satyagraha* must have no hatred in his heart, must wish ill to no one, have no evil thoughts, never tell a falsehood. Instead of mere refusal to act, this philosophy means action based on the refusal to do harm. You must do good even to your enemy, but this does not mean that you should by your passive consent help him to go on being bad; you must seek to break all ties with a wicked person.

You should do penance when you have committed a wrong act, but its wrongness must not be something you have conjured up out of your own mind; others must agree that this is the case. This doctrine of Gandhi's had two important practical values: By refusing to claim absolute truth he could work with people of any religious faith, or for that matter, of none. By insisting on a general agreement that something is wrong, he deftly turned aside all sorts of eccentric masochists who might want to punish themselves for imaginary ills.

Just how much success his nonviolent noncoöperation had in South Africa is hard to judge today. As soon as he went back to India, the Indians in South Africa pretty much abandoned his methods. As noted, there was some amelioration of the worst discrimination against the Indians over the next few years, and part of this was certainly the result of his activities and of the worldwide pressure of public opinion he succeeded in arousing.

A point to remember is that passive resistance was almost the only weapon the Indians had in South Africa. Strikes could be maintained only for very short periods; the strikers lived from hand to mouth at best, and after a few days without wages, they were on the verge of starvation. Sabotage of plants and equipment was not only alien to Gandhi's temperament but to that of most of his followers, beside needing, at least in some cases, special training and equipment.

Today in South Africa violent race discrimination is being practiced mainly against African Negroes. It is difficult to say what connection, if any, today's situation has with what Gandhi did.

We may anticipate our story and ask: Did *Satyagraha* in its final, full form, play an important role in eventually winning freedom for India? That it had some effect is certain; just how powerful it was is a matter that will be debated for generations to come. Gandhian resistance to the British flamed up periodically and then subsided again for long periods; sometimes the whole country was involved, sometimes only one area.

One of the striking cases came when about 100,000 Pathans on the Northwest Frontier adopted a modified form of Gandhi's philosophy, based upon their Moslem faith. The Pathans are a fierce, warlike people; less likely candidates for the doctrine of "love your enemies" would be hard to imagine. Nevertheless, their passive resistance to the British Government, coming to a climax in 1931, caused an enormous amount of trouble; the British hanged or shot an unspecified large number, but the movement survived another seven or eight years.

We should remember that *Satyagraha* was accompanied throughout the years of the struggle by some stronger tactics against the British. Here and there, bands of terrorists, some very large, committed isolated acts of sabotage. While the Indian National Congress was entirely under the Mahatma's influence, it never formally adopted nonviolence as its policy, and some members frequently excoriated the British rulers in most un-Gandhian language.

Most of the *Satyagraha* campaigns seemed at the time unsuccessful or at least inconclusive. On the other hand, they helped educate the people to the possibilities of united action; they brought women out of seclusion into active political life; they created nationwide and worldwide publicity for some of the grosser evils of British rule. In one case, a proposed drastic increase in land taxes in one area of Bombay Presidency was resisted successfully; in another, the government salt monopoly was broken to the extent that the peasants were thereafter allowed to manufacture salt for their own domestic use. Britain's series of concessions over the years to the growing power of the Indian National Congress was undoubtedly hastened and enlarged by the *Satyagraha* campaigns, and especially by the Indian boycott of textiles and of liquor.

It is true, of course, that a campaign of this sort won't work except against an enemy who himself has some decency of character. This meant, in India and South Africa, the British or other Europeans who had been brought up in substantially the British tradition. As we have seen, in the early 1930's several million Russian peasants, all devout Christians, used nonviolent noncoöperation against Stalin's orders that their lands be incorporated into state farms; the Russian dictator simply took away their food, left them to starve, and stole their possessions; it is impossible to see that the sacrifice of these millions of men, women, and children had any effect at all on the subsequent historical development, except that perhaps the serious disaffection, especially in the Ukraine, made things somewhat harder for Stalin in the Second World War. Hitler, too, would have gloated over the excuse that pacifist resistance would have given him to machine-gun every participant.

In India, in Gandhi's time, there were powerful factors making for eventual freedom in addition to what he did. There was some pressure on London from other parts of the British Commonwealth. During the thirty years from 1917, when America entered the First World War, until 1947, when India was finally granted self-rule, Great Britain was sensitive to adverse criticism from the United States; and this was especially true from 1939 to 1945, when she could hardly have survived in the Second World War without American aid. For various reasons, there was powerful sentiment in the United States, official and unofficial, for setting India free. The work of Gandhi and his followers undoubtedly hastened the loosening of the ties; but it is difficult to argue that without him those ties would never have been loosened at all.

While he was still in South Africa, Gandhi set up the pattern of group living that was to continue for the rest of his life. He abandoned the idea of having an isolated home for his own family, and created a community that usually consisted of thirty or forty people but might increase to as many as two hundred or more from time to time. This was called an *Ashram*, an ancient Indian word for a living-group which, originally, consisted of holy men, corresponding roughly to the European concept of a monastery. Its members, beginning with Gandhi himself, performed all their own daily labor, sharing in the tasks indiscriminately, and with no regard for caste taboos. His successive *Ashrams* were very far from self-supporting; for almost fifty years of his life, Gandhi raised huge sums of money from wealthy Indians, primarily to fight the battle for freedom for all Indians—at first in South Africa and afterward in India—but incidentally to cover the costs of his household. His lifelong friend and associate, the poet Mrs. Sarojini Naidu, once made a widely quoted remark, "It costs a lot of money to keep Gandhi poor."

As the Mahatma became more and more famous through the years, the claims on his time became ever greater; when he wanted to be out digging latrines, to bring himself down to the level of the Untouchables, he was more likely to be obliged to sit all day long in a room, or under a tree, greeting an interminable series of devout pilgrims. Before the pressure got quite so great, he did, however, participate in many practical activities. Medical service being almost nonexistent for the Hindus in South Africa, he became something of a doctor, administering medicines to his followers, who were probably benefited as much from the fact that the remedies came from him as from their actual therapeutic qualities. As an amateur obstetrician, he successfully delivered his wife's fourth child.

In 1907, there occurred an incident that was characteristic in several ways. A law was passed in the Transvaal requiring all Indians over the age of eight to register and be fingerprinted. They regarded this as an insult, and refused to obey; Gandhi, as a leader of the recalcitrants, was put into jail. Jan Smuts was the Government official in charge of enforcement. The Indians were raising such a furore over the law that he had Gandhi brought from prison to confer with him and offered to repeal the law if the Indians would register voluntarily.

Gandhi agreed to this, though he had great difficulty in persuading his angry fellow countrymen to go along with him. Indeed, one Pathan not only refused to register, but threatened to kill the first Indian who did so. Gandhi, fearless as usual, said he would be that first man, whereupon the Pathan did in fact strike him down, injuring him severely. Gandhi recovered fairly soon, and refused to prosecute his assailant, who, he said characteristically, was doing what he thought was right. Then Smuts repudiated his promise, and the law was reënacted. A huge uproar followed; at a public mass meeting thousands of Indians burned the registration certificates they had voluntarily signed, trusting, with their leader, in Smuts's word. Hundreds were put into jail, headed, of course, by Gandhi. The new law remained in force for some years.

Typically, in spite of this betrayal, Gandhi continued to work with Smuts, and to accept his word as to what he would do. Following the code of *Satyagraha*, all his life he trusted every opponent and went on doing so, no matter how many times he was betrayed. In the case of Smuts this policy bore valuable fruit; up to that time the South African had shown very few of the qualities of greatness that he afterward displayed, but working with Gandhi over the years, he gradually built a basis for solid understanding, and the repressive laws were mostly repealed. Not until Smuts lost his influence did South Africa begin to return to the barbaric practices that are so much in evidence today.

When Gandhi prepared to return home in 1914 on the eve of the First World War, the grateful Indian colony in South Africa proposed to give him an enormously valuable treasure of gold, silver and jewels—one that could have meant lifelong economic security for him. To the dismay of his wife and some of his friends, Gandhi refused to take it, believing that to do so would violate the principles he had laid down for himself. Instead, he had the treasure sold, and set up a public trust fund with the proceeds.

He returned to India after a visit to London, arriving in his native land early in 1915. By this time he was famous all over the Western world. In India itself, however, he was known to only a handful of educated people. The peasants, eighty percent of them illiterate, were aware of nothing beyond the immediate horizon of their daily work; and the spread of information was further handicapped by the scores of different languages used in various parts of the country.

For decades, the demand had been steadily growing among

the people of India for better treatment by the British, who had conquered them one hundred and fifty years ago and had ruled the country by force or the threat of force ever since. Most of the Indians lived in desperate poverty; rightly or wrongly, they attributed this at least partially to British rule. Also of great importance was the social snobbery which existed among the British as it has among almost all other European colonial powers throughout the world.

There have always been many Englishmen who believed in freedom and equality, but somehow they hardly ever managed to get into any important place in any colonial administration. Most of the British agreed with their famous military hero, Field Marshal Lord Roberts, who said, "It is [the] consciousness of the inherent superiority of the European which has won us India. However well educated and clever a native may be, and however brave he may have proved himself, I believe that no rank which we can bestow on him would cause him to be considered an equal by the British officer." As late as 1920, official British documents quoted with approval an even blunter statement by General Drake-Brockman: "Force is the only thing an Asiatic has any respect for."

Social intermingling was conducted according to a rigid etiquette: you had to be a very important Indian indeed to get invited to parties given by Englishmen of a rank far inferior to your own. Rarely was an Indian allowed to become a member of a British club, although these clubs were staffed by Indian servants. The thousands and thousands of Eurasians born in India were almost always the result of a liaison between an Englishman and an Indian woman. (It is ironic that one of the most beautiful and touching of Rudyard Kipling's short stories, *Without Benefit of Clergy*, describes such a situation with complete unconsciousness of the anomalous social situation involved.)

It was not until two years after Gandhi's return to India that he began to make a real impression on the Indians. In Bihar, a province in the Northeast near Nepal, there were

British-owned farms occupied by about a million sharecroppers. They could grow any crop they chose, but fifteen percent of the land had to be sown to indigo, and this crop went to the landlord as rent. The leases provided that if any tenant refused to plant indigo, his rent could be raised. Synthetic indigo had recently been invented in Germany, and had destroyed the market for the natural product. The landlords therefore ordered the tenants to stop planting it, but at the same time used the technical language of the leases to raise the rent because the tenants had obeyed their orders!

The sharecroppers knew that there was no longer any market for natural indigo, and resented the trick by which their rents were being raised. The landlords responded by strong-arm methods: houses were looted, cattle seized, protesting farmers beaten and thrown into jail. Frightened of the white man, thousands of Indians signed new leases under duress. Finally, some of their leaders who had heard of what Gandhi did in South Africa sent a spokesman to plead with him to come and help them, and after a long delay he consented.

As soon as he arrived, he was arrested and ordered to leave the area; when he said he wouldn't, he was haled into court. Thousands of farmers came and packed themselves around the courthouse; as was to happen many times in the future, the police had to ask Gandhi himself to appeal to the crowd to be orderly, and as always, he cheerfully complied. By now, the district was in an uproar and the authorities were frightened. They told Gandhi he would have to give bail; but when he refused, they released him anyhow, and a few days later, on orders from the Central Government at Delhi, the case was dropped.

Gandhi spent nearly a year in Bihar. He forced the landlords to abandon the increased rents, and even to give back part of the money they had already extorted. Conditions among the peasants were miserable, and with the aid of the wealthy friends he was already beginning to accumulate in India he brought in doctors, sanitary experts, and teachers.

When he finally left, he nominated a committee of well-educated Indians in the province, most of them lawyers, to see that the abuse of the peasants was not resumed. The men he chose were willing to act but they suggested they should be joined by an Englishman, a famous disciple of Gandhi, Charles F. Andrews, who came to India as a Christian missionary and was one of the first men to fall under the Mahatma's spell. Andrews was willing to serve, but Gandhi fiercely resisted (if anything he ever did could be called fierce). You only want him because he is English, he told the members of the committee. You are just displaying the usual Indian inferiority complex. Andrews did not serve.

At about this time, Gandhi made his first notable public address after returning to India, one that showed his astonishing moral courage. He was invited to speak at an important ceremony at the Hindu University in Benares. He was a little-known lawyer, recently back from twenty years in South Africa; the audience included many great princes and maharajahs and their ladies, magnificently clad, covered with jewels, and surrounded by retinues of servants. But Gandhi was not at all impressed. His speech was one long excoriation of the wealthy and highborn of India for not contributing more money to the fight for independence, for neglecting the needs of the suffering masses, and for abusing the privileges of rank and caste. True to the ideals he himself had practiced, he told his audience that no man should be exempt from menial labor; that the priests should help to clean the temple, and the maharajahs to clean the streets in front of their own palaces. His address had no visible effect in the way of reformation, but when it was over, one thing was certain: people knew who he was.

Now began a way of life for Gandhi that was to continue, with few exceptions, for thirty years. He lived in an *Ashram* with a group of his followers, all day and every day receiving streams of visitors, most of them simple Hindus who believed him to be an exceptionally holy man and sought his blessing, others rich and powerful political leaders working to set India free.

All sorts of people asked his advice; he gave it readily, often admitting afterward that it had been bad. Sometimes he showed profound insights. When a young man came to him saying he intended to kill himself, Gandhi surprised all around him by merely requesting the boy to think it over for a day. He said he might suggest some acts of atonement for past misbehavior, but if tomorrow the youth still wanted to take his own life, Gandhi had no objection. The following day, the young man agreed to go on living, and Gandhi afterward explained the lad had been so overwrought that if ordered not to commit suicide he would almost certainly have done so.

At other times, the Mahatma's shrewdness had a glint of humor in it. A holy man turned up at the *Ashram* wanting to be fed and cared for without doing any work, planning to spend his whole time in meditation. Gandhi said sharply, "Meditation and worship are not things like jewels to be kept locked up in a strong box. They must be seen in every act." The holy man went to work like everybody else.

From time to time Gandhi would make long tours through India in the interest of the independence movement. In his weak, high voice, he addressed huge mass meetings; most of the members of the crowds could not hear what he said, but the mere sight of him sent them into hysterical frenzy, which was in various degrees composed of religious adoration and the powerful impulse to throw off the British yoke.

For decades he endured the overpowering devotion of the masses, most of whom considered him to be a god, or at least to possess supernatural powers. When he traveled by train, the stations were jammed with thousands seeking a glimpse of him; sometimes the train could not move, and fire hoses had to be used to push back the mob. (Such intense adoration of religious leaders is a familiar aspect of Indian culture.)

The British responded to the fight for freedom with the only actions colonial governors have ever seemed capable of: repression. Time after time they put Gandhi and all his chief leaders into jail; in the course of his life he spent six years and 148 days in prison—249 days of this time in South Africa and the remainder in India. He was always a model prisoner, cheerfully doing everything he was told (unless he was fasting). His jailers, of whatever race, wound up with deep affection for him.

Gandhi's fasts are widely misunderstood in the West. It is thought he was trying to force his own release, or even to compel the British to take immediate steps toward Indian independence. On the contrary, his fasts were almost always for self-discipline, or a form of compulsion exerted toward his own followers when they ignored his advice and took a course that he thought was politically unwise or incompatible with the teachings of religion. "I have no recollection," said Gandhi, "of a single experiment of mine in fasting having been a fruitless effort." Sometimes on these occasions he took nothing but water; at other times he would add a little fruit juice or salt, or bicarbonate of soda. On several occasions it was his fixed intention to continue until he either got his way, or perished. In his later years, when he was venerated by almost every Indian, the British government was alarmed lest he should die while fasting in prison, and in some instances released him.

In 1919 occurred one of the most terrible incidents in the history of British-Indian relations, the Amritsar Massacre. Following the First World War, the Indian people were growing more restive than ever. Indian troops had been brought to France to fight and there had discovered that the supposedly godlike white man had feet of clay like anybody else, that Indian soldiers fought as well as Europeans, man for man. The Moslems had a special grievance after 1918—the harsh terms imposed by the victorious Allies on Turkey, a Moslem Power, and the removal of the Sultan, both a political and a religious leader.

Amritsar, a city of 150,000 in the Punjab, occupied largely by the fierce, bearded Sikhs, a sect that broke away from the main body of the Hindu religion several centuries ago, was the scene of demonstrations of growing intensity during the early months of 1919. Because of this, two leaders of the Indian National Congress, a Moslem and a Hindu, were exiled from the Punjab, and on April 9 there was a riot in which three Englishmen were killed. Brigadier General Reginald E. H. Dyer, a true Colonel Blimp type, was in command of the city, and a few days later he issued a proclamation forbidding processions and meetings. He took no trouble to see that it was circulated, however, and there is no evidence that any considerable number of people ever heard of it.

On April 13, Dyer got reports that a mass meeting was to be held in the city at a place called the Jallianwalla Bagh, a very large vacant lot almost entirely surrounded by walls or by continuous rows of houses. It had only a few small entrances, too narrow for a wheeled vehicle. Dyer decided to go to this place with some soldiers and, as he afterwards said, to shoot all the men. His lighthearted comment was, "I thought I would be doing a jolly lot of good." His official report on the affair said: "It was no longer a question of merely dispersing the crowd, but one of producing a sufficient moral effect not only on those who were present, but more especially throughout the Punjab. There could be no question of undue severity." The official Government Commission which investigated the matter and gave Dyer only a perfunctory reprimand, commented merely, "This was unfortunately a mistaken conception of his duty."

Dyer brought two armored cars with machine guns which he intended to use on the crowd, but the cars were too wide to get through the narrow passage into the area. He therefore entered on foot with about a hundred soldiers, half of whom had rifles and the other half, knives. He entered on high ground at one end of the field; at the other, 10,000 or more Indians were clustered around a speaker. Without any warning, Dyer ordered his fifty men to fire and to keep on firing, which they did. In all, 1,650 rounds were used; although the official reports say that 379 were killed and 1,100 wounded, no one knows whether these figures are accurate; some estimates of the number killed go as high as a thousand. As the crowd rushed to one side, where the wall was lowest and they hoped to scramble over, Dyer told his men to aim where the Indians were thickest, increasing the carnage.

The massacre had the results that should have been foreseen: all India was set ablaze. The Viceroy, Lord Chelmsford, and other leading British officials stood by Dyer. The Indian National Congress, led by Gandhi, demanded that India strike back with the only weapon at her command: nonviolent noncoöperation, including a boycott of all possible British goods and services. Finally waking up to the seriousness of the situation, Great Britain made a few concessions to the Indian desire for self-government, the Montagu-Chelmsford reforms, under which a few ministerial positions in the provinces were for the first time made available to Indians.

This was a totally inadequate gesture and many leading Nationalists said so; but Gandhi, following his usual policy of always believing the enemy until he proves unworthy, pleaded for acceptance. "To trust is a virtue," he said. "It is weakness that begets distrust." Reluctantly, his lieutenants yielded to his enormous prestige and influence, and called off the boycott.

The uneasy truce was to be of short duration. As time passed, the Indians saw more clearly that the gestures toward participation in the government meant little and were to be followed by nothing more. The Moslems, always better fighters and haters than the Hindus, continued to brood over the slight to the Mohammedan world embodied in the new British policy toward Turkey. Within about a year the Indian National Congress, with Gandhi in the lead, reinstated the boycott in deadly earnest.

Indian lawyers drastically curtailed their incomes by refusing to practice in British courts. Students and faculty members withdrew from British-controlled universities. The Moslems abstained from liquor because of their religion; now the Hindus also abstained, in order to cut British tax revenue. An important source of government income was the impost on cloth, whether imported from Manchester or woven in British-owned textile mills in India. Gandhi went campaigning against foreign cloth; hundreds of overwrought Indians in his audiences tore off their garments then and there and pitched them into big bonfires.

The leaders of the Congress decided to restore the lost art of home weaving; unable to find a hand spinning wheel anywhere else, they borrowed one from a museum, copied it, and distributed many thousands of duplicates to Indian households. Gandhi himself undertook to spin at least half an hour a day. "Agriculture and hand spinning," he pointed out, "are the two lungs of the national body. In losing the spinning wheel, we lost our left lung." Home weaving not only hurt the British revenue, but it gave the Indian farmer something to do in the four or five months of each year that he was not working in the fields.

The British as usual responded with nothing but force. Gandhi and other leaders were in and out of jail repeatedly. Mass meetings were broken up by policemen, who beat the crowd mercilessly with *lathis*, long, sturdy, wooden staffs. Following Gandhi's instructions, most of the crowds, most of the time, made no resistance but allowed themselves to be struck down to the earth and lay there.

The stalemate continued. For some years in the late 1920's Gandhi did what he was also to do in the late 1930's, and ostensibly withdrew from political life. His role as a spiritual leader became even more marked, if that was possible; using his religious influence, as always, for practical ends, he pursued one of his great objectives at this time: to seek amelioration of the lot of the Untouchables.

For many centuries, India has lived under a rigid caste system by which the people are isolated into separate groups; there are four chief castes, with hundreds of subcastes. Highest of all are the Brahmans, who were originally priests—though now they follow many occupations. Next come the Kshatriyas, at one time the rulers and warriors. The Vaisyas, the caste from which Gandhi came, began as tradesmen and farmers, and fourth came the laborers, the Sudras. Beneath all these, outcasts in the literal sense, come the sixty million or so Untouchables.

For centuries, caste lines were rigidly preserved economically as well as in every other way; you could not follow an occupation reserved to another caste, even one below your own. Intermarriage between castes was looked upon with horror. There is still great resistance today to such intermarriage, although the economic barriers have been somewhat relaxed.

The doctrine of reincarnation helped to fortify the caste system. Hindu religion teaches that your station in this life is the result of good or bad deeds through one or many previous incarnations and that by fulfilling your lot as well as possible now, you can improve your status in some future rebirth. It was comforting and simple for the Brahman to assume that his fortunate position had been earned through a good life on many previous visits to earth, and that the Untouchable was paying for past sins.

Gandhi used the doctrine of reincarnation for practical purposes. Pointing out that every act done in the present has its effect, and every action has its reaction, he argued that one can make of himself whatever he will, and so can a nation. By so doing he helped to offset the tendency of many Indians to despair, to resign themselves to accepting whatever fate should send them.

The Untouchables, who constitute perhaps one-sixth of the Indian population, have always been forced to live in deep poverty and ostracism. While most Indians dwell in what seem to Western eyes to be slums, the Untouchables' lot is the most wretched of all. Until modern medicine brought home the lesson that disease cannot be halted by imaginary lines, they rarely had any unpolluted source of water. They do the humblest work, sweeping the streets and cleaning lavatories. Their chief form of craftsmanship is work in leather, which members of the four superior castes will not undertake because of the special veneration their religion applies to cattle. The present government of India has tried hard to better the lot of the Untouchables, and most of the legal restrictions have been removed; but custom and tradition die hard—perhaps harder in India than almost anywhere else—and the Untouchables are still poor and more oppressed than any other group.

Gandhi's ideas about the caste system in general developed slowly. In 1920 he wrote that he considered the system "fundamental, natural and essential," and the following year he said that he regarded the "prohibition against intermarriage and interdining as essential for the rapid evolution of the soul." In 1927 his son fell in love with the daughter of one of his closest friends, Chakravarti Rajagopalachari, who belonged to a different caste, the Brahman; the two outraged fathers forbade the match, not only because of the difference in caste but in Gandhi's case from the decidedly old-fashioned point of view that marriages arranged by the families are better than love matches! The parents jointly demanded that the young couple wait five years, hoping that their affection would cool in that length of time. When it did not, the elder generation gave way and permitted the marriage.

Though as late as his fifty-eighth year Gandhi thought that marriages should be arranged by the families of young people, he came early to disapprove of child marriage, and for decades he campaigned against it. Sometimes a girl of four or five would be "married" (only by ceremony) to a full-grown man, perhaps even one in or beyond middle age. If the husband died, the child was condemned to permanent widowhood. This was better than the forbidden practice of *suttee,* the burning alive of the widow in her husband's funeral pyre, which even in Gandhi's early days had been pretty well stamped out; but it was still an intolerable and unnatural fate. Child marriage is now illegal.

While still a young man, Gandhi began his lifelong fight for a better lot for the Untouchables. In spite of his lingering conservatism, even while living in South Africa he brought members of this group into his home as lodgers, to the horror of

Kasturbai. By the time Gandhi's first *Ashram* was established in India, he insisted on having Untouchables live there in full equality with caste members; for a long time, he would not permit a marriage to take place at the *Ashram* unless one of the parties was an Untouchable. With a shrewd public-relations instinct, Gandhi tried to abolish the semantically bad word Untouchable, or the equally bad British phrase, "the Depressed Classes," and call them the *Harijans*, which means the Children of God. Hoping to break down arbitrary distinctions, he once said, "I am an Untouchable. I am a Hindu, I am a Moslem, a Christian, a Jew, a Buddhist."

At first his attitude outraged many wealthy Hindus, and they withdrew their financial support; before long, the *Ashram* was out of money. On one occasion when things were at their blackest, a mysterious stranger drove up in a limousine and put 13,000 rupees (about $2,600) in bills into Gandhi's hand. (He was later identified as a wealthy textile manufacturer from a nearby city.) Gradually, Gandhi's great spiritual authority broke down the religious prejudice of caste members close to him, and with great perturbation, they actually ate meals at the *Ashram* with Untouchables, or shared with them in kitchen labor.

In 1932, the British government, continuing its series of niggling concessions to India, proposed to let the Untouchables vote, but only for special Untouchable candidates, just as they had long before laid down a policy that Moslems could not vote for Hindus, and vice versa. The leader of the Untouchables, the brilliant Dr. Bhimrao Ambedkar, wanted to accept the proposal on the practical ground that half a loaf is better than nothing, but Gandhi opposed it, just as he had opposed the similar policy for Moslems and Hindus. Louis Fischer, in his *Gandhi: His Life and Message for the World,* points out the harm separate electorates caused:

> A Moslem could vote only for a Moslem candidate and a Hindu only for a Hindu. The mischief produced by this institution was incalculable, because it made religious differences the deciding factor in every political contest. It was as though

Catholics in England, the United States and France, could vote only for Catholic candidates to Parliament and all other offices, Protestants for only Protestant candidates and Jews for only Jews. The central problem was to bridge the gulf between Hindus and Moslems and thereby make India a nation, but separate electorates, by closing the door to political intermingling, destroyed the bridge and widened the gulf.

Gandhi decided to fast in protest against the divisions that were widening among Moslems, caste Hindus, and Untouchables. His blood pressure was high, and the doctors said if he continued to fast he would probably not survive. India was in an uproar. In the effort to persuade him to break his fast, many Hindu temples were thrown open to Untouchables for the first time. Prominent Hindus announced in the press that they had taken food from the hands of Untouchables, or had eaten with them in public. In the villages, members of this group were at last permitted to use the water from the common well. Thousands of organizations adopted resolutions against discrimination; telegrams announcing such actions were heaped in a pile six feet high in the yard of the prison where Gandhi was, as usual, in jail. Finally, he agreed to break his fast. Unfortunately, the fraternal emotions engendered by Gandhi's peril did not last, and India soon slipped back a long distance.

As the decade of the 1920's waned, British-Indian relations got steadily worse. Promised improvements did not materialize, or turned out to be insignificant. Increasing numbers of Indians repudiated Gandhi's pacifism; there were riots in which British property was destroyed and Englishmen were injured or killed. Gandhi was trying as usual through his nonviolent campaign to appeal to the better nature of the British. He said, "My ambition is no less than to convert the British people through nonviolence and thus make them see the wrong they have done to India." But he was also, when he had to be, a shrewd and practical politician. He now saw that he must yield somewhat to the rising storm.

When the British Labor Party came to power in 1929, the

Indians' hopes were aroused; the Party had always professed friendship for India and had advocated Dominion status, if not complete freedom. With Labor in the saddle, the Viceroy, Lord Irwin (afterward to become Earl of Halifax), made a public statement promising Dominion status at some indefinite date in the future. But the Labor Government had to retreat; it had only a bare majority in the House of Commons, and the Liberals and Conservatives threatened to join forces on this issue and throw it out of office. At a new conference between Lord Irwin and the leaders of the Indian National Congress, December 23, 1929, the Viceroy repudiated his previous tenuous pledge. The Congress met at once, and with Gandhi's agreement, came out for complete independence. A communication was sent to the Viceroy with a demand for an answer before New Year's Day.

Gandhi and the other Indian leaders gathered in his *Ashram* and waited as the minutes ticked toward midnight on New Year's Eve. When no answer came, the men present signed the Declaration of Independence. On January 26, millions of Indians took the pledge that under Gandhi's leadership they would fight on for freedom; January 26 is still India's equivalent to the American Fourth of July.

True to character, Gandhi had done his utmost up to the last minute to compromise with the British and avoid the final break. He wrote to Lord Irwin saying, "Whilst . . . I hold the British rule to be a curse, I do not intend harm to a single Englishman or to any legitimate interest he may have in India." On other occasions he summed up his attitude on colonialism: "Good government is no substitute for self-government. . . . The economics that permits one country to prey upon another is immoral. . . . Imperialism is a negation of God."

In his letter to Lord Irwin he specifically indicted British rule in India.

> Why do I regard the British rule as a curse? It has impoverished the dumb millions by a system of progressive exploitation and by a ruinous, expensive, military and civil administration

which the country can never afford. It has reduced us politically to serfdom. It has sapped the foundations of our culture. . . . I fear . . . there has never been any intention of granting . . . Dominion status to India in the immediate future.

He added that the taxation system "seems to be designed to crush the very life out of [the peasant]. Even the salt he must use to live is so taxed as to make the burden fall heaviest on him." The peasants, Gandhi gravely explained to the Viceroy, ate more salt per capita than the rich because they did manual labor and perspired more. To buy salt required three days' work by each peasant each year. The government was also fattening itself on profits from liquor and opium, which debauched the Indians. Gandhi complained that the Viceroy's salary was $85,000 a year, the equivalent of perhaps $200,000 a year today, while the average Indian's income was about $14 a year. Thus the Viceroy received a salary equal to the earnings of more than 6,000 Indians, while the British Prime Minister got only the equivalent of the earnings of ninety average Englishmen. Gandhi added a statement that was to prove enormously significant, that he intended to disobey the law that punished an Indian if he possessed salt obtained in any other way than from the official government salt monopoly.

One of the most dramatic single episodes in a life crowded with drama now began. On March 12, 1930, Gandhi started the historic "Salt March" from his *Ashram* to a point on the seacoast about 240 miles away. He left with seventy-eight men then living at the *Ashram*, and obligingly printed the names of all members of the group in his magazine, *Young India*— which was a convenience for the police. For twenty-four days the party walked, stopping each night in some village, averaging ten miles a day but on some days walking as many as fifteen. Gandhi, who was sixty-one, refused the offer of a horse, walked the entire distance, and showed less fatigue than many other younger members of the party. Each day he stopped to spin for an hour and to write in his diary; and several times each day, political meetings were held in the villages en route, where the pilgrims were joyously received, to urge the cause of civil disobedience and to collect funds to carry it on.

All India was soon in turmoil; people came from all over the country to join the march. The inhabitants of each village walked with Gandhi at least as far as the next one, and some of them continued on with him toward the sea. When on April 5 the pilgrims arrived at the coast at the little town of Dandi, the group had several thousand members. They held an all-night prayer meeting, and early in the morning followed Gandhi down to the beach. He waded out into the water a little, and then returned to the shore and picked up some salt, the result of evaporation of seawater in a small pool. This was technically a violation of the law, and was all that was needed. (The salt he picked up was later auctioned off for $500 to raise money for the cause.)

A new wave of resistance to the British, both violent and nonviolent, now swept the nation. Everywhere along the Indian coast peasants dipped pans into seawater and manufactured salt illegally. Gandhi and all the other leaders of the Congress were soon back in jail; the number of political prisoners quickly mounted to about 60,000.

A dreadful incident followed soon after at an official government salt works at the town of Dharsana. The Congress ordered a raid on the salt works by unarmed men who were to offer no resistance to the police. Webb Miller, a noted American correspondent for the United Press, was there and reported what happened. The Indians resolutely marched forward, a few at a time, toward the salt works, facing a line of police armed with heavy *lathis*. The police struck them down, fracturing many skulls or breaking shoulder bones. As each wave of Indians fell to the ground, another followed. Miller reported that after one raid he counted in the hospital 320 injured people, "many still insensible with fractured skulls, others writhing in agony from kicks in the testicles and stomach." A few of the police were sickened by the results of what they had to do, and sometimes refused to go on with it.

The brutality at Dharsana, and other similar incidents which set the country aflame, soon brought results. The Viceroy, who had ignored Gandhi's earlier communications, now conferred with him, and a compromise agreement was effected. As noted earlier, peasants were henceforth permitted to manufacture salt for their own use but not for sale. The harsher aspects of the censorship by the British Government of newspapers, magazines, and pamphlets were modified. The 60,000 political prisoners were released. Worldwide attention had again been drawn to the fact that the people were anything but happy under British rule. The Indian National Congress was permitted to participate in a Commonwealth Round Table Conference to take place soon in London.

In exchange, Gandhi agreed to call off the boycott of liquor and textiles, although the campaign for home spinning and weaving continued, and no disciple of his ever wore British-manufactured cloth. The propaganda battle was also brought to a temporary halt.

Nothing in Gandhi's whole career was more impressive than his ability to convert millions of Indians to *Satyagraha*. Many Americans tend to brush off this achievement on the ground that Indians are pacifists by nature or by religion, or both; but this is a false notion. It is true that some religions practiced in the subcontinent preach that taking life must be avoided if possible, but there are others that breed a different attitude. Only a few decades before Gandhi was born, the Government of India stamped out with great difficulty the doctrine of Thuggee, which in service to the Goddess Kali murdered hundreds of thousands of innocent people, usually unwary travelers, by strangulation. The Sepoy Rebellion (the Indian Mutiny) of 1857 was marked by scenes of great brutality. The Sikhs are famous as warriors and serve as policemen in many Asiatic countries. In the First World War, as noted above, Indian troops proved fully equal to white men when they were imported into Europe. In short, the people of India vary in their personal characteristics quite as much as do those of any other part of the world. Proof of Gandhi's extraordinary personal power while he lived is shown by the fact that following his death there was an explosion of dreadful violence between Hindus and Moslems.

The affair at Dharsana, and many similar scenes throughout India, deepened the bitterness between the Indians and the British, if that were possible. Rabindranath Tagore, the famous Indian poet, a supporter of, but not a very active participant in, the independence movement, second only in national prestige to Gandhi himself, wrote at the time:

> Europe [Great Britain] has completely lost her former moral prestige in Asia. She is no longer regarded as the champion throughout the world of fair dealing and the exponent of high principle, but as the upholder of Western race supremacy and the exploiter of those outside her own borders. For Europe, this is, in actual fact, a great moral defeat.

The struggle between the two nations went grimly on. A Round Table Conference held in London in 1930 came to nothing; the Indian Nationalist movement was not even represented. In 1931 a second Round Table Conference was held in London, and this time Gandhi was allowed to attend; he was let out of jail to do so and incarcerated again as soon as he returned to India. Under such circumstances it is hardly surprising that the conference failed; as Gandhi acidly remarked on another occasion, "You can wake a man only if he is really asleep; no effort that you make will produce any effect upon him if he is merely pretending to sleep."

The Indian, however, scored a personal success with the British public with his charm and wit. Though the meeting took place in the cool British autumn, he wore only his regular Indian costume—loin cloth, sandals and a shawl or blanket. Asked about this, he replied, "You people wear plus fours; mine are minus fours." Invited to tea at Buckingham Palace with King George V and Queen Mary, he refused to dress up for the occasion, remarking afterward, "The King had enough on for both of us."

While he often showed a keen sense of humor, he was sometimes literal-minded to a breathtaking degree. At a time when he still considered himself loyal to the British crown, he worried seriously about the national anthem which says: "Scatter her enemies And make them fall; Confound their politics, Frustrate their knavish tricks." Gandhi asked in complete earnestness, "How could we assume that the so-called 'enemies' were 'knavish'? And because they were enemies, were they bound to be in the wrong?"

As the stalemate continued, life in India again gradually moved back toward more normal conditions. Young people returned to the universities; many Indians who held various types of jobs under the British resumed them. The closing years of the 1930's were for Gandhi like those of the 1920's; ostensibly at least, he devoted himself chiefly to religion and the efforts to improve the lot of the Indians within the framework of the existing political situation. He continued to be venerated by the masses who insisted, to his deep displeasure, on trying to treat him as a god.

Through the years, the Mahatma attracted to himself, as already mentioned, many disciples; while most of them were Indians, some of the others came from all over the world. One of the most famous was Miss Madeline Slade, daughter of a high-ranking British naval officer. While still a young woman, she read about Gandhi in her home in Great Britain, and felt an irresistible urge to cast in her lot with his. She went to India, joined the *Ashram*, and stayed there; when he was away, they corresponded frequently, and some of these letters have been published and give a fascinating picture of the details of his life, more candid, since they were not intended for publication, even than his autobiography. He called her Mira, and she called him *Bapu*, or Father. In one letter he boasts of having got his weight up to ninety-five and a half pounds, after months of weighing less. In another, he is apologetic about traveling second class on the railroad instead of third. (This was not miserliness on his part: Aside from his determination to share the lot of the masses, he lived on donated money and wanted as much of it as possible for the needs of the *Ashram*, always on the verge of bankruptcy.)

Mira gave him a new spinning wheel; he did not like it and wrote to her listing its defects. But he would end up saying: "Enough, however, of criticism. I am not going lightly to leave aside a thing that has come charged with so much love. I am, therefore, going to continue the use of the wheel and report to you from time to time." In fact, he spun so much that he had to stop using his left arm for awhile.

All the members of the *Ashram* followed Gandhi in not destroying animal life, if it could be avoided, and Mira was no exception. She wrote to Gandhi about the mice in her bedroom:

> They found their way into my bed, sometimes nibbling my feet, sometimes running up and down my side and sometimes getting mixed up in my hair. My chief anxiety was not to squash them. And what with this anxiety and the fidgeting of the mice, sleep became a difficult problem until I hit on the device of using a mosquito net. This proved wholly successful.

She needed a different technique, however, with the scorpions and rats.

> In the cottage . . . I had caught and removed to the fields not less than fifty-two scorpions . . . I set about catching the rats and within a week removed over thirty to a distant upland.

Gandhi's attitude on not taking life was not rigid enough to satisfy some of the more fanatical Indian sects, like the Jains. On one occasion he condoned killing a pack of sick and miserable homeless dogs, and on another he agreed that a dying calf should be put out of its misery, things for which he was abused for years.

The coming of the Second World War brought a great new opportunity to India in her fight for freedom. While Gandhi had supported the British cause in the First World War, more than twenty years of bitter experience had elapsed since then. Other leaders of the Congress Party were now prepared to coöperate with the British in exchange for a firm promise of freedom when the War was over, but Gandhi's official position was one of neutrality; in his heart he may have been more pro-Ally than he seemed.

In any case, Britain would make no such bargain as the Indians proposed. Churchill, who in 1935 had said that "Gandhism and all it stands for must ultimately be grappled with and finally crushed," was now in full control as Prime Minister. On November 1, 1942, he made his famous statement that "I have not become the King's First Minister in order to preside at the liquidation of the British Empire." It was as though the British, even in their darkest hour, were deliberately seeking to alienate the Indians, who could have been of enormous assistance. When Gandhi asked for a conference with the Viceroy, now Lord Linlithgow, hoping for some sort of compromise, Linlithgow refused to see him.

In August, 1942, the Congress voted to resume civil disobedience. Though the censorship kept the news from the Western world, terrible riots broke out in many parts of India. Gandhi and the other leaders went back to jail. The British Government lost control of many districts, where the local inhabitants improvised rule for themselves; some Indians actually joined the War on the side of the Japanese.

The British first cut off Gandhi's lines of communication with the outside world, and then started a campaign of public propaganda blaming him for the violence. This false charge hurt him deeply. As he wrote to Linlithgow, by putting him into prison incommunicado, the British had destroyed his power to try to keep noncoöperation nonviolent. He began a new fast, announcing in advance that it would last twenty-one days; the doctors predicted that he would die, and he nearly did so, but somehow he survived.

Time dragged on. On February 22, 1944, Kasturbai, who had also been put into prison, died in Gandhi's arms. A few weeks later, Gandhi suffered a severe attack of benign tertian malaria, and once more fears were felt for his life. On May 6 he was released with his associates.

In July, 1945, about two and a half months after Germany surrendered and shortly before the atom bombs on Hiroshima and Nagasaki proved the last blow to reeling Japan, the war-weary British people voted the Labor Party into office. Clement Attlee, the new Prime Minister, was made of sterner stuff than Ramsay MacDonald had been sixteen years earlier. He immediately set action under way to give India Dominion status. Yet the news, after so many years of struggle, brought not peace and rejoicing to India, but heightened bitterness and tension. This was because of the quarrel between Moslems and Hindus over the form the new India should take.

The quarrel was never to be resolved, and for this the chief blame probably falls on the Moslem leader, Mohammed Ali Jinnah. The closer India came to freedom, the more obdurate Jinnah was in his long-standing demand that the Moslems, about a quarter of the total population, should have a separate country of their own, Pakistan. (Not all Moslems, by any means, concurred.) Since there were two widely separated regions in which they had a majority of the population, he stipulated that East and West Pakistan, in different parts of the subcontinent, should be set up; the first would be almost surrounded by Hindu territory, with one short border contiguous to Burma, and the second would face the new India, the Arabian Sea, Iran, and Afghanistan.

The British finally announced that they would quit India not later than August 15, 1948, and sent Lord Louis Mountbatten to India to close up shop as the twentieth and last Viceroy. Mountbatten, great-grandson of Queen Victoria, who had served brilliantly as an Admiral in the British Navy in the Second World War, captivated everyone by his charm, but the religious conflict was too deep to be ended, or even much ameliorated, by anything one man could do. The Indians wanted the country to remain united, under one government, and the British wanted this also. They set up a plan for a Federal Government, with strong Provincial Governments with great local authority, in various parts of the country.

Jinnah continued, like the fanatic he was, to insist on partition. Gandhi, strongly opposed to Jinnah, wavered between acceptance and rejection of the British scheme, liking the general idea but being dissatisfied with some of the details; he was followed halfheartedly by most of the leaders of the Hindu-dominated Congress Party. The overriding fact was that Jinnah was prepared to go to war to get his way, while the Hindus were not, and the British were by now concerned only to get out of India as soon as possible and on as decent terms as could be obtained.

Jinnah proclaimed August 16, 1946, as Direct Action Day. The Moslems raged through Calcutta for ninety-six hours, and in the fighting 5,000 persons of both religions, but mostly Hindus, were killed, and 15,000 wounded. Reprisals sprang up all over the country; in Bihar, 5,000 to 10,000 were killed; the Hindus were the chief aggressors and the victims were mostly Moslems.

Gandhi, seeing his whole life's work going down the drain and the Indian people who professed to love him turning to blood lust, was in a desperate frame of mind. As the Congress wavered nearer and nearer to accepting partition, he traveled up and down the country struggling desperately to rouse the people in favor of one united nation and also to halt the bloodshed. In the midst of all his other troubles, he had to stop and seek to reconcile his warring lieutenants, Sardar Vallabhbhai Patel and Jawaharlal Nehru. Patel was perhaps the strongest of the Indian leaders, just as Rajagopalachari was the most statesmanlike. Nehru was ideologically furthest from Gandhi, but for him the older man had a deep personal affection.

In his seventy-seventh year, the Mahatma went into East Bengal (now East Pakistan) to try to ease the tension. Nearly all of India is a bleak, inhospitable region, with impoverished soil and a bad climate, but this part presents especial difficulties; it is so remote and hard to traverse that the traveler feels enormously isolated. It is a vast swamp area, cut into fragments by the various mouths of the Ganges, a land with little wheeled transportation, where one must walk, crossing numerous fragile bamboo bridges strung high above the streams to prevent damage in time of floods. Gandhi's personality was still magic; wherever he went, there was usually momentary peace. Indians and Moslems embraced one another and swore friendship, but as soon as he had gone, fighting sprang up again. Yet in spite of his tremendous prestige, there were some times when his own life was actually in danger—usually from fanatical Hindus rather than from Moslems.

The Congress Party finally accepted the principle of partition, though both East and West Pakistan were made much smaller than Jinnah had at first demanded. In August, 1947, the two new states came into existence, with Nehru as Prime Minister of India and Jinnah, Governor General of Pakistan.

There followed in Northern India one of the most terrible mass riots in modern history—one not then fully reported to the outside world—conducted by armed individuals and mobs responsible to no one. Refugees fled across the country from districts that were about to come under the formal control of the other religion. There were no provisions for their care, and they were murdered, or starved, or died of disease by thousands along the roads.

Everywhere there was looting, rape, and killing. In districts like East Bengal, where the Moslems were about eighty percent of the population, thousands of Hindus were forcibly "converted." Large numbers of women were abducted and "married" to Moslems, insuring that their fanatical Hindu families would never take them back. J. B. Kripalani, President of the Congress, told of one well that yielded 107 bodies of Hindu women and children; the women had destroyed their children and themselves to avoid attack by Moslems. In another case, fifty Hindu women were killed by their fathers, brothers, and husbands, to avoid a similar fate. Hordes of refugees trampled down the grain in the wheat fields, destroying thousands of tons of potential food and adding to the horrors of the famine.

Gandhi, having worn himself out journeying around the countryside from one conflagration of religious hatred to another, decided on a new fast to try to stop the slaughter. He announced that it would be a fast to the death, and since his health as usual was precarious, the doctors again predicted he could not last very long. Leading Moslems and Hindus came to his bedside and promised that the fighting would stop—a promise which they were of course powerless to carry out, though temporarily things were better. When Gandhi demanded that the promise be put in writing, they readily complied, setting up a whole series of fair-sounding conditions. The Mahatma ended his fast after seventy-three hours.

Moslems owned vast amounts of property in the parts of India from which they were being expelled, just as Hindus owned substantial though probably lesser amounts in the areas soon to be incorporated into Pakistan. On January 13, 1948, Gandhi began another fast, which was to prove his last. He announced in advance that it was another attempt to bring an end to the religious war, but after a day or two, he said that it was also to require the new Indian Government to pay $125 million to Pakistan in compensation for its share of the assets left behind in the transfer of population. All the leaders of the Congress Party—except Gandhi—were unanimous that this could not be done. They sent a delegation to see him which explained elaborately why his proposal was impossible. Gandhi, his strength failing fast, responded merely by bursting into tears; the delegation announced that the compensation would be paid.

By now, the Mahatma was too weak to stand. When Indian leaders came to confer with him, he whispered his wishes to one of them, who repeated aloud what he had said. The most formal pledges were again made by the Hindus that Moslem life and property would be protected. On the fifth day of his fast, Gandhi seemed to be pondering whether to live or die. His decision was to live, and he called for a glass of orange juice.

He was a guest at this time in the Delhi home of a millionaire Hindu sympathizer, G. D. Birla, and for some time he had been conducting a daily prayer meeting in the spacious grounds of the residence. On the first day after his fast ended, he had to be carried to the meeting, where he prayed in a barely audible voice into a microphone connected to a loudspeaker.

By now, die-hard young Indian Nationalists had formed a secret terrorist organization aimed at the Moslems and at all Hindus who seemed to be supporting them, which of course meant Gandhi above all others. On January 20, 1948, one of the members of this terrorist group, Madan Lal, tried to kill Gandhi with a bomb at the daily prayer meeting; it went off but at some little distance.

On January 30, another of the conspirators, Nathuram Vinayak Godse, attended the meeting. He was a Brahman, editor and publisher of an extreme right-wing Hindu Nationalist weekly. Armed with a revolver, he crowded forward to the small raised platform from which Gandhi conducted the meetings. As the Indian leader mounted the steps, Godse pulled out his revolver and shot him three times. Gandhi said only, "Oh, God!" and collapsed, dying a few minutes later. Godse was at once arrested and hurried away by the police to avoid possible vengeance by the crowd. He was later tried and sentenced to be hanged.

The funeral, the traditional Hindu open-air cremation, was held at the junction of the Ganges and the Juana Rivers. It was attended by one of the largest crowds even known to assemble anywhere, estimated at four million persons.

Gandhi's scorn of material possessions is well illustrated by the worldly goods he left when he died: half a dozen articles of wearing apparel, three bowls, a pair of spectacles, a watch, a copy of the *Bhagavad Gita.*

Horrified by the murder which was the climax of the dreadful almost nationwide bloodbath, the country became somewhat more peaceable. Relations between the two states remained bad; they quarreled in particular over the possession of Kashmir, the beautiful valley in the Himalayan foothills in northwest India, but the transfer of populations, accomplished at such terrible cost, proved roughly effective in ending the riots and massacres.

Since the establishment of the precarious peace, both nations have worked hard to ameliorate conditions for their people. In both, and especially in India, these efforts have been almost swamped by the huge, never-ending increase in population, amounting at present to more than 14,000 a day. The Indian Government has encouraged birth control, with thus far negligible results. Gandhi himself recognized the dreadful problem of overpopulation and suggested that families have but one child. He was opposed to birth control except through continence, even though it is not incompatible with the teachings of Hinduism. He felt that the problem should be solved by voluntary chastity such as he had practiced since his middle thirties.

With all his faults and weaknesses—defects which he confessed in public, over and over, with a candor unparalleled in this generation—Gandhi remains a towering figure among the great leaders of the twentieth century. It is true that during his active life, the flames of anti-colonialism were burning fiercely all over the world; sooner or later, India would have obtained her freedom even if he had never lived. Yet the historic fact remains: When his countrymen needed a leader of heroic stature, he filled that role. And at the same time he gave the world the extraordinary lesson of his personal life: his devotion to truth, charity, and love of his fellowmen.

# 7. Chiang Kai-shek:
# The Warlord as Statesman

OF ALL THE MEN in this book Chiang Kai-shek probably has the most puzzling personality. On the surface a Hamlet-like introvert, he has nevertheless acted at times with great decision and complete ruthlessness. A tremendous egoist, with an indomitable drive to power and success, he has more than once, at crucial periods, suddenly resigned all his posts and gone to sulk in his tent until called back by his associates. Often very cruel to his enemies—he once ordered the execution of more than sixty members of the family of a General who had opposed him—at other times he permitted opponents who had been captured to escape, or even gave them large sums of money and sent them into exile abroad.

In conversation, especially with foreigners, he is markedly silent; Madame Chiang is usually present on these occasions and does the talking. Yet for many years he had a habit of calling weekly conferences of those of his officers who were near by. At these sessions he would read aloud the famous Testament of Dr. Sun Yat-sen, pausing after each sentence to let his audience repeat it in unison. Then he would lecture the men, sometimes for two hours, reporting everything that had gone wrong or been done badly since the last meeting;

his listeners had to stand up for this whole period. When he was through, he would say curtly, "Completed."

A tremendously hard worker, for most of his adult life Chiang rose at dawn and got in an hour's work before breakfast. Then he continued until lunch, after which he took a short nap; John Gunther in *Inside Asia* says that for a long period he went to sleep every day to a rendition of Schubert's *Ave Maria* on a phonograph. After his nap he worked again until tea time, and after that he meditated or prayed for half an hour. He liked to work lying on a sofa.

Like most other dictators, he has been abstemious. He does not smoke or take coffee or tea, and barely tastes of his glass of wine on ceremonial occasions. His only real recreations are walking or reading Chinese poetry. He eats either Chinese or occidental food, sparingly.

A favorite quotation of his is from Confucius, and gives something of a clue to his character:

> In order to propagate virtue to the world, one must first rule one's country.
> In order to rule the country, one must first rule one's family.
> In order to rule the family, one must first regulate one's body by moral training.
> In order to regulate the body, one must first regulate one's mind.
> In order to regulate the mind, one must first be sincere in one's intentions.
> In order to be sincere in intentions, one must first increase one's knowledge.

The greatest influence in his life, and a tremendous one indeed, is Madame Chiang, one of the three remarkable Soong sisters. She and all her family were devout Methodists, and when the marriage was impending, it was suggested to Chiang that he might well adopt that faith. He replied with some asperity that people would think poorly of one who changed his religion in order to win a bride. They were married in

**CHIANG KAI-SHEK**

"On the surface a Hamlet-like introvert, he has nevertheless acted at times with great decision and complete ruthlessness. Though a tremendous egoist . . . he has a sense of humor, wry and subdued."

1927, and within three years Madame (as she is known universally to the Chinese) had converted him. He took his religion seriously; on one occasion when he was going into battle against a group of Chinese enemies, with a slim chance of success, he prayed. A blinding snowstorm ensued, unusual in that place at that time of year. It helped Chiang to win, and he believed it was an answer to his prayer.

Most of his biographers speak of the Generalissimo's iron self-control; however, Theodore H. White and Annalee Jacoby, who had many opportunities to see him in action, say in *Thunder Out of China* that he sometimes engaged in violent tantrums in which he would throw crockery or beat any underling who came within his reach.

Chiang is not noted for his sense of humor, but he has one, wry and subdued. For many years his closest foreign friend and chief adviser was the Australian journalist W. H. Donald, who, as his name suggests, was of Scottish ancestry. Chiang assiduously collected Scottish jokes and told them in Donald's presence. Once, when the Australian suggested, "Let's shoot all the traitors and crooks," the Generalissimo drily replied, "Unfortunately, there is not enough ammunition in China."

For a long time, Chiang kept a private diary, and this once helped to save his life. In 1936, when the Chinese Civil War was raging, he was captured by a warlord, Chang Hsuehliang, who was sympathetic to the Communists and sought to force Chiang into a united front with them against the Japanese. Though his life was in danger, Chiang refused to compromise, or indeed, to negotiate with his captors at all. They found his diary in his possession, read it, and were apparently deeply impressed by its spiritual quality. They were also impressed by the message he sent to his wife immediately after being captured:

> As I have made up my mind to sacrifice my life, if necessary, for my country, please do not worry about me. I shall never allow myself to do anything to make my wife ashamed of me or become unworthy of being a follower of Dr. Sun Yat-sen. Since

I was born for the Revolution I will gladly die for the same cause. I will return my body unspotted to my parents. As to home affairs, I have nothing to say further than I wish you would, to gladden my spirit, regard my two sons [from an earlier marriage] as our own.

Madame Chiang, as famous for her bravery as is her husband, promptly joined him in the kidnapers' custody. At the moment that he learned he was to be forcibly detained, Chiang had tried to escape, climbed a wall, fallen into a ditch, and hurt his back; it was to trouble him at intervals for the rest of his life. Madame Chiang helped to care for him, and after a few days the kidnapers gave up and released him. Although he had made them no promises of any kind, he did in fact soon make a truce with the Communists, as he had done before and was to do again, under the pressure of events. Like the other agreements, this one soon fell apart.

In what sort of China did Chiang grow up, in the last decade of the nineteenth century? It was first of all a land of desperate poverty for the many, and great luxury for the few. All but a very small minority of the population were peasants, many of them working badly eroded or otherwise difficult land (sixty percent of China is at an altitude higher than 6,600 feet). Partly because of overuse of the land, devastating floods were frequent. Any crop failure, for any reason, brought famine in which many thousands sometimes died quietly in their villages, or fled a few miles to another area which, very likely, was as short of food as their own. Little attempt was made by the Chinese Government or outside agencies to alleviate these famines; when efforts were undertaken, it was found that the rice eaters of the South sometimes starved because they could not adjust to wheat, and the wheat eaters of the North rejected rice.

The popular Western idea of a big Chinese family with several generations living under one roof usually applied only to the middle and upper classes; poverty kept the rural population small. Most upper-class women had their feet distorted by binding, beginning in early childhood, so that they walked with an insecure wobbling motion which Chinese men found peculiarly attractive; bound feet were a status symbol, indicating that the upper-class woman had all her work done by servants or slaves. Peasant women on the other hand performed the hardest sort of physical toil in the fields.

The Chinese were ignorant of birth control, but they kept the population in balance by the surest technique of all: infanticide. Since only sons could inherit, girl babies were unwelcome, and millions of them were strangled at birth, or put out on the roadside to die. Trying to divide the land among several heirs resulted in carving up the tiny farms, usually only a few acres, into strips; as in Tsarist Russia, these made any sort of use of machinery almost impossible; production of food in China cost ten or twenty times as many man-hours as in the United States. Most peasants were tenants, and the landlords, avaricious and brutal, took fifty to eighty percent of the crop as rent. Tax collectors for the central Government, or the warlords, got much of the rest.

With such a huge population, about four hundred million even when Chiang was a boy, it is not surprising that human life was at a discount. Every year, nearly 30,000 corpses were picked up in the streets of Shanghai alone, some of them newborn girl babies, the remainder, people who had died of hunger or hunger-induced disease, or those whose relatives were too poor to afford a costly funeral.

Desperate families in the hinterland were often glad to sell their children into slavery or, in the case of girls, concubinage. Contractors for the Japanese-owned textile mills in Shanghai and other cities would go through the country buying the services of children, sometimes only five or six years old, to work long hours in these mills. They slept on rags under the machines they tended, locked in for the night, and were fed just enough rice to keep them efficient for hard work. The children were sold for only a few dollars, and their wages were paid to the entrepeneur. The contracts were usually for three or four years. Conditions in the British- and Chinese-owned mills were not much better, though contract labor was not permitted.

In general, the China in which Chiang grew up was very much as it had been for thousands of years. The men wore pigtails; these had fallen out of fashion by the middle of the seventeenth century but were made compulsory at that time by the Manchu conquerors to remind the people to whom they owed loyalty. Great cruelty was practiced to slaves and prisoners; the latter were sometimes exposed in cages, and would have starved if they had not been fed by their families and friends. Torture was the standard form of extorting confessions; it was only partially abandoned, well into the twentieth century.

When Chiang was born, the foreign Powers already had a firm grip on China. Its sparse large-scale industry was chiefly operated by foreigners in the "treaty ports." The foreign-owned factories actually made the poverty of the peasants worse; they had been accustomed to use their spare time to manufacture silk and to weave cloth, straw baskets, and hats, but they could not compete with the cheap factory goods turned out in the cities by coolie labor.

The central Government, with headquarters in Peking, was only partly in control of the country. The redoubtable old Dowager Empress was the real ruler, although the nominal Emperor was her nephew, Kwang Hsü, whom she had appointed after the death of her son, Tung Chih, in 1875. The rule was that of the Manchus. In theory they were still an army of occupation, ruling the land by force; in fact, after more than two centuries they had become indolent and corrupt. Though the great development of the warlords came after the Manchu power was overthrown in 1912, they existed decades before that in some parts of the country, a parallel to the robber barons in medieval Europe. They ruled strictly by terror, maintaining private armies, taxing the people heavily, issuing their own currency, which was backed by bullets, making constantly shifting networks of alliances with one another, accompanied by almost constant warfare. These struggles were not very lethal; the warlord who saw that his adversary was superior would usually be glad to be bought off, or alternatively, to pay heavy ransom to be allowed to continue to rule his little satrapy.

China was being slowly nibbled to death by the Great Powers, notably Japan, Germany, Great Britain, and France, all of which had seized territories and put them under their own rule. The United States also demanded special concessions and privileges, though she refrained from taking land.

The process of foreign domination began with the famous Opium War of 1839. The British had been importing opium into China to be sold to the people; the Chinese Emperor of the day tried to put a stop to this, and the British invaded the country and forced him to permit the commerce. An uneasy truce followed until the war broke out again in 1856, the British this time being joined by the French. The following year the Allied Forces captured Canton and Peking. Still another revolt began in 1860 and the British again occupied Peking. Russia now joined in the looting and seized a large area facing on the Pacific Ocean, ranging all the way down from the Sea of Okhotsk to the Sea of Japan, including what is now Russia's chief seaport, Vladivostok.

Over the years, the foreigners extended their control. Japan, especially, took over large areas of land and set up puppet Chinese regimes, or tried to. Several of the other powers had "concessions" in some of the larger cities.

The doctrine of extraterritoriality was forced upon China by the Great Powers. This meant that none of their citizens was subject to Chinese law; if they committed a crime, they could be arrested only by police of their own government and tried only in their own courts. Chinese police were not allowed to set foot in the foreign settlements, though the foreign police would sometimes capture there a Chinese suspected of a crime, and turn him over to the local authorities.

Beyond this, the foreign Powers set up their own post offices and other services. China borrowed money from them—sometimes forced upon her—and service on these loans became a first claim upon the Chinese customs duties. To make sure that these would be administered properly, they were put into the hands of foreigners, some of whom turned out to be able civil servants who made needed reforms in many parts of the government.

China for centuries had chosen many of its officials by civil-service examinations. These were very difficult, and men sometimes studied for them through their youth and even through middle age. While competitive examinations are better than the spoils system characteristic of some Western countries, these examinations were based mostly on ancient classical lore and had not much relationship to the jobs filled through them.

Bribery was universal in China and had become through long usage a virtually untouchable part of the system. Nearly all public officials, from the lowest to the highest, expected to get a certain amount of "squeeze" from those who came to them seeking their official services. Household servants who did the marketing could afford to work for almost nothing because they got squeeze from the merchants with whom they dealt.

A profoundly important factor, running deep into the Chinese culture, was "saving face"—avoidance of even the slightest degree of public humiliation. When Chiang Kai-shek was kidnaped, he refused for several days to eat the food offered him, thus causing his captors to lose much face. Westerners traveling through remote parts of China and carrying their own food could not use it if they were the guests of a Chinese; they had to eat local food, no matter how poor, and pay it extravagant compliments.

Loss of face often resulted in consequences startling to the Western mind. During the Second World War a group of soldiers being trained by Americans, exhausted by long hours of drill, fell asleep during a lull in practice maneuvers. They were all shot by their Chinese officers, who had lost face because of their actions. One soldier, who stole an apple from an orchard and ate it, contrary to orders, was publicly rebuked for doing so. He killed himself that night. Sometimes troops in untenable advanced positions, ordered to retreat, would refuse to do so, to save face.

The Chinese written language is the despair of foreigners, and of many Chinese as well. Each word is a separate picture, and always remains the same, so that, broadly speaking, there is no Chinese grammar. Originally, these were actual pictures showing the thing or the action described, but over many centuries, they have become stylized and formalized until the original relationship is all but lost. There are 40,000 to 50,000 of these picture words, but it is doubtful whether even the most learned scholar knows them all. By the age of ten, a child should know about 2,000, and a good newspaper, in the old days, used perhaps 7,000 or 8,000.

The difficulties created by the situation are formidable. It takes many years to memorize the ideographs with which an educated person is supposed to be familiar. It is almost impossible to index a book or to create a dictionary. Telegrams have to be coded into Arabic numerals and then decoded upon receipt.

For many years before the Second World War attempts were being made to simplify the language, and these are continuing both on Formosa (Taiwan), where Chiang Kai-shek took refuge after his defeat in 1949, and among the Communists who captured control of the mainland in that year. The effort is to reduce the number of written characters in common use to not more than 1,000. Books are now being published using this limited number of words, which might be compared to "basic English."

Although all literate Chinese can read the language as printed or written, there are many spoken dialects, some of which are incomprehensible to one another. To overcome this there have been efforts to make Mandarin, the classical language, universal; millions of Chinese students now learn both this and their native dialect.

The Communists have attempted to work out a phonetic alphabet on the Western model; this is not intended, however, to take the place of the ideographs, but merely to facilitate learning in the first few years. They have tried to make the ideographs less complicated; the five hundred most essential characters have been drastically reduced in the number of strokes required.

Chinese religion, as it used to be practiced on the mainland and survives today on Formosa and among the millions of Chinese overseas, is a complicated affair. There are hundreds of gods, some of whom operate only locally. There are also quantities of good and evil spirits. The religions based on Confucius, Lao-tse, and Buddha are not considered mutually exclusive, as Western faiths might be; any of them, or all three, can be fitted nicely into the hierarchy of Chinese gods.

Christianity came into China in an important way only after the unequal treaties were forced upon the country in the middle of the last century, and only under the protection of those treaties, the result being that the Christian missions became inextricably bound up with political matters. The missionaries suffered from the hatred of all foreigners; to offset this, some of them renounced their extraterritoriality, and put themselves under Chinese law, though others did not. It is estimated that at the most, Christian converts numbered only about one percent of the population, perhaps four or five million. Of these about nine-tenths became Catholics; the elaborate rituals of the Catholic Church, and especially its long list of saints, seemed to have a special appeal to the Chinese.

Chiang Kai-shek was born in 1887, in a little village near Shanghai. His ancestors were middle-class farmers and merchants, but his immediate family was poor. He was the eldest son of his father's third wife, and when the father died, while Chiang was still a child, his mother had a rough time of it. "Kai-shek" is a name he chose himself; it means "boundary stone"; he has another name, Chung-chen, which means "central righteousness."

From his early childhood he was determined to become a soldier, and as soon as he was old enough, he applied for and was admitted to the Paotang Military Academy. The Academy found, however, that he was lacking in some fundamentals, and as often happened in those days, he was sent to Japan, to the Imperial training school. It was a move that determined his whole future life. Dissatisfaction with the arbitrary, reactionary rule of the old Dowager Empress was widespread in China at this time, and many liberal young Chinese had entered the revolutionary movement. Some of these were in exile in Japan; Chiang met them and very soon fell under their spell.

The leader of all the revolutionary forces was a remarkable man, Dr. Sun Yat-sen. Born in 1866 to a poor farmer near the Portuguese colony of Macao, Sun was sent to Honolulu in the care of an elder brother and got most of his early education there. In 1891, he entered the new medical school in Hong Kong, being graduated in 1894. After China's humiliating defeat in the war with Japan a year later, Dr. Sun entered a revolutionary plot. It was discovered and most of his fellow conspirators were put to death, but he managed to smuggle himself out of the country.

Thereafter, he was for many years the chief figure in Chinese revolutionary activities, living abroad almost continuously. The millions of Chinese outside of China, in the Philippines, Hawaii, Malaya, and throughout the South Seas, were dissatisfied with the Manchu dynasty and contributed large amounts of money to Dr. Sun; the Dowager Empress responded by putting a price of £100,000 on his head—equal to a million dollars or more today. In an episode that sounds like something from the annals of Dr. Fu Manchu, Dr. Sun was once actually kidnaped on the streets of London and rushed into the Chinese Legation. His life was saved only when he managed to smuggle out a note to Sir James Cantlie, whom he had known when a medical student in Hong Kong. Sir James used his influence with the British Government which in turn put pressure on the Chinese, and Dr. Sun was released.

Japan's easy victory in the war of 1894–95 was followed by greatly increased aggression by her and by all the Western Powers. Japan seized Formosa and part of Manchuria, though Russia afterward forced her to draw back somewhat. Russia herself boldly built the Trans-Siberian Railroad across Manchuria. Great Britain took various bits of territory, including land on the Burmese frontier and the Kowloon Peninsula opposite Hong Kong. France got an area in Indo-China, and railroad and mining privileges. Germany seized Tsingtao, and railroad and mining concessions in Shantung. Russia next took the important twin harbor cities, Port Arthur and Dairen.

Nearly all the Powers put more pressure on China to borrow money from them for railroads and other improvements. The United States took no territory, but went on reiterating the demand first made by John Hay, Secretary of State, in 1899, for an Open Door policy. This was not actually intended to help the Chinese very much; it meant chiefly that the individual foreign Powers should not be unreasonably greedy at one another's expense.

The obvious fact that China lay helpless and open to exploitation forced some internal reforms. The Emperor, showing a spark of independence, organized new schools, reformed the archaic civil-service examinations, improved the courts and the civil code, and for the first time set up patent and copyright laws. He also began to reorganize the Army on the Western model. These improvements, as might be expected, incensed the reactionaries, of whom the Dowager Empress was the leader; through palace intrigue, she now made the Emperor a prisoner.

In 1900 occurred what the West calls the Boxer Uprising, whose core was a secret society called by the Chinese the Righteous Harmony Fists. The purpose was to kill all foreigners and Chinese Christians, and to end, once and for all, foreign occupation of Chinese soil. Scores of foreigners were killed, most of them missionaries, and thousands of Chinese Christians. Many foreigners gathered in Peking's Legation Quarter, which had been under extraterritoriality—among them a young American mining engineer named Herbert Hoover. They were besieged there by the Chinese, until an international army representing all the Powers fought its way in from the coast and rescued them. The slaughter of foreigners would have been much worse except that some of the warlords, especially in the West and South, at odds with Peking, refused to join the movement.

While the adolescent Chiang looked on, the nibbling to death of China continued at an accelerated rate which would have gone even faster were it not for the quarrels of the Great Powers among themselves. The Russo-Japanese War of 1904, fought partly over control of the Chinese province of Manchuria, speedily resulted in victory by Japan, paving the way for her annexation of Korea.

Somewhat chastened by the prompt defeat of the Boxer Uprising, the Dowager Empress now blew hot and cold, sometimes seeking the friendship of the Great Powers and at other times trying to sabotage them. She extended the movement to remodel the schools on a Western basis. Christian missionary schools were expanded and thousands of students were sent to Japan—among them young Chiang—or to Europe or to the United States. The latter country in 1908 returned its share of the indemnity extorted after the Boxer Uprising, on condition that it be used to let Chinese students study in American universities. The development proved of tremendous importance; in later years many of the high posts in the government were filled by men who had been trained in the United States and brought Western ideas home with them. Other reforms of this period included a promise of parliamentary government at some time in the future; the theoretical abolition of torture by the police—except in criminal cases; the abolition of slavery, which in view of the desperate poverty of the country had little tangible effect, and another in a long series of effort to stamp out the opium trade, Great Britain at last consenting.

Yet dissatisfaction with the Manchu regime was steadily mounting, intensified as students returned from other countries and reported on what they had seen. In 1908 both the Emperor and the Dowager Empress died; a child of two and a half years, Pu Yi, a nephew of the Emperor, was now put on the throne, and his father, a weak and ineffective individual, acted as Regent. Finally, in 1911, the troops supposedly loyal to the Manchu regime mutinied. The Manchus were forced out of office in many provinces, and a provisional republican government was set up at Nanking, Dr. Sun hastily returning from abroad to be its first President. Early in 1912, the boy Emperor, who could hardly have understood what was going on, was forced to abdicate, and the Chinese Republic at long last came into being.

When the collapse of the Manchu regime seemed imminent, Chiang Kai-shek went back secretly from Japan to work with the revolutionaries. He was by now, at twenty-four, technically an officer in the Japanese Army, and John Gunther in *Inside Asia* records the fact that he scrupulously returned his uniform and sword to the Japanese government—by mail!

The new Chinese Republic promptly fell upon hard times. Dr. Sun, named provisional President, had been out of the country so much that it was felt someone else should be made President. The post was given to the former Viceroy, Yuan Shih-kai, Dr. Sun accepting the lesser position of Director of Transport and Trade. Yuan turned out to be a traitor to the ideals of the Revolution. He now made himself a dictator, and it was obvious that he planned to become Emperor. By 1913 conditions were so bad that Dr. Sun started a new armed revolt. Yuan put it down easily, and Dr. Sun had to flee for his life to Japan. The new ruler used the excuse to declare the organization of Sun's followers, the Kuomintang, illegal. Its members were dismissed from Parliament, and Parliament itself was speedily dissolved.

The opening of the First World War, in September, 1914, gave Japan an opportunity to act alone in China without interference. She promptly seized the former German concession in Shantung. The following year she served her Twenty-one Demands on China, which was given only forty-eight hours in which to agree or take the consequences. The Japanese were to have their seizure of Shantung confirmed and their "rights" in Manchuria extended; they were to get important railroad and mining concessions, and even a degree of control of the Chinese police force. The United States, by now the only important neutral in the world, made a sharp protest, and the terms were watered down somewhat. However, Japan made a secret agreement with Great Britain and France that in return for her neutrality, she was to get large amounts of territory, including important islands in the Southwestern Pacific—agreements that were honored at the Paris Peace Conference of 1919.

In 1915 Chiang Kai-shek participated in an attempted military uprising near Shanghai, readily put down by the Government. What Chiang did for the next few years is rather obscure. His friends say that he was in the banking business in Shanghai under the tutelage of several wealthy Chinese bankers who took an interest in him and helped lay the foundations for his substantial personal fortune. His enemies say that he was only a clerk in the stock exchange, and engaged in dubious underground activities with the gangsters and racketeers who at this time and for many years thereafter had an "invisible government" in the city.

In 1917, after the United States had entered the war, there was great pressure on China to join the conflict. She did so on August 14, but there was little time for her to take effective action. She did, however, send a Labor Battalion of 175,-000 men to France; Chinese at that time were considered by the West to be only valuable to dig trenches and latrines—a point of view that was to change by the time the Chinese Communists entered the Korean War in 1950.

Among the laborers sent to France in 1917 was a young man named Chou En-lai, descended from a prosperous family of Manchu Mandarins. He stayed on after the end of the war to study in France, and returned to China to become the third most important figure in the Communist opposition to Chaing Kai-shek.

The central Government of China had practically ceased to exist. Dr. Sun, who by now controlled some of Southern China, set up an independent government of his own in Canton, but most of the country was in fact ruled by warlords, big and little. None of the Great Powers recognized Dr. Sun's government, a short-sighted action that they would afterward regret. Both Canton and the old Peking Government sent delegations to the Paris Peace Conference of 1919, and both were given some degree of recognition. They made a series of demands that China be set free from domination by foreign powers, all of which were refused. As a result, China would not sign the Treaty of Versailles which, among other acts of injustice, handed over to Japan control of the former German concession in Shantung Province. The Austrian Treaty omitted this obnoxious clause, and China signed that one, thus paving her way into the new League of Nations. One important concession made at Paris was that the German share of the Boxer Indemnity was cancelled; the victorious Allies were quite willing to put an end to imperialist actions in China by the defeated Central Powers while retaining everything of their own.

In 1920, the United States was responsible for formal adoption of the Chinese Consortium by all the chief Powers. This was described as a measure of justice to China but it was in fact, like John Hay's Open Door, little more than a scheme to give all the Powers an equal chance to force their loans upon the Chinese.

The next few years were more of the same. The great Washington Disarmament Conference of 1921–22 did very little for the Chinese except to permit them a world forum to present their grievances. The Conference actually confirmed Japan's "special interests" in Northeast China. However, the final Nine-Power Treaty said that Chinese territorial integrity ought to be respected, and set up machinery under which the foreign Powers were to consider the ultimate abolition of their own post offices in China, and even extraterritoriality. World public opinion had begun to swing to the side of China; under its influence, Japan grudgingly gave back the province of Shantung, though she kept control of the mines. A couple of years later, all the Powers followed the example of the United States and returned the money of the Boxer Indemnity, specifying that it must be used for cultural and educational purposes.

Of far more importance at this time was Russia's decision to come to the aid of Dr. Sun and the Kuomintang. The new Russian Communist Government had said in 1920 that it would help colonial people all over the world to get their freedom, but it was something of an innovation to apply this idea to a non-Communist, bourgeois revolutionary struggle like that of Dr. Sun. Several years later, this Russian policy was implemented by sending advisers from Moscow to work with Dr. Sun in his precarious Cantonese Government; the most important were the political expert, Michael Borodin, as he called himself, and the mysterious military expert known as Galen. They were of enormous value in organizing Sun's army. They also, with Sun's consent, were tremendously busy in increasing the size and activity of the Chinese Communist Party.

By now, Chiang Kai-shek was again taking a part in the revolution. By sheer force of personality he had come up through the ranks until he came to the attention of Dr. Sun. In 1925 he was sent to Russia for six months as liaison officer, and got on with the Russians well enough, though in later years he professed to have been greatly disillusioned by his visit. His son by his first marriage, on the other hand, lived in Russia for years, married a Russian girl, and was for a long time a dedicated Communist; he did not return to China until his father had gained control of most of the country.

In 1924, at Dr. Sun's insistence, Chiang had become director of the important Whampoa Military Academy; many of the men he trained there became invaluable to him as top officers in his army. In the same year, to symbolize the coöperation of the Communists with Dr. Sun's forces, an important Party leader, Mao Tse-tung, and seven other members, were elected to posts in the Kuomintang. Mao was the son of a "rich" peasant, owning nearly four acres in the Central China province of Hunan. His father beat and starved his whole family, and Mao left home as soon as he was able. He found his way to Peking University where he came under the influence of two left-wing professors, Li Ta-chao and Ch'en Tu-hsiu, who were to be the founders of the Chinese Communist Party. By 1925 Mao had risen in the Party to be one of its top leaders, and in that year, he was made chief propagandist for the Kuomintang Government at Canton.

To understand the relation between the Kuomintang and the Communists, at this time and later, we must remember that Dr. Sun's Revolution was a revolt against the tyranny and corruption of the Manchu dynasty, and little more. His famous Three Principles consisted of unity for the country, to be achieved by military means, the political education of the people, and after this had reached an advanced state, constitutional development, including elected officials and a parliament. He did not advocate the Communist doctrines of public ownership of the means of production, or breaking the grip of the landlords on the peasants, though as a liberal he opposed their most severe extortions.

Dr. Sun was easygoing and able to work with the Communists, but when he died in 1925, and Chiang became the dominant personality, the picture was changed. Chiang's ideas of the aims of the Revolution were even more limited than those of Dr. Sun. The truce with the Communists became increasingly an uneasy one, and Mao, sensing this, drifted away from Canton back to his native Hunan, where he began setting up small Communist guerrilla bands, composed primarily of peasants, who hid in the mountains.

At the time of Dr. Sun's death, Chiang was nominally only Commander-in-chief of the Kuomintang Army; that year he succeeded in capturing two of the three most southerly Chinese provinces, Kwantung and Kwangsi, and before the end of the year he had taken Canton. Tension between the right and left wings of the Kuomintang grew stronger. According to his own story, Chiang learned early in 1925 that the Communists were plotting to kidnap him, smuggle him on board a gunboat tied up at Canton, and kill him. He declared martial law in the nick of time, he says, and arrested the leading local Communists.

In 1926, his armies now being ready for action, he began a successful, rapid drive to the north. Borodin gave consent to this on behalf of Russia, and later got rebuked by Moscow for having done so. Chiang's army marched under radical slogans, probably more radical than its commander believed in. It was strongly anti-foreign, and some of the scenes of the Boxer Rebellion, a quarter of a century before, were repeated. Chiang dealt with the local warlords, some of them powerful men, in various ways, sometimes defeating them in the field, sometimes buying them off and incorporating their armies into his own.

Chiang's second wife, Mei-ling Soong, born in 1896 and a graduate of Wellesley College, was the youngest of the three famous Soong sisters. The oldest, Ai-ling, a graduate of Wesleyan College in Macon, Georgia, married H. H. Kung, at the time a child-welfare worker, but later to play an important role in Chiang's government. The middle daughter, Ching-ling, became secretary to Dr. Sun, and later married him. The three names of the sisters are attractive in translation: Ai-ling means the Lovable, Ching-ling means the Pure, and Mei-ling means the Beautiful.

There were also three brothers, of whom T. V. Soong was the most important. He was for nine years chairman of the National Bank of China, and did a good job in establishing a unified currency and fighting inflation. He is supposed to have accumulated a huge personal fortune, impressive even after he had lost a good part of it in the War. After a falling out with Chiang, he came to America, as did his two brothers.

H. H. Kung, who married Ai-ling and was a graduate of Harvard, was made director of the Central Bank. He, also, accumulated a large fortune.

Next to Madame Chiang, the best known of the six Soong brothers and sisters is Mrs. Sun, Ching-ling. After Dr. Sun's death in 1925, she continued his attitude of friendly toleration of the Communists, and when Chiang broke with them and began a reign of terror, she quarreled with him over this issue, left China and lived abroad for about twelve years. When her brother-in-law made one of his several truces with the Communists, in 1939, she was reconciled and returned to China, but when the civil conflict broke out with renewed fury after the end of the Second World War in 1945, she was alienated again, and this time permanently. How completely she is a Communist, no one can be sure, but she lives in Communist territory, is regarded by them as one of their chief public figures, and presumably has no more contact with the other members of her family.

Many people have expressed surprise that Chiang should have swung so far to the Right; but their puzzlement results from a misunderstanding both of the nature of Dr. Sun's Nationalist movement and of Chiang's character. While the Generalissimo has always believed himself to be completely loyal to Dr. Sun and his ideas, in fact he is and always has been far more conservative. He wanted China to be freed from the Manchus, but he has never been able to break away from the culture in which he was reared. In most essentials his own character has been as autocratic and dictatorial as that of any of the warlords of his youthful days. The veneer of democracy has been skillfully applied to him by Madame Chiang and others, but it is a veneer only.

By 1927, the break with the Communists was complete. Chiang's enemies say that he had to get support from the rich

Chinese bankers and merchants, and that his hostility to the Communists was part of the price he had to pay. Chiang himself says that the Communists betrayed and sabotaged him; both these explanations may be true. He had conquered all of China south of the Yangtse when he learned of a Communist uprising in the rear, in his home base of Canton. The Communists set up their own government, which claimed to speak for the Kuomintang. Chiang returned to Canton, crushed the uprising and began a bloodbath among the Communists. Edgar Snow, always hostile to Chiang, says in *The Other Side of the River* that there were at this time about 50,000 Communists in China, and that Chiang killed 40,000 of them. Whatever the number executed, there is no doubt that Chiang was harsh in the extreme. The Kuomintang had an extremely efficient secret police nicknamed "the Blue Shirts," who operated as the secret police always do under a dictatorship, creating a reign of terror of their own.

Now began a period that was to last for many years, in which Japan became even more aggressive in China. Her excuse before the world was that she was putting down a Communist uprising that threatened the whole Orient. Chiang and the Communists fought each other intermittently and also attacked the Japanese when opportunity offered; each party accused the other of being insufficiently zealous in fighting the invader. From 1930 to 1935, Chiang launched repeated assaults upon the Communist forces; several times when he seemed to be winning, Japanese military action, such as the invasion of Manchuria in 1931, forced him to divide his forces and lack the strength for a knockout blow. Mao was spreading his influence in several unconnected regions in Southeast China, and Chiang was unable to stamp out the Red guerrillas who came down into the plains for a quick strike and then retreated to their mountain fastnesses.

Fighting the Communists was useful to Chiang in several ways. It gave his armies indispensable battlefield practice. It also enabled him to invade the territory of any warlord on the ground that he was pursuing the Communist enemy—an excuse no local ruler could very well dispute. It was an effective answer to Japan's argument that she was invading China only to prevent a Communist revolution, since she fought Chiang, the enemy of Communism, as vigorously as she did the Communists themselves.

Stalin, by now dictator in Russia, was never very helpful to his Chinese comrades. The advisers he sent to China over a long period were there to aid Chiang; the Russian was quite prepared to betray Communism in China if he thought, as he did for a long time, that his interests would be better served by having Chiang in power. But while he was a poor friend, he was, after all, the only one the Chinese Communists had.

Their strength was concentrated in a few scattered pockets of resistance in Southeast China, cut off from direct contact with the Russians, and therefore, in October, 1934, they started what became famous as "the Long March," one of the most remarkable epic migrations in history. In about a year, they marched 6,000 miles across twelve provinces, beginning in Kiangsi, in southeast China not far from the coast, and ending a year later in Shensi, far to the northwest, not far from the border of Mongolia, which was under heavy Russian influence.

The entire Communist population, men, women and children, made the march, carrying all their valuable possessions, largely on their backs; they crossed eighteen mountain ranges, overran sixty-two cities, and averaged an almost unbelievable fifteen miles a day, resting one day in four. They began with about 100,000 men, of whom only 50,000 survived the almost daily skirmishes and the fifteen major battles fought with Chiang's forces. Once arrived at the Shensi town of Yenan, they set up an independent Communist state, whose first act was to declare war on Japan.

Meanwhile, that country was continuing her infiltration, especially in Manchuria. The Japanese arguments were several. First, they claimed they were doing little more than were the great European Powers. They also argued that they must have raw materials and markets for the badly overcrowded archipelago. Especially would they need food, coal, and oil in case they were to go to war with a maritime Power that could blockade their main trade routes; they were probably thinking of the United States, even ten years before Pearl Harbor.

In 1931 they seized the key Manchurian city of Mukden and proceeded to set up a dummy government of what they called Manchukuo. The little boy who had been put on the Manchu throne by the Dowager Empress in 1908, Pu Yi, was now a grown man and a collaborator with the Japanese, and they installed him as Emperor.

China appealed to the League of Nations, which at first temporized. It sent a committee, headed by the British Lord Lytton, to investigate a situation that was patent to the whole world. When the League finally got its courage up to declare Japan in the wrong, that country responded by withdrawing from the Geneva organization.

Fighting now broke out afresh in China. The Japanese landed military forces at Shanghai, and seized the far northern province of Jehol. Handicapped by his internal troubles with the Communists, in 1933 Chiang was forced to ask Japan for a truce.

The worldwide depression that had begun in 1929 had a serious effect on the Chinese economy. The countries of the West were on the gold standard, and when they went off gold in favor of a managed currency, it did not matter greatly to them that the rise in the price of this metal caused other prices to slump. Chiang Kai-shek, now in firm control of most of the country except those areas seized by Japan, was forced to nationalize silver and himself go to a managed currency.

He now tried to institute some badly needed reforms, though always within a limited range which did little or nothing to help the mass of the peasants. He tried with some success to introduce more Western ideas into education. Chinese medicine was of a traditional form centuries old, relying heavily on herbs and on acupuncture—thrusting hot or cold needles of various sizes into different parts of the body. Chiang did not dare to do away with it, and it is still practiced widely today. He did, however, try to set up some schools to teach Western medicine, to supplement those of the missionaries. Other reforms included a national post office and a national tariff system. Internal trade had for centuries been handicapped by tariffs between province and province, city and city, called *likin*; he attacked this problem.

Japan steadily continued her aggressions with an increasing tempo. Having bought the Russian interest in the Chinese Eastern Railway, she sent her troops into two more northern provinces, Hopei and Chahar. Finally, in July, 1937, she decided the time had come for full-scale war. On the flimsy pretext that a Japanese soldier had been kidnaped—a story that proved to be false—she attacked on a big scale around Shanghai. Some authorities believe that she intended to annex only the five northernmost provinces, but every war, once begun, gets out of the control of the aggressor, and she had to keep pushing forward. Chiang's soldiers fought well, by the Chinese standards of the day, but his staff work was bad, and he was soon pushed back. The capital, which was also his headquarters, had to be moved to Nanking, then Hankow, and finally to Chungking, beyond the mountainous gorges of the Yangtse. The Japanese speedily knocked out the ineffective little Chinese Air Force, and Chiang was without air cover until the American General Claire Chennault was engaged to recruit American fliers at high salaries, to fight as mercenaries. His squadron became known as the Flying Tigers, legendary throughout Asia for their skill and daring.

In December, 1937, Japanese planes bombed an American gunboat, the *Panay*, lying in the Yangtse near Nanking. When the crew was forced to leave the sinking vessel, they were machine-gunned from the air while in the small boats and afterward, when they tried to hide in the freezing marshes along the shore. The Japanese colonel who ordered the attack said he had been told to clear the river of ships, and that the limiting word "Chinese" had been left out in the transmission; in fact, it seems much more likely that the attack was a typical piece of Japanese arrogance, to show the Chinese that they were not afraid of the white man. However, the ensuing uproar in the United States frightened the Japanese Government, not yet ready for the war they were to start four years later. The American bill for damages of $2,200,000 was paid instantly without demur, and a popular collection was taken up for the survivors.

As the Japanese conquered the whole coast, millions of Chinese fled westward before them, mostly on foot, through an area with very few railroads and still fewer roads suitable for heavy vehicular traffic. It is estimated that sixteen million Chinese abandoned their homes to avoid coming under control of the Japanese, who acted with the wanton cruelty they later displayed against white prisoners in the Second World War.

The Chinese tore up railroads as they moved west, carried the rails by hand, and relaid them farther on. Whole factories were dismantled and the parts were moved; about 400 factories, with 200,000 tons of equipment were loaded on barges, which were then dragged by hand up the Yangtse through the rapids by a technique many centuries old: long ropes were attached to the prow of each vessel, and hundreds of coolies pulled on each rope, straining forward along a precarious footpath on the bank. When the disassembled factories arrived at Chungking, they were put back together; since there was a bad shortage of metal, even steel mills were built with only bamboo beams supporting the roof. Chiang's men collected copper coins from the peasants and melted them down. Human excrement, always the chief source of manure for China, was employed for nitrates needed for ammunition.

Life was hard in Chungking—heavy dust and dreadful heat in summer; thick mud and bitter cold in winter. Japanese air raids were frequent, by night or by day, or both; when the alarm sounded, much of the population took refuge in deep caves dug into the steep cliffs that descended from the town to the river bank. In this time of national peril, one uneasy truce succeeded another between Chiang and the Communists; finally the Communist armies and guerrillas were given their own territory to defend, in the northwest.

The universities in the territory where the Japanese were advancing were evacuated to the southwest; most of the faculty and students simply walked nearly two hundred miles. The chief universities were consolidated into one, called National Southwest University, at the town of Kunming. In spite of the tremendous difficulties under which they labored, two years after the War began the number of students had risen from 32,000 to 40,000. As is true all over the world, many of the students showed signs of radicalism, which troubled Chiang. He set up his own Youth Corps, heavily indoctrinated with Kuomintang principles, and enrolled them in the university, with orders that they must not be flunked—a condition any student would consider as paradise.

The War was conducted, especially on the Chinese side, on principles immemorial in the Orient. The loss of life in battle was usually not very great, though the armies were always half-starved and were decimated by disease. Secret trade continued to flourish between the opposing armies; the Japanese sold cloth, rubber tires, medicine, and gasoline to the Chinese and got in exchange tungsten, tin, and antimony. The Chinese in unoccupied territory had little trouble in getting letters through to their friends behind the Japanese lines.

When France fell to the Nazis in 1940, it had a pronounced effect on the situation in China. The Japanese persuaded the defeated French Government to cut off the railroad which was Chiang's last link to the coast, and also to permit them to occupy the northern part of Indo-China. The British and Dutch were also blackmailed by Japan; the British agreed to close for three months the road north through Burma into Chiang's territory in China, and the Dutch agreed to sell oil to the Japanese from their refineries in the East Indies.

It was the United States which persuaded these countries

to show more courage. After America had herself long continued to sell scrap iron, steel, and oil to Japan, she finally embargoed these exports, and convinced the Dutch and British they should stiffen their attitude. Some historians believe that the Japanese sneak attack on the United States at Pearl Harbor in December of 1941 came because the Japanese believed they must win the war quickly before their supplies gave out; others think that to conquer the United States was an essential part of their program, formulated decades earlier, to dominate the entire Western Pacific and Asia.

The attack on Pearl Harbor, which sounded Japan's ultimate doom, saved Chiang Kai-shek. The fact that the United States was in the War gave a tremendous boost to Chinese morale, even though America at first could offer her little but moral support. With incredible rapidity, the Japanese now overran the Philippines, all the countries of Southeast Asia, and the Dutch East Indies. The United States could do little except to begin the slow and painful process of capturing the vast South Sea Archipelago, island by island.

The Japanese probably blundered badly, after winning Burma, in not advancing into India. This vast country was still seething with revolt against British rule, and had not yet received any firm promise of independence in the visible future. The Indians hated the white man, as did the Chinese themselves, the Burmese, Malays, and Indonesians, not only for political and economic exploitation but for their open contempt for "inferior people" with dark skins. Europeans finally paid a terrible price for the signs in Shanghai parks saying, "Chinese and dogs not permitted" (spiritually if not literally true); for the refusal to allow Orientals to ride in the same elevators; for the social snobbery which drew a color line in their clubs and at their dinner tables; for—in Indonesia, for example—the refusal to permit more than a handful of natives to get a college education.

In many areas, the native inhabitants at first welcomed the Japanese as liberators. In Burma, they gave the invaders much assistance. White and Jacoby report that tin cans were laid on the ground in a V to show Japanese fliers where to drop their bombs. In the Dutch East Indies, the natives gave little aid to the Dutch resistance, feeling they could hardly be worse off under one conqueror than another. In Singapore, the large Chinese population, loyal to Chiang, wanted to form a volunteer militia to help fight off the Japanese who were advancing down the Malay Peninsula, but the contemptuous British, still under the delusion that the Chinese could not fight, refused to accept their aid until it was too late.

Surprisingly enough, the Japanese proved just as scornful of other Asiatics as were the Europeans. No one knows what might have happened in India if they had coöperated with the Indian Nationalists, but they believed themselves to be divinely superior to other nations and rejected all collaborators. News of their mistreatment of the natives in every land they had conquered soon leaked through the censorship, and alienated those who might have been their friends. Faced with an indifferent or hostile population, and with great difficulties in transporting supplies for their troops, their drive into India soon came to a halt.

The American effort to get military supplies to Chiang at Chungking was also terribly difficult. In 1939 the Chinese, with heroic efforts, had built a road from Kunming in Southwest China to the town of Lashio in Burma; it offered a meager supply line except when closed by the British. In 1942, however, the Japanese conquered Burma and seized the southern end of the road. In 1944 the Allies, starting from Assam in eastern India, reconquered part of northern Burma; and in the face of enormous obstacles, American engineers built a new road from Ledo, India, to a point intersecting the old Burma Road where Chiang's men were still in control. The new section ran 478 miles across mountain ranges, down into swamps and jungles. It cost $148 million, and took a full year to complete, being finished only about six months before the surrender of the Japanese in August, 1945.

For two and a half years before that, the only contact between Chiang and his Western Allies was the air route from India. It was by far the most hazardous in the world, going hundreds of miles over lofty, uninhabited mountain terrain, where a landing was impossible; for long periods more planes and pilots were lost flying "the Hump," as it was called, than in combat in all of Asia. By the end of the War, the amazing figure of 80,000 tons a month of military supplies was being carried in on this route, including, of course, all the gasoline necessary for the return flights.

The chief American military figure in the Chinese area of operation at this time was General Joseph W. Stilwell, a tough, blunt-spoken, irascible old soldier. He had lived in China, spoke Chinese fluently, and was Chiang's chief military aide. When the Japanese came down from the north, cut Burma in two, and forced the Allies to fall back to India, General Stilwell astonished everybody by walking out with his men, executing the most difficult of all military maneuvers, a successful wholesale retreat. In an era when communiqués always tried to gloss over every setback, he astonished the world by observing, when he reached India, "I claim that we took a hell of a licking."

Stilwell was deeply angered by the incompetence of the Chinese military leaders, their disregard for the hardships of their soldiers, the graft and corruption that were practically universal. His private diaries, when first published, had been discreetly censored, but twenty years later, some of his frank comments were made public. Speaking of the Allied retreat from Burma, he wrote:

> What a commentary on the Chinese General Staff—no preparations, no concern, they just sit and let me go to it. Through stupidity, fear and a defense attitude they lost a grand chance to slap the Japs back at Toungoo [in Burma]. The basic reason is C.K.S's [Chiang's] meddling. . . . The Chinese Army and Division Commanders failed to obey. . . . They are chiselers and grafters. . . .

Madame loves power She eats up publicity and flattery.

C.K.S has been boss so long, so many yes men, he has idea he is infallible on any subject.

C.K.S.'s ignorance and fatuous complacency are appalling, the little dummy.

The Chinese Red Cross is a racket. Stealing and the sale of medicine are rampant. . . . Higher-ups in the Army steal the soldiers' food.

By ample testimony, Stilwell did not overstate conditions. When a contingent of Chinese soldiers was sent to Burma to help the Americans and British to try to defend that country, many of them died on the way of exhaustion and malnutrition; of those who survived, American doctors found that ten to fifteen per cent had tuberculosis or malaria. They had been fed polished rice and so little else that beri-beri was endemic. Sent to India, given decent food and clothing by the Americans, and retrained, the improvement in the Chinese troops was amazing. Repeatedly, they expressed surprise that they received their entire stipulated pay, intact; they could not understand how the American officers were getting their graft, as they assumed was of course being done.

While some Chinese soldiers were volunteers, many others were drafted, though if they had money, they could buy their way out. Press gangs picked up able-bodied men on the roads and in the fields. No matter how ill, a soldier stayed with his company if he was able to walk, since otherwise he would have no food or shelter. So far as his family was concerned, a man who went into the Army simply disappeared; even if he could read and write, which was highly unlikely, he had no way of getting news of himself back to his native village.

In China itself, the War settled down into a stalemate. The Japanese ruled the entire coast, some eight provinces, and about one hundred million people; but with American help, Chiang held on stubbornly in the interior, and so did the

Chinese Communists in the northwest. The Communists had won the allegiance of many peasants by promising them, under the old Russian formula, land, peace, and bread, though for practical reasons they continued for a time to work with the landlords, merely reducing the worst extortions. Each of Chiang's Generals was a law to himself in the territory he held. They extorted heavy taxes from the peasantry, and some of them enriched themselves in other ways, including the illicit opium traffic.

The Americans, who kept the war going for Chiang, found conditions difficult. Huge quantities of their supplies, brought in over the Hump at such a heavy cost in men and machines, were stolen and sold to the Japanese on the black market, or sometimes back to the Americans themselves. Chinese money was heavily inflated, but the Americans were forced to buy it at a high price in American dollars; some Chinese commanders made fortunes by holding these dollars.

By the end of 1944, Chiang would endure Stilwell's sharp tongue no longer. Wires were pulled in Washington and he was recalled. On hearing that Chiang himself would now devote his full energies to directing the War, the General wrote in his diary, "God help China." He was succeeded by General Albert C. Wedemeyer.

In his book, *Soviet Russia in China*, Chiang noted candidly a curious fact about himself. Repeatedly President Roosevelt sent top-level advisers to him and repeatedly, he says, he was not frank with them, so that they failed to understand the total situation. This was true of the United States Ambassador during the War, Clarence Gauss. It was also true of two emissaries the American President sent in August, 1944—Donald Nelson, an expert on factory production, and Patrick J. Hurley, whose job it was to try to make Chiang and Stilwell get along together.

It is probably a fact that by now the most effective fighting against the Japanese was being done by the Chinese Communist guerrillas. They had for years lived by four rules formulated by Mao Tse-tung, though they have been practiced by all guerrillas everywhere, from time immemorial: Retreat when the enemy advances; harass him when he halts; attack if he tries to avoid an engagement; pursue if he retreats.

By day, the guerrillas were innocent farmers peacefully working in their fields; by night, they retrieved their well-hidden guns, struck at the Japanese, and then ran away. They attacked lines of communication, set fire to stores, shot sentries. Sometimes they laid homemade mines in a complete circle around a Japanese camp, so that the first men to leave in the morning were likely to be killed. Their own headquarters were in remote Chinese villages; these also were encircled with mines, leaving only one safe path that was changed at frequent intervals. The bewildered Japanese could only respond by taking hostages and shooting them, which did nothing to conciliate the Chinese. The invaders found it almost impossible to get quislings to act on their behalf locally; anyone who served in this way had a brief life expectancy.

The stalemated war in China ended with the Japanese surrender in August, 1945, after the United States had dropped atom bombs on Hiroshima and Nagasaki. China was now free of the invaders for the first time in many decades, but the unanswered question still remained: Who was to rule the country?

A new, liberal constitution was written in 1946 which was supposed to end one-party rule by the Kuomintang, but did not. Chiang, who had fought the Communists intermittently for almost twenty years, liked them no better than he had in the past. President Truman sent General George C. Marshall to China to try to bring peace between the warring factions, and for a short time it looked as though he might succeed. A plan was worked out to merge the Kuomintang and Communist armies; but then everything fell apart again. In his book Chiang says that with General Marshall he once again failed to be candid.

The Russians, who had occupied Manchuria, now withdrew. Chiang rushed his troops in, trying to get ahead of the Communists; afterward he felt this had been a tactical error, that he should instead have put his case before the United Nations. His lines were overextended, and the Communists were able to drive his men back. They were aided by huge supplies captured by the Russians from the Japanese at the end of the War and now handed over to the poorly-equipped Chinese Reds.

With Manchuria in their hands, the Communists started a drive south, with successes as startling as those of Chiang Kai-shek moving north from Canton more than twenty years earlier. By the end of 1948, they had captured almost the entire country north of the Yangtse. They were aided by the fact that Chiang's troops were exhausted and dispirited by many years of fighting, while the Communists had the high morale of zealots. The Kuomintang was handicapped by sharp dissension among its leaders, divided into right and left wings.

Now Chiang's forces began a bitter series of retreats paralleling those made twelve years earlier before the Japanese. In April, 1949, the Communists captured Nanking, which was then the Kuomintang capital. The Nationalists fell back to Canton, which surrendered six months later. Another retreat to Chungking, and that city, too, gave up after only six weeks. Three months before this, anticipating victory, the Communists had called a national convention in Peking; while the documents were phrased to sound as though all parties were to be included, the Reds were in complete control. On October 1, the Chinese People's Republic was formed.

Earlier in the year, Chiang had followed his familiar pattern and retired for a time from public life, but in December he came back. With the aid of the United States Navy, the almost miraculous task was accomplished of moving half a million of his soldiers, and a vast horde of civilians—perhaps as many as 1,500,000—to the island of Formosa, where a new government was set up in the city of Taipei. Two Chinas had at last come into being.

When Chiang was driven from the mainland, a bitter debate began in the United States that was to continue for many years. During the whole time from the end of the War to the

Communist victory four years later, the United States had given complete support to the Nationalists; in all, and including the War period, they got $9 billion in supplies of every kind. Many Americans, however, believed that our aid had been insufficient. During much of the decade of the 1950's Senator Joseph R. McCarthy of Wisconsin was engaged in his great campaign to root out Communists in various branches of the United States Government, and he and others charged that Chiang had been deliberately betrayed by secret Communist sympathizers in the U.S. State Department. Particularly active in criticism was Senator William F. Knowland of California, who soon acquired the nickname of "the Senator from Formosa." A strong journalistic supporter of Chiang was Henry R. Luce, publisher of *Time, Life,* and other periodicals, who had been born of missionary parents in China and had spent his boyhood there. Many conservative newspapers, most of them affiliated with the Republican Party, which had opposed President Roosevelt and continued to resist those of the Rooseveltian policies that were pursued by President Truman, joined in the attack.

The defenders of the Government's policy argued that no matter what the United States had tried to do, this country could not have brought about a Nationalist victory. They pointed out that the Communists had the enormously high morale of fanatics, zealous believers in a cause, while the Nationalists, quarreling among themselves, shot through with graft, corruption and disaffection, lacked the spirit to fight. Great quantities of American supplies were either captured by the Chinese Reds or secretly sold to them. Millions of dollars' worth of medicines and other supplies disappeared, to turn up later on the black market.

The Communists had won the peasants by cracking down on the landlords and by promising a distribution of land; Chiang was identified in the minds of these people with the landlords, ruthless tax collectors, and money-lenders. To insure a Nationalist victory, the United States would have needed to send in hundreds of thousands of American soldiers, after the end of the bitterest war in its history, and with a staggering problem in logistics in trying to transport them across the Pacific and keep them supplied.

This debate continues to rage, with no real meeting of minds. As the years have passed, however, there has been an important change in American opinion regarding the possibility of a successful invasion of the mainland by Chiang's forces, which at first had seemed quite feasible. During this whole time, Formosa has been a military protectorate of the United States, huge sums being given to Chiang, and the Formosa Straits being patrolled by the United States Seventh Fleet.

The Nationalists continued to cling to two small islands very near the Chinese coast, Quemoy and Matsu. For a long time the Communists ignored these islands, but in 1958 they began heavy bombardment of both of them, which went on for several years without having any strategic results one way or the other.

Chiang's rule on Formosa was cast in the same mold as his previous rule on the mainland. To placate the Americans, he talked of democratic government and free speech, but he succeeded in effectively muzzling any substantial criticism. His son by his first wife, Chiang Ching-kuo, was his assistant in setting up an effective secret police. Informers were well rewarded for reporting dissatisfaction in the population and as always happens under these circumstances, some of them became *agents provocateurs* in the endeavor to drum up business. From time to time Chiang would agree to improve the situation, as when he promised to stop reviewing court decisions and increasing the severity of punishments which he deemed too light, but his periods of reformation were not of long duration. At the beginning of 1965, foreign observers believed there were signs that Chiang Kai-shek, now seventy-seven, was planning to hand over the reins of government to Chiang Ching-kuo.

There were three groups on Formosa with differing ambitions. Before 1895, the island had been occupied for many centuries by the Chinese, and the aboriginal Formosans fared no better than did the Indians in the United States. In 1895, Japan took the island as part of the loot extorted from China in the war that ended that year. The Japanese introduced hydroelectric power, improved the irrigation system, and increased the agricultural output. They made the Japanese language compulsory in the schools, so much so that it is still the *lingua franca* used by Chinese groups speaking different dialects.

At the Cairo Conference in 1943, Roosevelt and Churchill agreed that after the war Formosa should be returned to the Chinese Nationalists. The administrators sent from the mainland after the end of the war in 1945 proved highly unpopular, and there was an unsuccessful revolt by the natives in 1947. With the beginning of the Korean War in 1950, the United States, reversing its recent policy, decided that Formosa was an essential part of its own defense perimeter, and sent the Seventh Fleet to patrol the hundred-mile-wide straits between the island and the Chinese coast. In 1956 a Mutual Security Agreement was signed between the United States and the Chinese Nationalists; it was, of course, an extremely one-sided document, under which the United States undertook to defend Formosa and the Pescadores, a tiny group of islands about thirty miles west of Formosa itself.

In the next eight years the United States gave Chiang about a billion additional dollars in direct assistance, and military aid of perhaps an equal amount. The troops Chiang brought with him from the mainland in 1949 were getting old, but American military missions helped to train and supply new recruits; how many of them are actually fit for war is widely disputed, but the number may be around half a million.

The Nationalists' difficulties have in recent years been augmented by the population explosion. In 1963, the high birth rate and low death rate were resulting in an increase of about thirty-two per thousand per year, and there were eleven million people crowded into an island area of less than 14,000 square miles, about half of which is so mountainous as to be unusable. There were five million children under fifteen years of age. One obvious answer would be birth control, but the mores of the old Chinese civilization are opposed to it, and it is further disliked because the Communists, after various changes in policy, began to favor it.

Formosa's economic problems are formidable, and would be even more serious if it were not for the huge sums spent annually by the United States. The island has little to export, and a program of industrialization which might blot up some of the unemployment is difficult. A psychological handicap is the fact that the aging Chinese who came from the mainland with the Generalissimo consider themselves only temporary residents, and have little interest in long-range development.

Since the United Nations began as an organization of the victors in the Second World War, Chiang Kai-shek's "Republic of China" received an important role. In 1965, it was still one of the five permanent members of the Security Council, with the United States, Great Britain, France and the Soviet Union. Since on all substantive matters an affirmative vote of seven nations is required, including all five of the permanent members, China, like the four other Powers, has an effective veto.

For the first decade and a half of the existence of the [Communist] People's Republic of China, the United States and Chiang succeeded in keeping it out of the United Nations. Sentiment for its admission was rising, however, and election to the Assembly seemed only a matter of time, assuming its leaders were willing to accept.

Chiang, now in his late seventies, showed no signs of alteration in his character or purposes. He still insisted that he hoped and expected to reconquer the mainland in the near future, though hardly anyone in the world outside his immediate entourage believed there was the remotest chance of this. Whether he really believed in the plan himself, or even knew what he really believed, no one could say. Both warlords and statesmen are inscrutable.

# 8. Hirohito:
# The Biologist as a God

EMPEROR HIROHITO of Japan differs in several important ways from the other men discussed in this book. Each of them rose to eminence through his own efforts. While three of them —Roosevelt, Churchill, and Gandhi—came from families that were fairly prosperous, four others—Stalin, Hitler, Mussolini, and Chiang Kai-shek—had childhoods of poverty. None of the seven was aided very much in his climb by anything other than his innate strength of character.

Hirohito, on the other hand, was born to the most exalted position in his country, and in some ways, in the world, and was brought up among tremendous riches, though by tradition he was trained to austerity. In one sense he was, until the end of the Second World War, the richest man in the world, since in theory he owned Japan and everything in it.

Up to 1945, no ruler in history was ever venerated more than the Japanese Emperor. He was considered to be of divine origin, the direct descendant of the Sun Goddess, Ameratsu, and thus had religious as well as political significance. It is hard for any Occidental to grasp the attitude toward the Japanese Emperor in modern times. No one was allowed to look at him directly; when he rode through the streets on his famous white horse, familiar to Americans through newsreel pictures, every Japanese bowed low from the waist and kept his eyes cast down. When he took a train trip, all blinds had to be drawn in the windows of houses overlooking the rail line. No one was permitted at any time to be at a higher elevation than the Emperor; when a tower was being added to a Tokyo police station, it was abandoned after the builders realized that from it one could look down into the garden of the Imperial Palace.

When *Time* magazine had Hirohito on its cover, the editors were asked to print a notice requesting their readers not to handle the magazine upside down or to put anything on top of it; the brilliant special issue of *Fortune* on Japan was suppressed in that country because the cover was adorned with the Imperial chrysanthemum. Before the War, the Emperor was not supposed to wear any article of clothing, even underwear, twice. His discarded garments were given away individually to loyal subjects, who received them with veneration. Tailors did not dare lay a tape measure on the exalted form of the sovereign, but had to make their measurements by estimates from some distance. Even worse, doctors for a long time were not permitted to touch any member of the Imperial family. Even after the introduction of Western medical ideas, they had to wear gloves.

The rules regarding the Emperor and his family were rigidly prescribed. John Gunther tells us in *Inside Asia* that on one occasion, an Empress died suddenly while she was visiting in the country. Since all members of the royal family were supposed to expire in the Imperial Palace, her body was dressed in her customary garments, and she was brought back to Tokyo in a sealed railway carriage, put into her own bed, and the death was then announced.

The adulation of the Emperor, which amounted to mass hysteria, was drilled into all children at an early age. Every Japanese school had portraits of the Emperor and Empress, and these were brought out and displayed to the genuflecting

**EMPEROR HIROHITO**
"A mild-mannered little man, with slightly prominent teeth, a swarthy complexion and thick-lensed spectacles."

students at stated, infrequent intervals, in an atmosphere of the utmost reverence and tension. The schoolmaster who had to approach the stage and unveil the portraits had to follow a rigidly ordained pattern; if he varied from it in any serious degree, it was not uncommon for him to commit suicide in his humiliation. (This fact is not quite as sensational as it may sound to Americans; the Japanese culture condones suicide more readily than would be true in the West.)

Willard Price, in *Japan and the Son of Heaven*, reports that the army officer who was attached to each school would end the picture-showing ceremony with an address to the children, working up to the highest pitch of fervor and ending with, "What is your dearest wish?" The children would answer in unison, "To die for the Emperor!" Sometimes they had to be watched to make sure that they did not try to kill themselves then and there with pocket knives.

In the Second World War, thousands of Japanese soldiers went on fighting against hopeless odds, rather than surrender and "betray the Emperor"—in itself considered a form of spiritual suicide. Price reports a dialogue that took place on many occasions when one of them was captured:

> "Why did you fight and kill Americans?"
> "Because of the Emperor."
> "Do you believe that the Emperor is God?"
> "Yes."

Since they fought so stubbornly, the Americans expected that the few who permitted themselves to be captured would refuse all information; but on the contrary, many of them talked freely and gave valuable details about the deployment of Japanese forces. The point was that in their own eyes as well as those of their families and friends, having surrendered they were considered dead, with no particular odium attached to their subsequent conduct.

Toward the end of the War, when Japan's situation was growing desperate, many scores of Japanese youths became *kamikaze* fliers; in planes loaded with explosives, they would try to crash against an American battleship, which meant certain death for themselves. The *kamikaze* did in fact do tremendous damage to the American fleet, though not enough to turn the tide of war.

One should not give the impression that the worship of the Emperor, and willingness to die for him, were universal. In some cases the *kamikaze* "volunteered" because the alternative was to be shot. There were draft dodgers in Japan, as in every other country; some of them tried self-mutilation to avoid military service. Once they got into the Armed Services, however, the incessant patriotic propaganda usually had its effect.

Hirohito, the object of this extraordinary veneration, is a mild-mannered little man, with slightly prominent teeth, a swarthy complexion, and thick-lensed spectacles; some observers believe that all Japanese weaken their eyes by the ordeal of learning the written language (though this is not usually said of the Chinese whose writing is similar and equally difficult).

Hirohito is the first Japanese Emperor to make an attempt to live in modern style. Born in 1901, he went to Europe as a young man, the first heir to the throne ever to leave Japan. His hobby is marine biology and authorities in this field have said that he is quite good, for an amateur; his specialty is the hydrozoa, a group among which the jellyfish are probably the most familiar. He is fond of classical Western music, which he hears on a phonograph. Before the War, he spent his summers at the seaside and used to get up at six in the morning to chop wood.

By nature he has always been casual and friendly, but the Army, anxious to maintain the gulf between him and his subjects, frowned on his efforts at informality. When he was growing up, experts in economics, zoölogy, literature, and art used to visit the Imperial Palace in Tokyo and deliver solemn lectures to an audience of one. He delights in keeping an elaborate journal, and loves to type out cards for his index of marine biological information. As a child he was fascinated by Aesop's Fables, which he read and reread, and of which he wrote imitations. He has also written many *Tanka* and *Hokku*, traditional Japanese poems of five lines and thirty-one syllables and three lines and seventeen syllables, respectively. He is the patron of the annual poetry competition, in which hundreds of thousands of people join. There are no prizes; the honor of winning is reward enough. The Emperor and other members of the Royal Family write poems for the competition, but are not eligible to win.

A characteristic poem by Hirohito is this:

> As I
> was visiting
> the Shinto Point in Kii
> clouds were drifting far
> over the sea

One of his poems, written in 1938, in the middle of the war with China, caused a sensation. It said:

> Peaceful
> is morning in the shrine garden;
> world conditions it is hoped
> will also be
> peaceful.

This was interpreted in some quarters as meaning that he wanted the war to be ended, an idea extremely disturbing to the Japanese militarists, then at the peak of their power.

When once asked what was his favorite poem he did not choose one of his own, but an old one which says, "The light of the sun and moon withholds no favors; they shine equally upon all."

In the old days, the Emperor was prevented from having more than the slightest contact with foreigners, though this rule is now somewhat relaxed. The Army, intent on maintaining his role as a God, discouraged any friendships with persons outside the Imperial Palace, a group of buildings in Tokyo which with their surrounding gardens occupy an area about one-third as large as New York's Central Park. One prewar custom has been maintained, that of two very large Imperial garden parties each year, celebrating the cherry blossoms in the spring and the chrysanthemums in the fall. To these parties, attended by thousands, some foreigners are invited, including correspondents for the foreign press, but under these circumstances, any real contact with the Emperor is impossible.

Hirohito was the first Japanese Emperor to marry for love. The Empress, two years younger than he, was not a member of the family of the Fujiwara, from whom consorts for the Emperor were traditionally chosen. His counsellors approved the choice, however; his father, Emperor Taisho, developed insanity, and a fresh blood line was considered desirable. Hirohito has had six children, four of them girls. By ancient Japanese custom, his brothers tried not to have any children until the Emperor's first son was born, which occurred in 1933.

Because of his father's mental decline, Hirohito had to become Regent at the age of twenty. After the death of his father, he ascended the throne at twenty-five. The ceremonies involved were elaborate to the last degree, involving three sacred objects supposedly handed down from ancient times: a mirror, a necklace, and a sword. The sword is a duplicate of the original, which was lost many years ago. The mirror is also believed to be a duplicate; the necklace is authentic.

Despite the extraordinary veneration of the Emperor, he was at this time little more than a puppet, controlled by the military. To understand how this came about, it is necessary to take a quick glance back into history.

The first recorded Emperor, Jimmu, was supposed to be a fifth-generation descendant of the Sun Goddess, and to have ruled in about the sixth century B.C. Although the Japanese hate to admit it, they were illiterate barbarians until a thousand years later, when reading and writing and such arts as pottery were introduced from China.

There are several widely held misconceptions about the history of Japan. It is commonly said that Hirohito is the one-hundred-twenty-fourth occupant of the throne in a direct line of descent, but this is almost certainly not true. Until quite recent times, not only were plural marriages common for the Emperors, but they had large numbers of concubines as well; human nature being what it is, there can be no doubt that many offspring considered the sons and daughters of Emperors were in fact fathered by other men. Babies were also adopted by the Imperial Family, and sometimes were even smuggled into the Imperial household by their parents. Any one of this mixed conglomeration, with blood lines quite impossible to trace, might become heir to the throne.

Another misconception is that the significant role and the adulation of Hirohito before the Second World War continued a tradition that stretched back into the indefinite past. On the contrary, for about six centuries, until 1868, the Emperors were helpless prisoners in the Imperial Palace. At one time there were actually two of them, both claiming the throne. The real rulers were successive Shoguns, members of one of several powerful families; the rule was passed on from one member to another until some other family took control by force of arms. In the 1850's, the Shoguns were the Tokugawa family, who were soon to be overthrown by a combination of the Satsumas and the Choshus.

Still another misconception is the notion that Japan had always been closed until Commodore Perry visited the country in 1853 and forced it into relations with the West. In fact, in 1543 a Portuguese vessel was wrecked on the Japanese coast, and the sailors managed to get ashore. They were received with friendship, and the natives picked up some European ideas from them; for instance, they succeeded in casting rough imitations of the ship's cannon.

News of the development spread, and very soon Catholic missionaries arrived and began converting the Japanese. The Jesuits were especially strong, and played a useful role as intermediaries between Japan and China, which were quarreling with one another. Soon there were various Christian sects with strong missionary activity. Unfortunately, they fell to fighting among themselves and with the Japanese. Finally, in 1637, the Shogun of that day became disgusted and expelled the foreigners, closing down all their missions.

Japan did now remain sealed off until Commodore Perry's famous visit in 1853. The organization of the country was feudal, with little feeling of nationalism. Beneath the Shogun, but giving him little or no allegiance, were the feudal barons, called the Daimyo. Each of these warlords had his private army of Samurai, with a strict code among themselves, called Bushido. They were famous for their long hair, worn on the top of the head, and for their even longer swords. They were a law to themselves; they had the disagreeable habit of murdering anyone who was, or was thought to be, disrespectful to them, and there was no superior authority to hold them to account. For that matter, any important person could mistreat anyone of a lower rank with relative impunity.

Commodore Perry was sent to Japan by the United States to demand that the Japanese stop mistreating American sailors wrecked on their shores. He was soon joined by British forces, and the Japanese reluctantly accepted their presence. Then the tide turned the other way and Western ideas became enormously popular. Christianity was reintroduced and speedily found many converts.

This development seemed dangerous to the members of the ruling clique, who decided upon a bold counter stroke. They believed that the Emperor, virtually a prisoner in the Palace, would be more amenable to their ideas than any future Shogun, and would prove a useful symbol for their propaganda. In 1868, therefore, the Emperor was formally restored to power. A little later, an Imperial army based on conscription came into existence, to offset the Samurai, who still owed their allegiance to the feudal barons. These private armies were pensioned off, but were sufficiently dissatisfied to stage a series of local revolts, which were put down without too much trouble. Universal (male) education was now introduced for the first time, with heavy emphasis on morality and loyalty to the throne.

About this time several successive delegations of elder statesmen traveled abroad, to see for themselves what the outside world was like; the sentiment of the country was such that the earliest of these had to make their visits in secret, lest they be executed on their return. They brought back many Western ideas, which soon included railroads, steamboats, the telegraph, a postal system, and such social habits as Western dancing, card playing, and the art of photography, to which Japan is now probably more addicted than any other country.

There were even more serious results from these explorations of the West. A delegation visited Prince Bismarck, then at the height of his power in Germany, and he advised them to counteract the tendency toward liberal and radical ideas that was beginning to be apparent, by increased emphasis on veneration of the Emperor, and on religion. He is supposed to have told them that the Army and Navy should control the country—advice the Japanese hardly needed, since military power had been supreme in Japan for many centuries.

Now began the extraordinary veneration of the Emperor which reached its climax more than sixty years later, in the 1930's. The tradition of his descent from the Sun Goddess was already implanted, but now it was reëmphasized in every possible way. At the same time the Shinto religion was brought forward to compete more strongly with Buddhism and Christianity.

The Japanese, like the Chinese, saw nothing wrong in adhering to several religions at once; they practiced Buddhism, Confucianism, and Shintoism all together, and would have added Christianity (as in fact some of them secretly did) if the missionaries had consented.

Shintoism is less a religion than a set of traditional rituals and customs, involving popular festivals and pilgrimages to famous shrines. The Shintoists believe in thousands of gods and goddesses, most but not all beneficent in purpose. There are many millions of lesser deities, some of them attached to a single place, perhaps only a rock or a tree. The dead can come back to exercise an important, often baneful, influence; ancestor worship, a significant part of Japanese life, is an attempt to placate these ghosts. Indeed, Shintoism is largely an effort to prevent harm by the spirits of the dead; people who adhere to several religions usually base their practical code of behavior on Confucius, and turn to Buddha for the answers to spiritual and metaphysical problems; even today, many homes have both Buddhist and Shinto shrines.

The militarists of the 1870's saw in Shintoism a useful tool for their purposes and pushed it hard. The legend of the Sun Goddess, from whom the Emperor was supposed to be descended, gave a divine origin not only to the Emperor himself, but to all the Japanese people; as a result, Japan had an enormous superiority complex, which helped to justify the aggression toward China and other countries. Shintoism was made the state religion, in spite of the fact that there are several sects, differing slightly from one another.

Though this is still the most popular form of worship, it is no longer supported by the state. Emperor Hirohito gave it a heavy blow when on New Year's Day, 1946, he formally renounced the theory of his divine origin. General Douglas Mac-Arthur, Supreme Commander for the Allied Powers in the occupation of Japan, disestablished Shintoism as the state religion and forbade the use of public funds for it.

Toward the end of the 1950's, about eighty million persons were professing one or another of a dozen forms of Shintoism. There were roughly forty million supporters of various Buddhist sects (with much overlapping), and some six hundred thousand Christians, also divided among numerous denominations.

The pattern of life set up in the 1870's was to continue for about two-thirds of a century. The military were the real rulers. The Army, which had at first been modeled on the French, was hastily converted to an imitation of Germany's after France was defeated by Prussia in 1870. A new constitution was adopted in 1889, based chiefly on Germany's, but it did nothing to change the balance of power between the civil and military authorities.

Japan shared fully in the long process of the Western Powers who were engaged in "nibbling China to death"; the only restraint, as noted, was the jealousy of the nations which caused two or three of them to gang up when any one became too aggressive. Japan coveted in particular the Korean Peninsula which hung down so temptingly near to her own southern island. The Chinese, who had been meddling in the Kingdom of Korea for many centuries, had taken it over completely early in the seventeenth century but had not succeeded in suppressing the patriotic loyalty of its inhabitants. In 1894 there was a Korean revolt against China, and Japan promptly sent in an army with the typical Oriental explanation that she was doing so only to help China. Her real intentions quickly became obvious and helped to produce the Sino-Japanese War of 1894–95 which ended, as was inevitable, in a Japanese victory. Nominally, both Powers now recognized Korea's independence, but everyone knew that this was only a piece of public hypocrisy.

Japan had also coveted the Liaotung Peninsula, which depends from the Asiatic continent like a smaller Korea, a short distance to the west. She now extorted from China this peninsula, the island of Formosa (Taiwan), and the little Pescadores lying between that island and the mainland, as well as a big indemnity in gold, and additional treaty ports in China itself, where she could manufacture, duty free, goods to be bought by the Chinese. However, the seizure of Liaotung was too much for the Europeans, and they forced Japan to return the Peninsula—whereupon Russia herself seized the territory, including the valuable cities at its tip, Dairen and Port Arthur.

The Japanese bided their time, but they did not forget the insult to their pride. In 1902 they signed the Anglo-Japanese Alliance which was to continue for two decades and was to exert an important force on world history. It was based on the fear of Russian aggression by both countries, but did not require either Power to come to the aid of the other unless attacked simultaneously by two or more enemies. The Alliance probably helped Japan to start her war with Russia two years later; her easy victory left her the strongest Oriental power, and she did not hesitate to annex Korea in 1910.

The Anglo-Japanese Alliance, which had been renewed in 1911, brought Japan into the First World War. Her assistance was of little value to the Allies, except in compelling Germany to give up the Chinese territory she was occupying and her islands in the Pacific. Japan herself took over these islands, nominally under League of Nations mandate; in fact, she promptly made them part of her empire and secretly set about fortifying them, in violation of the mandate terms. She had wanted a declaration of the equality of all races in the Versailles treaty of peace, and was bitterly disappointed when she did not get it.

Fascism took power in Italy in 1923, the year of Hitler's first unsuccessful attempt to seize the reins in Germany. It was paralleled by a rapid similar development in Japan. The Army and Navy had always exerted great power; under the 1889 constitution they could bring down any Japanese government simply by having the Secretary for the Army resign from the Cabinet. Of enormous influence was the unofficial body of Elder Statesmen, who pretended to advise the Emperor, but in fact dictated to him; their views almost always coincided with those of the military men.

Japan's population increased enormously in the last decades of the nineteenth century and the early part of the twentieth. Like Great Britain, she had to import food and raw materials, and to export manufactured goods to pay for them; and this fact, combined with her national pride and her feeling of superiority based on the supposed divine origin of the Japanese people, shaped her foreign policy. These motives lay behind the annexation of Korea and the repeated extensions of Japanese influence in China.

The Bolshevik Revolution of 1917 gave Japan a chance for further adventures on the Asiatic mainland. As we have seen, the Allies were hostile to the Revolution, one of whose early acts was to make a separate peace with Germany; they landed an expedition in Archangel, in northern Russia, and they agreed to a joint Japanese-American occupation of eastern Siberia from Vladivostock westward along the line of the Trans-Siberian Railroad. After the Armistice in November, 1918, the American troops were withdrawn, but it took years to get the Japanese to leave.

The national pride of the Japanese was hurt by two developments of the early 1920's. At the Naval Disarmament Conference of 1921–22, the American Government suggested that the naval vessels of the three chief powers be limited as to tonnage. The United States and Great Britain were to have equality, and the Japanese Navy was to be forty percent smaller. Japan was furious, but was not in a position to refuse. Other agreements now destroyed the Anglo-Japanese Alliance in favor of multilateral treaties designed chiefly to protect Chinese independence.

Another blow to Japanese pride came with the new United States Immigration Law of 1924. European powers were given annual quotas based on their representation in the existing American population, totalling about 154,000 annually, but Asiatics were entirely excluded, as they had been from some other countries—notably Australia. A further blow to Japanese pride was the passage of laws in California and some other American states forbidding land ownership by individuals from countries whose nationals were ineligible for citizenship. These laws were forced through by white farmers who objected to competition by the Japanese, who worked hard, lived sparsely, and produced at low cost.

In the 1920's, the growth of Japanese home industry accelerated. Industrial workers were badly exploited, and many of them turned to Communism; as in the United States and Western Europe, the Russian experiment had an influence far beyond the actual membership of the Japanese Communist Party. Exports of silk increased greatly, and the number of small tenant farmers growing silk worms was much enlarged. The rise of liberal and radical ideas was met by repression by the Government, which was more than ever influenced by the Armed Forces.

Prime Minister Hara Takashi, the first holder of that post to come from the ranks of the commoners, counted himself a conservative; but when he tried to reduce the power of the Army, he was assassinated, in 1921. Nine years later Prime Minister Osachi Hamaguchi was killed for the same reason. A secret organization, the Black Dragon Society, became powerful. It and other similar groups were colored by the nostalgia for the past that has produced right-wing extremists in many other countries in modern times. They objected to all the chief political parties, none of which was sufficiently conservative for them; to the preoccupation of big business with material gain; and to the popularity of Western ideas. These Fascist groups were responsible over the years for many assassinations of political and business figures.

As in Italy and Germany, the Japanese Fascists talked a form of radicalism they made no effort to bring into being. They spoke of nationalizing property, putting strict limits on individual wealth, and abolishing the peerage. In the greatly expanded Army and Navy, most of the junior officers were by now ignorant farm boys, who fell easy prey to this sort of talk. The right-wing influence was especially strong in the Army units on the Asiatic mainland, who were occupying much of Manchuria, and especially the Liaotung Peninsula. In 1928, without consulting the home government, the military men murdered Marshal Chang Tso-lin, the Manchurian warlord, who had proved intractable.

A year earlier, in 1927, had come the famous incident of the Tanaka Memorandum, of which Baron Giichi Tanaka, the Prime Minister, was supposed to be the author. The Japanese did not admit that the document was authentic, but certainly their subsequent actions sought to fulfill its recommendations. Said the Memorandum:

> The way to gain actual rights in Manchuria and Mongolia is to use the region as a base and under the pretense of trade and commerce penetrate the rest of China. Armed by the rights

already secured, we shall seize the resources all over the country. Having China's entire resources at our disposal, we shall proceed to conquer India, the [South Sea] Archipelago, Asia Minor, Central Asia, and even Europe.

Toward the end of the decade, several things adversely affected Japanese prosperity. In 1928 the Chinese, in despair of resisting Japan with arms, instituted a sweeping boycott of Japanese goods of every type; China was Japan's best customer, and the boycott hurt.

In 1929 began the worldwide Depression, sparked by a severe break in the American stock market. The Japanese exports of silk to the United States were severely damaged, and with the subsequent development of synthetic fabrics, they never came back to their former level. The results were disastrous both for farmers and for silk weavers in the towns and cities.

The Depression only increased the fanaticism of the Fascists. Japan's population was growing by a million a year, but emigration was impossible. Alarmed by low prices for Japanese exports, other countries around the world instituted tariffs or embargoes. The Nipponese response was to try even harder to make a vassal of China; in September, 1931, the Army proceeded to overrun all Manchuria. The commanders in the field were acting as a law to themselves, aided by sympathizers at home.

In 1932, another Prime Minister, Inukai Tsuyoshi, was assassinated, and in 1936, there was still another bloodbath which included the Finance Minister. The Prime Minister of the day, Okada Keisuke, escaped only because the assassins killed his brother by mistake, giving him a chance to escape. For several days a rebellious regiment actually held downtown Tokyo, though eventually troops loyal to the Emperor managed to recapture the city. In November of that year, Japan made an alliance with Nazi Germany aimed against the Russians and Communism, and soon Italy also joined. In 1937 began the full-scale war with China.

What was the role of the Emperor in all this? When he became Regent for his insane father, he was only twenty, and completely a puppet. For some years after he became Emperor he seems to have been equally quiescent. Yet he had no real sympathy with the Fascist tendencies. His interest in marine biology made him follow Western science, and his own leanings were toward political liberalism on the European or American model. But he was still virtually a prisoner in the Imperial Palace; as John Gunther remarks, Japanese politics for many years consisted in a struggle for control of the Emperor, who was a rubber stamp for whatever faction was in power.

His first real effort to assert himself seems to have come in 1931, when the Army's invasion of Manchuria became a flagrant repudiation of international law and the policies of the League of Nations. When he protested to the Elder Statesmen and the chief leaders of the Government, he was told flatly that he was risking forcible removal from his throne. In spite of this, he ordered his troops not to cross the Great Wall into China proper; his action threw the High Command into confusion, and the movement of the Army was halted for several weeks. Then the military men decided to defy the Emperor and went ahead. He did nothing.

When the full-scale war with China began with military action at Shanghai, in 1937, the Emperor at first did not commit himself one way or the other. Later, however, he made enigmatic statements that implied he supported the attack.

If Hirohito had been a strong character, the whole course of modern history might have been different. For sixty years, the militarist clique who ruled Japan had been building up an image of the Emperor as all-wise, all-good and virtually infallible. In doing so, they risked the chance that someone might come to the throne who would be able to overthrow the image makers. But Hirohito, like all hereditary rulers, had been trained from childhood to play the role allotted to him by those about him. When the test came, he failed.

Throughout the 1930's, the ruling clique, the Japanese "Establishment," continued to paint the picture of a country mercilessly harried by enemies bent on destroying her. The Great Powers continued their opposition to her efforts to take over control of China; her title for her policy, The Greater East Asia Co-Prosperity Sphere, which seemed to the Japanese people a reasonable statement of her ambitions, appeared to the West to be laughable when it was not sinister.

The Japanese were, or pretended to be, outraged that China should reject their offers of "coöperation," which were extended in the form of bombing Chinese towns from the air and looting and murdering by ground troops. The increase in the Army and Navy went on at a furious rate; the five-five-three ratio in capital ships, set up so hopefully at the Washington Conference on Limitation of Armament in 1921–22 had long since been repudiated. The United States continued to sell scrap steel to Japan, though many American citizens protested; the U.S. Government feared to exacerbate the situation by an embargo, though the gloomy prophecies came true, and much of this steel was eventually made into bullets and shot back at American soldiers.

Japan's industry was remarkably efficient; she had modern machinery in her factories, operated by workers who got starvation wages and lived like prisoners. Many of them came from the villages where poverty was even worse than in the towns; dormitories were attached to the factories, and the operatives were kept locked up, day and night, except for a rare day off, sometimes one in fourteen. As a result, Japanese goods could be sold in the export market at fantastically low prices; some of them were inferior, but others were of good quality. The mill owners imported cotton from India, made it into shirts, sent it back to India, paid import duties, and still were able to undersell handmade Indian shirts.

Japanese business was largely controlled by five huge firms, larger in proportion to the total national wealth than anything in the United States. Of these, two were known around the world. The Mitsui consortium had control of cotton, rayon, mining, and metals, among many other things; the Mitsubishi group was interested chiefly in banking, shipping, and insurance. The millionaire businessmen were comparatively enlightened, and most of them did not sympathize with the plans of the militarists to conquer the world by force of arms, but they were powerless, kept in line by the threat of assassination. The politicians were equally powerless; with about one Prime Minister in three murdered while in office, the top men lived in constant fear, trying to keep their movements secret, occupying large houses with secret exits, and never sleeping in the same bed twice.

Japan's censorship was highly effective. She had passed a "Dangerous Thoughts Law" under which people could be arrested, not for any overt act, but merely on suspicion of lacking loyalty to the prevailing policy. In the three years, 1933–35, some 60,000 persons were arrested on this charge. Ninety per cent of them were never tried at all, though they were kept in prison, often for long periods.

All foreigners came under suspicion, and many of them were constantly trailed by the secret police. An American journalist living in Japan is supposed to have written to a friend in the United States, saying, "I don't know if this letter will ever arrive, because the Japanese censor may open it." He received a note from the Japanese post office: "The statement in your letter is not correct. We do not open letters."

Another foreigner was found with chest X-rays in his possession, and had a hard time convincing the police that these were not spy photographs.

When the common people were given a chance, they demonstrated their lack of sympathy with the Fascist tendency; in 1937 only about ten percent of them voted for the political party frankly supporting the militarists. By the end of the decade, however, the civilian Government was badly disorganized, with the two chief political parties almost leaderless and ineffective. In 1938, a National Mobilization Law was passed, giving the Government, by now almost completely in the hands of the Army and Navy and their sympathizers, rigid control over exports, imports, prices, and wages.

Just when the Japanese militarists decided to make war on the United States is not known, any more than we can be certain when Hitler secretly planned that Germany should conquer all of Europe by force of arms, but the plans must have been formulated years before the attack on Pearl Harbor. The militarists were greatly helped when Stalin signed a nonaggression treaty with Japan, giving her a free hand in the Pacific. The United States had strongly protested, as had other Powers, the inexcusable aggression in China. The rest of the world was too busy with the Second World War to take any real action against Japan, but the United States was still technically neutral. It had finally embargoed steel and oil to Japan, actions that could be represented to the Japanese people as an attempt to isolate and weaken them.

Going to war with the United States with its incomparably superior industrial organization and its wealth of needed raw materials, seems to Westerners an act of suicide. The answer is that the Japanese militarists were still living in the eighteenth century, not realizing that war was by now something that engaged a country's total resources, and that the opponent with the greater assets was almost sure to win.

John Toland, in *But Not in Shame,* gives a good summary of the events in the fateful last third of 1941. On September 6, a top-secret Imperial Conference was held in Tokyo, with the Emperor and the chief civilian and military leaders in attendance. Admiral Osami Nagano, Chief of the General Staff of the Navy, summed up Japan's situation as he saw it. He said she was facing shortages of many essential raw materials imported from abroad. She was growing weaker while the United States was growing stronger. The clear inference was that the situation must not be allowed to deteriorate farther. Baron Yoshimichi Hara, President of the Privy Council, who did not belong to the war faction, argued that diplomacy could still be used to solve Japan's problems and was preferable to the appeal to arms.

It was traditional for the Emperor to remain silent at Imperial conferences, but now Hirohito, to everyone's amazement, spoke up. His words were cryptic, in the Japanese style, but their import was unmistakable. He felt that the policy of the Army and Navy was ambiguous, and recalled a poem written by his grandfather, the Emperor Meiji, the first ruler after the Restoration of 1868:

> When all the earth's oceans are one,
> Why do the waves seethe and the wind rage?

The Emperor added, "I have always read and appreciated this poem and kept in my heart the Emperor Meiji's spirit of peace. It has been my wish to perpetuate this spirit."

There was a long, shocked silence, and then Admiral Nagano assured the Emperor that the Armed Services were not bent on war. He said they considered diplomatic negotiations of the utmost importance, and would not appeal to arms unless that seemed the only possible course. These ideas were then made the formal policy of the conference. This of course made war almost certain; it was highly unlikely that the United States would suddenly reverse its course.

The wheels continued to grind. In Washington, the two envoys, Saburo Kurusu and Kichisaburo Nomura, saw Secretary of State Cordell Hull, only to be told sternly that Japan must end her war against China. On October 12, Premier Fumimaro Konoye called an emergency meeting of his Cabinet, and asked General Hideki Tojo how he could hope to win a war with such a powerful opponent as the United States? Tojo replied in effect that victory was not certain, but that a great nation like Japan must be prepared to take risks; four days later Konoye resigned, and was succeeded by Tojo.

On November 26, Secretary Hull sent a note demanding withdrawal of all Japanese forces from China. The militarists triumphantly asserted that this was an ultimatum, that further diplomacy was useless, that Japan must now strike without warning. On December first, just a week before Pearl Harbor, a new conference was held, with the Emperor and all the top civilian and military leaders present. While the Emperor remained silent, everyone else insisted that war was the only recourse, and all except Hirohito signed an official document confirming the decision. Later that same day the Emperor yielded to the overpowering moral pressure, and signed too. Next day a radio message went to the fleet of aircraft carriers that had started for Hawaii November 26 and was now half way there, telling Admiral Chuichi Nagumo, commander of the task force, to attack Pearl Harbor. The War was on.

When the fleet returned to Japan after its stunning victory, its personnel were of course national heroes, and especially the fliers who had led the first and second groups of planes, Commander Mitsuo Fuchida and Lieutenant Commander Shigekazu Shimazaki. Finally Hirohito himself expressed the desire to meet them. What his motives were we do not know, but at any rate, the meeting was arranged. The fliers were too low in the military hierarchy to enter the presence of the Emperor, and had to be given temporary higher rank as Special Assistants to the Chief of the Naval Staff.

Gordon W. Prange reports in his book, *Tora, Tora, Tora!,* the pathetic questions Hirohito asked. Had any hospital ship been bombed? Had any civilian or unarmed training planes been shot down? He was told the answer was No in both cases. In the mood of most Japanese at that moment, bombing hospital ships or shooting down noncombatant planes would have been of little significance. In the Emperor, the marine biologist and humanitarian momentarily took precedence over the leader of the nation.


Of the Emperor's activities for the duration of the war, little needs to be said. The Japanese of course took precautions for his safety, and American fliers in the latter days of the war when regular air raids on the home islands became possible, had orders to spare the Palace grounds. In spite of this, however, the main building was hit during a raid, and burned down. The purpose of the order was to avoid wounding or killing the Emperor, on the ground that this would make the Japanese fight even harder. The Imperial family followed the routine of all rulers in wartime, living even more austerely than before, doing hospital work, and in general trying to bolster civilian morale.

As the end of the war approached, and the star of the militarists began to wane, Hirohito became more effective in public affairs than he had ever been in his life. Long before most of the men around him, he saw that the struggle was hopeless and that Japan must sue for peace, and he began to throw his weight, such as it was, against the bitter-enders. He played an important role in the peace feelers that were sent to the Allies by way of Russia, which unfortunately were couched in such circumlocutions that their significance was seemingly not grasped by President Truman and most of the others at the Potsdam Conference. Stalin presumably understood them, but he had no intention of letting the war with Japan end until he had made his token entrance into it, and had thus laid a basis for his territorial and other demands in the Far East, after the surrender.

With the dropping of atom bombs on Hiroshima, August 6, 1945, and Nagasaki three days later, Hirohito saw that suing for peace was imperative. Many of the leaders wanted to go on and lead the country into what would in effect be a national suicide, but eventually they were overruled. Japan, in asking for peace, made only one condition, that the Emperor be kept on the throne. The United States, which played the chief role in the peace negotiations as it had done in winning the war in the Pacific, was divided on this point. Many Americans felt that future peace would be more secure if the Imperial system were discarded and Japan were made a simple republic on the Western model; others believed that the nation would fall apart and end in chaos if this were done. Though the first reply to the Japanese overture was noncommittal on this point, the second group won and Hirohito was allowed to stay on the throne—a fact that probably interested him less than almost anyone else.

How to announce the surrender to the Japanese people was a problem. During the War they had been lied to constantly, with Japanese victories exaggerated. Japan's heaviest losses had been in her Navy, which, after the battle of Leyte Gulf, in the Philippines, was all but destroyed; her Army was still largely intact, and its leaders believed it could make a strong defense of the home archipelago. The Americans agreed with this; one of the strong arguments for dropping the atom bomb was the belief that the invasion would cost at least a million casualties. This belief was mistaken; Japan's industrial and military potential had been almost destroyed by the highly effective, nearly ceaseless American air raids toward the end of the war; American submarines and planes had cut down the import of needed raw materials almost to nothing. Most of the cities lay in ruins, including especially Tokyo, where the total casualties were even greater than at Hiroshima or Nagasaki.

After the Japanese Government had decided to surrender, there was bitter opposition at home by many fanatics, some of whom committed hara-kiri in front of the palace gates. The decision was made that the Emperor himself should announce the end of the War in a radio address. This was prerecorded, and the bitter-enders, knowing this, broke into the Imperial Palace seeking to find the recording and destroy it before it could be broadcast. Luckily, they failed.

The Japanese people were thunderstruck by the news, but the fact that the Emperor himself had made the announcement probably helped them to accept it. Soon the United States had sent in occupying forces; the Japanese Army and Navy units were disarmed, and the nation settled down to the task of reconstruction.

On January first, 1946, Hirohito carried out one of the most extraordinary incidents of modern times. In a radio address he told the Japanese people that he was not a god, but a man like themselves; that he derived his position from the power of the people, and that the Emperor should be thought of as no more than a symbol of the unity of all elements in Japanese life. The impact of this statement must have been stunning, especially to the older generation; but they had suffered so much in the War and the surrender that they were presumably in a state of shock. At any rate, Hirohito's altered status was accepted quietly by most of the people.

With equal quiet, the Emperor stood aside and saw revolutionary changes introduced in quick succession by the American Occupation, which was to continue until the Peace Treaty went into effect in 1952. The Occupation was headed from the beginning to 1951 by General MacArthur, a man with a powerful, driving personality. In theory, MacArthur was subject to two Allied Commissions, one composed of the United States, Great Britain, and Russia, the other of Great Britain, Russia, and China (then still ruled by Chiang Kai-shek). In fact, MacArthur ignored them both.

Hordes of American experts on politics, economics, agriculture, and other subjects were brought to Tokyo, and proceeded to institute changes in Japanese institutions as sweeping as had ever been seen anywhere in so short a time. The Americans wrote a new Constitution in about a week, hurrying to get it completed before the other Allies could bring forward a different scheme. A Parliament was hastily elected to adopt the Constitution, which went into effect early in May, 1947.

Women were given the vote and other forms of equal rights, including divorce, heretofore a male prerogative. The House of Peers and all titles except those of the Imperial family were abolished, the House of Peers being succeeded by a House of Councillors rather like the United States Senate, with a six-year term. Most of the power resided, however, in a House of Representatives with a four-year term. As in Great Britain, a Prime Minister was chosen from the dominant group in the Parliament. Schemes were set up to turn tenant farmers into small landholders. An effort was made to unscramble the giant cartels. The secret police and censorship were abolished, and the school textbooks hastily rewritten to remove the hysterical Emperor-worship.

As happened in Germany, a number of top military and governmental figures were tried as war criminals. A few were executed, and a larger number got prison sentences, some of them for life.

The Emperor, continuing on the throne, found his whole life drastically altered. The changes were paralleled by a revolutionary modification of the face of Japanese culture, and to understand the first, we need to take a look at the second.

The formal surrender to the Allies was even more of a shock to Japan than the actual defeat in the field. The people felt that their entire system of moral values had been proved wrong, and they did not know how to improvise a new way of life for themselves. As A. M. Rosenthal remarked in the *New York Times*, Japan had no great historic documents like the American Declaration of Independence, no national heroes like Washington and Lincoln, whose teachings were appropriate to the new day. The vast changes brought by the American Occupation, which were openly opposed by very few, added to the confusion. The Japanese did not now know quite who they were, or who they wanted to be.

From one of the most militaristic nations on earth, the country suddenly became one of the most pacifist; for a time her few remaining soldiers did not dare venture forth alone on the streets in uniform lest they be attacked. In 1945, with the lessons of the War fresh, the Allies had demanded that Japan be completely disarmed, and wrote a clause to that effect into the new Constitution, but then as the Cold War got more bitter, the United States reversed its policy and demanded a degree of Japanese rearmament, which was accepted with great reluctance. It also maintained extensive Navy and Air Force installations of its own on Japanese soil. In 1964, American military personnel numbered about 50,000 men, and a billion and a third dollars had been spent by the United States on its military establishment. Japan had spent twice that much, and had an army of about 200,000 men, 140,000 tons of naval vessels, and 1,400 planes, a situation that was bitterly resented by millions.

Some of the changes hopefully inaugurated by the Allies after 1945 did not last. The great cartels gradually reëstablished themselves, especially after the end of the Occupation in 1952. Many women, especially in rural areas, were reluctant to use the new freedom thrust upon them and continued in their highly subservient role, a role symbolized by their kneeling to welcome their husbands when they returned home at the end of the day.

Shintoism got a heavy blow when it was disestablished as the state religion. Cynical Japanese said of Buddhism that it lived only on the tourist trade, and Christianity managed to attract only one-half of one percent of the population. Torn adrift from all their old moorings, many people abandoned the moral code of previous generations. As everywhere else in the world, juvenile delinquency arose. Sexual liberty had always been accepted for men, especially in urban areas, and it was now extended, to some degree, to women; some wives, who had evidently not condoned their husbands' infidelities as readily as had been assumed, indulged in extra-marital affairs as a means of revenge.

While some Japanese were still hostile to the United States, among the majority the craze for American gadgets and forms of entertainment rose to unparalleled heights. Jazz became the musical language of youth. Western dress was almost universal on city streets. American television programs—and often the worst of them—were seen on Japanese television, which reached four out of five families—a remarkably high level for such a poor country. The typical Japanese home was a weird mixture of the old and the new, with a Shinto or Buddhist shrine perhaps crowded in beside a TV set, and an electric washing machine nearby.

The situation of most young people has become difficult in the extreme. Competition to get into high school and college is intense, and the entrance examinations are formidable; four out of five fail to get into the universities on their first attempt, and some of those who are disappointed kill themselves. Most students are desperately poor, and large numbers work their way through by employment at fifteen or twenty cents an hour. Though the winter weather is bitterly cold, students in a college dormitory voted against having heat that would have cost only a couple of dollars per year per person.

In theory, young people are now supposed to marry for love, but in fact at least half the marriages are arranged by the parents as in the old days, and in rural areas the proportion is near to one hundred percent. Japan, it is interesting to note, has gone from one of the highest birth rates in the world to one of the lowest, largely because abortion not only is legal, but has social sanction.

About one-third of the people have Leftist political leanings; only a small minority are Communists, but there are several Socialist parties, most of which collaborate readily with the Communists. As is true all over the world, the rift between Russian and Chinese Communists has divided and confused Japanese Leftists. Radicalism is very strong among the intellectuals, and especially among high school and college teachers, and the result is that these views are far more widespread among young people than their elders. It was young Communists who led the demonstrations in 1960 which caused President Eisenhower to cancel his projected visit to Japan that year; they were an unsuccessful attempt to prevent a renewal of the military treaty between Japan and the United States.

In recent years, Japan has had an amazingly high rate of industrial growth, more than ten percent a year, and for some time her exports increased sixteen percent a year, three times the world average. There are several reasons for this. She started from a low level; much of her factory equipment was destroyed during the War and has been replaced by new and improved machinery, and she has paid very low wages, giving her a great advantage in foreign trade. Before the War, sixty percent of her exports were to the Asiatic mainland, next door; today only one-third go to Asia, one-third to North America, and one-third to the rest of the world, mainly to Europe. Wages are now rising, and the competitive advantage is exports is disappearing. In spite of her new industrialization, Japan's output per worker is not very high; in 1963 it was only about one-fifth that in the United States.

In theory, at least, country girls no longer come to the cities to be prostitutes for a few years in order to earn a suitable dowry for their weddings, but they do work in factories for the same period and for the same purpose. Young men also move from the country to the cities, as modern agricultural methods reduce the need for farm labor. As part of the industrial proletariat, they are easy victims for radical propaganda. The gap between these workers and the upper class of managers, financiers, and bureaucrats has been widening in recent years. The well-to-do are heavily overrepresented in Parliament. The trade unions, which were encouraged by the Americans during the Occupation, today show heavy Leftist tendencies.

Japan is a good illustration of the fact that cultural evolution cannot be hurried. The more the American influence recedes in time, the more the changes that were pushed through tend to be obliterated. The most dramatic alterations in Japanese culture today result from other causes, the impact of television, the popularity of Western dress, movies, music, and other things, the influence of Russian communism, the weakening of religion. While the family remains more a center of moral authority than in most Western nations, its influence is being reduced as an increasing number of its members work outside the home for wages.

The Emperor's renunciation of his godhead seems by now to have been almost completely accepted in the cities, which were centers of skepticism even before the War, and it is possible that indifference to him is growing. When a thousand city dwellers were asked in 1963 whether the throne should be abolished, only sixty percent said it should be kept. A few

Leftists thought it should go, and the rest professed not to care. It is chiefly in remote rural areas that some attempt is being made to return to the myth that Hirohito is descended from the Sun Goddess. In these regions a handful of people, perhaps the Japanese equivalent of the American extreme Right, want to abolish foreign innovations, turn back the clock, and restore the glories of the old Japan of the Samurai.

It is against this background that the Emperor and his family have tried to pick up the pieces and make a new, profoundly altered way of life for themselves. They live simply and abstemiously, as they always have, and as, indeed, all Japanese do (to the despair of advertising men who try to introduce American standards of conspicuous consumption). After the Palace was destroyed, the Emperor lived for years in a modest structure that was once his library; not until recently was the famous architect, Junzo Yoshimura, who is well known in America, engaged to design a new dwelling place.

Hirohito's personal fortune used to be reckoned at about $1 billion, if you ignore the more grandiose idea that he owned the entire Japanese Empire; today all his wealth is swept away, and he lives on an annual grant from Parliament of some $140,000. No longer do worshipping crowds bow deeply in the streets as he passes by, not venturing to look upon his sacred person; on the contrary, he is cheered just like any important and popular figure in America or Western Europe. He lays cornerstones and appears on television, with no quickening of the national pulse. When he descended from an airplane after his first aerial journey, the Japanese photographers, now irreverent like their kind the world over, shouted, "Take off your hat." Yet vestiges of the old days still appear. When he made an inspection tour of a factory, a workman, presumably trying to live up to the new order of things, impulsively tried to shake hands (which would have resulted in a death sentence before the War). Hirohito hesitated a second, and then said, "Let us do it in the Japanese way," whereupon, without touching each other, both bowed.

Nearly eighteen years after the end of the War, the Emperor did in fact shake hands with one of his subjects, for the first time and by accident. Greeting a long line of visitors, he mistook a minor official of his own court for a visiting diplomat from Thailand, and pressed his fingers. The incident made headlines around the world. The hapless man must have thanked his stars that the incident did not occur before 1946 and force him to suicide.

The change in Hirohito's status has not meant that he is any less busy than before. He keeps regular office hours, sitting at his desk from ten to twelve and two to four. While his real activity is hardly any greater than when the Fascists were in control, he has to sign fifty or sixty documents of all kinds, every day. He receives many foreign visitors; though he knows some French and English, on these occasions he feels more comfortable using an interpreter.

His chief exercise is a brisk daily walk through the Palace grounds. Of his three meals, two are of Western-style food, which he prefers. His vacations are spent in the mountains or at the seashore where he can work as a biologist. He watches television, sees films in his private movie theatre, listens to the phonograph, and continues to write short poems.

Several times each year he makes a brief official tour through the provinces. While he does his best to be friendly and informal on these tours, it is quite clear that he is still shy and introverted, and does not really like the role he has to play.

The postwar revolution in the status of the Imperial Family is nowhere better shown than in the life of Crown Prince Akihito. For the first time in recorded history, the heir to the throne has married a commoner, Michiko Shoda, daughter of a wealthy flour-mill owner, whom he met on a tennis court. In the past, the Imperial children have always been taken away at about the age of three and brought up independently, but Akihito is rearing his son, born in 1960, in his own house.

In 1963, the Crown Prince had to resort to the law to stop the publication of a long serial novel in a monthly magazine.

Though labeled fiction, it used the real names of Akihito and Michiko, and discussed their private lives with a frankness exceeding even that of a New York or London tabloid newspaper.

Still more shocking to Japanese sensibilities was a plot in the same year to kidnap Hirohito's youngest daughter, Princess Suga, and hold her for ransom. Like her brother, she is married to a commoner, a prosperous banker, and the kidnapers thought they could ask $140,000 for her safe return. For reasons inexplicable to the occidental mind, they believed that because she was the Emperor's daughter, the police would not interfere. The plot miscarried when one of the conspirators lost his nerve and betrayed his fellows.

In recent years, complaints have been heard that court officials were trying again to isolate the Emperor from the mass of the people, and probably this development should have been expected. The more he can be hemmed in, the greater the degree of power those around him can exercise, even though, as in Great Britain, he reigns but does not govern. His popular following, in spite of all evidence to the contrary, may still be substantial; if he chose to appeal to the people over the heads of the Cabinet on some specific issue, no one knows what might happen.

At the same time, it is hard to imagine a situation in which this could take place. The Emperor shows no wish to influence the course of events, and even if he did, his personality and the traditions of the throne would make such an effort almost impossible.

No one has recognized this better than Hirohito himself. On his sixtieth birthday he remarked ruefully that "he had done nothing really worthwhile in his life," and this judgment was substantially correct. But for the accident of birth, as we have said, he could have lived out his days as a modestly successful biologist. It is the irony of history that such a man occupied the Japanese throne in an era of crisis when a stronger character in his place might have thwarted the rise of Japanese Fascism and avoided a terrible war.

# Postscript

THOSE who cannot remember the past," said Santayana, "are condemned to repeat it," and Hegel, even more pessimistic, observed that "the only thing we learn from history is that we learn nothing from history." Neither of these statements is wholly true; yet they may help to sting us into considering what are the chief lessons of the recent past that may be useful in the future.

One of these is how terrifyingly thin is the veneer of civilization. The paranoiac Hitler was able to persuade most of the Germans to swallow his nonsensical notions about a master race—notions that unfortunately are still endorsed by many people in every country, including the United States. He found thousands who at his bidding, and without any apparent compunction, helped to kill several million innocent victims with the efficiency of a big Chicago abattoir, in many cases after inflicting indescribable tortures upon them. Evidently latent sadism lurks much nearer to the surface, even in supposedly civilized twentieth-century communities, than we had supposed.

The fires of nationalism, fanned by the events described in this book, and now burning so fiercely in Africa and Asia, reveal some important facets of human personality. In some cases, the countries that have demanded and obtained their independence face a period during which they will be much worse off in every material sense than they were as colonies. People who have been rated as second-class citizens anywhere in the world have begun in recent decades to resent it with fierce anger, and they refuse to wait any longer for their wrongs to be righted. Human dignity is now seen to be the most precious of all possessions. In some cases, in the liberated parts of Africa for example, people are still being exploited, but the exploiters are men of their own race, and the yoke therefore seems easier to bear—at least at first. That millions of people whose ancestors accepted an inferior status are now unwilling to do so is the most revolutionary change in human psychology in all history, and one whose effects we are only beginning to feel.

A chief lesson to be learned from the recent past is the folly of appeasement, whether internal or external. The Bolsheviks in Russia were a small minority when they were allowed to take power. Hitler began with only a handful of followers and his movement grew slowly for almost a decade. The same was true of Italian Fascism, for a briefer period. Even in Japan, control by the Fascists was not inevitable. In all the countries, it was a failure of will by the forces in opposition that allowed the totalitarians to come to power. At first they were tolerated; by the time the danger had been realized, it was—or seemed to be—too late.

When Hitler invaded the Rhineland he told his Army commanders that if France and Great Britain showed any signs of resisting his action, the troops should be withdrawn at once. If these two nations had moved, which at the time involved little risk, the Second World War might have been averted. Japanese aggression against China could have been halted at any time if the rest of the Great Powers had acted resolutely and in concert. The overwhelming fact is that there is no such thing as a safe, small amount of anti-democracy that can be tolerated without danger.

We urgently need to understand better than we do the forces that create a Hitler, a Stalin, or a Tojo. Part of the answer lies in the realm of abnormal psychology, part in the realm of mass response to such a pathological individual. The scientists who study human behavior are making some progress in solving these riddles.

Another important lesson found in the events I have described is the significance of propaganda in the modern world. It cannot alone insure victory, but it can greatly facilitate the conditions that make victory possible. The dictators succeeded —at least for a time—in direct proportion to their skill in manipulating the media of mass communication. No technique has yet been created that can immunize any population from the effects of propaganda skillfully disseminated, and the truth or falsity of such propaganda does not seem to be—at least temporarily—the decisive factor.

That the democracies should clean their own houses, should practice what they preach, goes without saying. While the impulse toward totalitarianism rises from complex and profound social forces, in every country where it has come to power it has done so among a people who were cynical about the good faith and humanitarian intentions of the existing government.

Both Communists and Fascists have excused their actions by recourse to justifications that are no longer valid, if they ever were. Germany in the 1930's had everything to gain and nothing to lose by honest and friendly coöperation with her neighbors. Japan could have obtained all she needed if she had traded fairly with an independent China instead of making war on her. Mussolini's pretext for attacking Ethiopia was proved to be nonsense when, after he had captured the country, Italian settlers refused to go there.

All the Fascist dictatorships said they were overpopulated and must conquer new land to which to send their excess people. The claims of overpopulation were mostly false; but even if they had been true, demographers know that emigration is not the answer. The solution, aside from voluntary control of the birthrate, lies in increasing the standard of living by technological advance and internal economic readjustment.

Almost all colonialism has been based on long-outmoded theories. To put the matter in its lowest, most sordid terms, the colonial Powers would have made far larger profits in modern times if they had sought the good will of their subject peoples, educated them, raised their standard of living, and then traded with them as independent equals.

Nearly all the worst things that have happened on the international scene in the past few decades have taken place because the rulers believed in a set of myths that had been exposed years earlier. It is a tragic fact that those who knew have lacked power and those in power have lacked knowledge. For the future welfare of the world we need two things. The first is better communication between these groups. The second is that the dominant fraction in every country shall realize, and act upon, the grim truth that in the atomic age resort to war by any nuclear power is intolerable and must be prevented at any cost. Mankind has many grave problems; but few indeed are those that cannot be ameliorated or solved by the combination of scientific advance and human goodwill.

# Bibliography

MANY books have been written about the eight men discussed in this volume, and the number is growing rapidly; it would be easy to put down a very long bibliography on each of them. I am, however, not writing for scholars who are specialists in this field, and are quite capable of making their own bibliographies; I am writing for laymen, and am listing only books that such individuals might want to read. I believe that these volumes contain substantially all the material likely to be of interest to the average person.

### ROOSEVELT

Baillie, Hugh, *High Tension.* New York: Harper & Row, 1959.

Burns, James M., *Roosevelt, The Lion and the Fox.* New York: Harcourt, Brace & Company, 1956.

Brogan, Denis W., *Roosevelt and the New Deal.* New York: Oxford University Press, 1952.

Butcher, Capt. Harry C., *My Three Years with Eisenhower.* New York: Simon & Schuster, 1946.

Fay, Bernard, *Roosevelt and His America.* Boston: Little, Brown & Company, 1934.

Flynn, John T., *The Roosevelt Myth.* New York: Devin-Adair, 1948.

Freidel, Frank B., *Franklin D. Roosevelt: The Apprenticeship,* 1952; *Roosevelt: The Ordeal,* 1954; *Roosevelt: The Triumph,* 1956. Boston: Little, Brown & Company.

Gunther, John, *Roosevelt in Retrospect*. New York: Harper & Row, 1950.

Hallgren, Mauritz, *The Gay Reformer*. New York: Alfred A. Knopf, 1935.

Hoyt, Edwin P., *The Tempering Years*. New York: Charles Scribner's Sons, 1963.

Lindley, Ernest K., *Franklin D. Roosevelt: A Career in Progressive Democracy*. Indianapolis: Bobbs Merrill, 1931.

Perkins, Frances, *The Roosevelt I Knew*. New York: Viking Press, 1946.

Robinson, Edgar E., *The Roosevelt Leadership*. Philadelphia: J. B. Lippincott Company, 1955.

Roosevelt, Eleanor, *Autobiography*. New York: Harper & Row, 1961.

Roosevelt, Franklin D., *Public Papers and Addresses*. New York: Harper & Row, Macmillan, and Random House, various dates.

——, *His Personal Letters*. New York: Duell, Sloan & Pearce, 1947.

——, *Selected Messages and Public Addresses*. New York: Oxford University Press, 1933.

Rosenman, Samuel I., *Working with Roosevelt*. New York: Harper & Row, 1952.

Schary, Dore, *Sunrise at Campobello* (a play). New York: Random House, 1958.

Schlesinger, Arthur M., Jr., *The Crisis of the Old Order*, 1957; *The Coming of the New Deal*, 1958; *The Politics of Upheaval*, 1960. Boston: Houghton Mifflin Company.

Sherwood, Robert E., *Roosevelt and Hopkins, An Intimate History*. New York: Harper & Row, 1948.

Smith, Merriman, *Thank You, Mr. President*. New York: Harper & Row, 1946.

Tugwell, Rexford Guy, *The Democratic Roosevelt*. New York: Doubleday & Company, 1957.

CHURCHILL

Bryant, Sir Arthur, *Triumph in the West*. Garden City, N. Y.: Doubleday & Company, 1959.

——, *The Turn of the Tide*. Garden City, N. Y.: Doubleday & Company, 1957.

Churchill, Sir Winston, *A Churchill Reader,* edited by C. R. Coate and P. D. Bunyan. Boston: Houghton Mifflin & Company, 1954.

———, *The Second World War.* 1. *The Gathering Storm.* 2. *Their Finest Hour.* 3. *The Grand Alliance.* 4. *The Hinge of Fate.* 5. *Closing the Ring.* 6. *Triumph and Tragedy.* Boston: Houghton Mifflin & Company, 1948–1953.

———, *The Unrelenting Struggle; War Speeches.* Edited by Charles Eade. Boston: Little, Brown & Company, 1942.

———, *While England Slept; A Survey of World Affairs, 1932 to 1938.* New York: G. P. Putnam's Sons, 1938.

———, *The World Crisis.* Four volumes. New York: Charles Scribner's Sons, 1923 to 1929.

Cowles, Virginia, *Winston Churchill: The Era and the Man.* London: Hamilton, 1953.

De Mendelssohn, Peter, *The Age of Churchill.* New York: Alfred A. Knopf, 1961.

Fishman, Jack, *My Darling Clementine, the Story of Lady Churchill.* New York: D. McKay, 1963.

Pawle, Gerald, *The War and Colonel Warden.* New York: Alfred A. Knopf, 1963.

Taylor, Robert Lewis, *Winston Churchill, an Informal Study of Greatness.* Garden City, N. Y.: Doubleday & Company, 1952.

Thompson, Walter Henry, *I Was Churchill's Shadow.* London: C. Johnson, 1951.

HITLER

Biddle, Francis, *In Brief Authority.* Garden City, N. Y.: Doubleday & Company, 1962.

Bradley, Gen. Omar N., *A Soldier's Story.* New York: Holt, Rinehart & Winston, 1951.

Bryant, Sir Arthur, *The Turn of the Tide.* New York: Doubleday & Company, 1957.

Bullock, Alan, *Hitler, A Study in Tyranny.* New York: Harper & Row, 1960.

Ciano, Count Galeazzo, *The Ciano Diaries, 1939–1943.* Edited by Hugh Wilson. Garden City, N. Y.: Doubleday & Company, 1946.

———, *Ciano's Hidden Diary, 1937–1938.* New York: E. P. Dutton & Company, 1953.

Deakin, F. W., *The Brutal Friendship*. New York: Harper & Row, 1963.

Gilbert, Felix, editor, *Hitler Directs His War*. New York: Oxford University Press, 1951.

Gunther, John, *Inside Europe*. New York: Harper & Row, 1938.

Heiden, Konrad, *Der Führer*. Boston: Houghton Mifflin Company, 1944.

Hitler, Adolf, *Mein Kampf*. New York: Reynal & Hitchcock, 1939.

Howe, Quincy, *The World between the Wars*. New York: Simon & Schuster, 1953.

Shirer, William L., *Berlin Diary*. New York: Alfred A. Knopf, 1941.

————, *End of a Berlin Diary*. New York: Alfred A. Knopf, 1947.

————, *The Rise and Fall of the Third Reich*. New York: Simon & Schuster, 1960.

Taylor, Telford, *Sword and Swastika*. New York: Simon & Schuster, 1952.

Tobias, Fritz, *The Reichstag Fire*. New York: G. P. Putnam's Sons, 1964.

Trevor-Roper, Hugh, *The Last Days of Hitler*. New York: The Macmillan Company, 1947.

Wiskemann, Elizabeth, *The Rome-Berlin Axis*. New York: Oxford University Press, 1949.

STALIN

Armstrong, Hamilton Fish, *Tito and Goliath*. New York: The Macmillan Company, 1955.

Deutscher, Isaac, *Stalin, A Political Biography*. New York: Oxford University Press, 1949.

Duranty, Walter, *Stalin and Company*. New York: William Sloane Associates, 1949.

Eastman, Max, *Stalin's Russia and the Crisis in Socialism*. New York: W. W. Norton & Company, 1940.

Fischer, Louis, *Life and Death of Stalin*. New York: Harper & Row, 1952.

Gunther, John, *Inside Europe*. New York: Harper & Row, 1938.

Harriman, Averell, *Peace with Russia?* New York: Simon & Schuster, 1959.

Howe, Quincy, *The World between the Wars*. New York: Simon & Schuster, 1953.

Kennan, George, *Russia and the West under Lenin and Stalin.* Boston: Little, Brown & Company, 1961.

Levine, Isaac Don, *Stalin.* New York: Cosmopolitan Book Corporation, 1931.

Ludwig, Emil, *Stalin.* New York: G. P. Putnam's Sons, 1942.

Lyons, Eugene, *Stalin, Tsar of All the Russians.* Philadelphia: J. B. Lippincott, 1940.

Orlov, Alexander, *The Secret History of Stalin's Crimes.* New York: Random House, 1953.

Reichers, Col. Lou, *The Flying Years.* New York: Holt, Rinehart & Winston, 1956.

Salisbury, Harrison, *The Northern Palmyra Affair* (a novel). New York: Harper & Row, 1963.

Shulman, Marshall, *Stalin's Foreign Policy Reappraised.* Cambridge: Harvard University Press, 1963.

General Sikorski Historical Institute, editor, *Documents on Polish-Soviet Relations, 1939–45.* London: Heinemann & Company, 1961.

Stalin, Joseph, *Stalin's Correspondence with Churchill, Attlee, Roosevelt and Truman, 1941–45.* New York: Dutton & Company, 1958.

Trotsky, Leon, *Stalin.* New York: Harper & Row, 1941.

Wolfe, Bertram, *Three Who Made a Revolution.* New York: Dial Press, 1948.

### MUSSOLINI

Ciano, Count Galeazzo, *The Ciano Diaries, 1939–43.* Edited by Hugh Wilson. Garden City, N. Y.: Doubleday & Company, 1946.

———, *Ciano's Hidden Diary, 1937–38.* New York: E. P. Dutton & Company, 1953.

Deakin, F. W., *The Brutal Friendship.* New York: Harper & Row, 1963.

Fermi, Laura, *Mussolini.* Chicago: University of Chicago Press, 1961.

Gunther, John, *Inside Europe.* New York: Harper & Row, 1938.

Howe, Quincy, *The World between the Wars.* New York: Simon & Schuster, 1953.

Seldes, George, *Sawdust Caesar.* New York: Harper & Row, 1935.

Sarfatti, Margherita, *The Life of Benito Mussolini*. New York: F. A. Stokes, 1925.

Hibbert, Christopher, *Il Duce*. Boston: Little, Brown & Company, 1962.

Finer, Herman, *Mussolini's Italy*. New York: Holt, Rinehart & Winston, 1935.

GANDHI

Andrews, C. F., *Mahatma Gandhi's Ideas*. New York: The Macmillan Company, 1930.

Bondurant, Joan, *Conquest of Violence: The Gandhian Philosophy of Conflict*. Princeton: Princeton University Press, 1958.

Catlin, George E., *In the Path of Mahatma Gandhi*. Chicago: H. Regnery, 1950.

Fischer, Louis, *Gandhi: His Life and Message for the World*. New York: New American Library, 1954.

———, *The Life of Mahatma Gandhi*. New York: Harper & Row, 1950.

Gandhi, Mohandas Karamchand, *All Men Are Brothers*. New York: Columbia University Press, 1959.

———, *Autobiography*. Washington: Public Affairs Press, 1948.

———, *The Gandhi Reader*, edited by Homer A. Jack. Bloomington, Indiana: University of Indiana Press, 1956.

———, *Gandhi's Letters to a Disciple*. New York: Harper & Row, 1950.

Miller, Webb, *I Found No Peace*. New York: Simon & Schuster, 1936.

Nanda, B. R., *Mahatma Gandhi, A Biography*. Boston: Beacon Press, 1958.

Naidu, Mrs. Sarojini, *Mahatma Gandhi, His Life, Writing and Speeches*. Madras: Ganesch & Company, 1921.

Sheean, Vincent, *Mahatma Gandhi*. New York: Alfred A. Knopf, 1955.

Shridharani, Krishnalal, *War without Violence: A Study of Gandhi's Method and Its Accomplishments*. New York: Harcourt Brace, 1939.

Wolpert, Stanley, *Nine Hours to Rama*. New York: Random House, 1962.

### CHIANG KAI-SHEK

Chiang Kai-shek, *China's Destiny*. New York: The Macmillan Company, 1947.

——, *Soviet Russia in China*. New York: Farrar, Straus & Cudahy, 1957.

Gunther, John, *Inside Asia*. New York: Harper & Row, 1939.

Hahn, Emily, *Chiang Kai-shek, An Authorized Biography*. Garden City, N. Y.: Doubleday & Company, 1955.

——, *China Only Yesterday: 1850–1950*. Garden City, N. Y.: Doubleday & Company, 1963.

——, *The Soong Sisters*. New York: Doubleday, Doran, 1943.

Howe, Quincy, *The World between the Wars*. New York: Simon & Schuster, 1953.

McKenna, Richard, *The Sand Pebbles* (a novel). New York: Harper & Row, 1963.

Snow, Edgar, *The Other Side of the River*. New York: Random House, 1962.

White, Theodore H. and Jacoby, Annalee, *Thunder out of China*. New York: William Sloane Associates, 1946.


### HIROHITO

Benedict, Ruth, *The Chrysanthemum and the Sword*. Boston: Houghton Mifflin and Company, 1946.

Busch, Noel, *Two Minutes to Noon*. New York: Simon & Schuster, 1962.

Butow, Robert J. C., *Tojo and the Coming of the War*. Princeton: Princeton University Press, 1961.

Feis, Herbert, *Japan Subdued*. Princeton: Princeton University Press, 1961.

Futara, Count Yoshinori and Sawada, Setsuzo, *The Crown Prince's European Tour*. Osaka: Osaka Mainichi, 1926.

Gunther, John, *Inside Asia*. New York: Harper & Row, 1939.

Howe, Quincy, *The World between the Wars*. New York: Simon & Schuster, 1953.

Lord, Walter, *Day of Infamy*. New York: Holt, Rinehart and Winston, 1957.

Prange, Gordon W., *Tora, Tora, Tora!* Pleasantville, N. Y.: The Reader's Digest, 1963.

Price, Willard, *Japan and the Son of Heaven*. New York: Duell, Sloan & Pearce, 1945.

Togo, Shigenori, *The Cause of Japan*. New York: Simon & Schuster, 1956.

Toland, John, *But Not in Shame*. New York: Random House, 1961.

Vining, Elizabeth Gray, *Return to Japan*. Philadelphia: J. B. Lippincott, 1960.

————, *Windows for the Crown Prince*. Philadelphia: J. P. Lippincott, 1952.

# Index